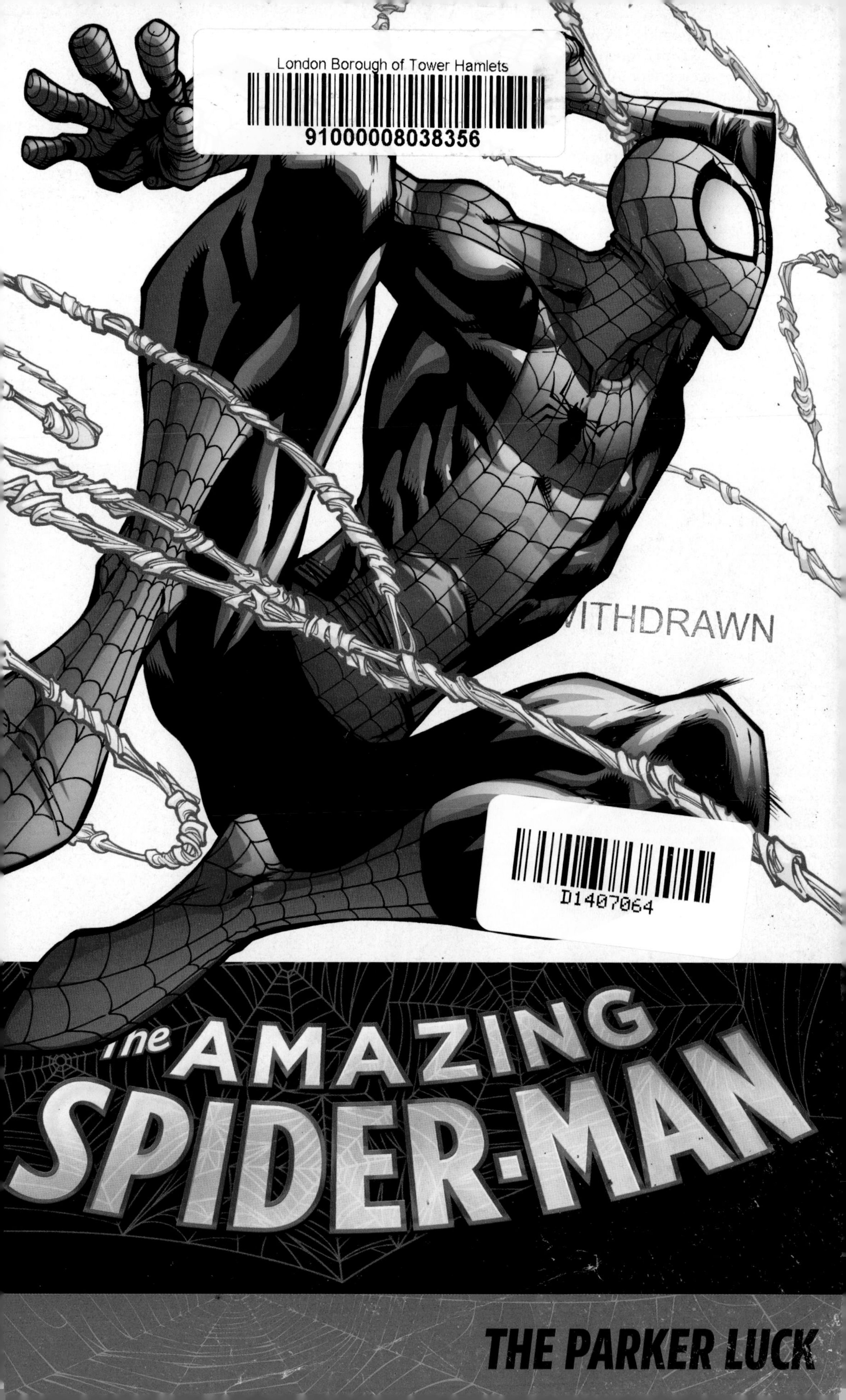

The AMAZING SPIDER-MAN

THE PARKER LUCK

Collection Editor: **Jennifer Grünwald**
Assistant Editor: **Sarah Brunstad**
Associate Managing Editor: **Alex Starbuck**
Editor, Special Projects: **Mark D. Beazley**
Senior Editor, Special Projects: **Jeff Youngquist**
SVP Print, Sales & Marketing: **David Gabriel**
Book Designer: **Rodolfo Muraguchi**

Editor in Chief: **Axel Alonso**
Chief Creative Officer: **Joe Quesada**
Publisher: **Dan Buckley**
Executive Producer: **Alan Fine**

10 9 8 7 6 5 4 3 2 1

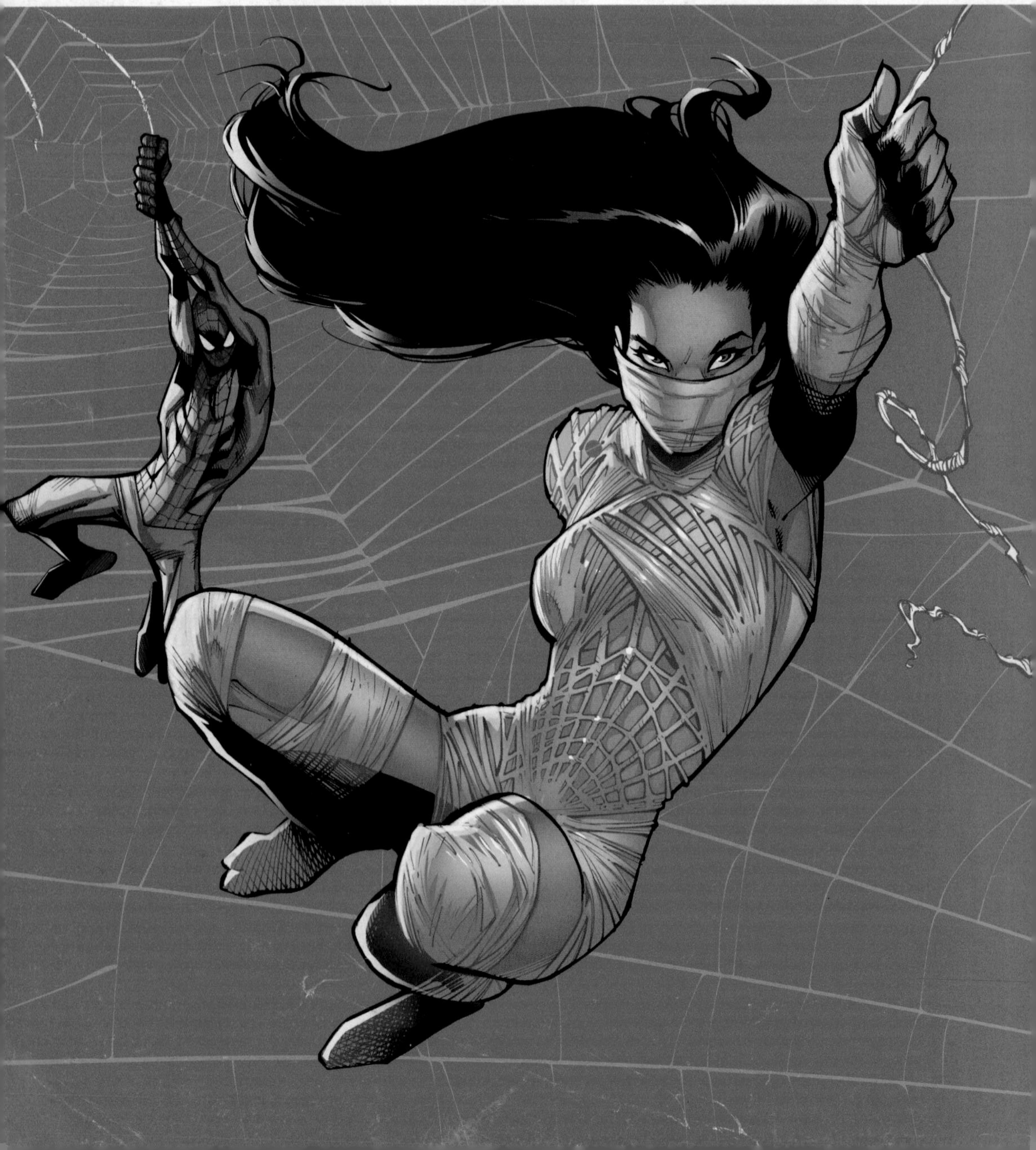

The AMAZING SPIDER-MAN

THE PARKER LUCK

WRITER:
DAN SLOTT

PENCILER:
HUMBERTO RAMOS

INKER:
VICTOR OLAZABA

COLORIST:
EDGAR DELGADO

"RECAPTURING THAT OLD SPARK"
WRITERS: **DAN SLOTT** & **CHRISTOS GAGE**
PENCILER/COLORIST: **JAVIER RODRIGUEZ**
INKER: **ALVARO LOPEZ**

"CROSSED PATHS"
WRITERS: **DAN SLOTT** & **CHRISTOS GAGE**
PENCILER: **GIUSEPPE CAMUNCOLI**
INKERS: **JOHN DELL** & **CAM SMITH**
COLORIST: **ANTONIO FABELA**

"HOW MY STUFF WORKS"
WRITER: **JOE CARAMAGNA**
ARTIST: **CHRIS ELIOPOULOS**
COLORIST: **JIM CHARALAMPIDIS**

LETTERER: **CHRIS ELIOPOULOS**
COVER ART: **HUMBERTO RAMOS**
& **EDGAR DELGADO**
ASSOCIATE EDITOR: **ELLIE PYLE**
EDITOR: **NICK LOWE**

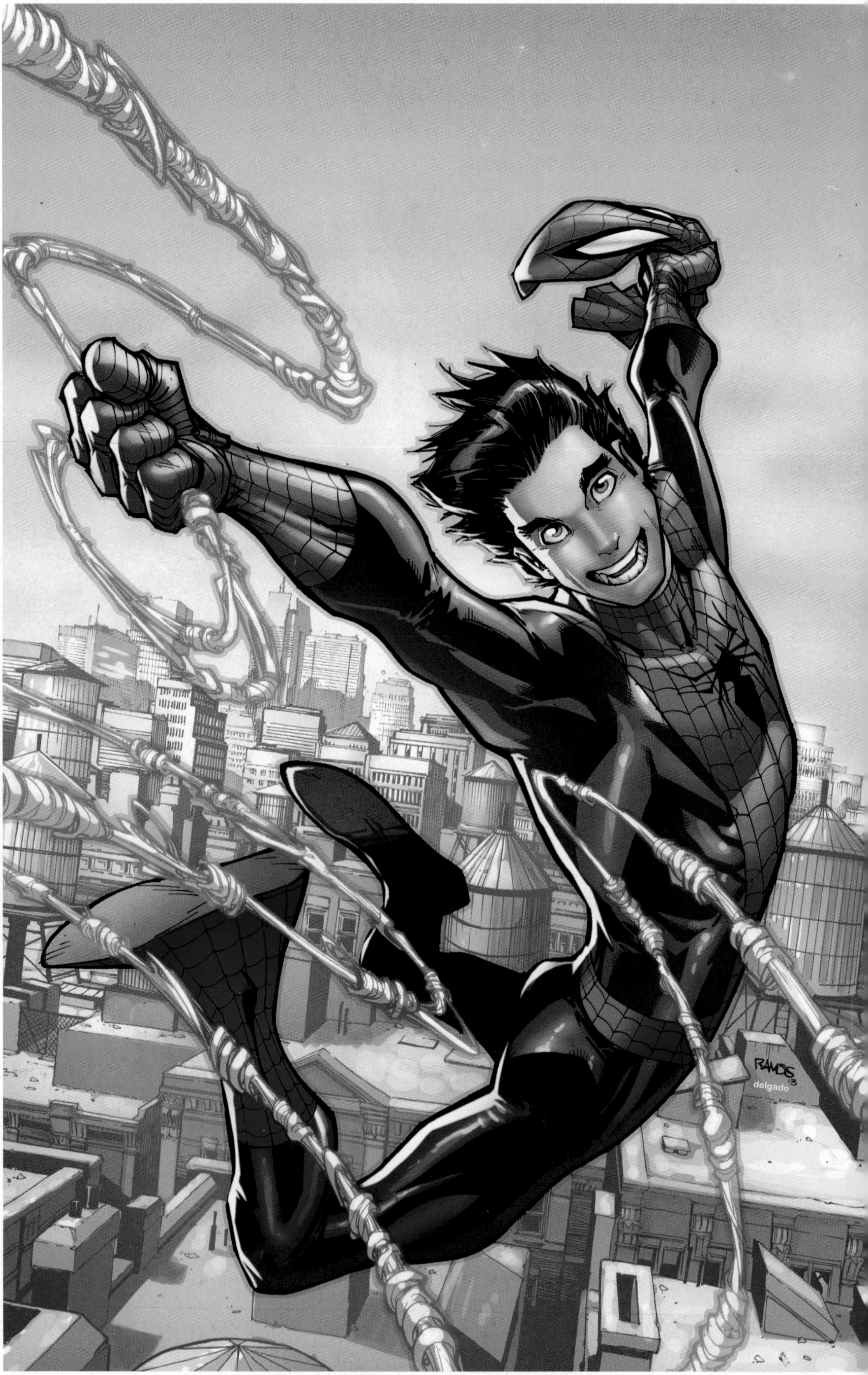
RAMOS '13
delgado

1

AN ALL-NEW CHAPTER IN A STORY 50-PLUS YEARS IN THE MAKING...

the AMAZING SPIDER-MAN IN

LUCKY TO BE ALIVE

DAN SLOTT WRITER | HUMBERTO RAMOS PENCILER | VICTOR OLAZABA INKER | EDGAR DELGADO COLORS | WITH LOVE TO STAN & STEVE

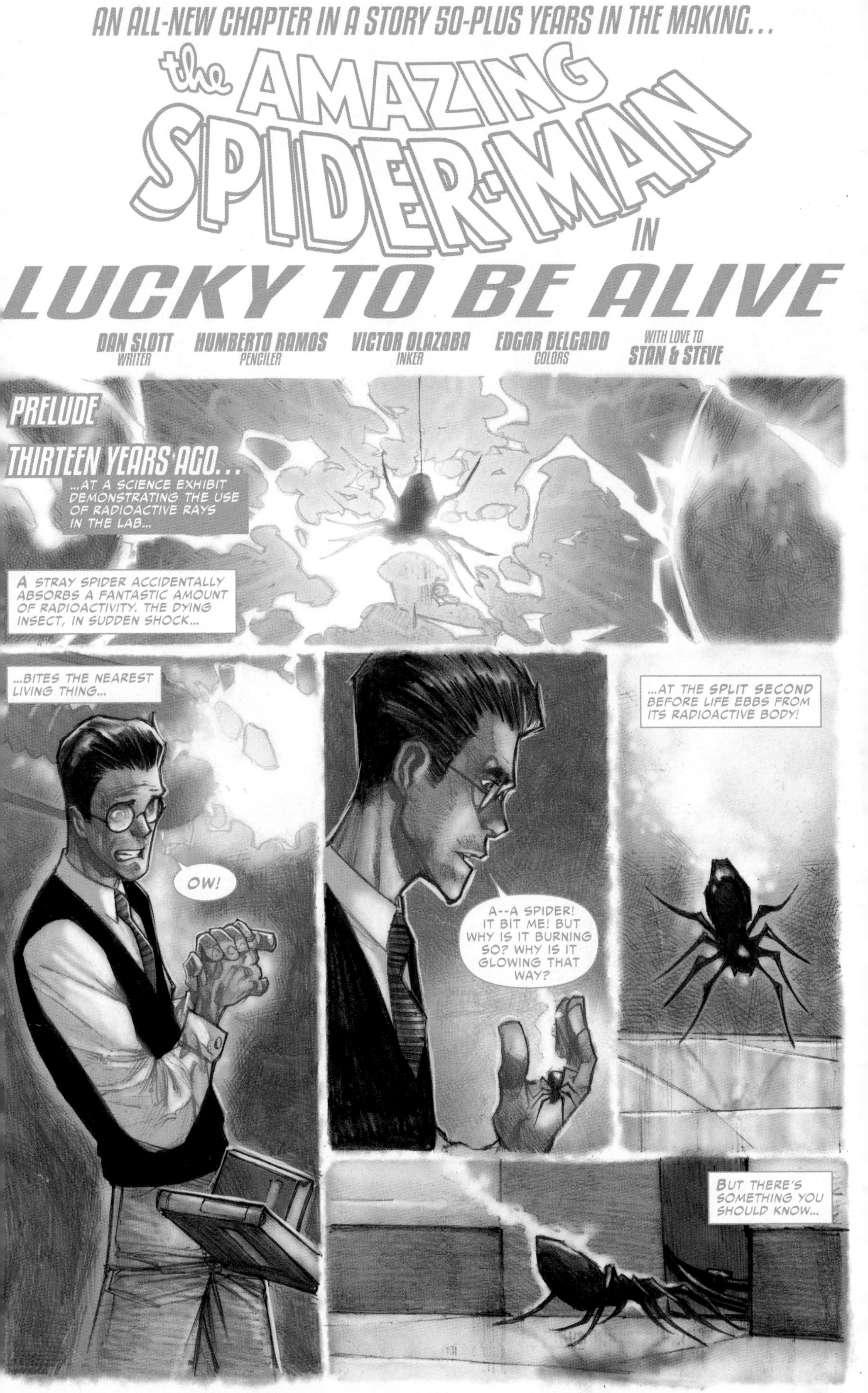
PRELUDE
THIRTEEN YEARS AGO...
...AT A SCIENCE EXHIBIT DEMONSTRATING THE USE OF RADIOACTIVE RAYS IN THE LAB...
A STRAY SPIDER ACCIDENTALLY ABSORBS A FANTASTIC AMOUNT OF RADIOACTIVITY. THE DYING INSECT, IN SUDDEN SHOCK...
...BITES THE NEAREST LIVING THING...
OW!
A--A SPIDER! IT BIT ME! BUT WHY IS IT BURNING SO? WHY IS IT GLOWING THAT WAY?
...AT THE SPLIT SECOND BEFORE LIFE EBBS FROM ITS RADIOACTIVE BODY!
BUT THERE'S SOMETHING YOU SHOULD KNOW...

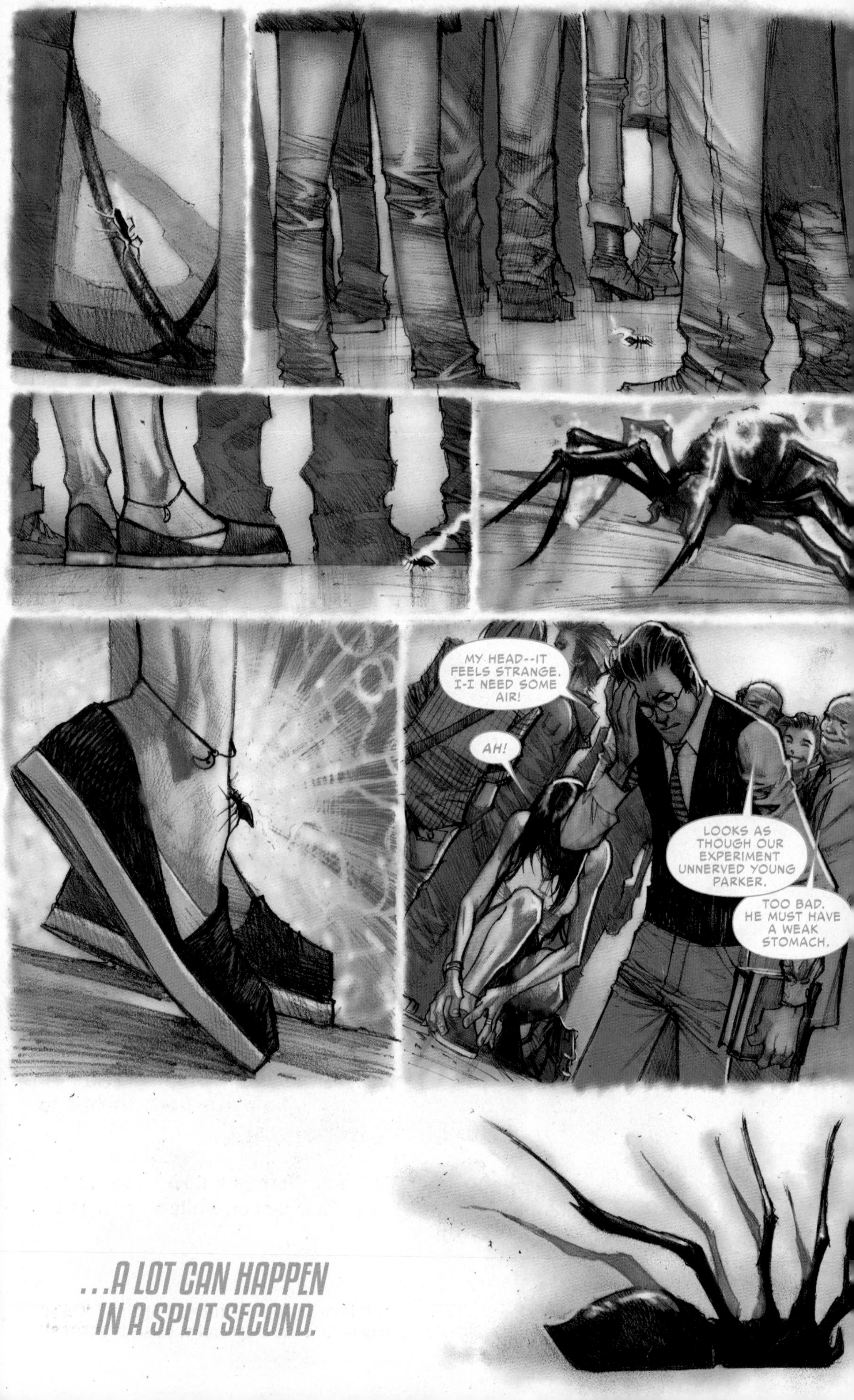
MY HEAD--IT FEELS STRANGE. I-I NEED SOME AIR!
AH!
LOOKS AS THOUGH OUR EXPERIMENT UNNERVED YOUNG PARKER.
TOO BAD. HE MUST HAVE A WEAK STOMACH.
...A LOT CAN HAPPEN IN A SPLIT SECOND.

ears ago, high school student PETER PARKER was bitten by a radioactive spider and gained the peed, agility, and proportional strength of a spider as well as the ability to stick to walls and a spider-ense that warned him of imminent danger. After learning that with great power there must also come great responsibility, he became the crime-fighting super hero...

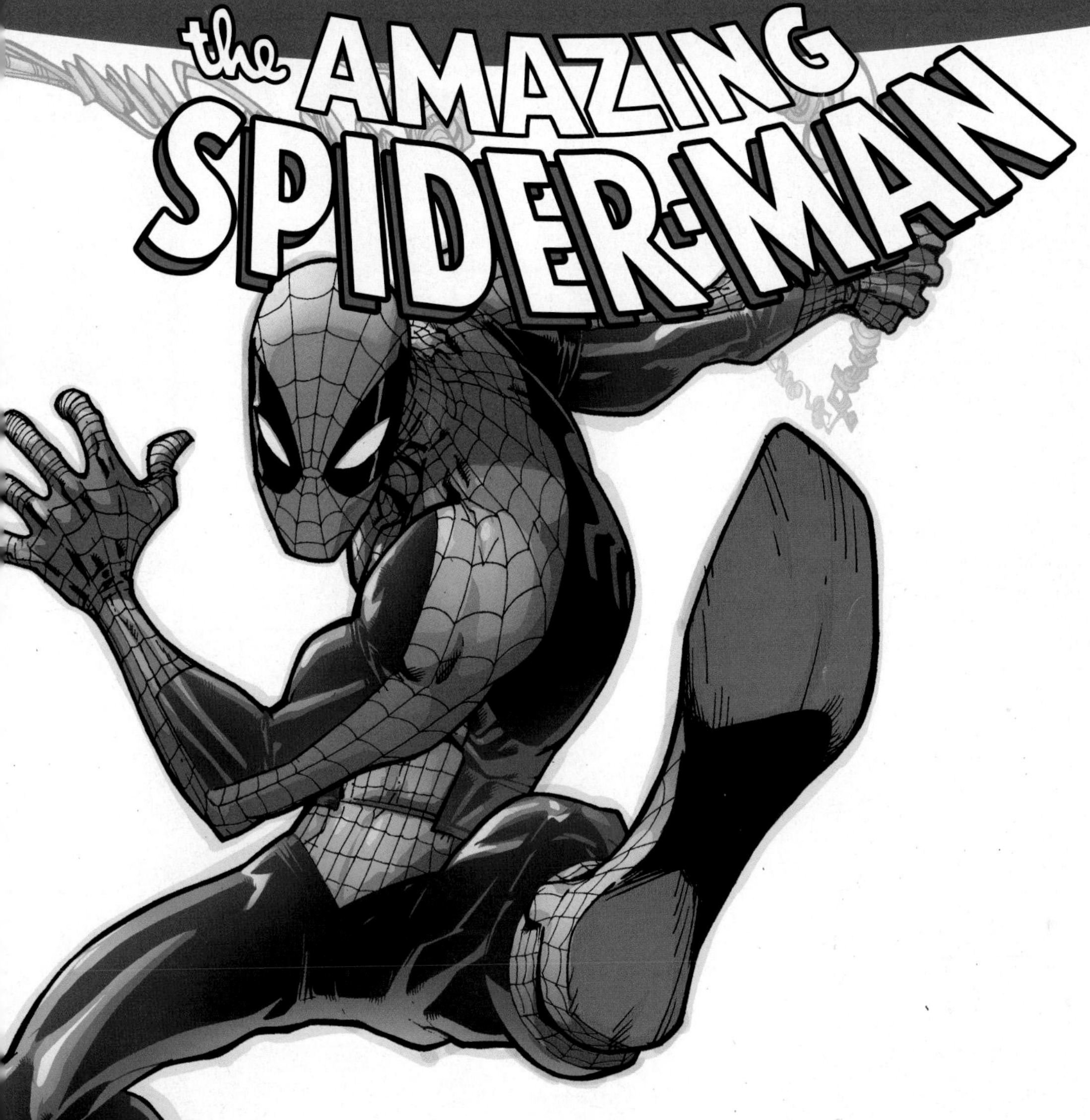

the AMAZING
SPIDER-MAN

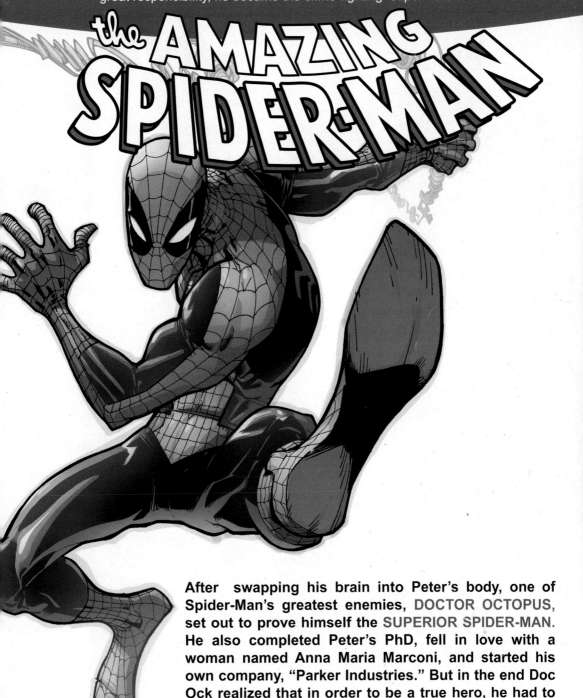

After swapping his brain into Peter's body, one of Spider-Man's greatest enemies, DOCTOR OCTOPUS, set out to prove himself the SUPERIOR SPIDER-MAN. He also completed Peter's PhD, fell in love with a woman named Anna Maria Marconi, and started his own company, "Parker Industries." But in the end Doc Ock realized that in order to be a true hero, he had to sacrifice himself.

Now, Peter Parker is back! He has a new lease on life and absolutely no idea what went on while he was gone.

When you see this: AR, open up the MARVEL AR APP (available on applicable Apple ® iOS or Android TM devices) and use your camera-enabled device to unlock extra-special exclusive features!*

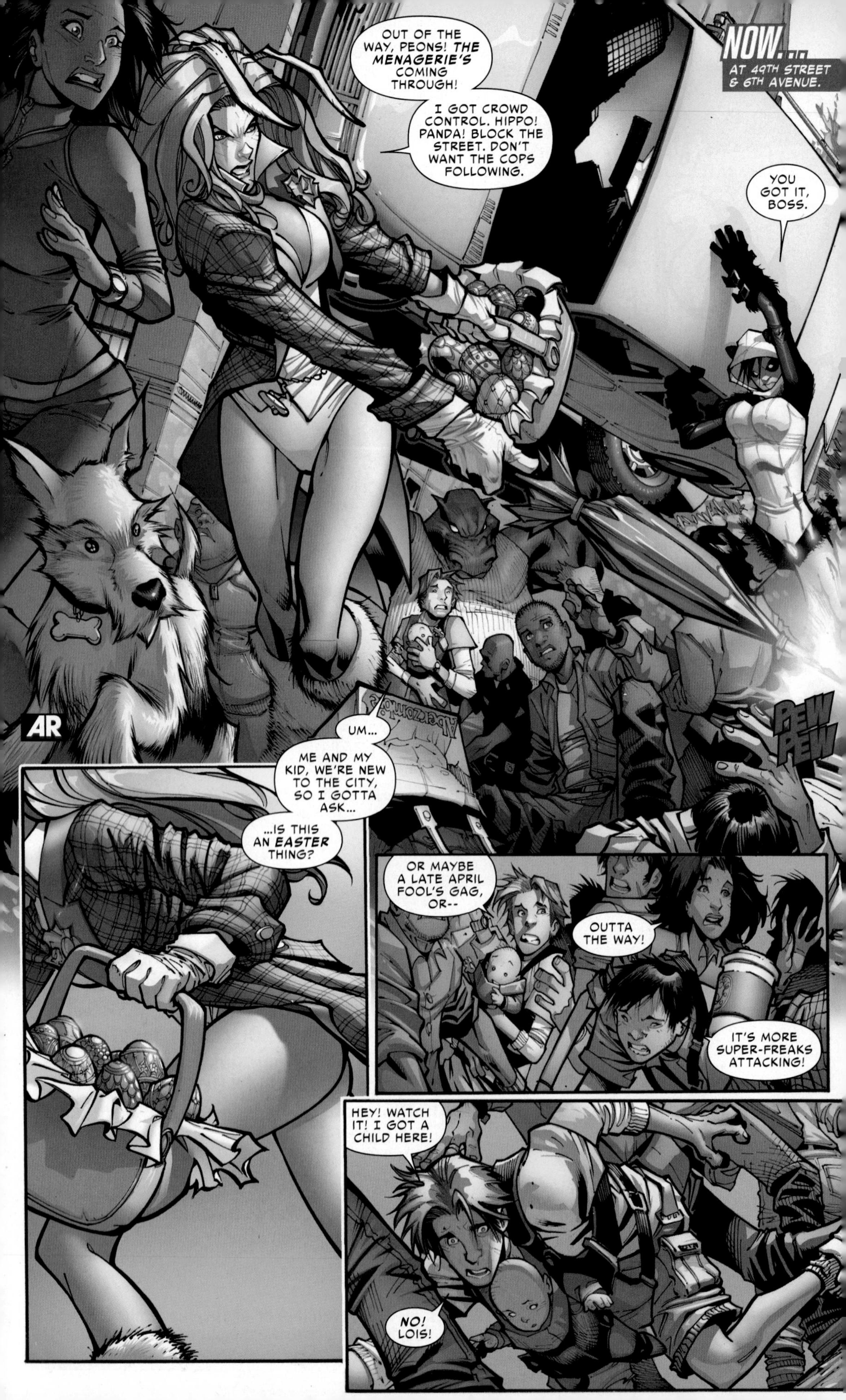

NOW...
AT 49TH STREET & 6TH AVENUE.
OUT OF THE WAY, PEONS! THE MENAGERIE'S COMING THROUGH!
I GOT CROWD CONTROL. HIPPO! PANDA! BLOCK THE STREET. DON'T WANT THE COPS FOLLOWING.
YOU GOT IT, BOSS.
PEW PEW
UM...
ME AND MY KID, WE'RE NEW TO THE CITY, SO I GOTTA ASK...
...IS THIS AN EASTER THING?
OR MAYBE A LATE APRIL FOOL'S GAG, OR--
OUTTA THE WAY!
IT'S MORE SUPER-FREAKS ATTACKING!
HEY! WATCH IT! I GOT A CHILD HERE!
NO! LOIS!

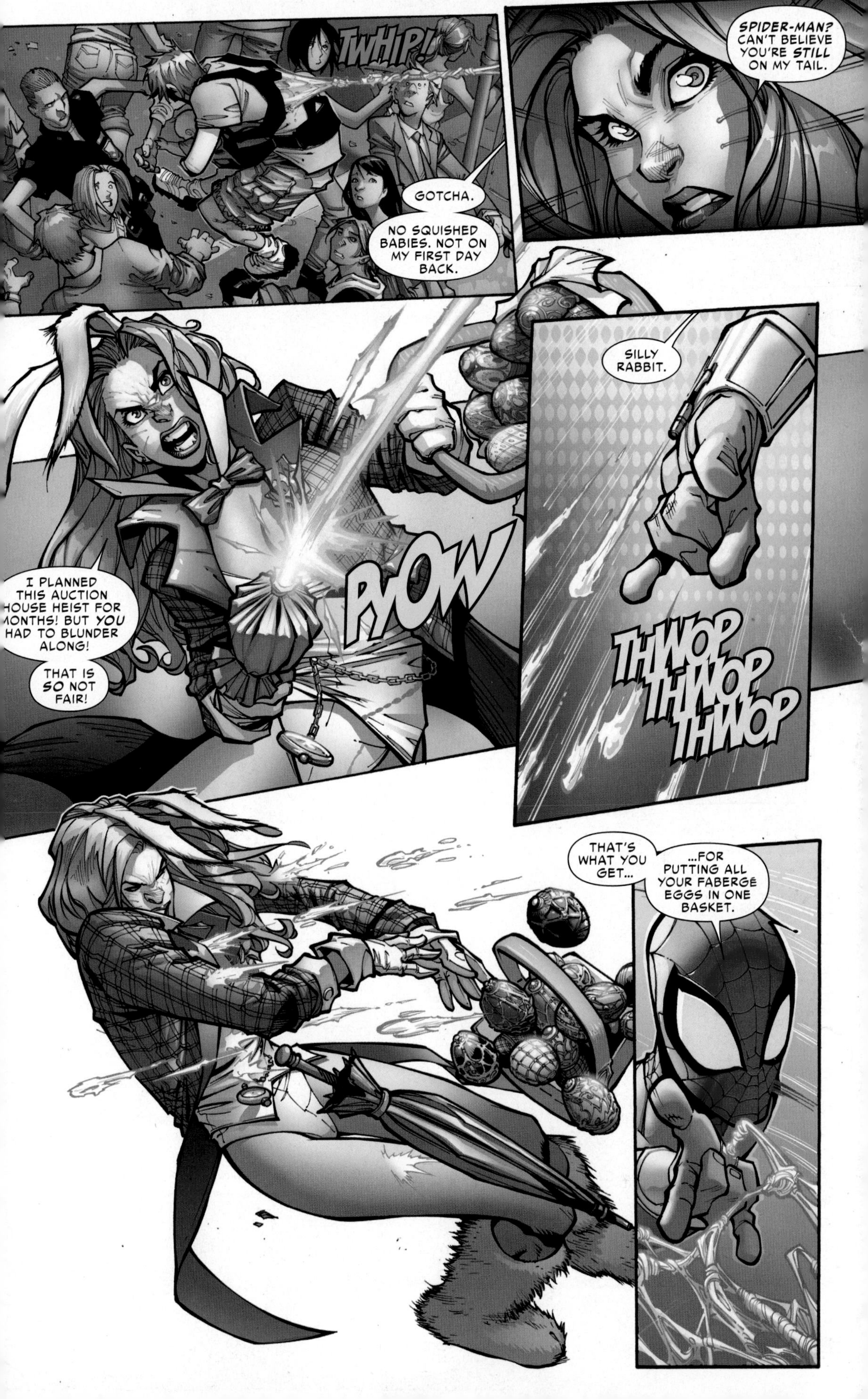
TWHIP!
GOTCHA.
NO SQUISHED BABIES. NOT ON MY FIRST DAY BACK.
SPIDER-MAN? CAN'T BELIEVE YOU'RE STILL ON MY TAIL.
SILLY RABBIT.
PYOW
I PLANNED THIS AUCTION HOUSE HEIST FOR MONTHS! BUT YOU HAD TO BLUNDER ALONG!
THAT IS SO NOT FAIR!
THWOP THWOP THWOP
THAT'S WHAT YOU GET...
...FOR PUTTING ALL YOUR FABERGÉ EGGS IN ONE BASKET.

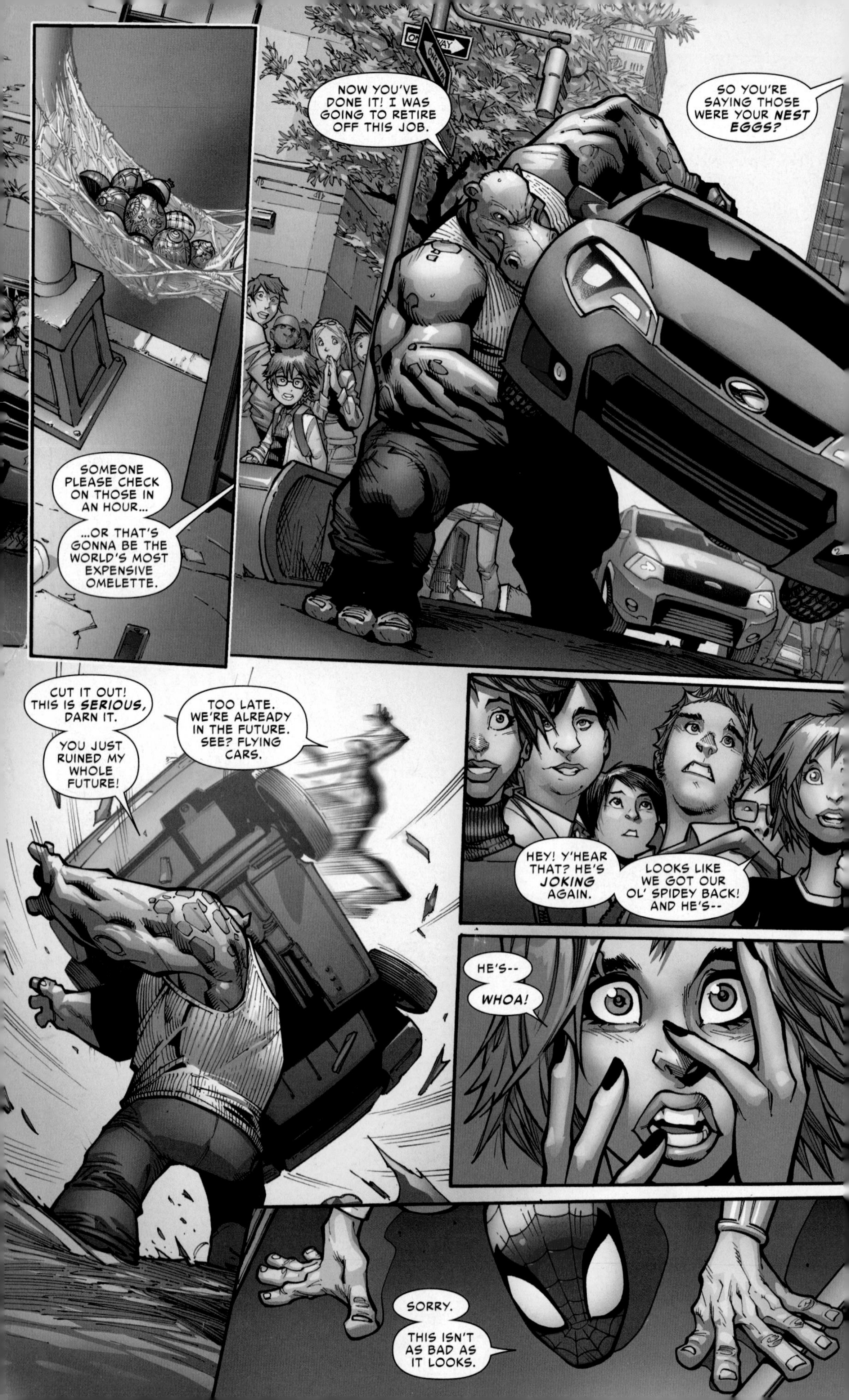
ONE WAY
ONE WAY
NOW YOU'VE DONE IT! I WAS GOING TO RETIRE OFF THIS JOB.
SO YOU'RE SAYING THOSE WERE YOUR NEST EGGS?
SOMEONE PLEASE CHECK ON THOSE IN AN HOUR...
...OR THAT'S GONNA BE THE WORLD'S MOST EXPENSIVE OMELETTE.
CUT IT OUT! THIS IS SERIOUS, DARN IT.
YOU JUST RUINED MY WHOLE FUTURE!
TOO LATE. WE'RE ALREADY IN THE FUTURE. SEE? FLYING CARS.
HEY! Y'HEAR THAT? HE'S JOKING AGAIN.
LOOKS LIKE WE GOT OUR OL' SPIDEY BACK! AND HE'S--
HE'S--
WHOA!
SORRY.
THIS ISN'T AS BAD AS IT LOOKS.

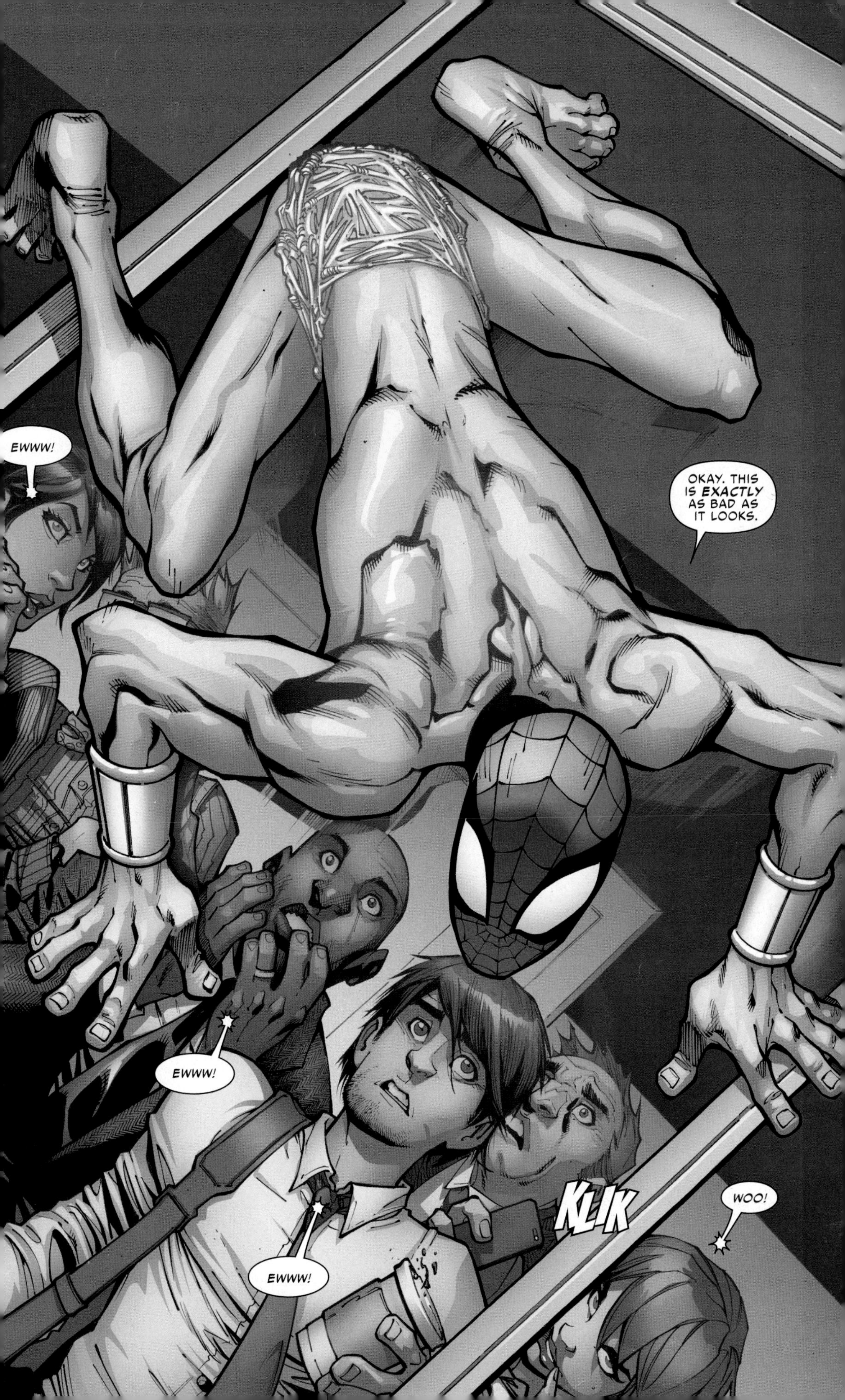
EWWW!
OKAY. THIS IS EXACTLY AS BAD AS IT LOOKS.
EWWW!
KLIK
WOO!
EWWW!

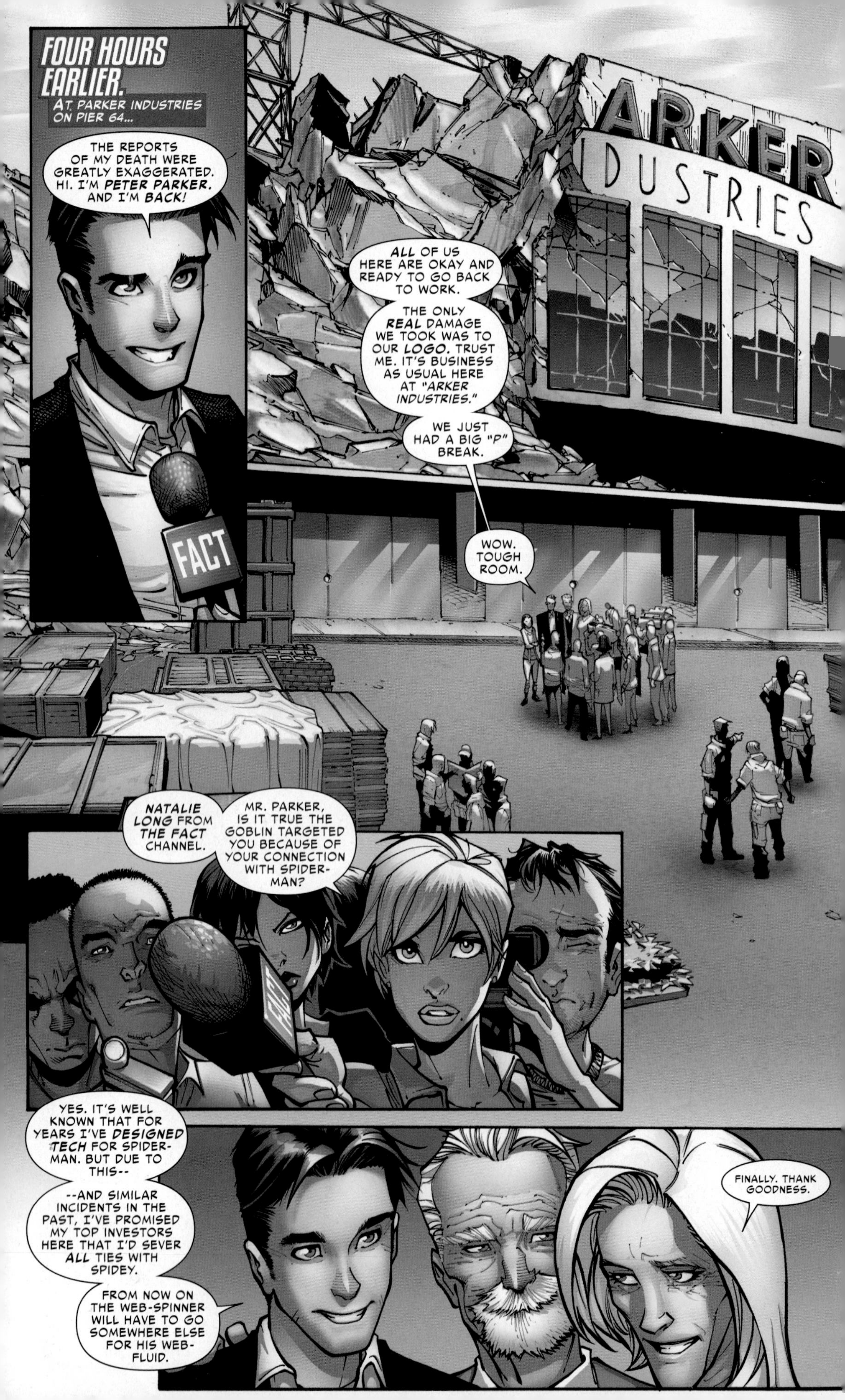
FOUR HOURS EARLIER.
AT PARKER INDUSTRIES ON PIER 64...
THE REPORTS OF MY DEATH WERE GREATLY EXAGGERATED. HI. I'M PETER PARKER. AND I'M BACK!
FACT
ARKER INDUSTRIES
ALL OF US HERE ARE OKAY AND READY TO GO BACK TO WORK.
THE ONLY REAL DAMAGE WE TOOK WAS TO OUR LOGO. TRUST ME. IT'S BUSINESS AS USUAL HERE AT "ARKER INDUSTRIES."
WE JUST HAD A BIG "P" BREAK.
WOW. TOUGH ROOM.
NATALIE LONG FROM THE FACT CHANNEL.
MR. PARKER, IS IT TRUE THE GOBLIN TARGETED YOU BECAUSE OF YOUR CONNECTION WITH SPIDER-MAN?
YES. IT'S WELL KNOWN THAT FOR YEARS I'VE DESIGNED TECH FOR SPIDER-MAN. BUT DUE TO THIS--
--AND SIMILAR INCIDENTS IN THE PAST, I'VE PROMISED MY TOP INVESTORS HERE THAT I'D SEVER ALL TIES WITH SPIDEY.
FROM NOW ON THE WEB-SPINNER WILL HAVE TO GO SOMEWHERE ELSE FOR HIS WEB-FLUID.
FINALLY. THANK GOODNESS.

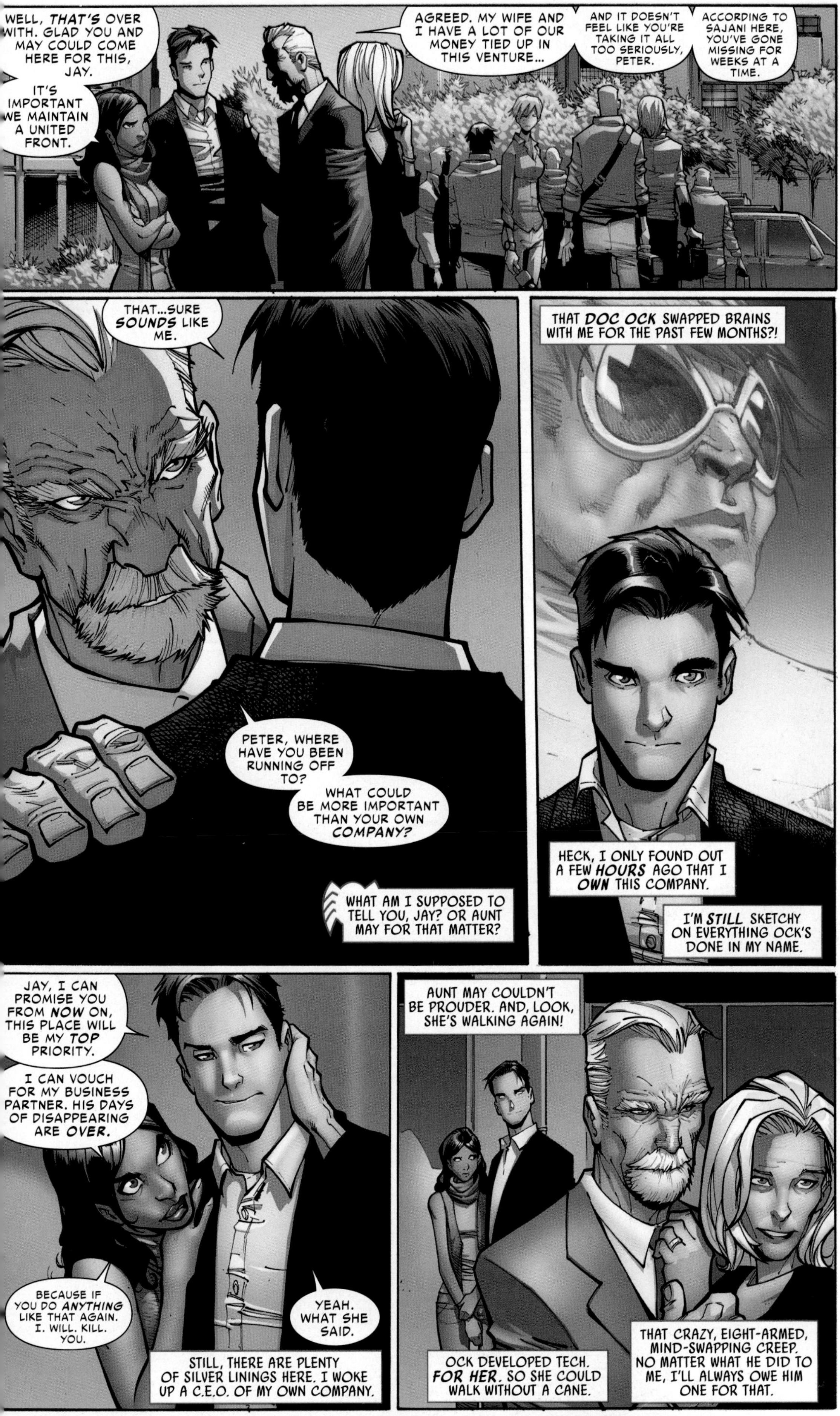
WELL, THAT'S OVER WITH. GLAD YOU AND MAY COULD COME HERE FOR THIS, JAY.
IT'S IMPORTANT WE MAINTAIN A UNITED FRONT.
AGREED. MY WIFE AND I HAVE A LOT OF OUR MONEY TIED UP IN THIS VENTURE...
AND IT DOESN'T FEEL LIKE YOU'RE TAKING IT ALL TOO SERIOUSLY, PETER.
ACCORDING TO SAJANI HERE, YOU'VE GONE MISSING FOR WEEKS AT A TIME.
THAT...SURE SOUNDS LIKE ME.
PETER, WHERE HAVE YOU BEEN RUNNING OFF TO?
WHAT COULD BE MORE IMPORTANT THAN YOUR OWN COMPANY?
WHAT AM I SUPPOSED TO TELL YOU, JAY? OR AUNT MAY FOR THAT MATTER?
THAT DOC OCK SWAPPED BRAINS WITH ME FOR THE PAST FEW MONTHS?!
HECK, I ONLY FOUND OUT A FEW HOURS AGO THAT I OWN THIS COMPANY.
I'M STILL SKETCHY ON EVERYTHING OCK'S DONE IN MY NAME.
JAY, I CAN PROMISE YOU FROM NOW ON, THIS PLACE WILL BE MY TOP PRIORITY.
I CAN VOUCH FOR MY BUSINESS PARTNER. HIS DAYS OF DISAPPEARING ARE OVER.
BECAUSE IF YOU DO ANYTHING LIKE THAT AGAIN. I. WILL. KILL. YOU.
YEAH. WHAT SHE SAID.
STILL, THERE ARE PLENTY OF SILVER LININGS HERE. I WOKE UP A C.E.O. OF MY OWN COMPANY.
AUNT MAY COULDN'T BE PROUDER. AND, LOOK, SHE'S WALKING AGAIN!
OCK DEVELOPED TECH. FOR HER. SO SHE COULD WALK WITHOUT A CANE.
THAT CRAZY, EIGHT-ARMED, MIND-SWAPPING CREEP. NO MATTER WHAT HE DID TO ME, I'LL ALWAYS OWE HIM ONE FOR THAT.

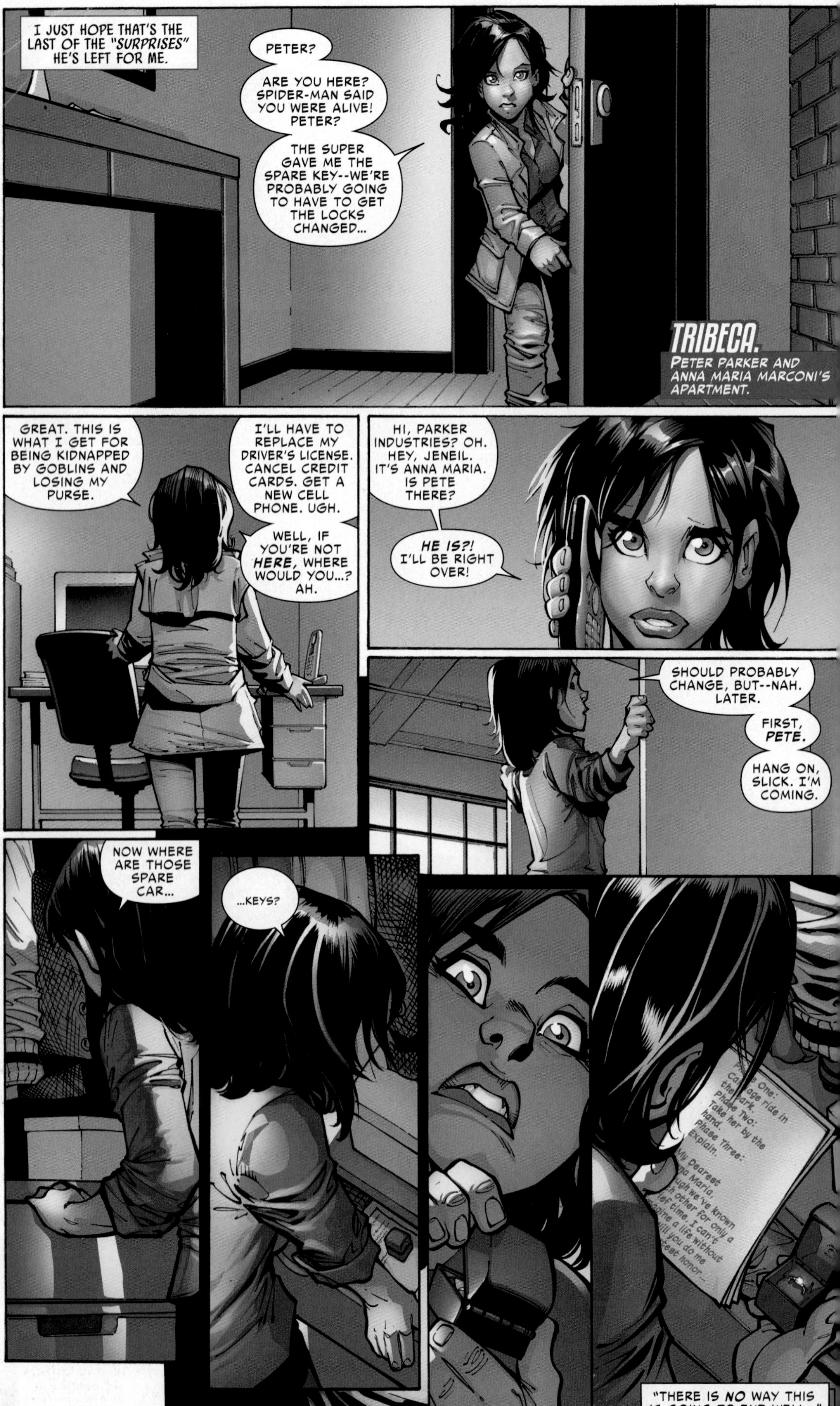

I JUST HOPE THAT'S THE LAST OF THE "SURPRISES" HE'S LEFT FOR ME.
PETER?
ARE YOU HERE? SPIDER-MAN SAID YOU WERE ALIVE! PETER?
THE SUPER GAVE ME THE SPARE KEY--WE'RE PROBABLY GOING TO HAVE TO GET THE LOCKS CHANGED...
TRIBECA.
PETER PARKER AND ANNA MARIA MARCONI'S APARTMENT.
GREAT. THIS IS WHAT I GET FOR BEING KIDNAPPED BY GOBLINS AND LOSING MY PURSE.
I'LL HAVE TO REPLACE MY DRIVER'S LICENSE. CANCEL CREDIT CARDS. GET A NEW CELL PHONE. UGH.
WELL, IF YOU'RE NOT HERE, WHERE WOULD YOU...? AH.
HI, PARKER INDUSTRIES? OH. HEY, JENEIL. IT'S ANNA MARIA. IS PETE THERE?
HE IS?! I'LL BE RIGHT OVER!
SHOULD PROBABLY CHANGE, BUT--NAH. LATER.
FIRST, PETE.
HANG ON, SLICK. I'M COMING.
NOW WHERE ARE THOSE SPARE CAR...
...KEYS?
Phase Two:
Take her by the
hand.
Phase Three:
Explain.
My Dearest
Maria,
we've known
other for only a
time, I can't
a life without
you do me
honor...
"THERE IS NO WAY THIS IS GOING TO END WELL..."

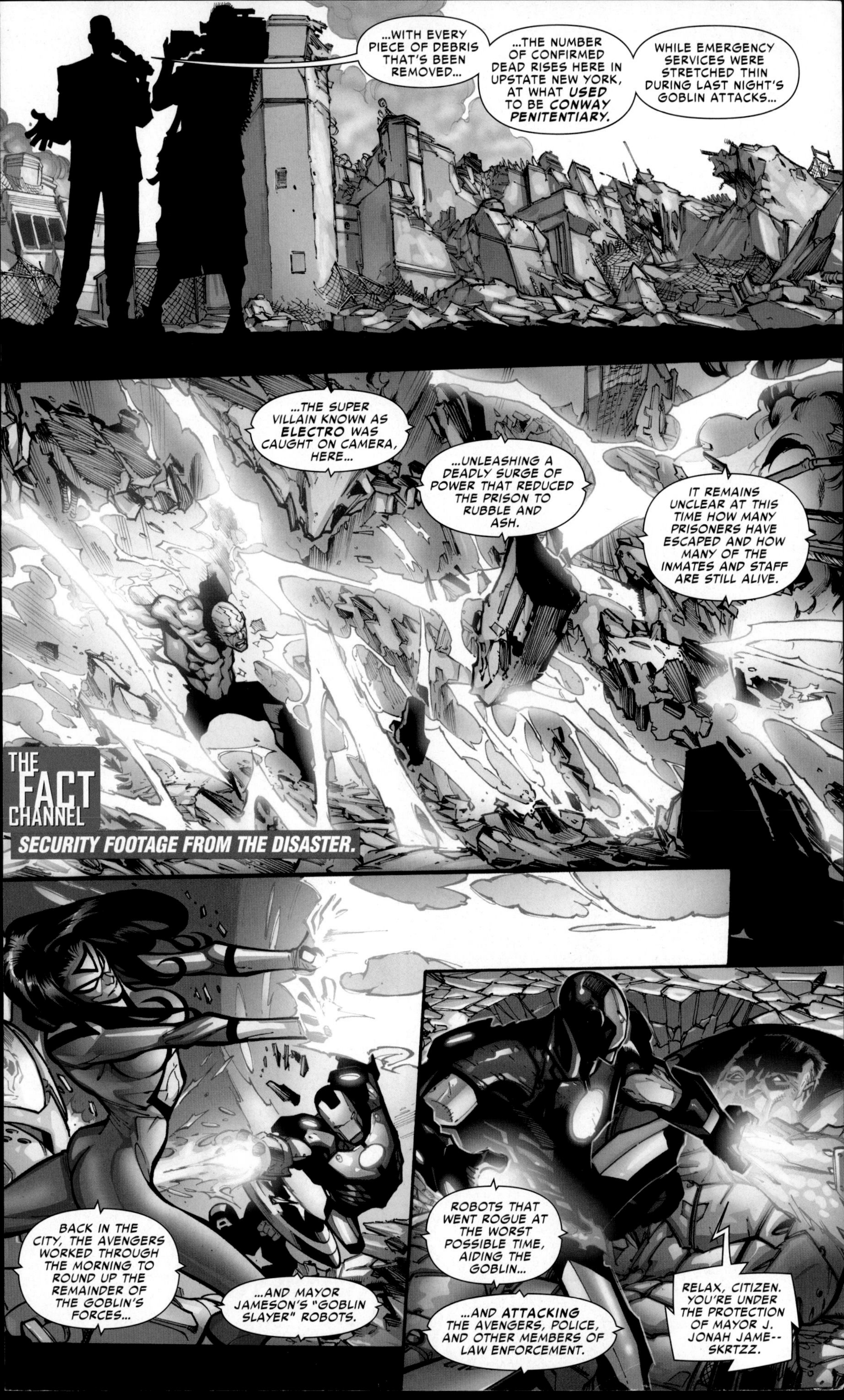
...WITH EVERY PIECE OF DEBRIS THAT'S BEEN REMOVED...
...THE NUMBER OF CONFIRMED DEAD RISES HERE IN UPSTATE NEW YORK, AT WHAT USED TO BE CONWAY PENITENTIARY.
WHILE EMERGENCY SERVICES WERE STRETCHED THIN DURING LAST NIGHT'S GOBLIN ATTACKS...
...THE SUPER VILLAIN KNOWN AS ELECTRO WAS CAUGHT ON CAMERA, HERE...
...UNLEASHING A DEADLY SURGE OF POWER THAT REDUCED THE PRISON TO RUBBLE AND ASH.
IT REMAINS UNCLEAR AT THIS TIME HOW MANY PRISONERS HAVE ESCAPED AND HOW MANY OF THE INMATES AND STAFF ARE STILL ALIVE.
THE FACT CHANNEL
SECURITY FOOTAGE FROM THE DISASTER.
BACK IN THE CITY, THE AVENGERS WORKED THROUGH THE MORNING TO ROUND UP THE REMAINDER OF THE GOBLIN'S FORCES...
...AND MAYOR JAMESON'S "GOBLIN SLAYER" ROBOTS.
ROBOTS THAT WENT ROGUE AT THE WORST POSSIBLE TIME, AIDING THE GOBLIN...
...AND ATTACKING THE AVENGERS, POLICE, AND OTHER MEMBERS OF LAW ENFORCEMENT.
RELAX, CITIZEN. YOU'RE UNDER THE PROTECTION OF MAYOR J. JONAH JAME-- SKRTZZ.

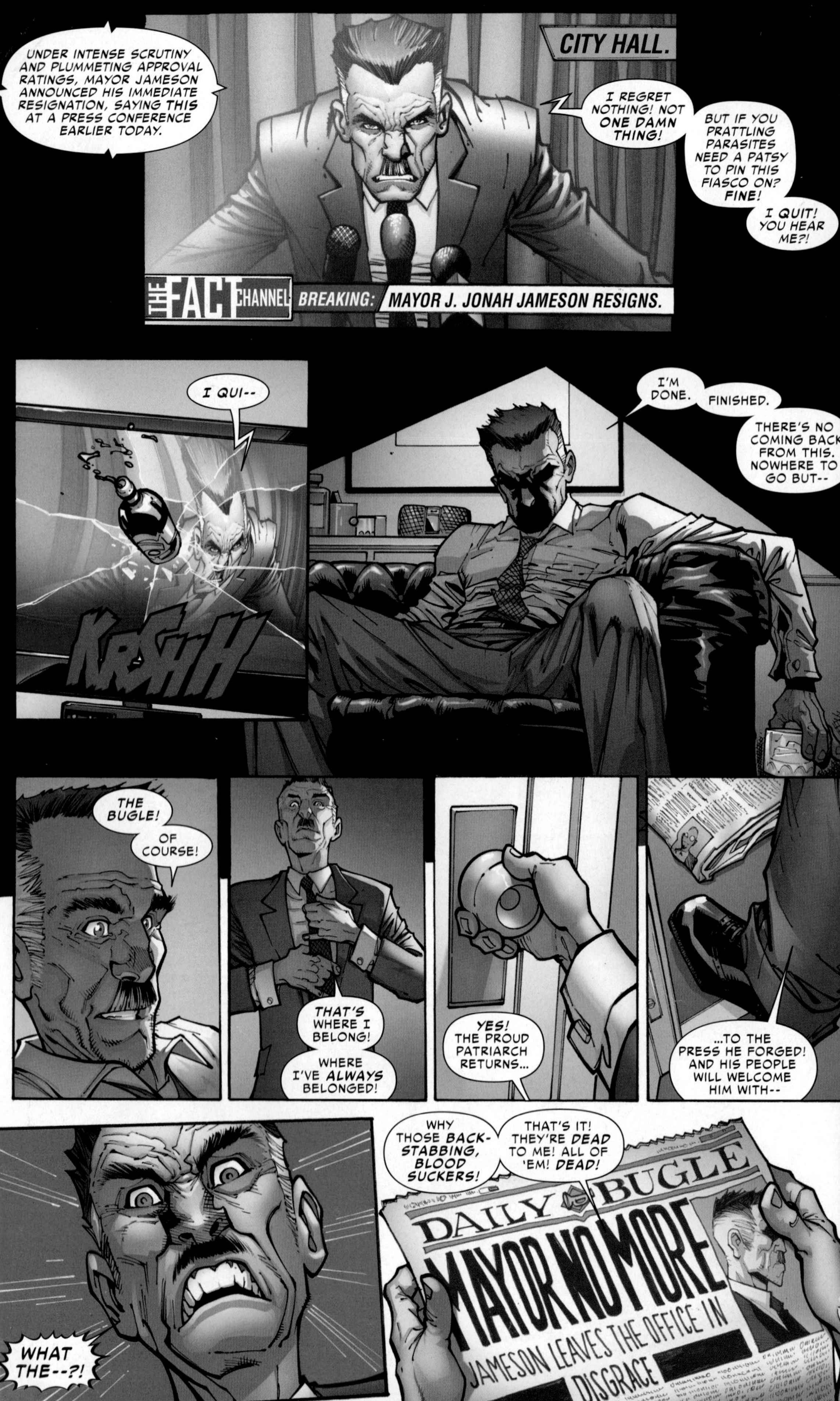
CITY HALL.
UNDER INTENSE SCRUTINY AND PLUMMETING APPROVAL RATINGS, MAYOR JAMESON ANNOUNCED HIS IMMEDIATE RESIGNATION, SAYING THIS AT A PRESS CONFERENCE EARLIER TODAY.
I REGRET NOTHING! NOT ONE DAMN THING!
BUT IF YOU PRATTLING PARASITES NEED A PATSY TO PIN THIS FIASCO ON? FINE!
I QUIT! YOU HEAR ME?!
THE FACT CHANNEL
BREAKING: MAYOR J. JONAH JAMESON RESIGNS.
I QUI--
KRSHH
I'M DONE.
FINISHED.
THERE'S NO COMING BACK FROM THIS. NOWHERE TO GO BUT--
THE BUGLE!
OF COURSE!
THAT'S WHERE I BELONG!
WHERE I'VE ALWAYS BELONGED!
YES! THE PROUD PATRIARCH RETURNS...
...TO THE PRESS HE FORGED! AND HIS PEOPLE WILL WELCOME HIM WITH--
WHAT THE--?!
WHY THOSE BACK-STABBING, BLOOD SUCKERS!
THAT'S IT! THEY'RE DEAD TO ME! ALL OF 'EM! DEAD!
DAILY BUGLE
MAYOR NO MORE
JAMESON LEAVES THE OFFICE IN DISGRACE

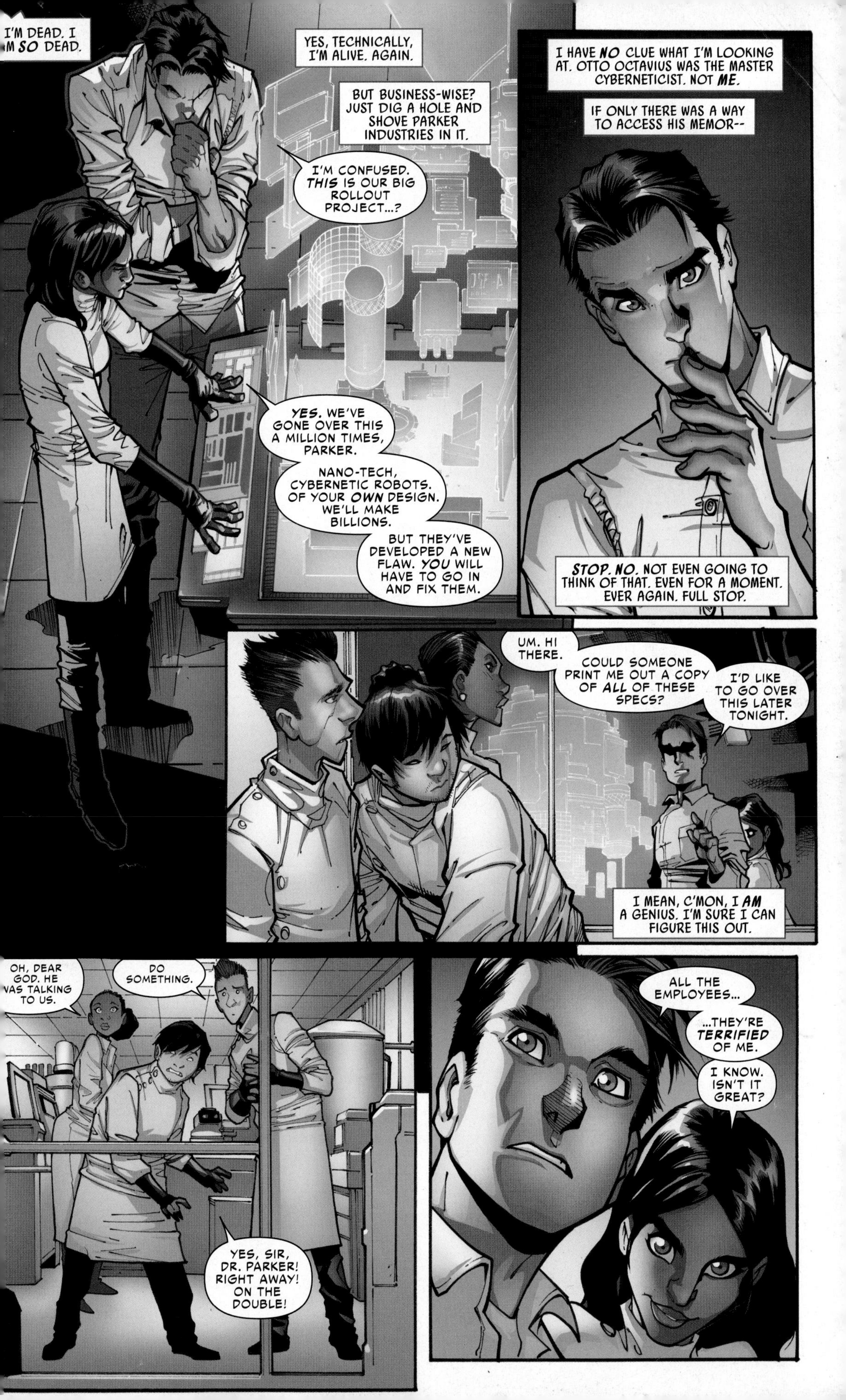
I'M DEAD. I
AM SO DEAD.
YES, TECHNICALLY, I'M ALIVE. AGAIN.
BUT BUSINESS-WISE? JUST DIG A HOLE AND SHOVE PARKER INDUSTRIES IN IT.
I'M CONFUSED. THIS IS OUR BIG ROLLOUT PROJECT...?
YES. WE'VE GONE OVER THIS A MILLION TIMES, PARKER.
NANO-TECH, CYBERNETIC ROBOTS. OF YOUR OWN DESIGN. WE'LL MAKE BILLIONS.
BUT THEY'VE DEVELOPED A NEW FLAW. YOU WILL HAVE TO GO IN AND FIX THEM.
I HAVE NO CLUE WHAT I'M LOOKING AT. OTTO OCTAVIUS WAS THE MASTER CYBERNETICIST. NOT ME.
IF ONLY THERE WAS A WAY TO ACCESS HIS MEMOR--
STOP. NO. NOT EVEN GOING TO THINK OF THAT. EVEN FOR A MOMENT. EVER AGAIN. FULL STOP.
UM. HI THERE.
COULD SOMEONE PRINT ME OUT A COPY OF ALL OF THESE SPECS?
I'D LIKE TO GO OVER THIS LATER TONIGHT.
I MEAN, C'MON, I AM A GENIUS. I'M SURE I CAN FIGURE THIS OUT.
OH, DEAR GOD. HE
WAS TALKING TO US.
DO SOMETHING.
YES, SIR, DR. PARKER! RIGHT AWAY! ON THE DOUBLE!
ALL THE EMPLOYEES...
...THEY'RE TERRIFIED OF ME.
I KNOW. ISN'T IT GREAT?

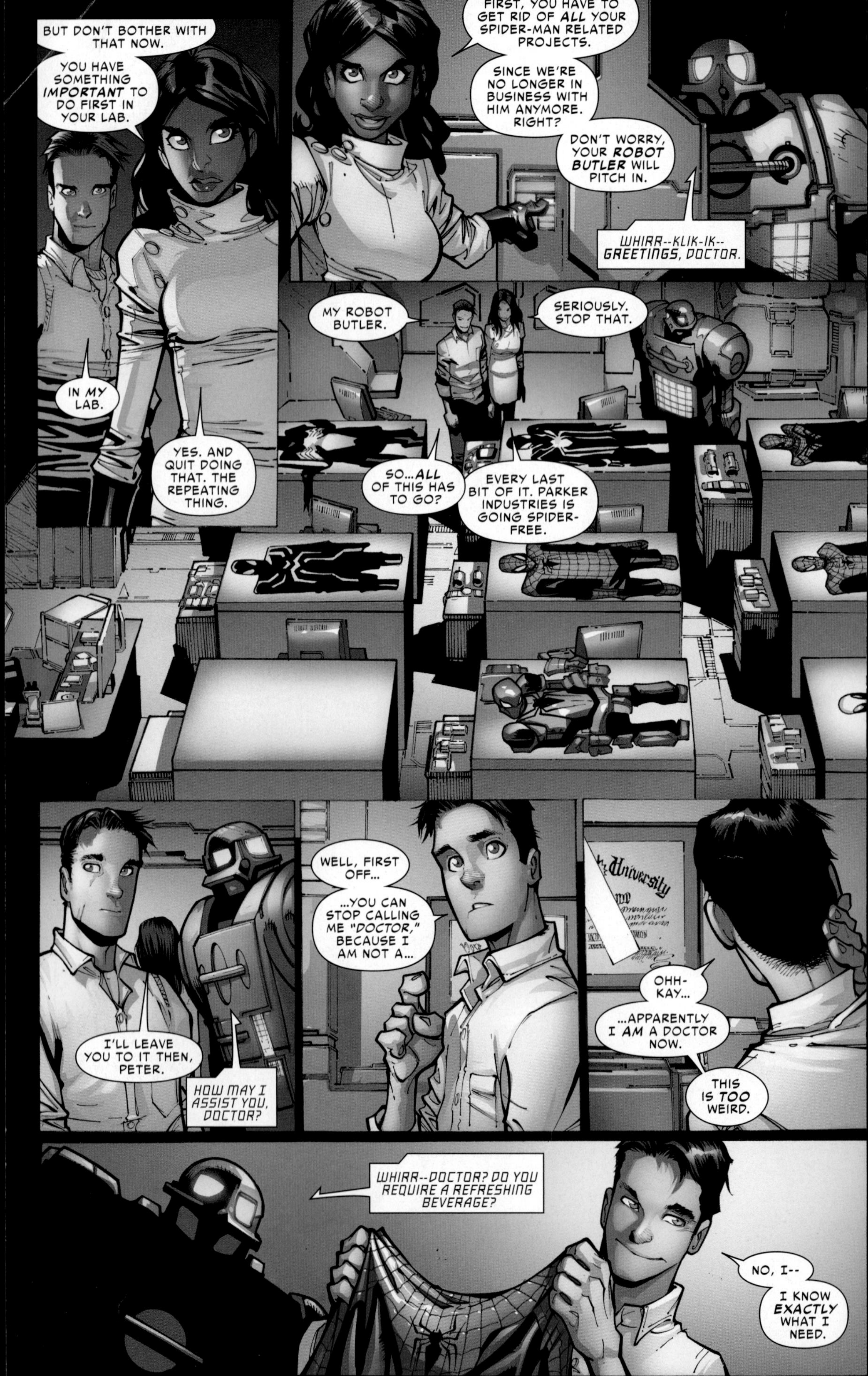
BUT DON'T BOTHER WITH THAT NOW.
YOU HAVE SOMETHING *IMPORTANT* TO DO FIRST IN YOUR LAB.
IN *MY* LAB.
YES. AND QUIT DOING THAT. THE REPEATING THING.
FIRST, YOU HAVE TO GET RID OF *ALL* YOUR SPIDER-MAN RELATED PROJECTS.
SINCE WE'RE NO LONGER IN BUSINESS WITH HIM ANYMORE. RIGHT?
DON'T WORRY, YOUR *ROBOT BUTLER* WILL PITCH IN.
WHIRR--KLIK-IK-- GREETINGS, DOCTOR.
MY ROBOT BUTLER.
SERIOUSLY. STOP THAT.
SO...*ALL* OF THIS HAS TO GO?
EVERY LAST BIT OF IT. PARKER INDUSTRIES IS GOING SPIDER-FREE.
I'LL LEAVE YOU TO IT THEN, PETER.
HOW MAY I ASSIST YOU, DOCTOR?
WELL, FIRST OFF...
...YOU CAN STOP CALLING ME *"DOCTOR,"* BECAUSE I AM NOT A...
OHH-KAY...
...APPARENTLY I *AM* A DOCTOR NOW.
THIS IS *TOO* WEIRD.
WHIRR--DOCTOR? DO YOU REQUIRE A REFRESHING BEVERAGE?
NO, I--
I KNOW *EXACTLY* WHAT I NEED.

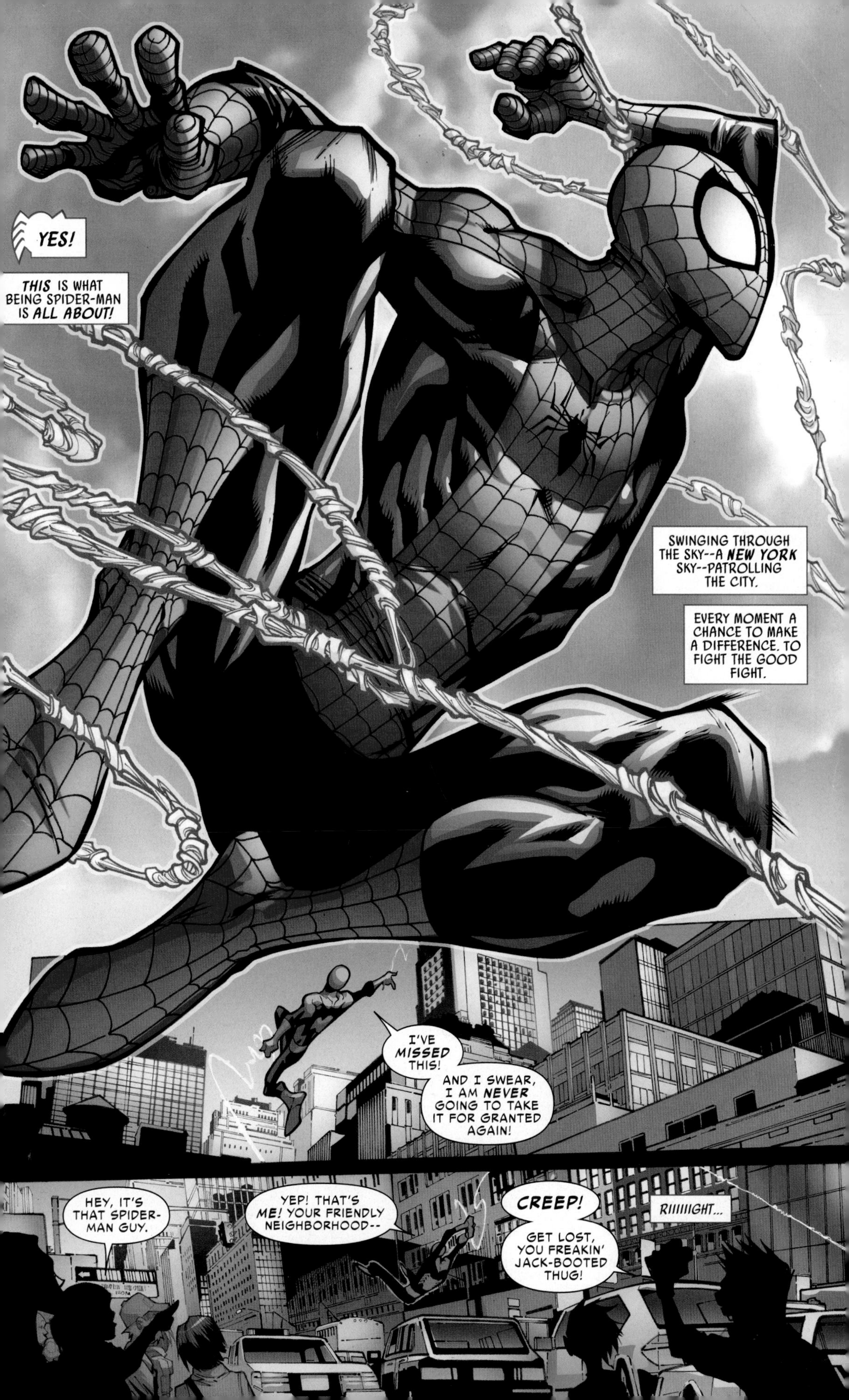
YES!
THIS IS WHAT BEING SPIDER-MAN IS ALL ABOUT!
SWINGING THROUGH THE SKY--A NEW YORK SKY--PATROLLING THE CITY.
EVERY MOMENT A CHANCE TO MAKE A DIFFERENCE. TO FIGHT THE GOOD FIGHT.
I'VE MISSED THIS!
AND I SWEAR, I AM NEVER GOING TO TAKE IT FOR GRANTED AGAIN!
HEY, IT'S THAT SPIDER-MAN GUY.
YEP! THAT'S ME! YOUR FRIENDLY NEIGHBORHOOD--
CREEP!
GET LOST, YOU FREAKIN' JACK-BOOTED THUG!
RIIIIIGHT...

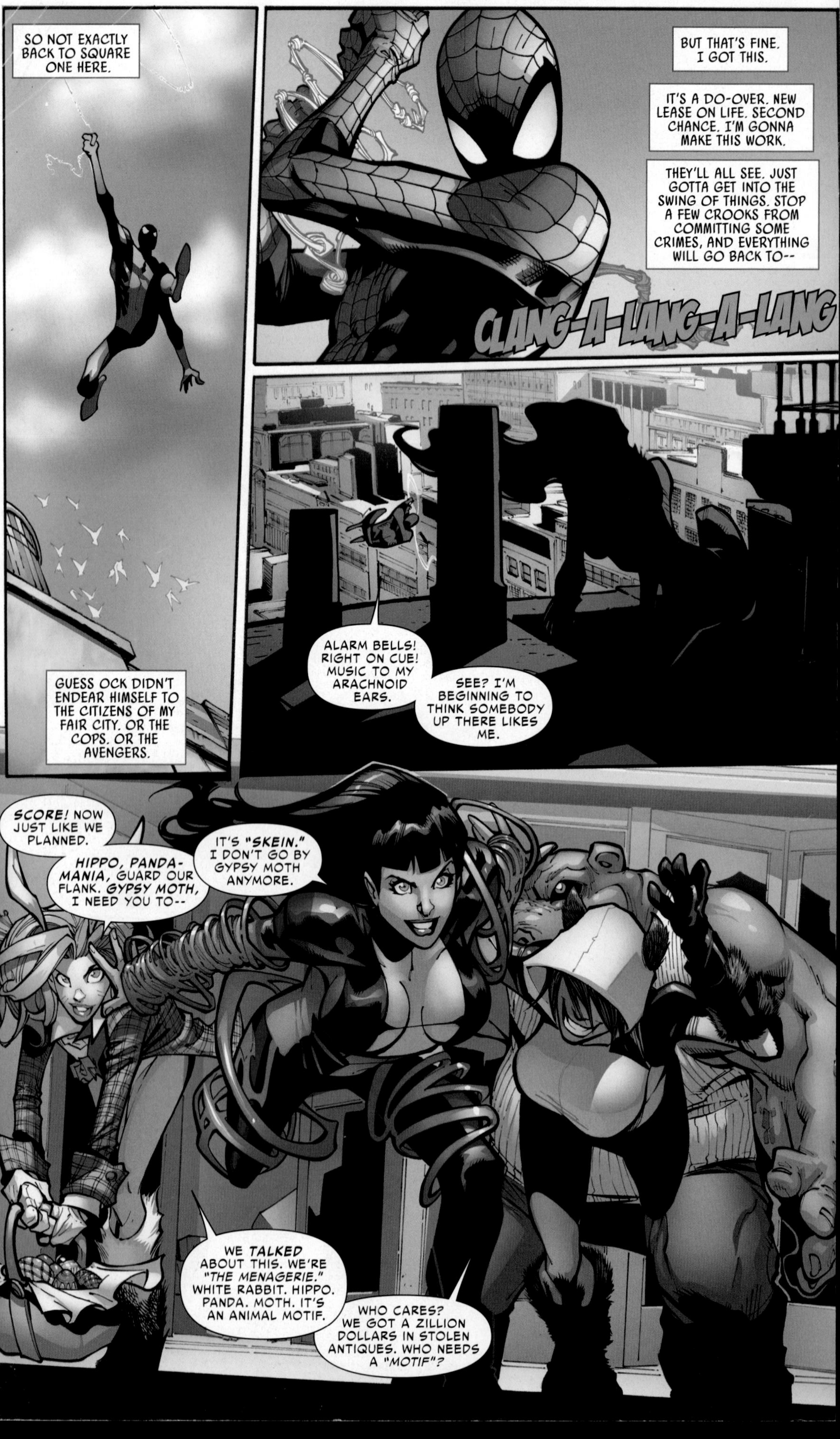
SO NOT EXACTLY BACK TO SQUARE ONE HERE.
BUT THAT'S FINE. I GOT THIS.
IT'S A DO-OVER. NEW LEASE ON LIFE. SECOND CHANCE. I'M GONNA MAKE THIS WORK.
THEY'LL ALL SEE. JUST GOTTA GET INTO THE SWING OF THINGS. STOP A FEW CROOKS FROM COMMITTING SOME CRIMES, AND EVERYTHING WILL GO BACK TO--
CLANG-A-LANG-A-LANG
GUESS OCK DIDN'T ENDEAR HIMSELF TO THE CITIZENS OF MY FAIR CITY. OR THE COPS. OR THE AVENGERS.
ALARM BELLS! RIGHT ON CUE! MUSIC TO MY ARACHNOID EARS.
SEE? I'M BEGINNING TO THINK SOMEBODY UP THERE LIKES ME.
SCORE! NOW JUST LIKE WE PLANNED.
HIPPO, PANDA-MANIA, GUARD OUR FLANK. GYPSY MOTH, I NEED YOU TO--
IT'S "SKEIN." I DON'T GO BY GYPSY MOTH ANYMORE.
WE TALKED ABOUT THIS. WE'RE "THE MENAGERIE." WHITE RABBIT. HIPPO. PANDA. MOTH. IT'S AN ANIMAL MOTIF.
WHO CARES? WE GOT A ZILLION DOLLARS IN STOLEN ANTIQUES. WHO NEEDS A "MOTIF"?

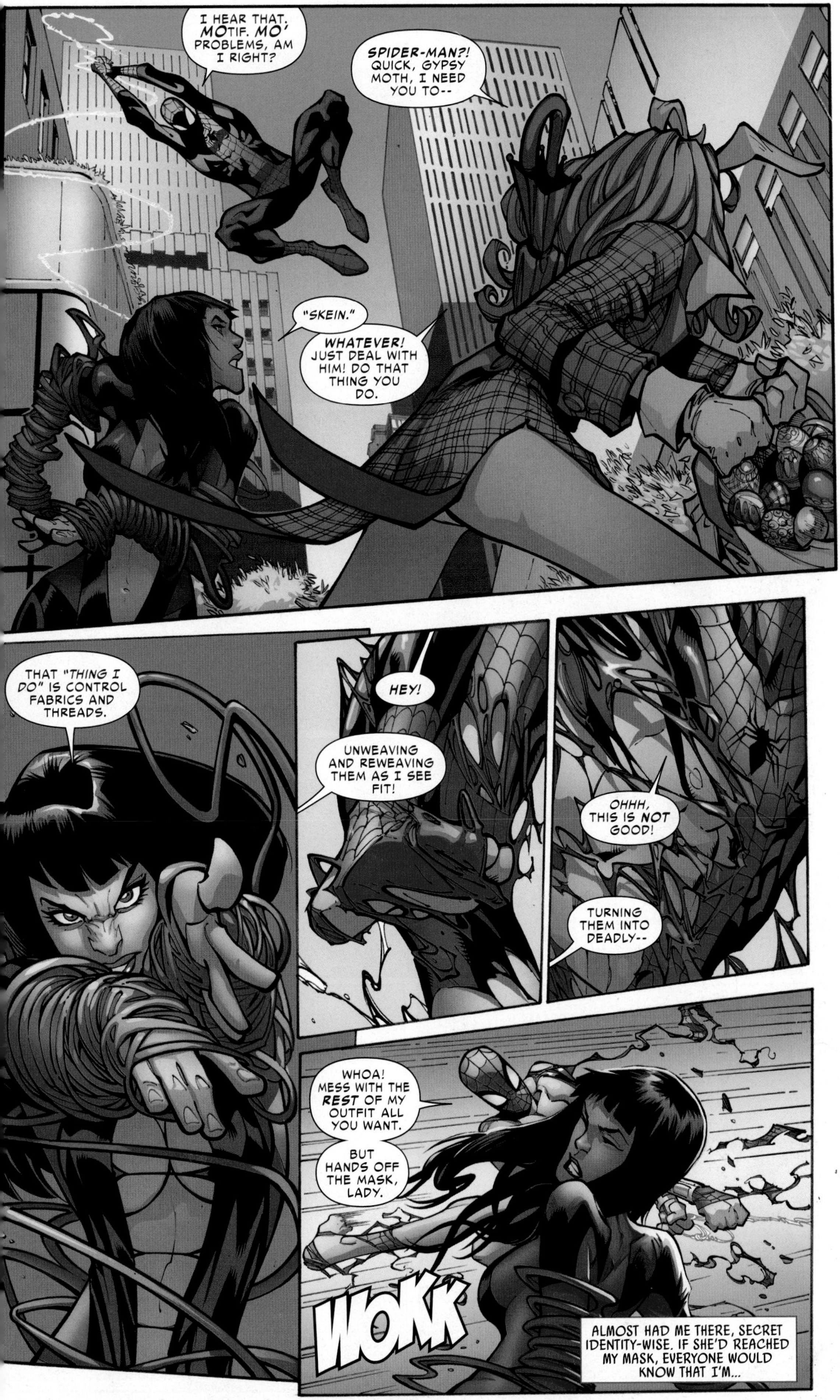
I HEAR THAT. MOTIF. MO' PROBLEMS, AM I RIGHT?
SPIDER-MAN?! QUICK, GYPSY MOTH, I NEED YOU TO--
"SKEIN."
WHATEVER! JUST DEAL WITH HIM! DO THAT THING YOU DO.
THAT "THING I DO" IS CONTROL FABRICS AND THREADS.
HEY!
UNWEAVING AND REWEAVING THEM AS I SEE FIT!
OHHH, THIS IS NOT GOOD!
TURNING THEM INTO DEADLY--
WHOA! MESS WITH THE REST OF MY OUTFIT ALL YOU WANT.
BUT HANDS OFF THE MASK, LADY.
WOKK
ALMOST HAD ME THERE, SECRET IDENTITY-WISE. IF SHE'D REACHED MY MASK, EVERYONE WOULD KNOW THAT I'M...

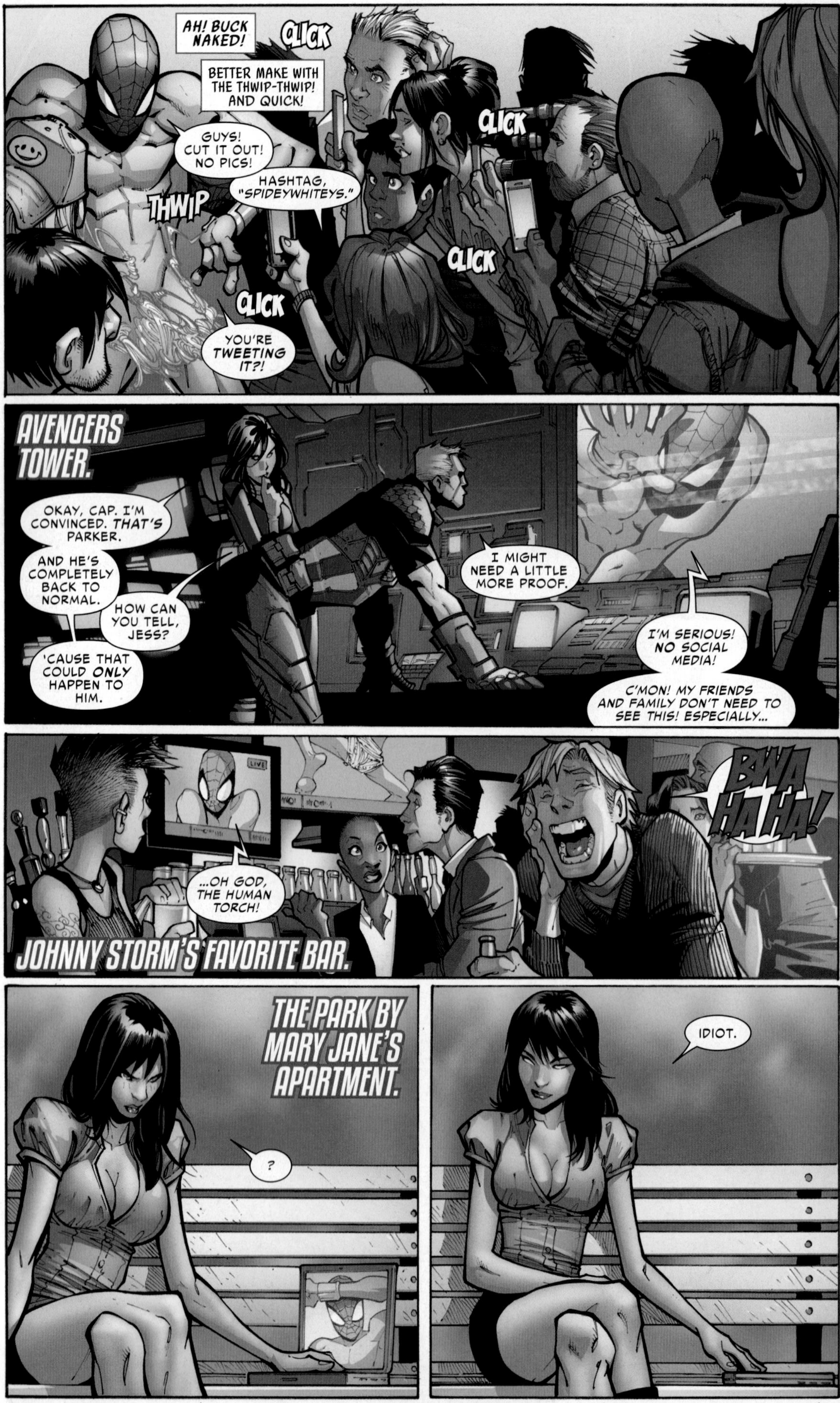
AH! BUCK NAKED!
CLICK
BETTER MAKE WITH THE THWIP-THWIP! AND QUICK!
GUYS! CUT IT OUT! NO PICS!
CLICK
HASHTAG, "SPIDEYWHITEYS."
THWIP
CLICK
CLICK
YOU'RE TWEETING IT?!
AVENGERS TOWER.
OKAY, CAP. I'M CONVINCED. THAT'S PARKER.
AND HE'S COMPLETELY BACK TO NORMAL.
HOW CAN YOU TELL, JESS?
'CAUSE THAT COULD ONLY HAPPEN TO HIM.
I MIGHT NEED A LITTLE MORE PROOF.
I'M SERIOUS! NO SOCIAL MEDIA!
C'MON! MY FRIENDS AND FAMILY DON'T NEED TO SEE THIS! ESPECIALLY...
LIVE
...OH GOD, THE HUMAN TORCH!
BWA HA HA!
JOHNNY STORM'S FAVORITE BAR.
THE PARK BY MARY JANE'S APARTMENT.
?
IDIOT.

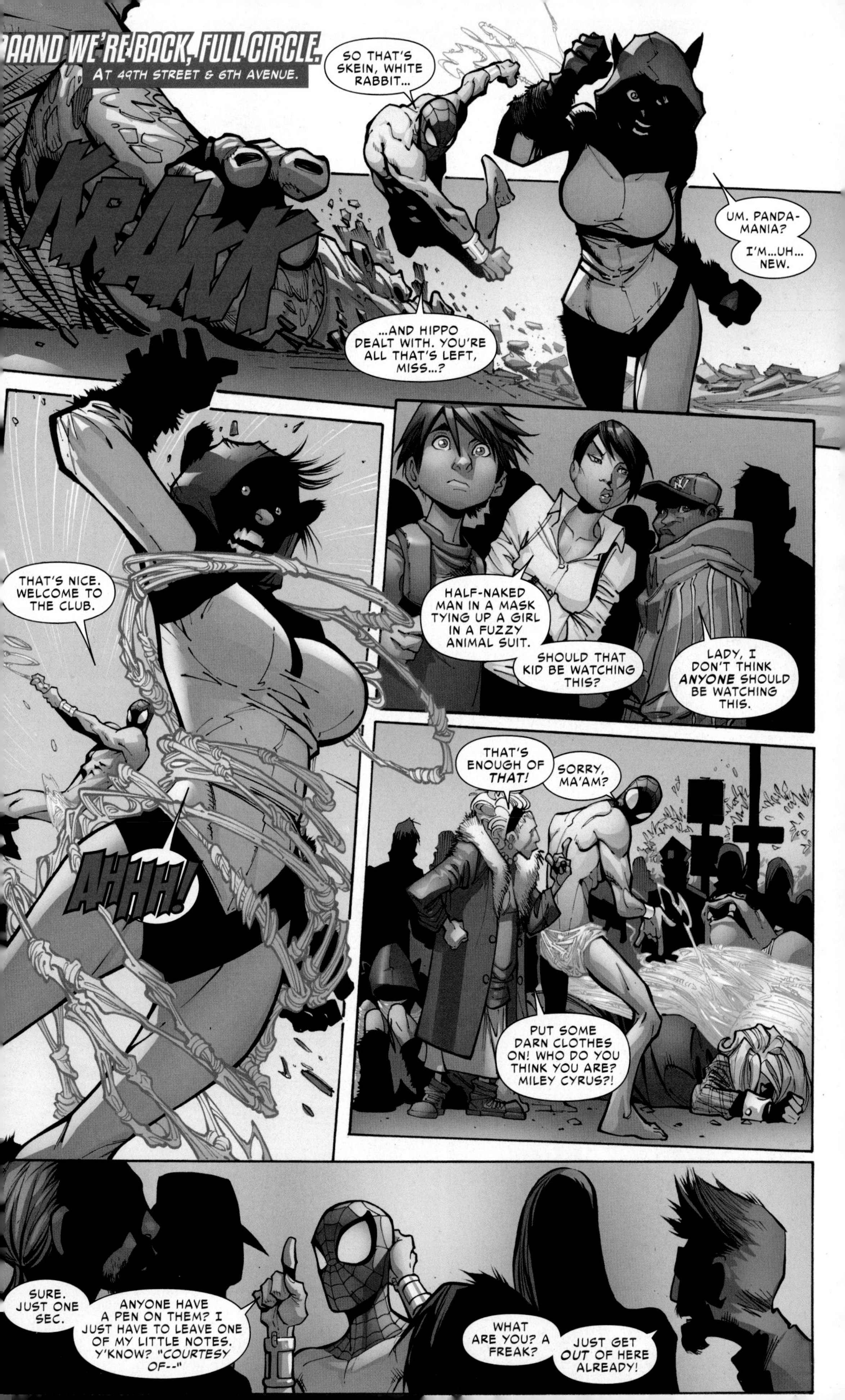
AAND WE'RE BACK, FULL CIRCLE.
AT 49TH STREET & 6TH AVENUE.
KRAKK
SO THAT'S SKEIN, WHITE RABBIT...
...AND HIPPO DEALT WITH. YOU'RE ALL THAT'S LEFT, MISS...?
UM. PANDA-MANIA?
I'M...UH... NEW.
THAT'S NICE. WELCOME TO THE CLUB.
AHHH!
HALF-NAKED MAN IN A MASK TYING UP A GIRL IN A FUZZY ANIMAL SUIT.
SHOULD THAT KID BE WATCHING THIS?
LADY, I DON'T THINK ANYONE SHOULD BE WATCHING THIS.
THAT'S ENOUGH OF THAT!
SORRY, MA'AM?
PUT SOME DARN CLOTHES ON! WHO DO YOU THINK YOU ARE? MILEY CYRUS?!
SURE. JUST ONE SEC.
ANYONE HAVE A PEN ON THEM? I JUST HAVE TO LEAVE ONE OF MY LITTLE NOTES. Y'KNOW? "COURTESY OF--"
WHAT ARE YOU? A FREAK?
JUST GET OUT OF HERE ALREADY!

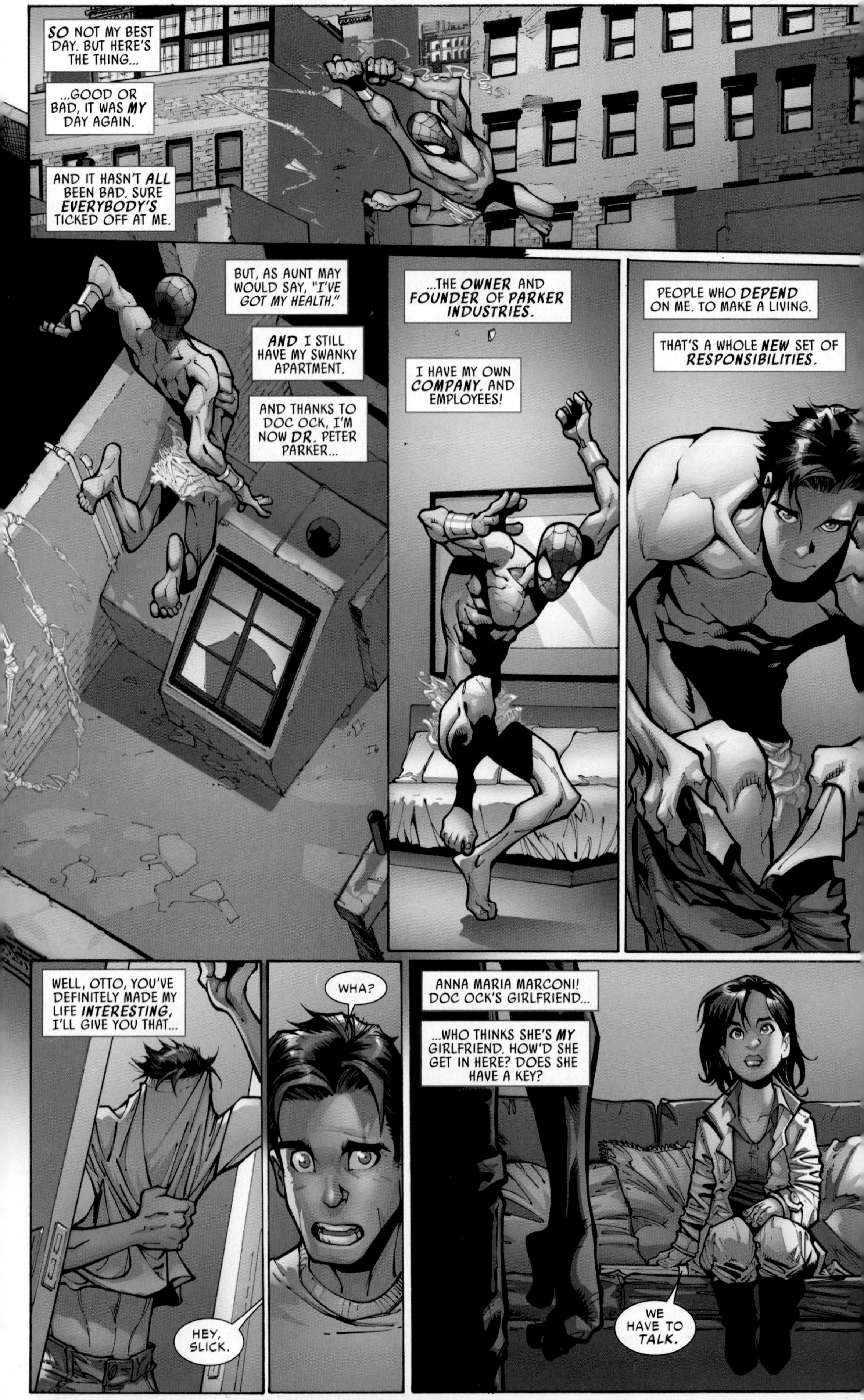
SO NOT MY BEST DAY. BUT HERE'S THE THING...
...GOOD OR BAD, IT WAS MY DAY AGAIN.
AND IT HASN'T ALL BEEN BAD. SURE EVERYBODY'S TICKED OFF AT ME.
BUT, AS AUNT MAY WOULD SAY, "I'VE GOT MY HEALTH."
AND I STILL HAVE MY SWANKY APARTMENT.
AND THANKS TO DOC OCK, I'M NOW DR. PETER PARKER...
...THE OWNER AND FOUNDER OF PARKER INDUSTRIES.
I HAVE MY OWN COMPANY. AND EMPLOYEES!
PEOPLE WHO DEPEND ON ME. TO MAKE A LIVING.
THAT'S A WHOLE NEW SET OF RESPONSIBILITIES.
WELL, OTTO, YOU'VE DEFINITELY MADE MY LIFE INTERESTING, I'LL GIVE YOU THAT...
HEY, SLICK.
WHA?
ANNA MARIA MARCONI! DOC OCK'S GIRLFRIEND...
...WHO THINKS SHE'S MY GIRLFRIEND. HOW'D SHE GET IN HERE? DOES SHE HAVE A KEY?
WE HAVE TO TALK.

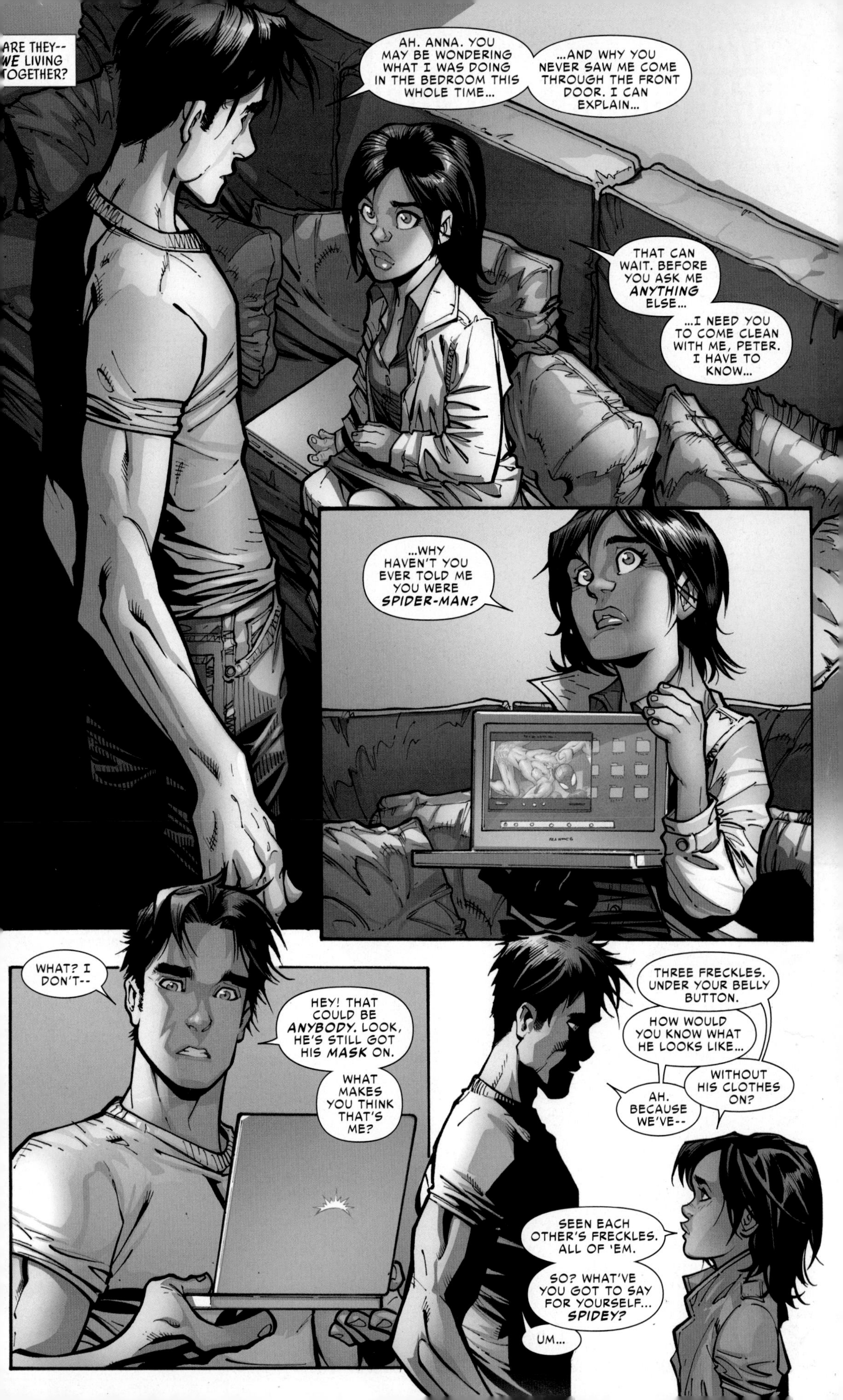
ARE THEY-- WE LIVING TOGETHER?
AH. ANNA. YOU MAY BE WONDERING WHAT I WAS DOING IN THE BEDROOM THIS WHOLE TIME...
...AND WHY YOU NEVER SAW ME COME THROUGH THE FRONT DOOR. I CAN EXPLAIN...
THAT CAN WAIT. BEFORE YOU ASK ME ANYTHING ELSE...
...I NEED YOU TO COME CLEAN WITH ME, PETER. I HAVE TO KNOW...
...WHY HAVEN'T YOU EVER TOLD ME YOU WERE SPIDER-MAN?
WHAT? I DON'T--
HEY! THAT COULD BE ANYBODY. LOOK, HE'S STILL GOT HIS MASK ON.
WHAT MAKES YOU THINK THAT'S ME?
THREE FRECKLES. UNDER YOUR BELLY BUTTON.
HOW WOULD YOU KNOW WHAT HE LOOKS LIKE...
WITHOUT HIS CLOTHES ON?
AH. BECAUSE WE'VE--
SEEN EACH OTHER'S FRECKLES. ALL OF 'EM.
SO? WHAT'VE YOU GOT TO SAY FOR YOURSELF... SPIDEY?
UM...

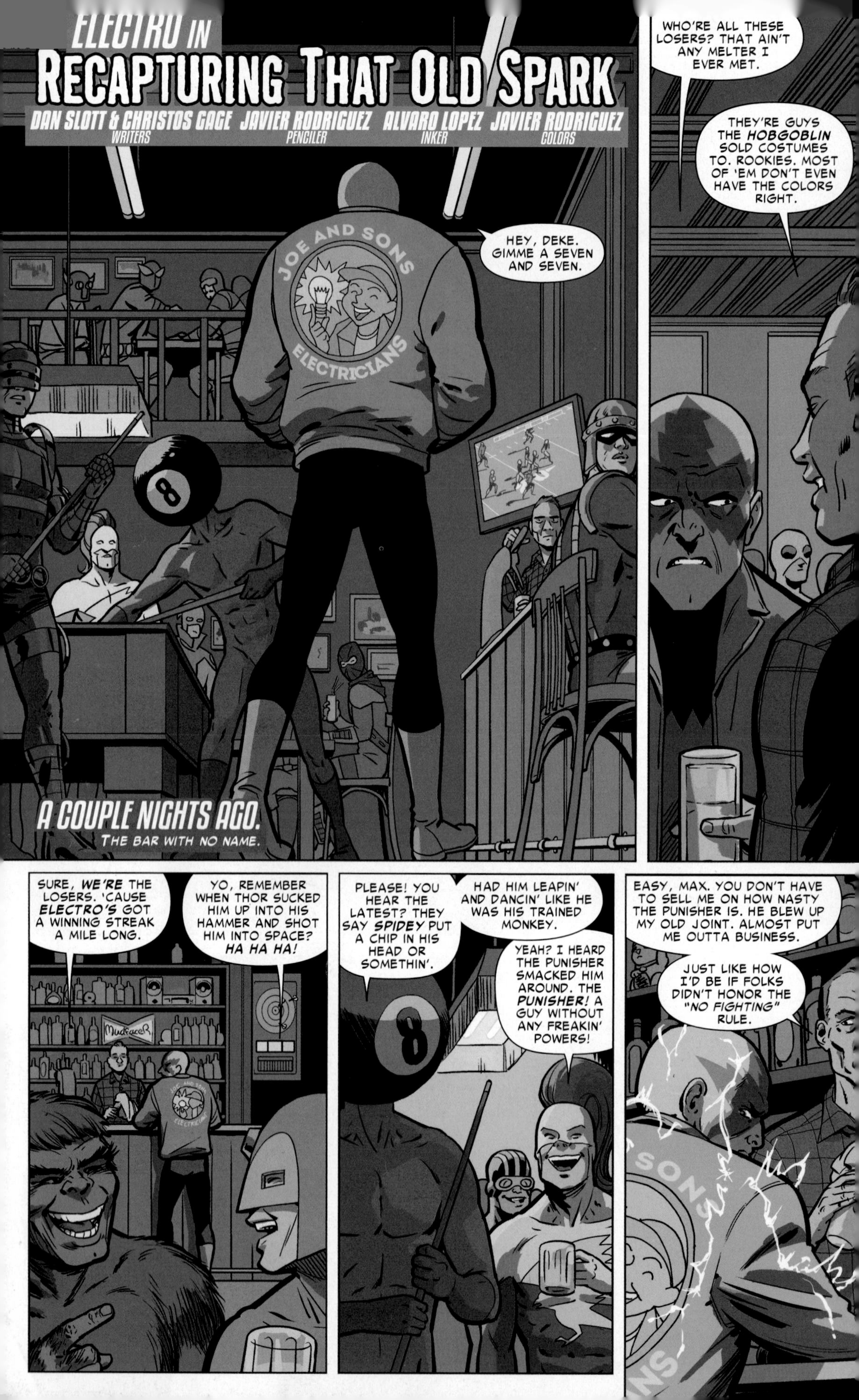
ELECTRO IN
RECAPTURING THAT OLD SPARK
DAN SLOTT & CHRISTOS GAGE WRITERS
JAVIER RODRIGUEZ PENCILER
ALVARO LOPEZ INKER
JAVIER RODRIGUEZ COLORS
A COUPLE NIGHTS AGO.
THE BAR WITH NO NAME.
HEY, DEKE. GIMME A SEVEN AND SEVEN.
JOE AND SONS ELECTRICIANS
WHO'RE ALL THESE LOSERS? THAT AIN'T ANY MELTER I EVER MET.
THEY'RE GUYS THE HOBGOBLIN SOLD COSTUMES TO. ROOKIES. MOST OF 'EM DON'T EVEN HAVE THE COLORS RIGHT.
SURE, WE'RE THE LOSERS. 'CAUSE ELECTRO'S GOT A WINNING STREAK A MILE LONG.
YO, REMEMBER WHEN THOR SUCKED HIM UP INTO HIS HAMMER AND SHOT HIM INTO SPACE? HA HA HA!
PLEASE! YOU HEAR THE LATEST? THEY SAY SPIDEY PUT A CHIP IN HIS HEAD OR SOMETHIN'.
HAD HIM LEAPIN' AND DANCIN' LIKE HE WAS HIS TRAINED MONKEY.
YEAH? I HEARD THE PUNISHER SMACKED HIM AROUND. THE PUNISHER! A GUY WITHOUT ANY FREAKIN' POWERS!
EASY, MAX. YOU DON'T HAVE TO SELL ME ON HOW NASTY THE PUNISHER IS. HE BLEW UP MY OLD JOINT. ALMOST PUT ME OUTTA BUSINESS.
JUST LIKE HOW I'D BE IF FOLKS DIDN'T HONOR THE "NO FIGHTING" RULE.

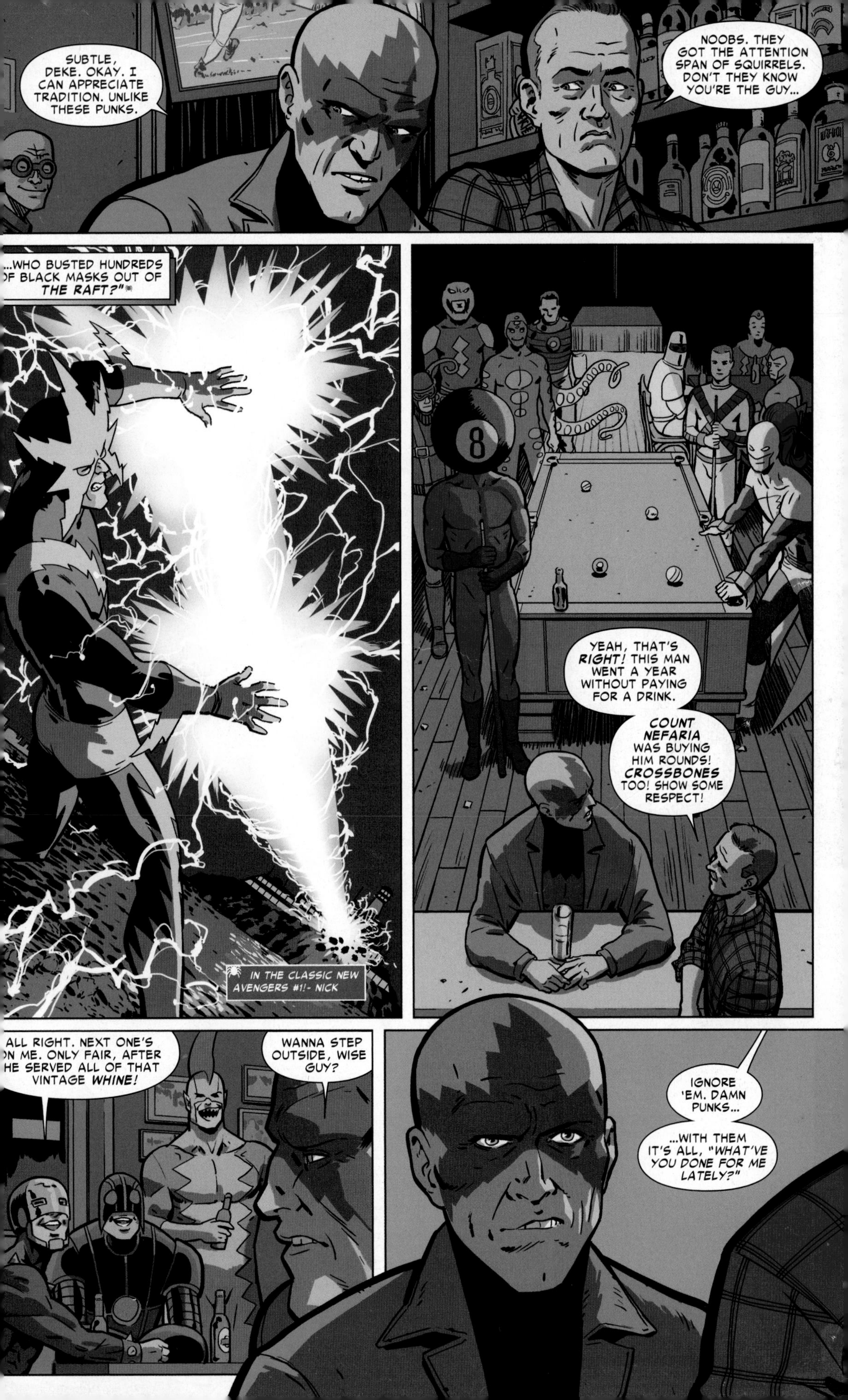
SUBTLE, DEKE. OKAY. I CAN APPRECIATE TRADITION. UNLIKE THESE PUNKS.
NOOBS. THEY GOT THE ATTENTION SPAN OF SQUIRRELS. DON'T THEY KNOW YOU'RE THE GUY...
...WHO BUSTED HUNDREDS OF BLACK MASKS OUT OF THE RAFT?"
IN THE CLASSIC NEW AVENGERS #1!- NICK
YEAH, THAT'S RIGHT! THIS MAN WENT A YEAR WITHOUT PAYING FOR A DRINK.
COUNT NEFARIA WAS BUYING HIM ROUNDS! CROSSBONES TOO! SHOW SOME RESPECT!
ALL RIGHT. NEXT ONE'S ON ME. ONLY FAIR, AFTER HE SERVED ALL OF THAT VINTAGE WHINE!
WANNA STEP OUTSIDE, WISE GUY?
IGNORE 'EM. DAMN PUNKS...
...WITH THEM IT'S ALL, "WHAT'VE YOU DONE FOR ME LATELY?"

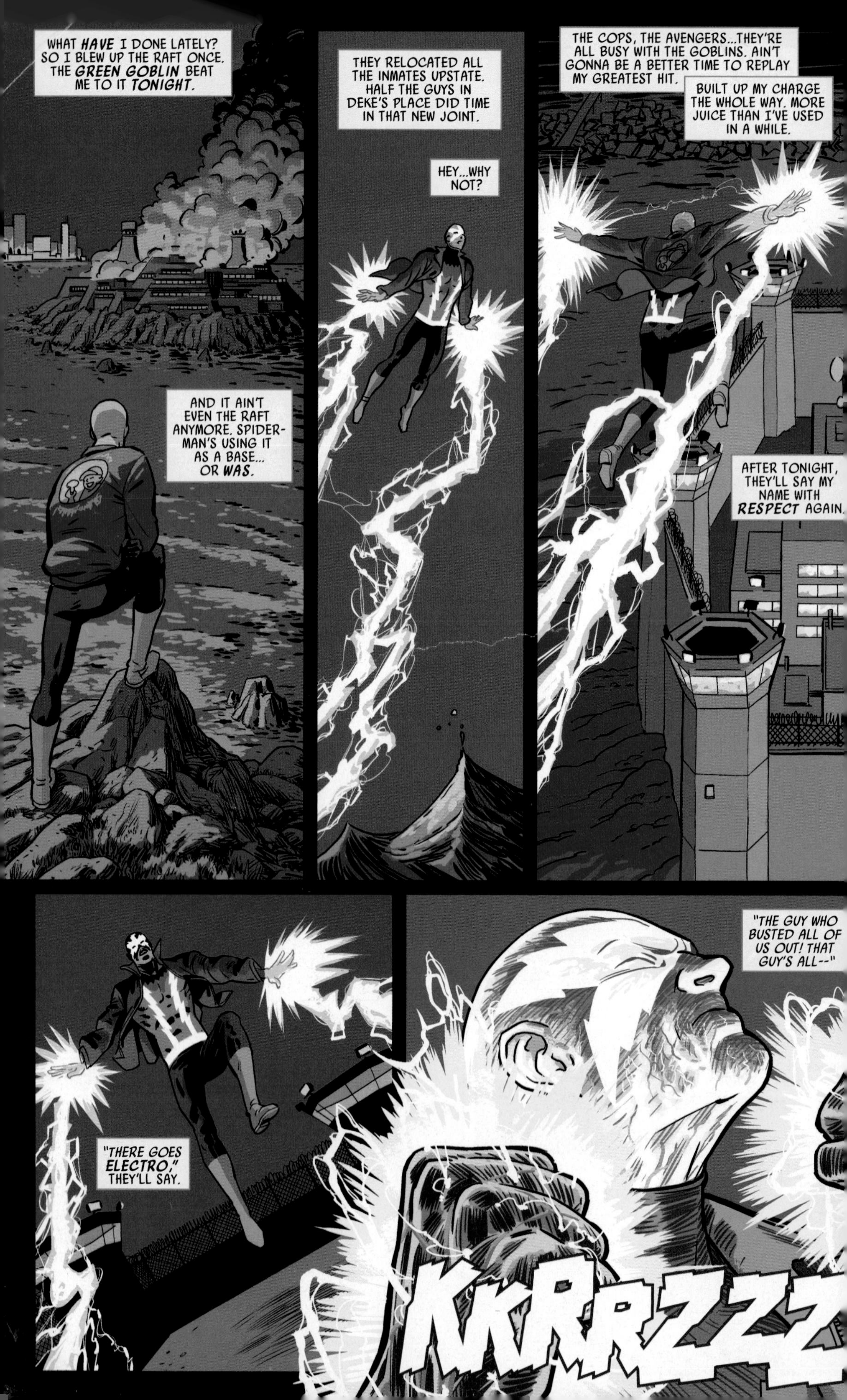
WHAT HAVE I DONE LATELY? SO I BLEW UP THE RAFT ONCE. THE GREEN GOBLIN BEAT ME TO IT TONIGHT.
AND IT AIN'T EVEN THE RAFT ANYMORE. SPIDER-MAN'S USING IT AS A BASE... OR WAS.
THEY RELOCATED ALL THE INMATES UPSTATE. HALF THE GUYS IN DEKE'S PLACE DID TIME IN THAT NEW JOINT.
HEY...WHY NOT?
THE COPS, THE AVENGERS...THEY'RE ALL BUSY WITH THE GOBLINS. AIN'T GONNA BE A BETTER TIME TO REPLAY MY GREATEST HIT.
BUILT UP MY CHARGE THE WHOLE WAY. MORE JUICE THAN I'VE USED IN A WHILE.
AFTER TONIGHT, THEY'LL SAY MY NAME WITH RESPECT AGAIN.
"THERE GOES ELECTRO," THEY'LL SAY.
"THE GUY WHO BUSTED ALL OF US OUT! THAT GUY'S ALL--"
KKRRZZZ

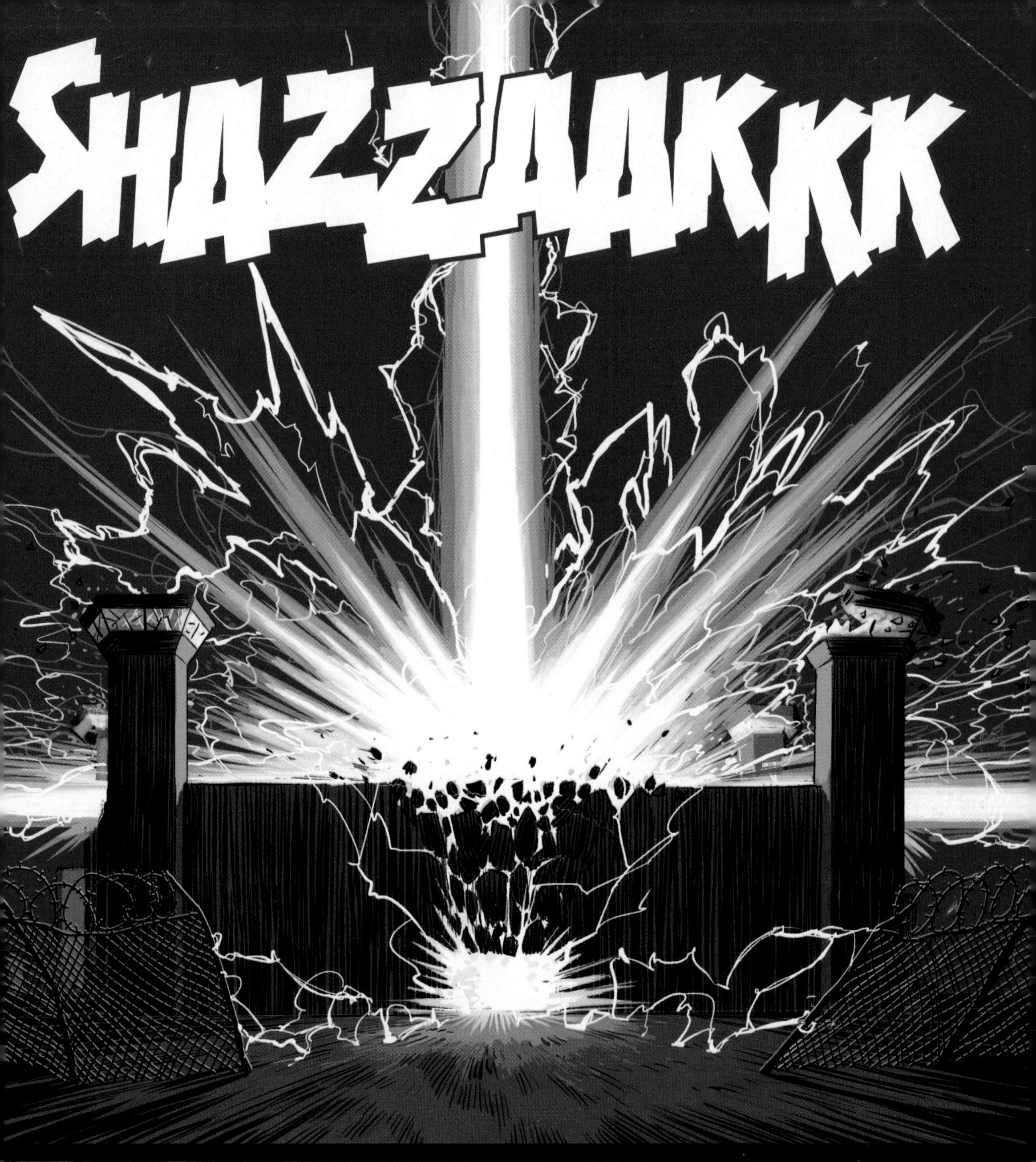
SHAZZAAKKK

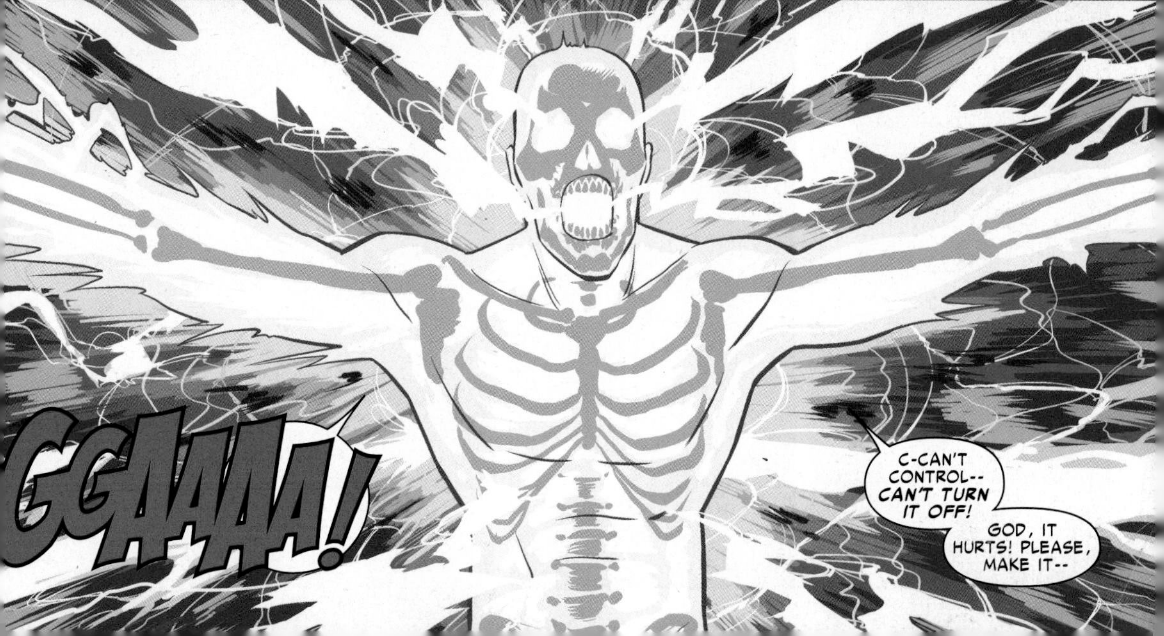
GGAAAA!
C-CAN'T CONTROL-- CAN'T TURN IT OFF!
GOD, IT HURTS! PLEASE, MAKE IT--

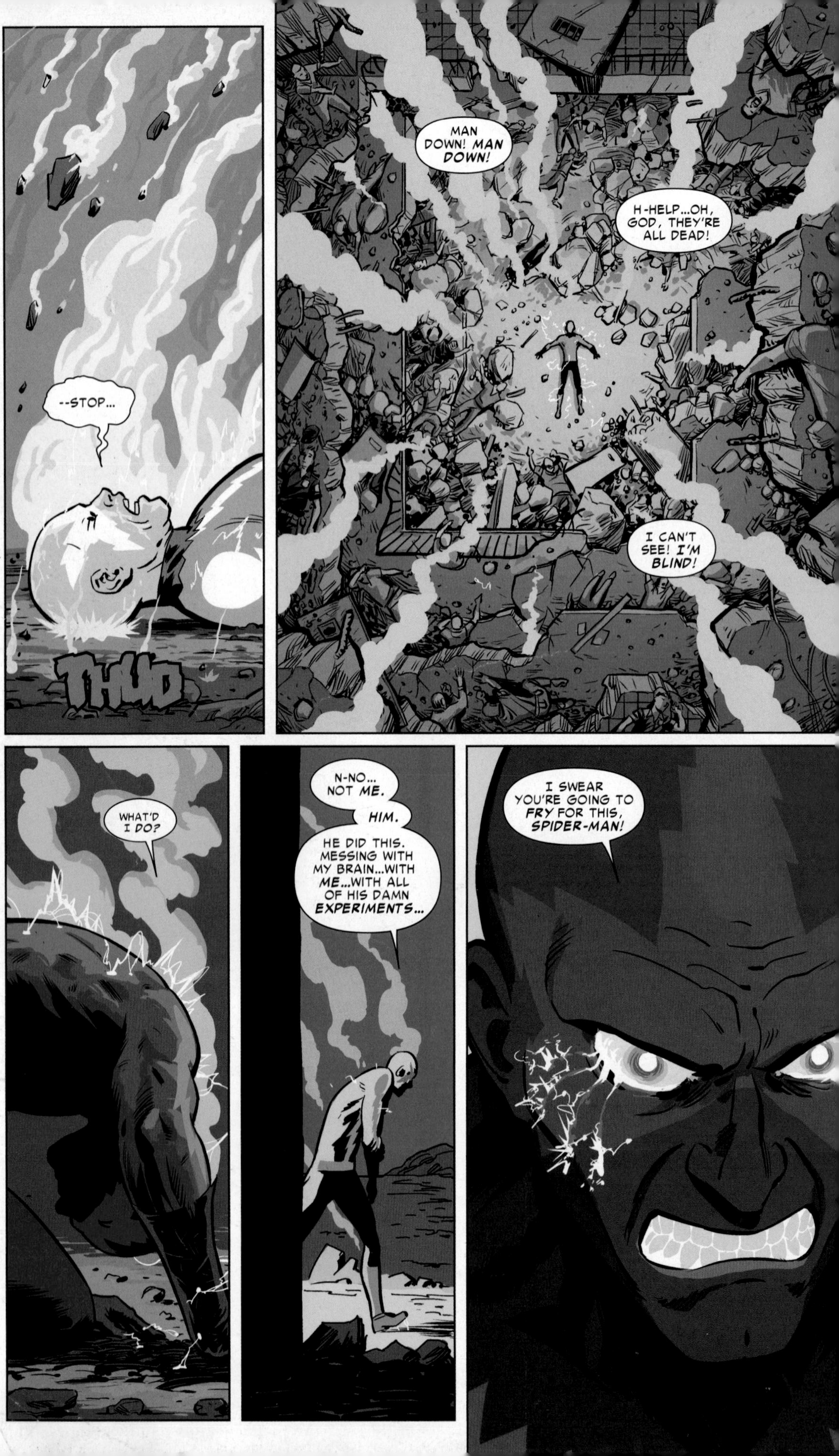
--STOP...
THUD
MAN DOWN! MAN DOWN!
H-HELP...OH, GOD, THEY'RE ALL DEAD!
I CAN'T SEE! I'M BLIND!
WHAT'D I DO?
N-NO... NOT ME.
HIM.
HE DID THIS. MESSING WITH MY BRAIN...WITH ME...WITH ALL OF HIS DAMN EXPERIMENTS...
I SWEAR YOU'RE GOING TO FRY FOR THIS, SPIDER-MAN!

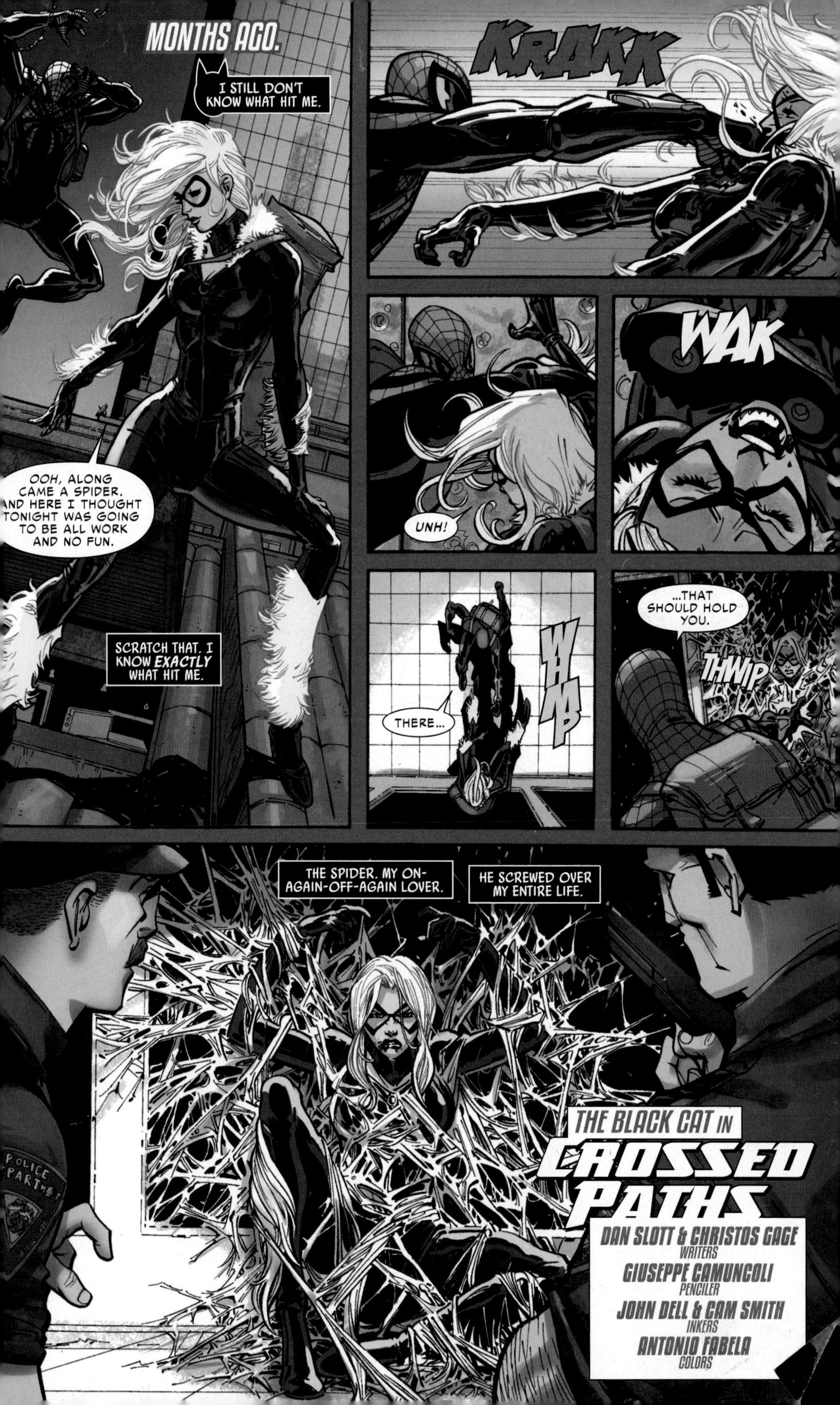
MONTHS AGO.
I STILL DON'T KNOW WHAT HIT ME.
OOH, ALONG CAME A SPIDER. AND HERE I THOUGHT TONIGHT WAS GOING TO BE ALL WORK AND NO FUN.
SCRATCH THAT. I KNOW EXACTLY WHAT HIT ME.
KRAKK
UNH!
WAK
WHAP
THERE...
...THAT SHOULD HOLD YOU.
THWIP
THE SPIDER. MY ON-AGAIN-OFF-AGAIN LOVER.
HE SCREWED OVER MY ENTIRE LIFE.
THE BLACK CAT IN
CROSSED PATHS
DAN SLOTT & CHRISTOS GAGE
WRITERS
GIUSEPPE CAMUNCOLI
PENCILER
JOHN DELL & CAM SMITH
INKERS
ANTONIO FABELA
COLORS

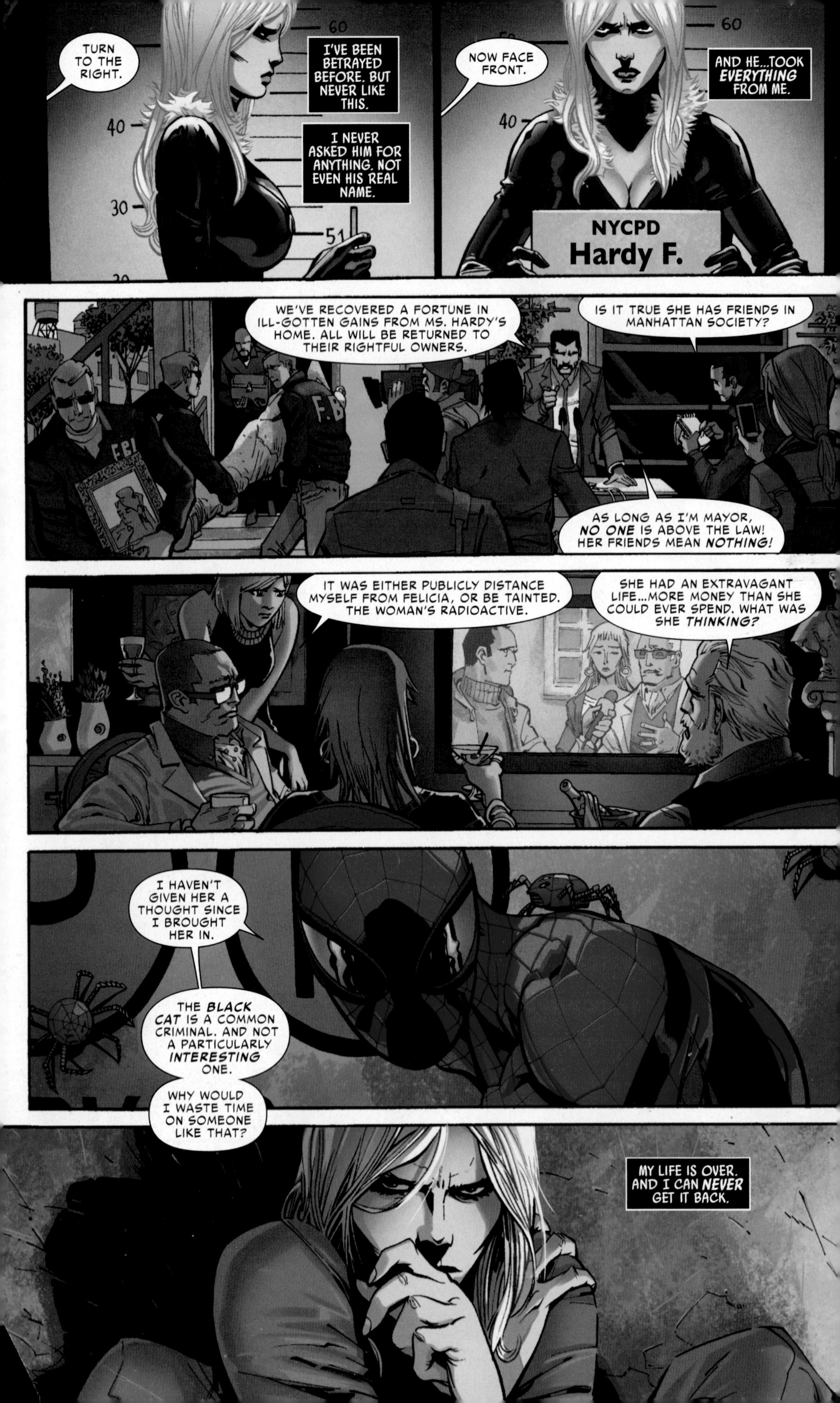
TURN TO THE RIGHT.
I'VE BEEN BETRAYED BEFORE. BUT NEVER LIKE THIS.
I NEVER ASKED HIM FOR ANYTHING. NOT EVEN HIS REAL NAME.
NOW FACE FRONT.
AND HE...TOOK EVERYTHING FROM ME.
NYCPD
Hardy F.
WE'VE RECOVERED A FORTUNE IN ILL-GOTTEN GAINS FROM MS. HARDY'S HOME. ALL WILL BE RETURNED TO THEIR RIGHTFUL OWNERS.
IS IT TRUE SHE HAS FRIENDS IN MANHATTAN SOCIETY?
AS LONG AS I'M MAYOR, NO ONE IS ABOVE THE LAW! HER FRIENDS MEAN NOTHING!
IT WAS EITHER PUBLICLY DISTANCE MYSELF FROM FELICIA, OR BE TAINTED. THE WOMAN'S RADIOACTIVE.
SHE HAD AN EXTRAVAGANT LIFE...MORE MONEY THAN SHE COULD EVER SPEND. WHAT WAS SHE THINKING?
I HAVEN'T GIVEN HER A THOUGHT SINCE I BROUGHT HER IN.
THE BLACK CAT IS A COMMON CRIMINAL. AND NOT A PARTICULARLY INTERESTING ONE.
WHY WOULD I WASTE TIME ON SOMEONE LIKE THAT?
MY LIFE IS OVER. AND I CAN NEVER GET IT BACK.

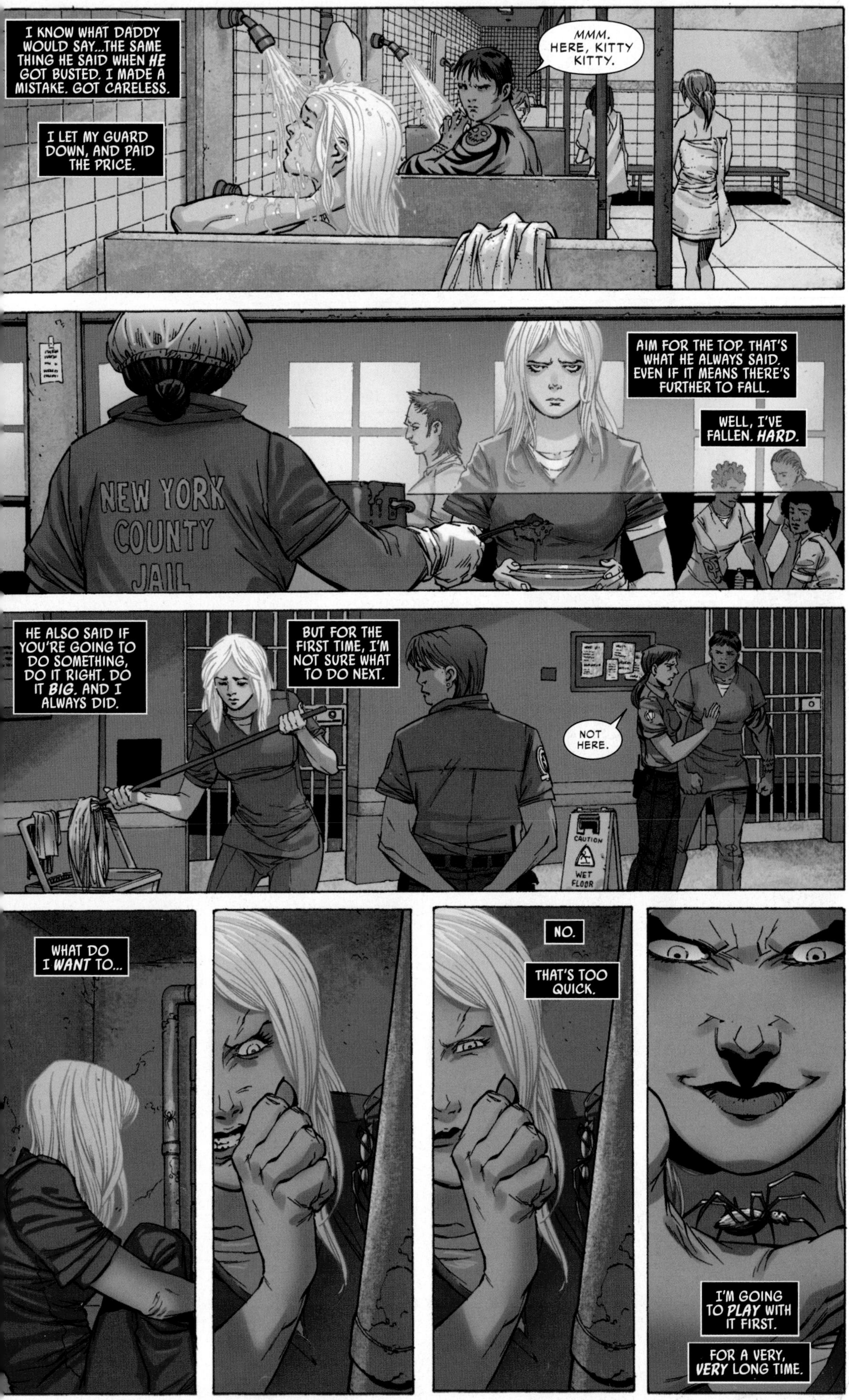
I KNOW WHAT DADDY WOULD SAY...THE SAME THING HE SAID WHEN HE GOT BUSTED. I MADE A MISTAKE. GOT CARELESS.
MMM. HERE, KITTY KITTY.
I LET MY GUARD DOWN, AND PAID THE PRICE.
NEW YORK COUNTY JAIL
AIM FOR THE TOP. THAT'S WHAT HE ALWAYS SAID. EVEN IF IT MEANS THERE'S FURTHER TO FALL.
WELL, I'VE FALLEN. HARD.
HE ALSO SAID IF YOU'RE GOING TO DO SOMETHING, DO IT RIGHT. DO IT BIG. AND I ALWAYS DID.
BUT FOR THE FIRST TIME, I'M NOT SURE WHAT TO DO NEXT.
NOT HERE.
CAUTION
WET FLOOR
WHAT DO I WANT TO...
NO.
THAT'S TOO QUICK.
I'M GOING TO PLAY WITH IT FIRST.
FOR A VERY, VERY LONG TIME.

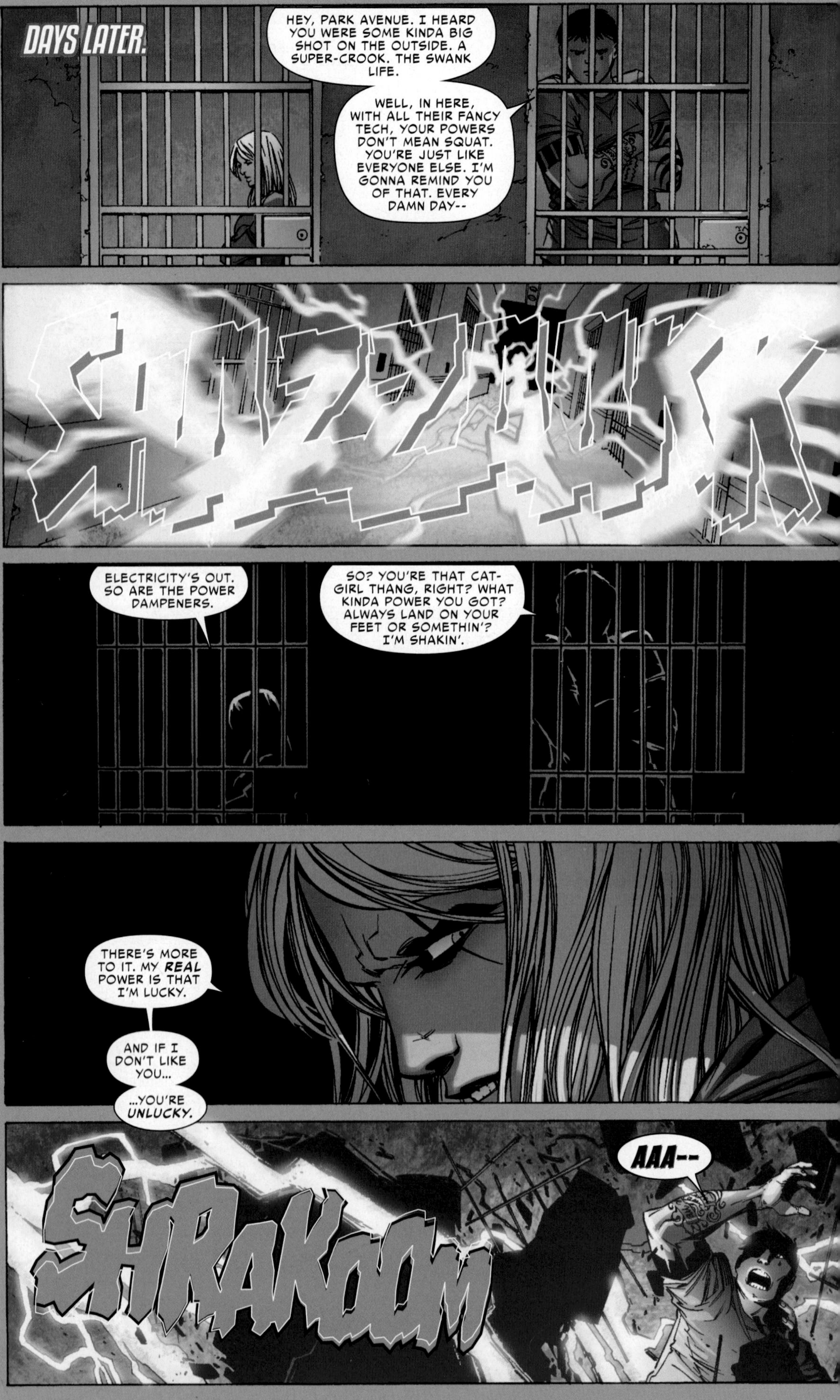
DAYS LATER.
HEY, PARK AVENUE. I HEARD YOU WERE SOME KINDA BIG SHOT ON THE OUTSIDE. A SUPER-CROOK. THE SWANK LIFE.
WELL, IN HERE, WITH ALL THEIR FANCY TECH, YOUR POWERS DON'T MEAN SQUAT. YOU'RE JUST LIKE EVERYONE ELSE. I'M GONNA REMIND YOU OF THAT. EVERY DAMN DAY--
ELECTRICITY'S OUT. SO ARE THE POWER DAMPENERS.
SO? YOU'RE THAT CAT-GIRL THANG, RIGHT? WHAT KINDA POWER YOU GOT? ALWAYS LAND ON YOUR FEET OR SOMETHIN'? I'M SHAKIN'.
THERE'S MORE TO IT. MY REAL POWER IS THAT I'M LUCKY.
AND IF I DON'T LIKE YOU...
...YOU'RE UNLUCKY.
AAA--
SHRAKOOM

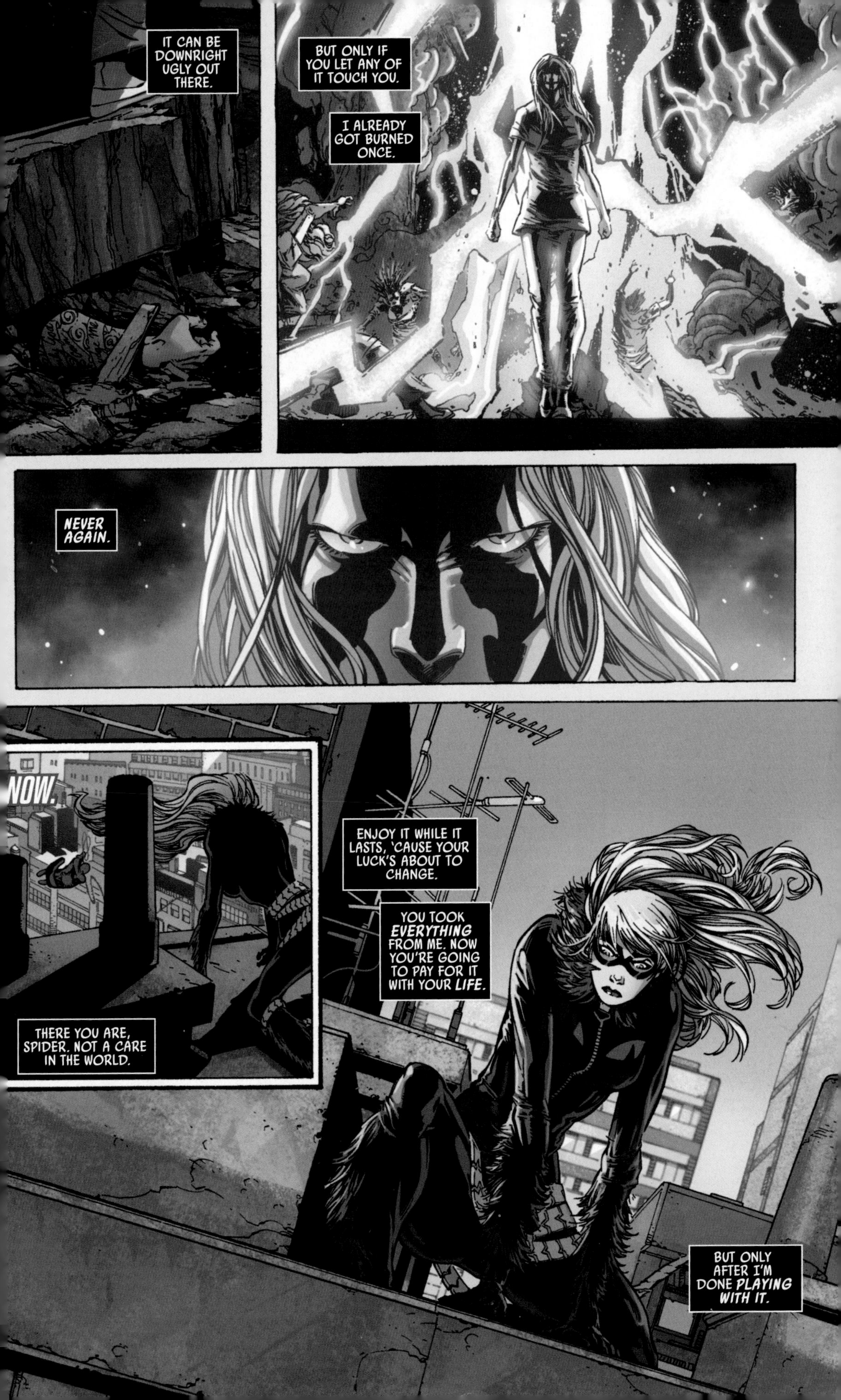
IT CAN BE DOWNRIGHT UGLY OUT THERE.
BUT ONLY IF YOU LET ANY OF IT TOUCH YOU.
I ALREADY GOT BURNED ONCE.
NEVER AGAIN.
NOW.
THERE YOU ARE, SPIDER. NOT A CARE IN THE WORLD.
ENJOY IT WHILE IT LASTS, 'CAUSE YOUR LUCK'S ABOUT TO CHANGE.
YOU TOOK EVERYTHING FROM ME. NOW YOU'RE GOING TO PAY FOR IT WITH YOUR LIFE.
BUT ONLY AFTER I'M DONE PLAYING WITH IT.

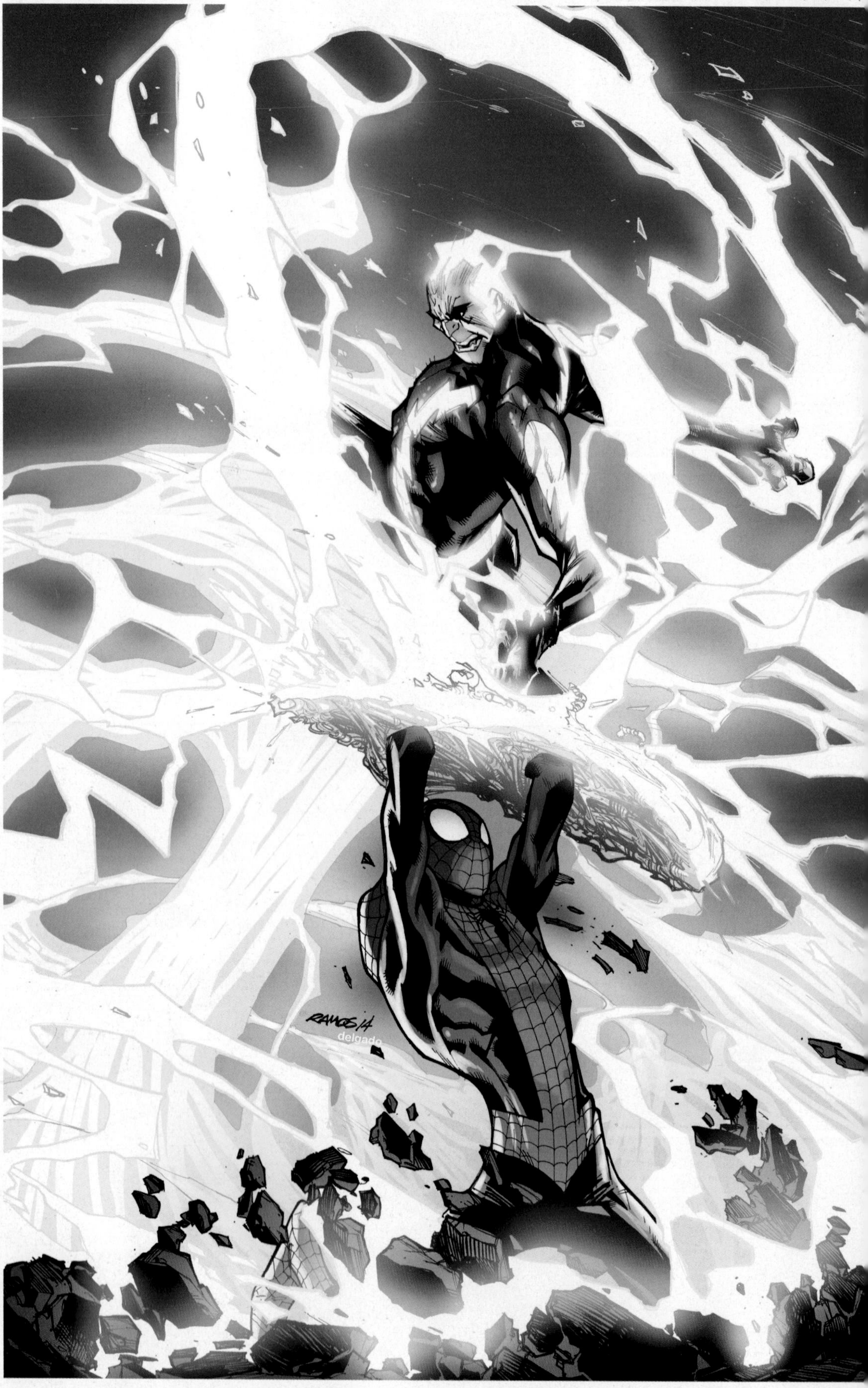
RAMOS/14
delgado

2

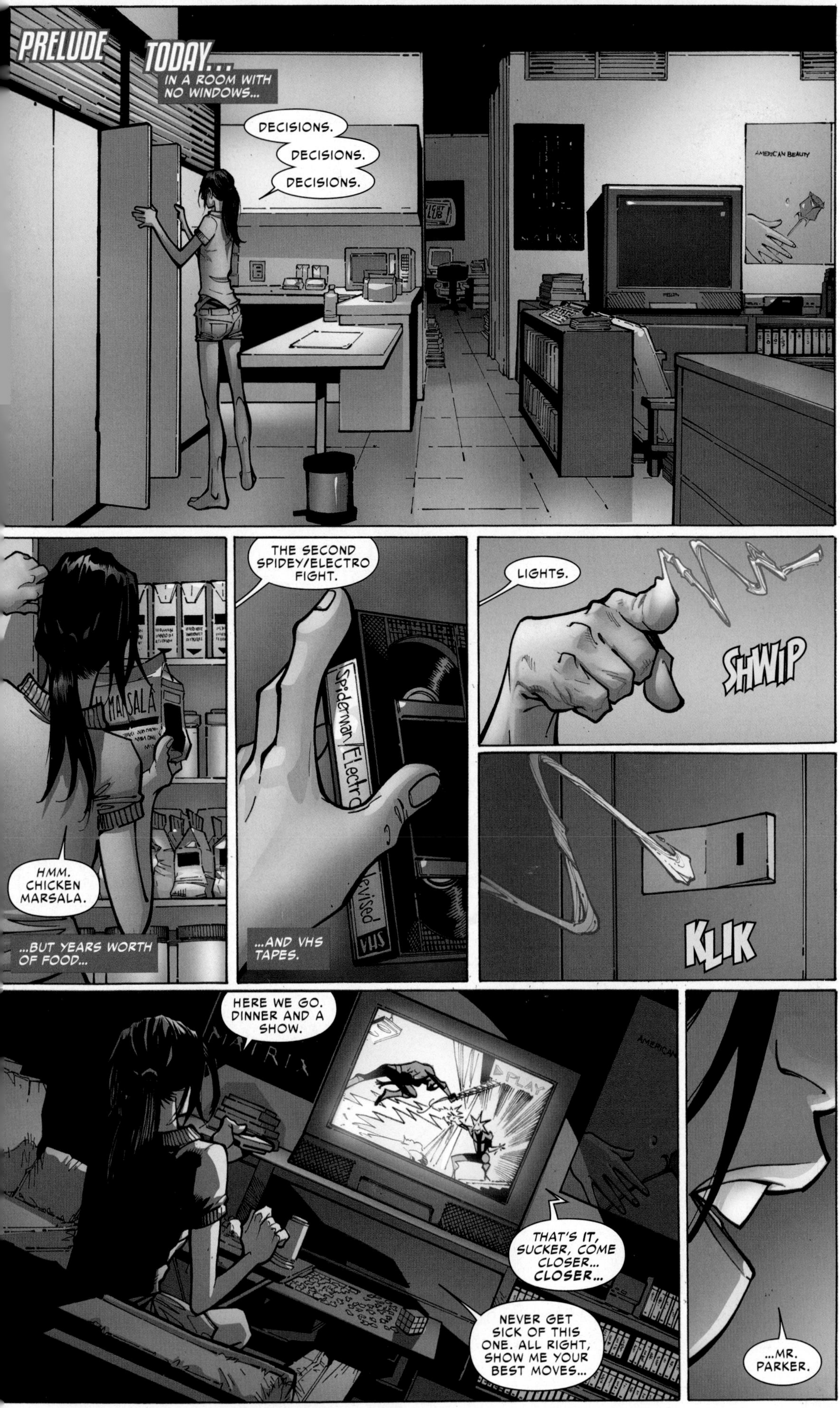
PRELUDE
TODAY...
IN A ROOM WITH NO WINDOWS...
DECISIONS.
DECISIONS.
DECISIONS.
AMERICAN BEAUTY
HMM. CHICKEN MARSALA.
...BUT YEARS WORTH OF FOOD...
THE SECOND SPIDEY/ELECTRO FIGHT.
Spiderman/Electro
...AND VHS TAPES.
LIGHTS.
SHWIP
KLIK
HERE WE GO. DINNER AND A SHOW.
PLAY
THAT'S IT, SUCKER, COME CLOSER... CLOSER...
NEVER GET SICK OF THIS ONE. ALL RIGHT, SHOW ME YOUR BEST MOVES...
...MR. PARKER.

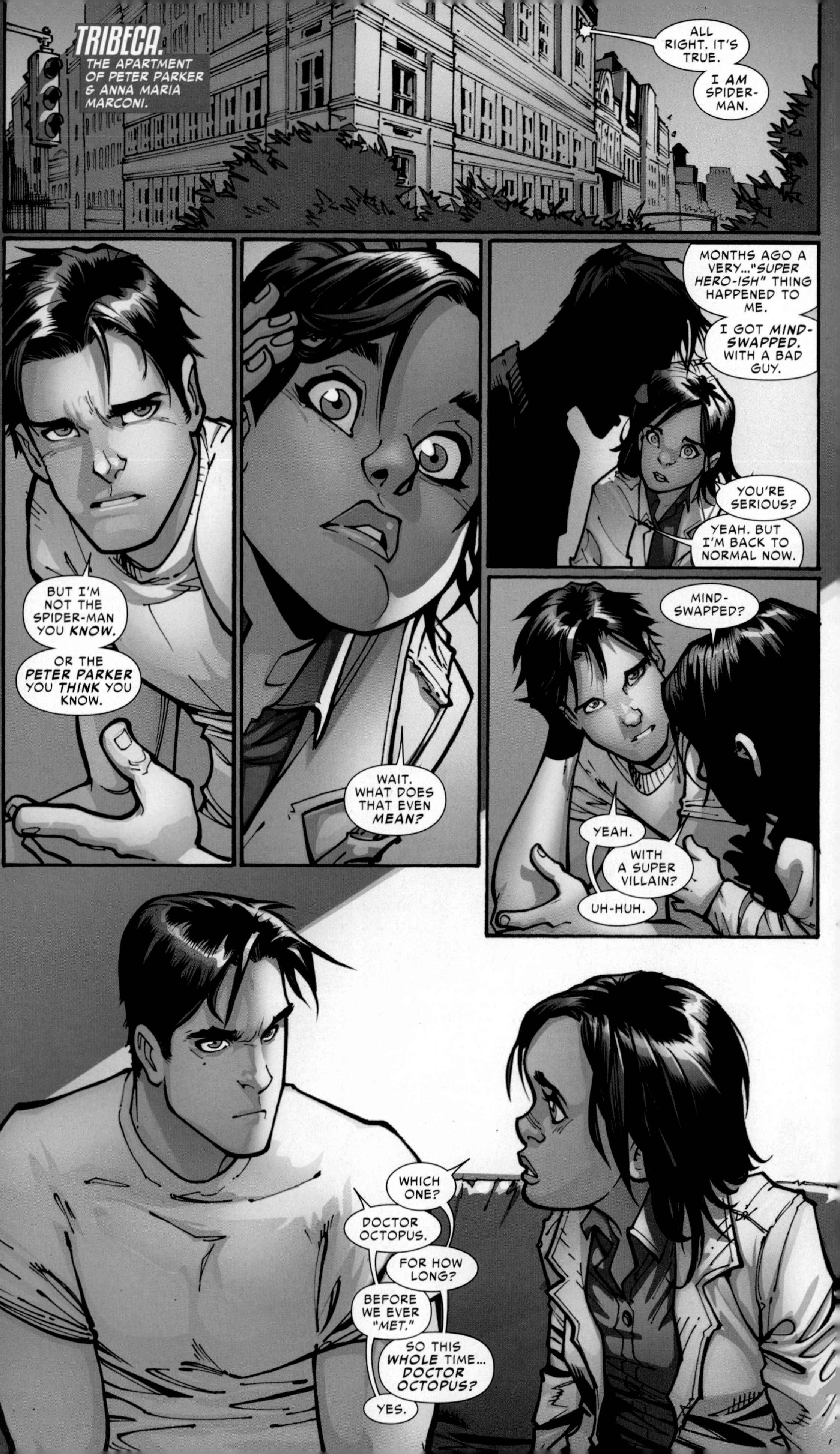
TRIBECA.
THE APARTMENT OF PETER PARKER & ANNA MARIA MARCONI.
ALL RIGHT. IT'S TRUE.
I AM SPIDER-MAN.
BUT I'M NOT THE SPIDER-MAN YOU KNOW.
OR THE PETER PARKER YOU THINK YOU KNOW.
WAIT. WHAT DOES THAT EVEN MEAN?
MONTHS AGO A VERY..."SUPER HERO-ISH" THING HAPPENED TO ME.
I GOT MIND-SWAPPED. WITH A BAD GUY.
YOU'RE SERIOUS?
YEAH. BUT I'M BACK TO NORMAL NOW.
MIND-SWAPPED?
YEAH.
WITH A SUPER VILLAIN?
UH-HUH.
WHICH ONE?
DOCTOR OCTOPUS.
FOR HOW LONG?
BEFORE WE EVER "MET."
SO THIS WHOLE TIME... DOCTOR OCTOPUS?
YES.

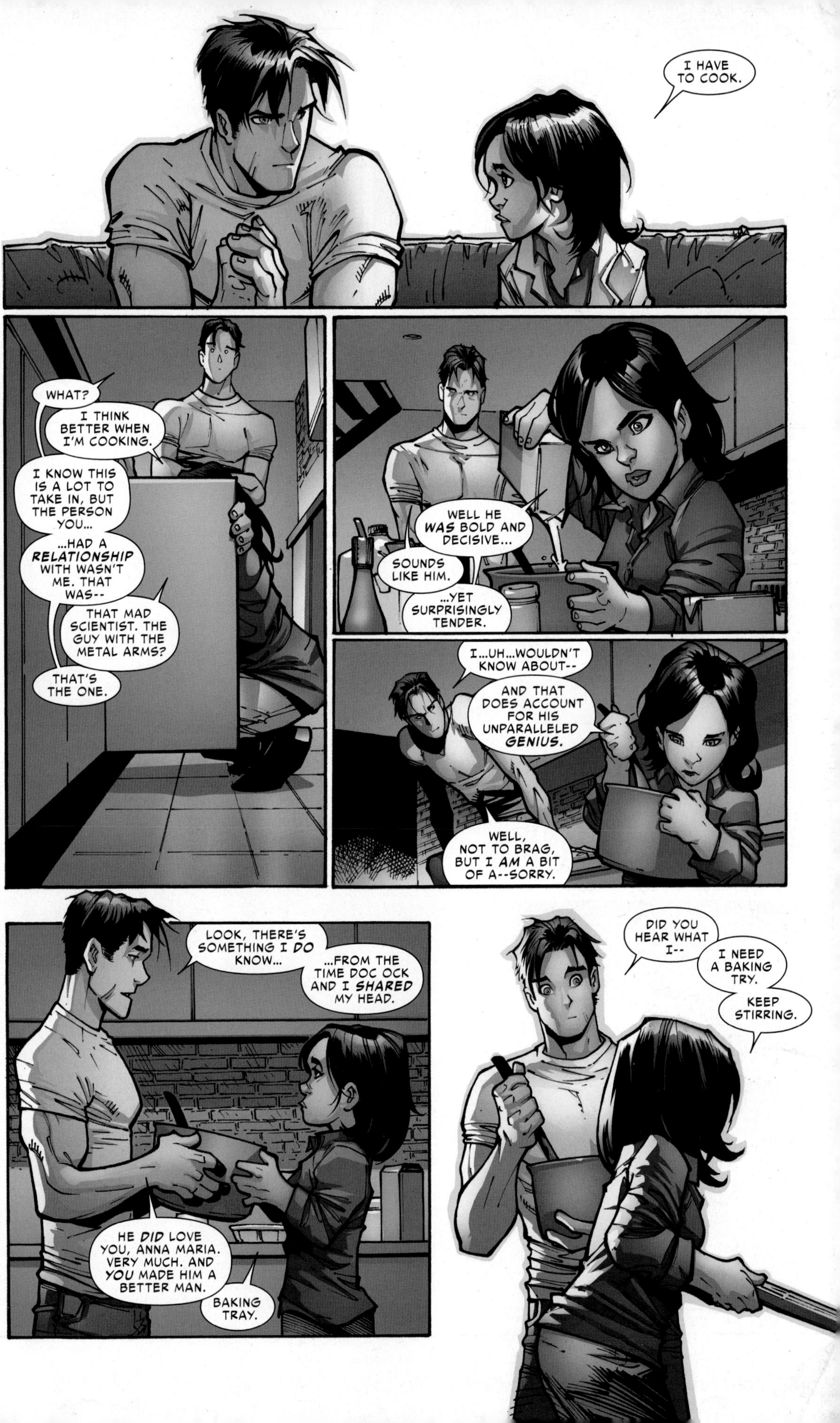
I HAVE TO COOK.
WHAT?
I THINK BETTER WHEN I'M COOKING.
I KNOW THIS IS A LOT TO TAKE IN, BUT THE PERSON YOU...
...HAD A RELATIONSHIP WITH WASN'T ME. THAT WAS--
THAT MAD SCIENTIST. THE GUY WITH THE METAL ARMS?
THAT'S THE ONE.
WELL HE WAS BOLD AND DECISIVE...
SOUNDS LIKE HIM.
...YET SURPRISINGLY TENDER.
I...UH...WOULDN'T KNOW ABOUT--
AND THAT DOES ACCOUNT FOR HIS UNPARALLELED GENIUS.
WELL, NOT TO BRAG, BUT I AM A BIT OF A--SORRY.
LOOK, THERE'S SOMETHING I DO KNOW...
...FROM THE TIME DOC OCK AND I SHARED MY HEAD.
HE DID LOVE YOU, ANNA MARIA. VERY MUCH. AND YOU MADE HIM A BETTER MAN.
BAKING TRAY.
DID YOU HEAR WHAT I--
I NEED A BAKING TRY.
KEEP STIRRING.

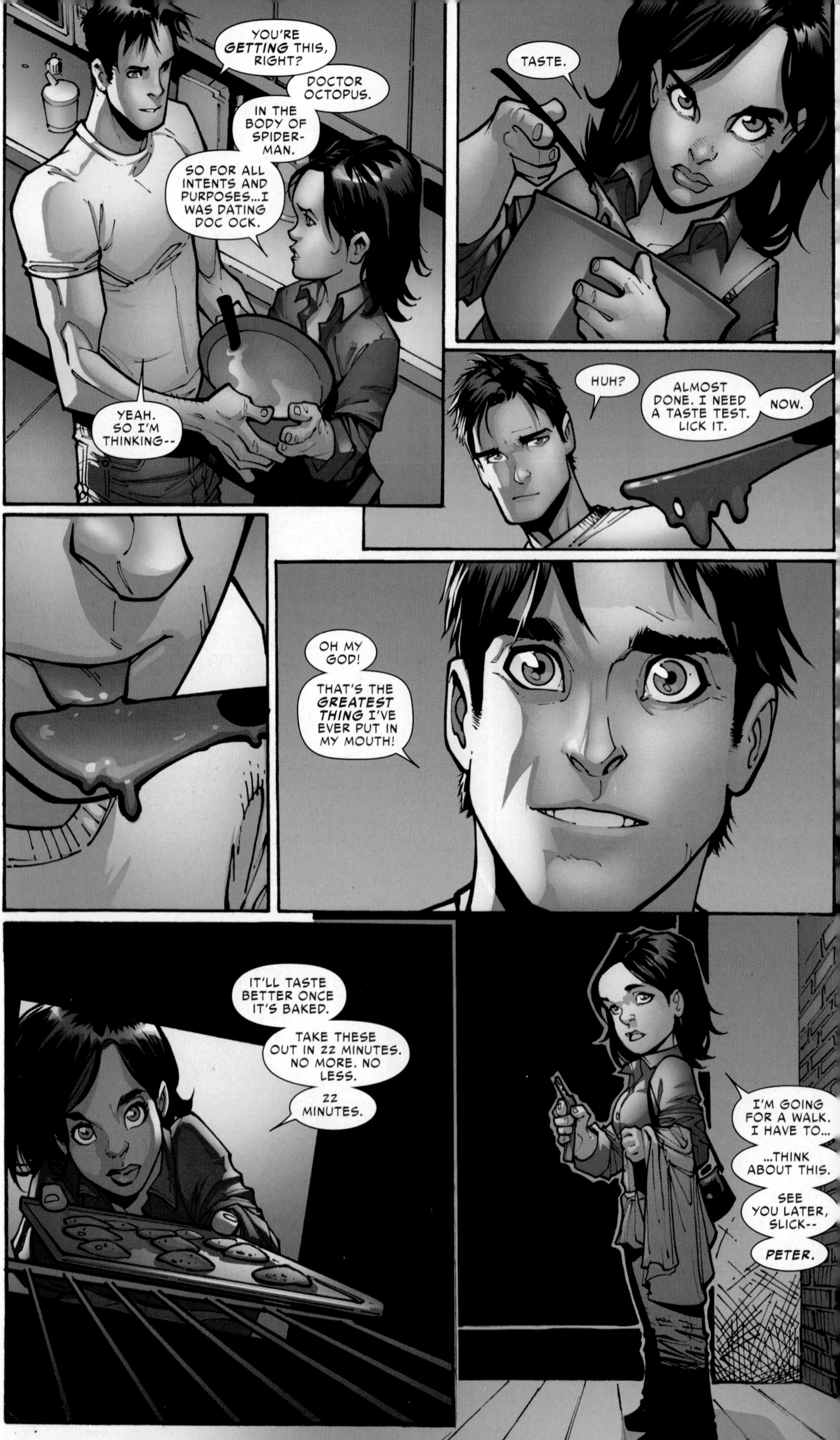
YOU'RE GETTING THIS, RIGHT?
DOCTOR OCTOPUS.
IN THE BODY OF SPIDER-MAN.
SO FOR ALL INTENTS AND PURPOSES...I WAS DATING DOC OCK.
YEAH. SO I'M THINKING--
TASTE.
HUH?
ALMOST DONE. I NEED A TASTE TEST. LICK IT.
NOW.
OH MY GOD!
THAT'S THE GREATEST THING I'VE EVER PUT IN MY MOUTH!
IT'LL TASTE BETTER ONCE IT'S BAKED.
TAKE THESE OUT IN 22 MINUTES. NO MORE. NO LESS.
22 MINUTES.
I'M GOING FOR A WALK. I HAVE TO...
...THINK ABOUT THIS.
SEE YOU LATER, SLICK--
PETER.

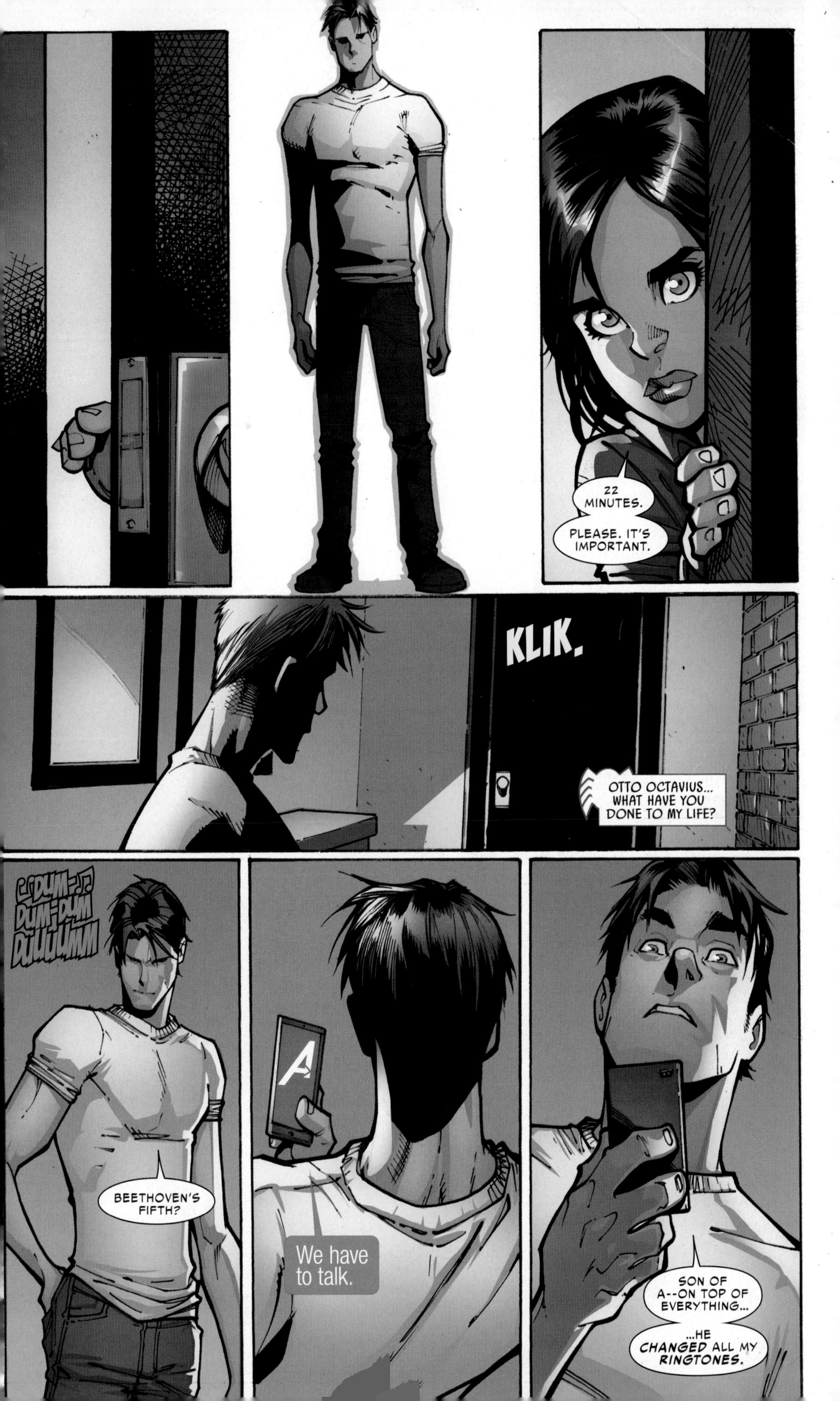
22 MINUTES.
PLEASE. IT'S IMPORTANT.
KLIK.
OTTO OCTAVIUS... WHAT HAVE YOU DONE TO MY LIFE?
DUM-DUM-DUM DUUUUMM
BEETHOVEN'S FIFTH?
We have to talk.
SON OF A--ON TOP OF EVERYTHING...
...HE CHANGED ALL MY RINGTONES.

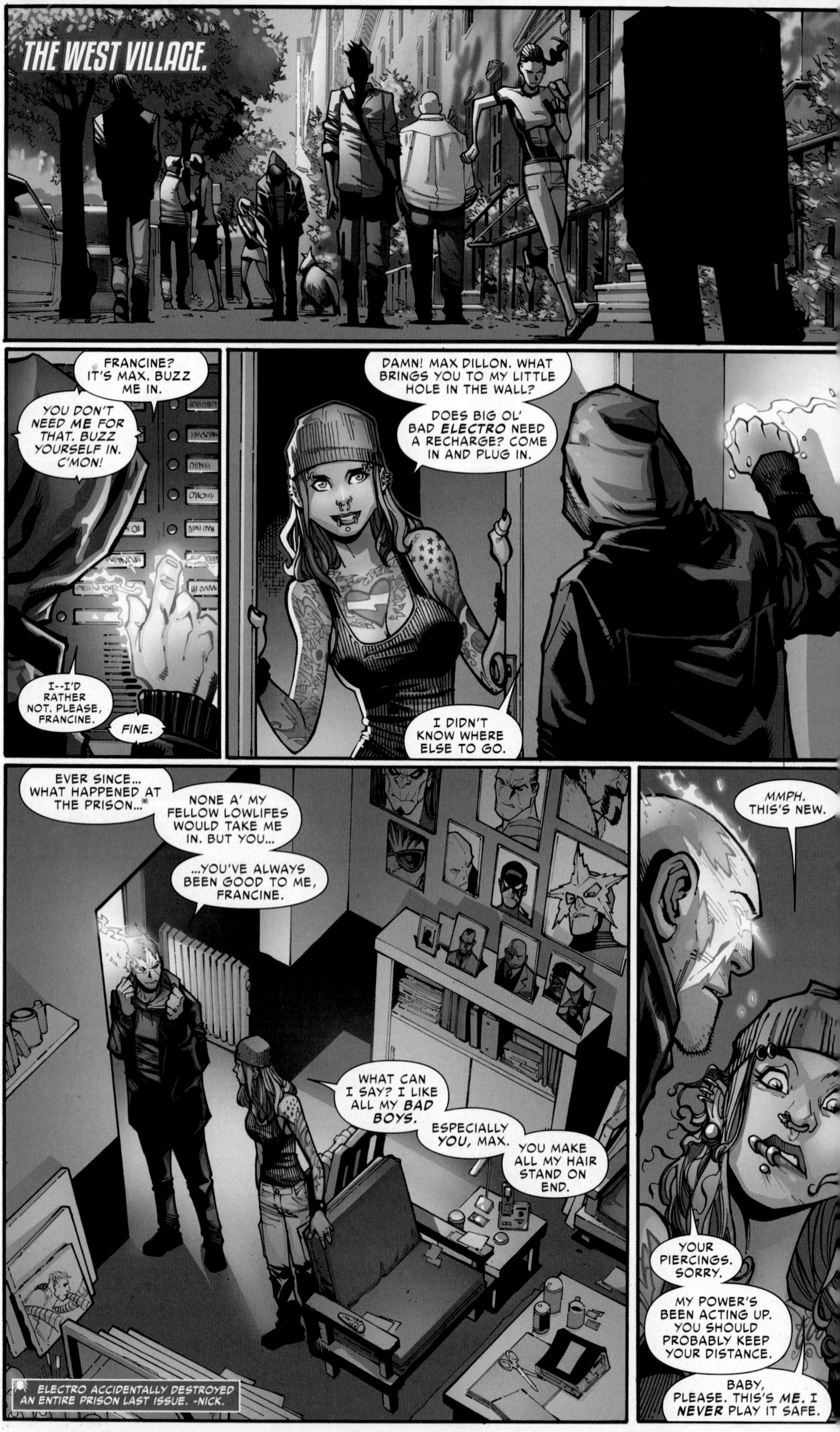
THE WEST VILLAGE.
FRANCINE? IT'S MAX. BUZZ ME IN.
YOU DON'T NEED ME FOR THAT. BUZZ YOURSELF IN. C'MON!
I--I'D RATHER NOT. PLEASE, FRANCINE.
FINE.
DAMN! MAX DILLON. WHAT BRINGS YOU TO MY LITTLE HOLE IN THE WALL?
DOES BIG OL' BAD ELECTRO NEED A RECHARGE? COME IN AND PLUG IN.
I DIDN'T KNOW WHERE ELSE TO GO.
EVER SINCE... WHAT HAPPENED AT THE PRISON...*
NONE A' MY FELLOW LOWLIFES WOULD TAKE ME IN. BUT YOU...
...YOU'VE ALWAYS BEEN GOOD TO ME, FRANCINE.
WHAT CAN I SAY? I LIKE ALL MY BAD BOYS.
ESPECIALLY YOU, MAX.
YOU MAKE ALL MY HAIR STAND ON END.
*ELECTRO ACCIDENTALLY DESTROYED AN ENTIRE PRISON LAST ISSUE. -NICK.
MMPH. THIS'S NEW.
YOUR PIERCINGS. SORRY.
MY POWER'S BEEN ACTING UP. YOU SHOULD PROBABLY KEEP YOUR DISTANCE.
BABY, PLEASE. THIS'S ME. I NEVER PLAY IT SAFE.

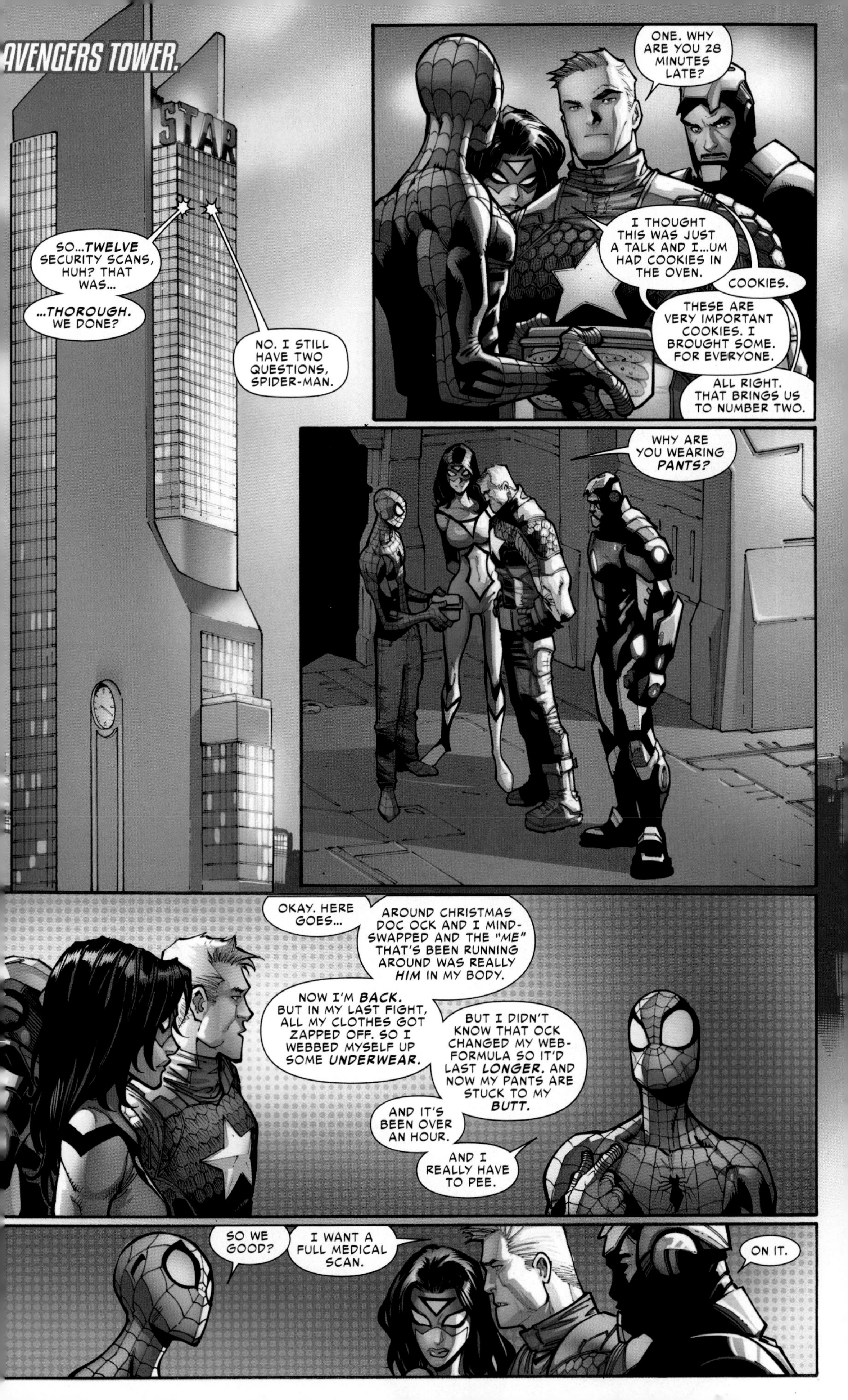
AVENGERS TOWER.
STAR
SO...TWELVE SECURITY SCANS, HUH? THAT WAS...
...THOROUGH. WE DONE?
NO. I STILL HAVE TWO QUESTIONS, SPIDER-MAN.
ONE. WHY ARE YOU 28 MINUTES LATE?
I THOUGHT THIS WAS JUST A TALK AND I...UM HAD COOKIES IN THE OVEN.
COOKIES.
THESE ARE VERY IMPORTANT COOKIES. I BROUGHT SOME. FOR EVERYONE.
ALL RIGHT. THAT BRINGS US TO NUMBER TWO.
WHY ARE YOU WEARING PANTS?
OKAY. HERE GOES...
AROUND CHRISTMAS DOC OCK AND I MIND-SWAPPED AND THE "ME" THAT'S BEEN RUNNING AROUND WAS REALLY HIM IN MY BODY.
NOW I'M BACK. BUT IN MY LAST FIGHT, ALL MY CLOTHES GOT ZAPPED OFF. SO I WEBBED MYSELF UP SOME UNDERWEAR.
BUT I DIDN'T KNOW THAT OCK CHANGED MY WEB-FORMULA SO IT'D LAST LONGER. AND NOW MY PANTS ARE STUCK TO MY BUTT.
AND IT'S BEEN OVER AN HOUR.
AND I REALLY HAVE TO PEE.
SO WE GOOD?
I WANT A FULL MEDICAL SCAN.
ON IT.

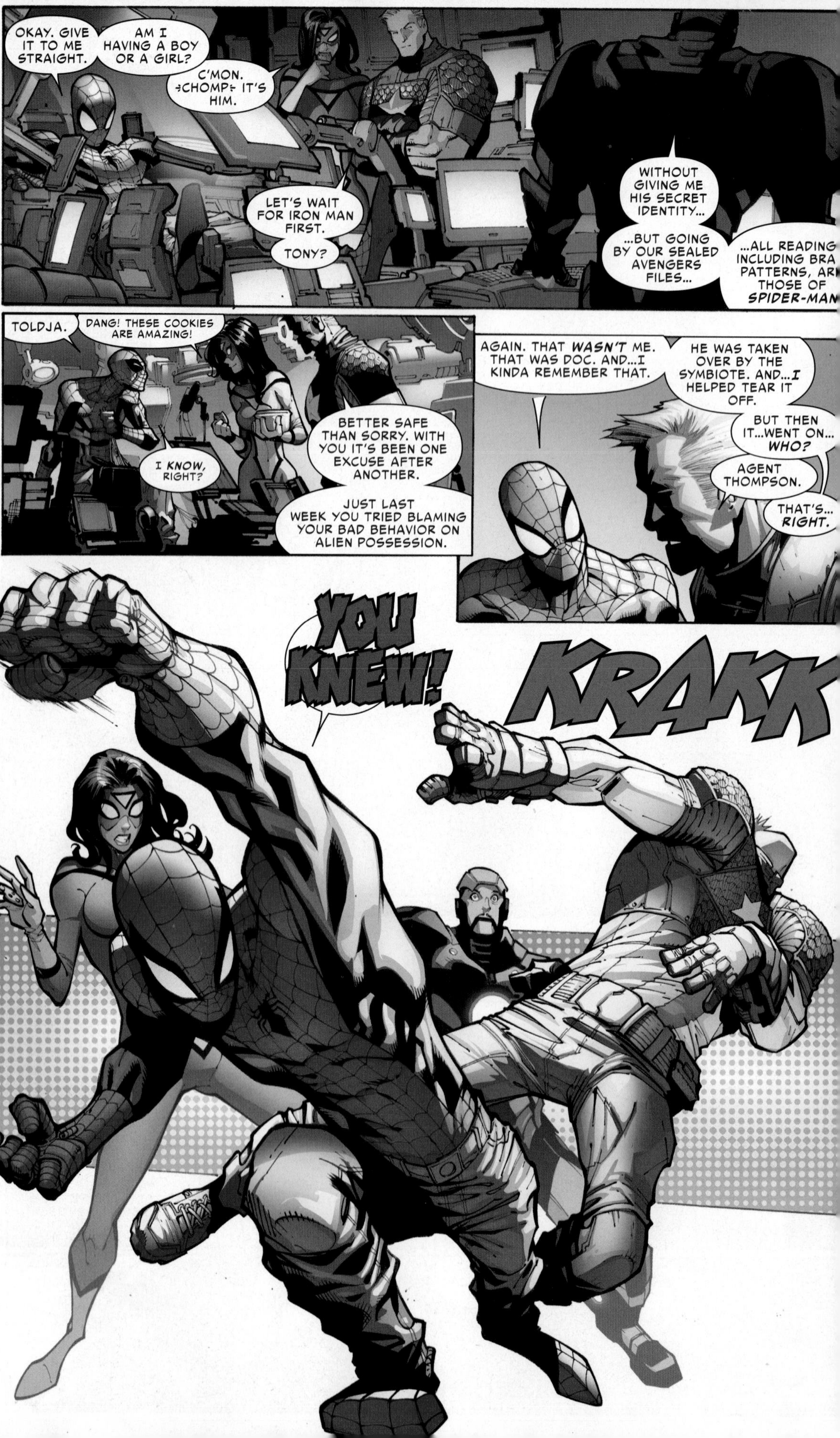
OKAY. GIVE IT TO ME STRAIGHT.
AM I HAVING A BOY OR A GIRL?
C'MON. ≠CHOMP≠ IT'S HIM.
LET'S WAIT FOR IRON MAN FIRST.
TONY?
WITHOUT GIVING ME HIS SECRET IDENTITY...
...BUT GOING BY OUR SEALED AVENGERS FILES...
...ALL READING INCLUDING BRA PATTERNS, AR THOSE OF SPIDER-MAN
TOLDJA.
DANG! THESE COOKIES ARE AMAZING!
I KNOW, RIGHT?
BETTER SAFE THAN SORRY. WITH YOU IT'S BEEN ONE EXCUSE AFTER ANOTHER.
JUST LAST WEEK YOU TRIED BLAMING YOUR BAD BEHAVIOR ON ALIEN POSSESSION.
AGAIN. THAT WASN'T ME. THAT WAS DOC. AND...I KINDA REMEMBER THAT.
HE WAS TAKEN OVER BY THE SYMBIOTE. AND...I HELPED TEAR IT OFF.
BUT THEN IT...WENT ON... WHO?
AGENT THOMPSON.
THAT'S... RIGHT.
YOU KNEW!
KRAKK

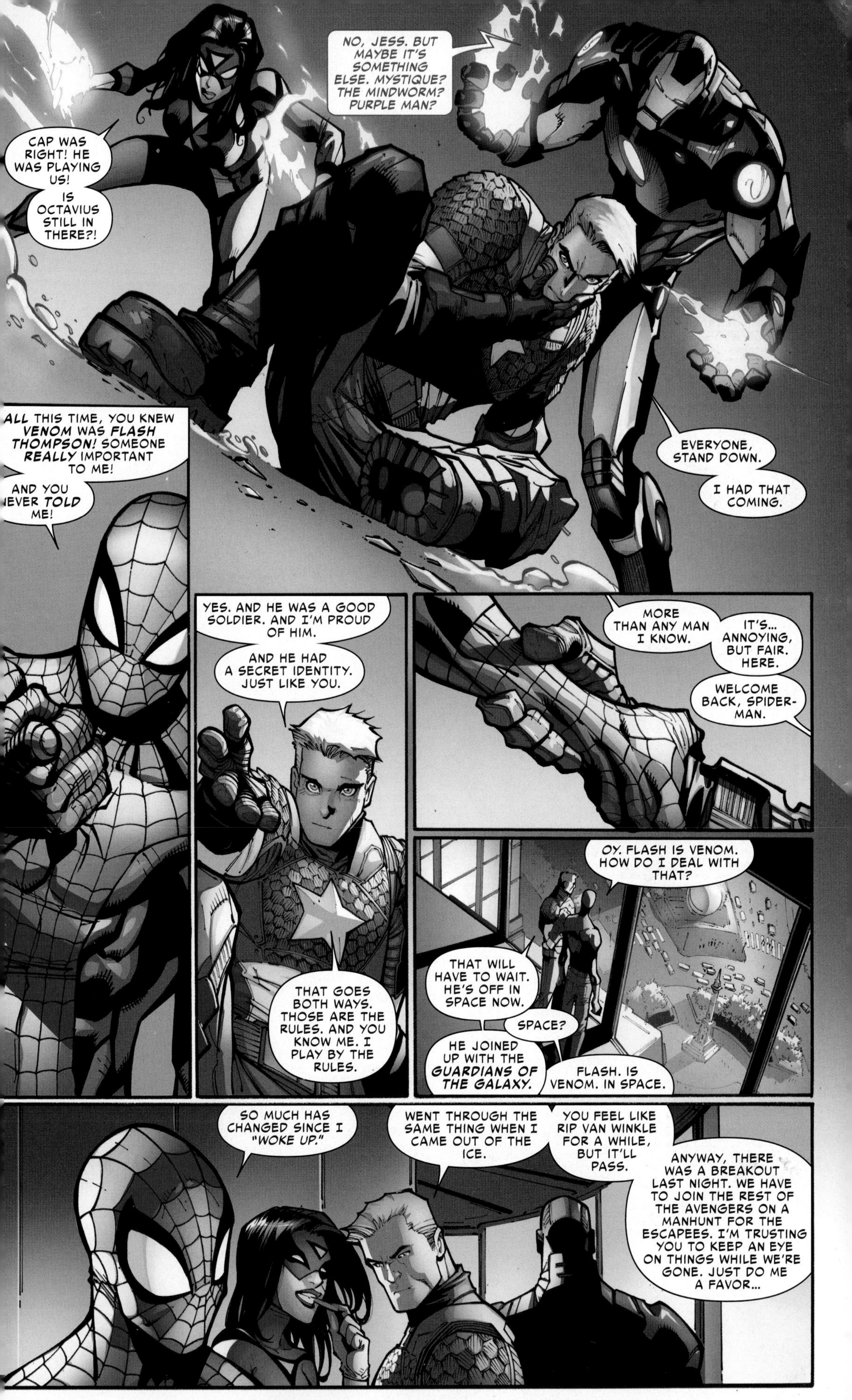
CAP WAS RIGHT! HE WAS PLAYING US!
IS OCTAVIUS STILL IN THERE?!
NO, JESS. BUT MAYBE IT'S SOMETHING ELSE. MYSTIQUE? THE MINDWORM? PURPLE MAN?
EVERYONE, STAND DOWN.
I HAD THAT COMING.
ALL THIS TIME, YOU KNEW VENOM WAS FLASH THOMPSON! SOMEONE REALLY IMPORTANT TO ME!
AND YOU NEVER TOLD ME!
YES. AND HE WAS A GOOD SOLDIER. AND I'M PROUD OF HIM.
AND HE HAD A SECRET IDENTITY. JUST LIKE YOU.
THAT GOES BOTH WAYS. THOSE ARE THE RULES. AND YOU KNOW ME. I PLAY BY THE RULES.
MORE THAN ANY MAN I KNOW.
IT'S... ANNOYING, BUT FAIR. HERE.
WELCOME BACK, SPIDER-MAN.
OY. FLASH IS VENOM. HOW DO I DEAL WITH THAT?
THAT WILL HAVE TO WAIT. HE'S OFF IN SPACE NOW.
SPACE?
HE JOINED UP WITH THE GUARDIANS OF THE GALAXY.
FLASH. IS VENOM. IN SPACE.
SO MUCH HAS CHANGED SINCE I "WOKE UP."
WENT THROUGH THE SAME THING WHEN I CAME OUT OF THE ICE.
YOU FEEL LIKE RIP VAN WINKLE FOR A WHILE, BUT IT'LL PASS.
ANYWAY, THERE WAS A BREAKOUT LAST NIGHT. WE HAVE TO JOIN THE REST OF THE AVENGERS ON A MANHUNT FOR THE ESCAPEES. I'M TRUSTING YOU TO KEEP AN EYE ON THINGS WHILE WE'RE GONE. JUST DO ME A FAVOR...

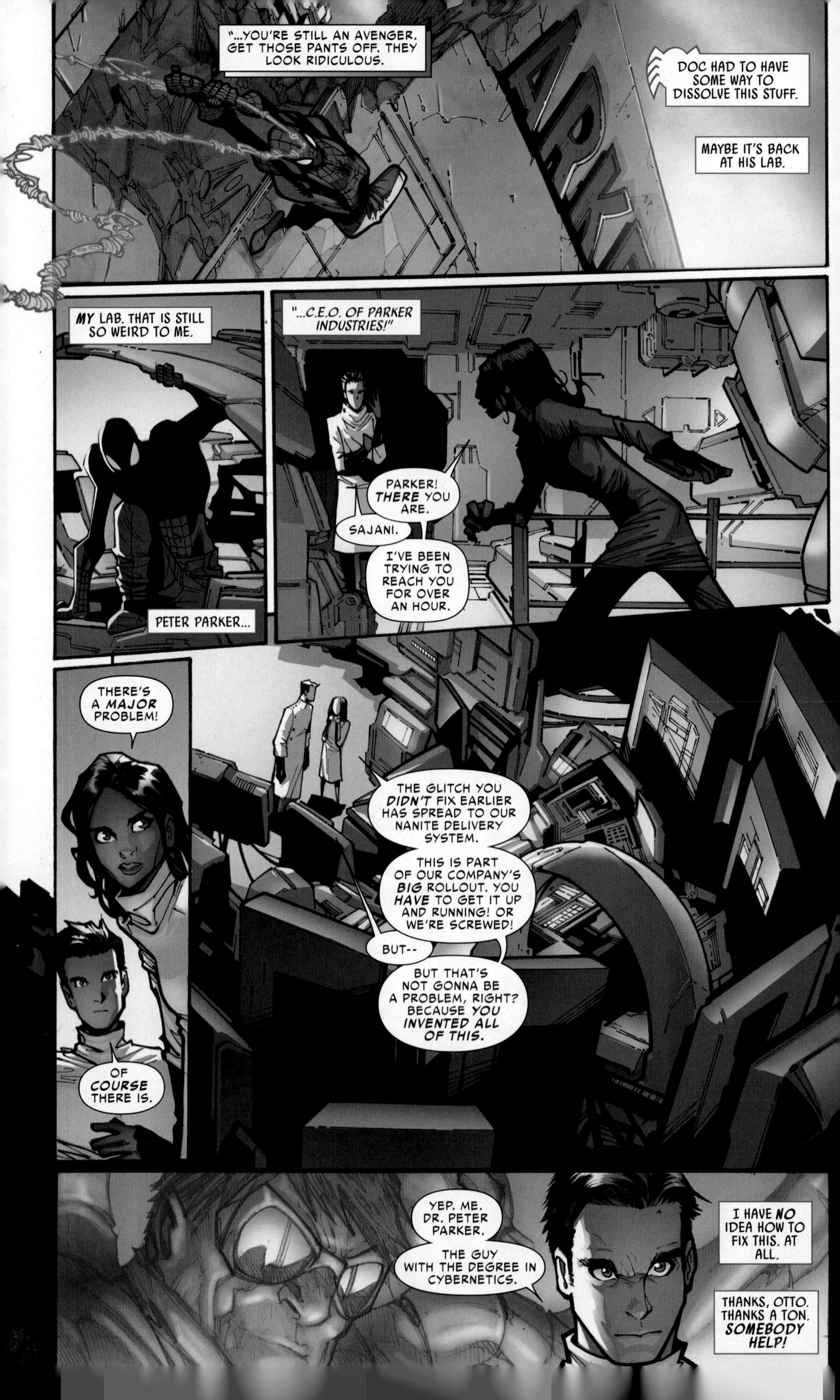
"...YOU'RE STILL AN AVENGER. GET THOSE PANTS OFF. THEY LOOK RIDICULOUS.
DOC HAD TO HAVE SOME WAY TO DISSOLVE THIS STUFF.
MAYBE IT'S BACK AT HIS LAB.
MY LAB. THAT IS STILL SO WEIRD TO ME.
PETER PARKER...
"...C.E.O. OF PARKER INDUSTRIES!"
PARKER! THERE YOU ARE.
SAJANI.
I'VE BEEN TRYING TO REACH YOU FOR OVER AN HOUR.
THERE'S A MAJOR PROBLEM!
THE GLITCH YOU DIDN'T FIX EARLIER HAS SPREAD TO OUR NANITE DELIVERY SYSTEM.
THIS IS PART OF OUR COMPANY'S BIG ROLLOUT. YOU HAVE TO GET IT UP AND RUNNING! OR WE'RE SCREWED!
BUT--
BUT THAT'S NOT GONNA BE A PROBLEM, RIGHT? BECAUSE YOU INVENTED ALL OF THIS.
OF COURSE THERE IS.
YEP. ME. DR. PETER PARKER.
THE GUY WITH THE DEGREE IN CYBERNETICS.
I HAVE NO IDEA HOW TO FIX THIS. AT ALL.
THANKS, OTTO. THANKS A TON. SOMEBODY HELP!

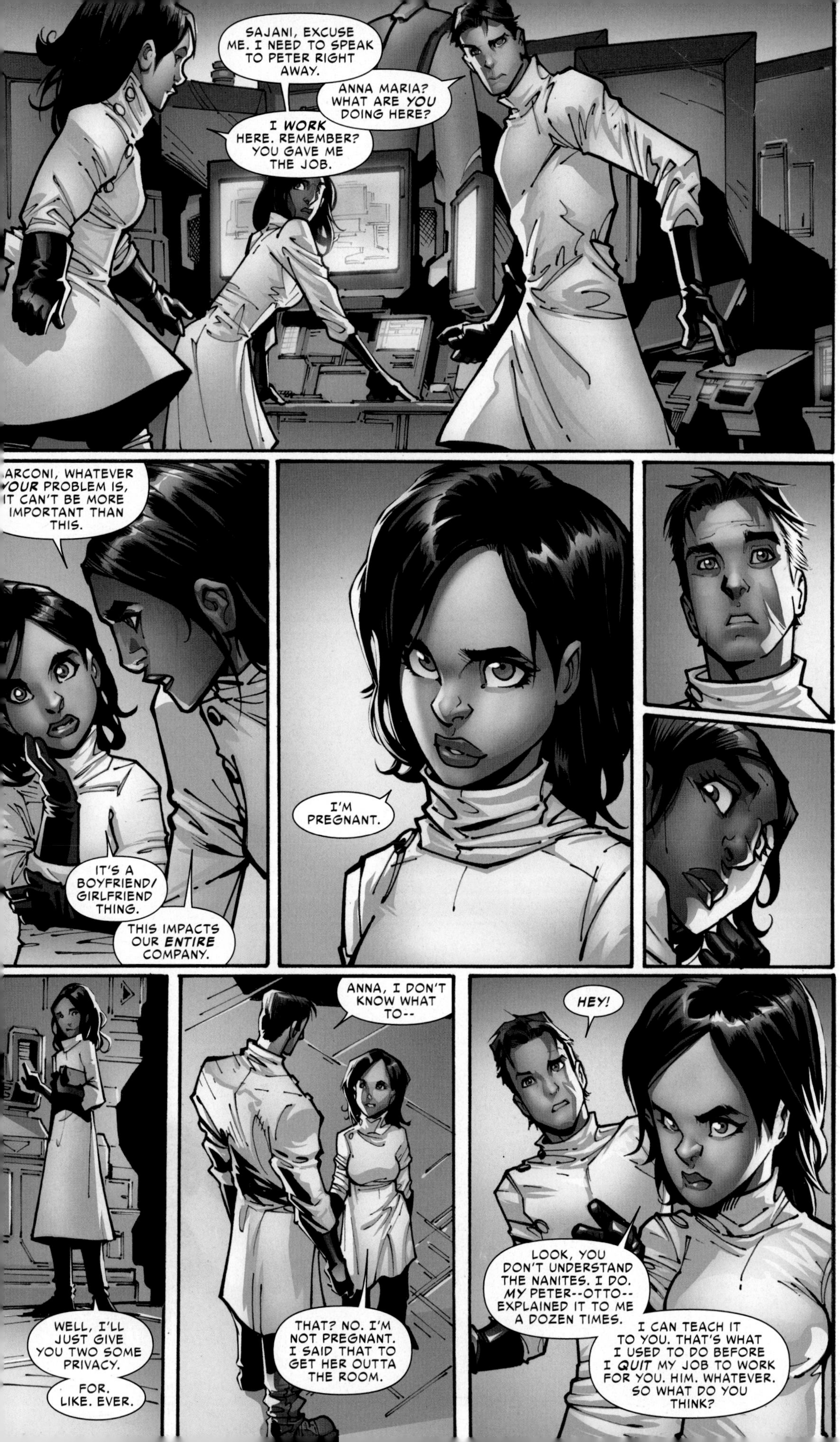

SAJANI, EXCUSE ME. I NEED TO SPEAK TO PETER RIGHT AWAY.
ANNA MARIA? WHAT ARE YOU DOING HERE?
I WORK HERE. REMEMBER? YOU GAVE ME THE JOB.
ARCONI, WHATEVER YOUR PROBLEM IS, IT CAN'T BE MORE IMPORTANT THAN THIS.
IT'S A BOYFRIEND/ GIRLFRIEND THING.
THIS IMPACTS OUR ENTIRE COMPANY.
I'M PREGNANT.
WELL, I'LL JUST GIVE YOU TWO SOME PRIVACY.
FOR. LIKE. EVER.
ANNA, I DON'T KNOW WHAT TO--
THAT? NO. I'M NOT PREGNANT. I SAID THAT TO GET HER OUTTA THE ROOM.
HEY!
LOOK, YOU DON'T UNDERSTAND THE NANITES. I DO. MY PETER--OTTO-- EXPLAINED IT TO ME A DOZEN TIMES.
I CAN TEACH IT TO YOU. THAT'S WHAT I USED TO DO BEFORE I QUIT MY JOB TO WORK FOR YOU. HIM. WHATEVER. SO WHAT DO YOU THINK?

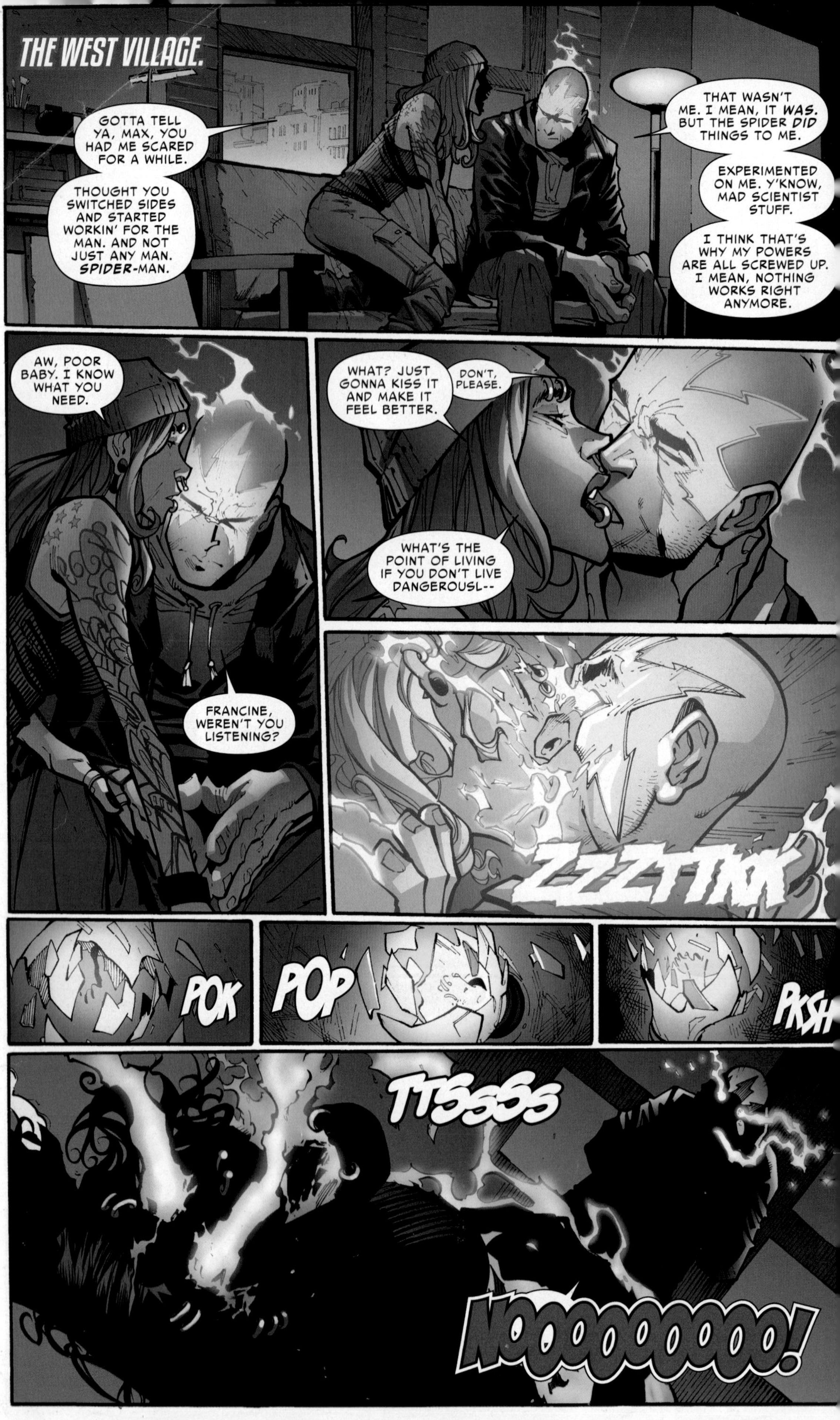
THE WEST VILLAGE.
GOTTA TELL YA, MAX, YOU HAD ME SCARED FOR A WHILE.
THOUGHT YOU SWITCHED SIDES AND STARTED WORKIN' FOR THE MAN. AND NOT JUST ANY MAN. SPIDER-MAN.
THAT WASN'T ME. I MEAN, IT WAS. BUT THE SPIDER DID THINGS TO ME.
EXPERIMENTED ON ME. Y'KNOW, MAD SCIENTIST STUFF.
I THINK THAT'S WHY MY POWERS ARE ALL SCREWED UP. I MEAN, NOTHING WORKS RIGHT ANYMORE.
AW, POOR BABY. I KNOW WHAT YOU NEED.
FRANCINE, WEREN'T YOU LISTENING?
WHAT? JUST GONNA KISS IT AND MAKE IT FEEL BETTER.
DON'T, PLEASE.
WHAT'S THE POINT OF LIVING IF YOU DON'T LIVE DANGEROUSL--
ZZZTTKK
POK
POP
PKSH
TTSSSS
NOOOOOOOOO!

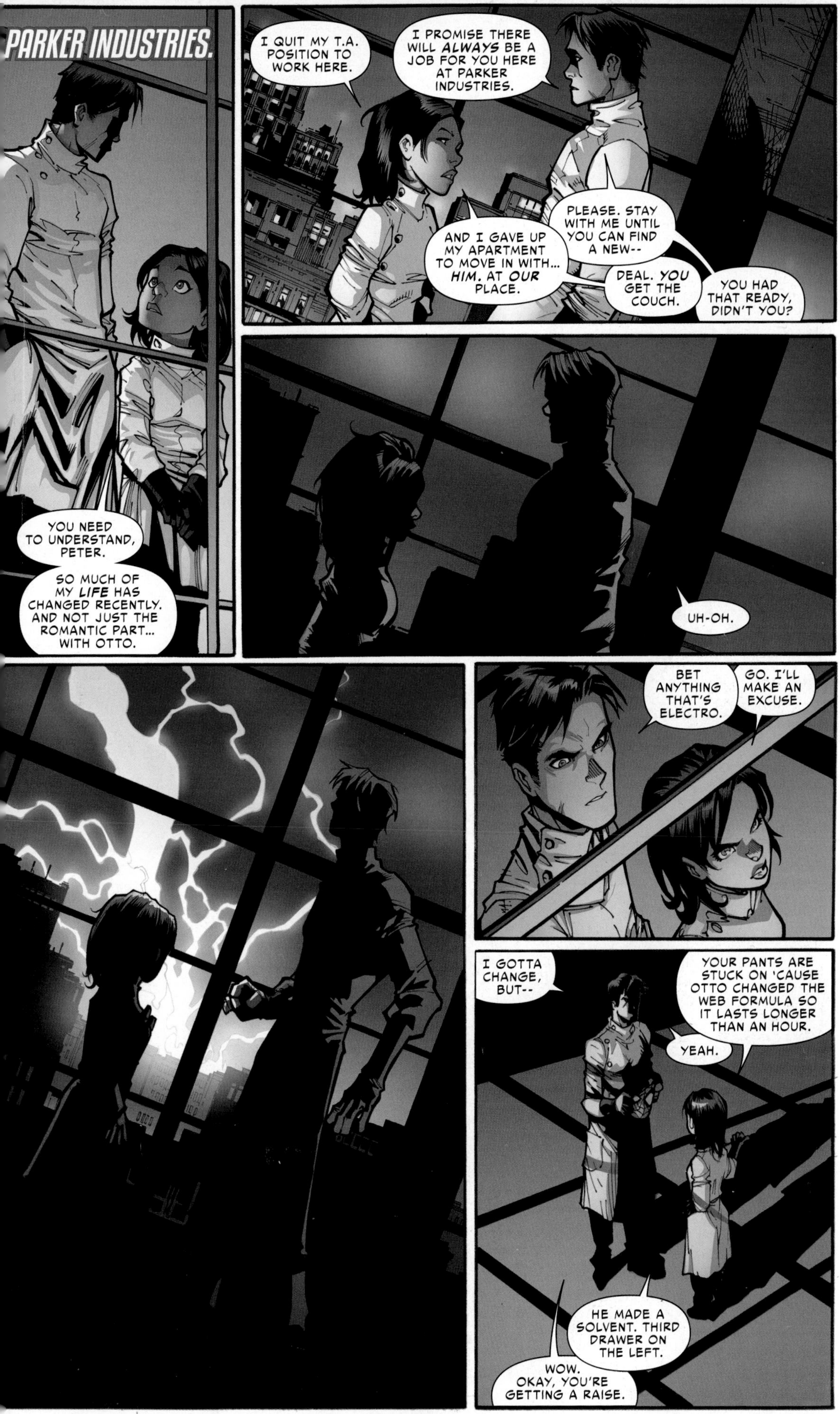

PARKER INDUSTRIES.
YOU NEED TO UNDERSTAND, PETER.
SO MUCH OF MY LIFE HAS CHANGED RECENTLY. AND NOT JUST THE ROMANTIC PART... WITH OTTO.
I QUIT MY T.A. POSITION TO WORK HERE.
I PROMISE THERE WILL ALWAYS BE A JOB FOR YOU HERE AT PARKER INDUSTRIES.
AND I GAVE UP MY APARTMENT TO MOVE IN WITH... HIM. AT OUR PLACE.
PLEASE. STAY WITH ME UNTIL YOU CAN FIND A NEW--
DEAL. YOU GET THE COUCH.
YOU HAD THAT READY, DIDN'T YOU?
UH-OH.
BET ANYTHING THAT'S ELECTRO.
GO. I'LL MAKE AN EXCUSE.
I GOTTA CHANGE, BUT--
YOUR PANTS ARE STUCK ON 'CAUSE OTTO CHANGED THE WEB FORMULA SO IT LASTS LONGER THAN AN HOUR.
YEAH.
HE MADE A SOLVENT. THIRD DRAWER ON THE LEFT.
WOW. OKAY, YOU'RE GETTING A RAISE.

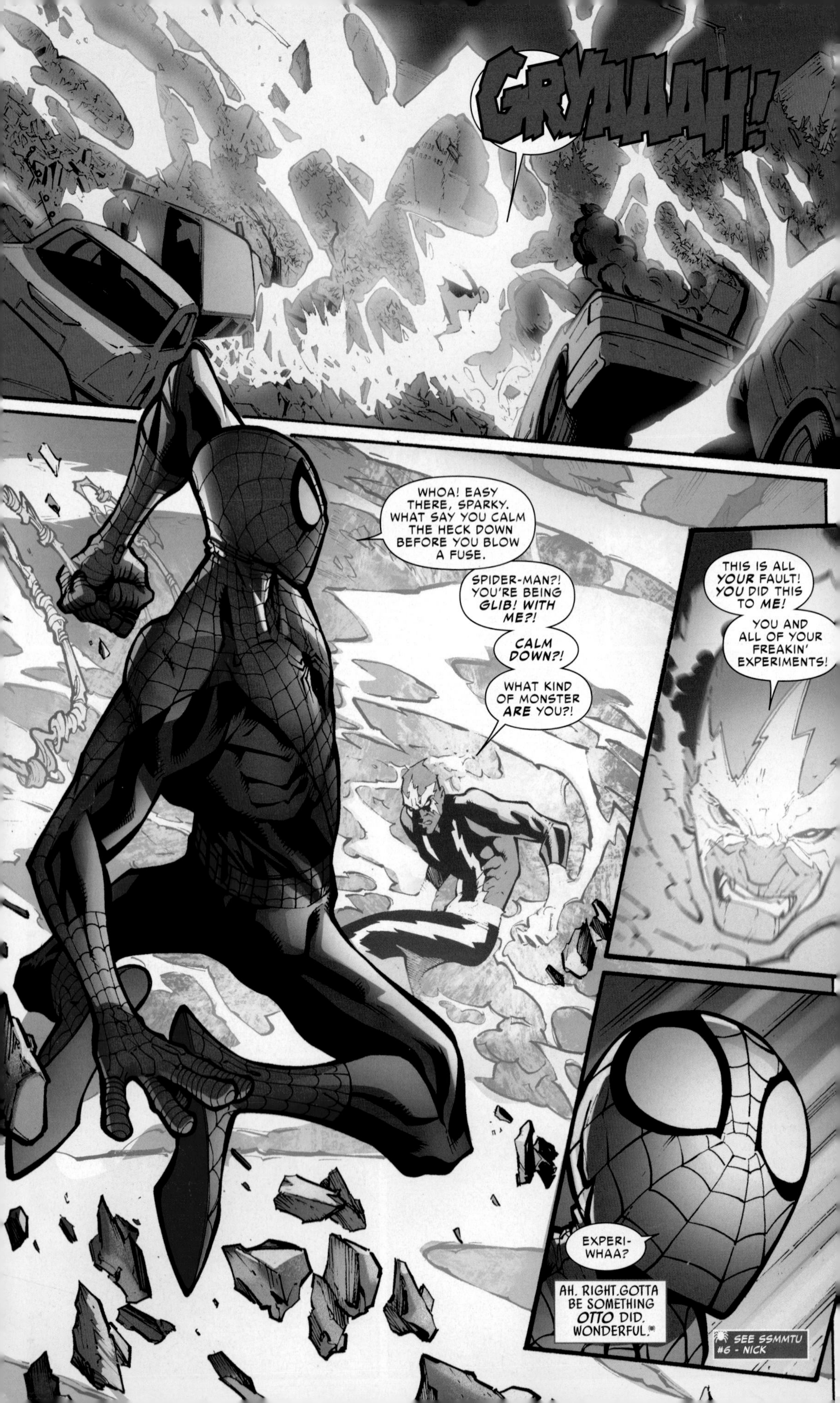
GRYAAAAH!
WHOA! EASY THERE, SPARKY. WHAT SAY YOU CALM THE HECK DOWN BEFORE YOU BLOW A FUSE.
SPIDER-MAN?! YOU'RE BEING GLIB! WITH ME?!
CALM DOWN?!
WHAT KIND OF MONSTER ARE YOU?!
THIS IS ALL YOUR FAULT! YOU DID THIS TO ME!
YOU AND ALL OF YOUR FREAKIN' EXPERIMENTS!
EXPERI-WHAA?
AH. RIGHT. GOTTA BE SOMETHING OTTO DID. WONDERFUL.
SEE SSMMTU #6 - NICK

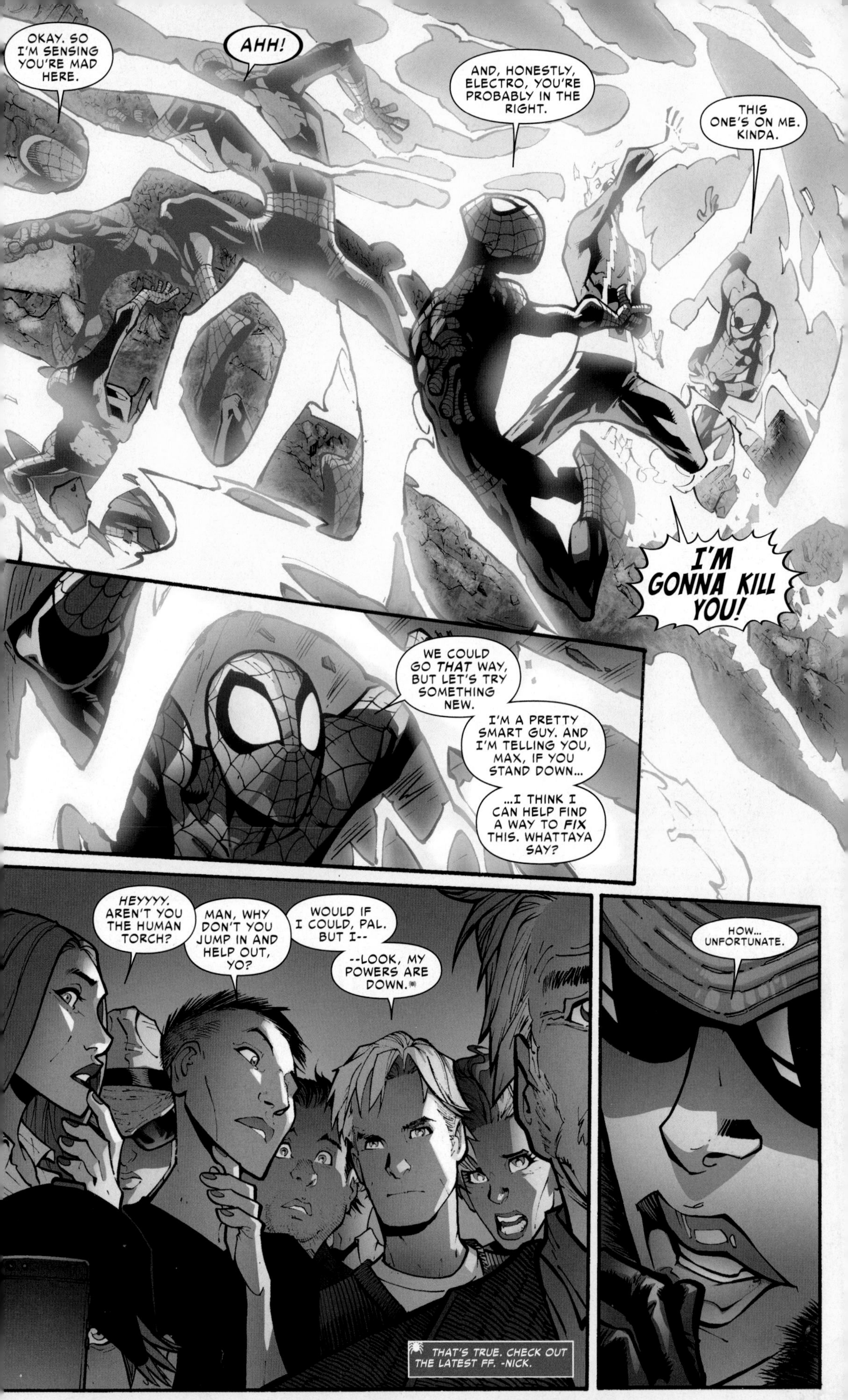

OKAY. SO I'M SENSING YOU'RE MAD HERE.
AHH!
AND, HONESTLY, ELECTRO, YOU'RE PROBABLY IN THE RIGHT.
THIS ONE'S ON ME. KINDA.
I'M GONNA KILL YOU!
WE COULD GO THAT WAY, BUT LET'S TRY SOMETHING NEW.
I'M A PRETTY SMART GUY. AND I'M TELLING YOU, MAX, IF YOU STAND DOWN...
...I THINK I CAN HELP FIND A WAY TO FIX THIS. WHATTAYA SAY?
HEYYYY. AREN'T YOU THE HUMAN TORCH?
MAN, WHY DON'T YOU JUMP IN AND HELP OUT, YO?
WOULD IF I COULD, PAL. BUT I--
--LOOK, MY POWERS ARE DOWN.
THAT'S TRUE. CHECK OUT THE LATEST FF. -NICK.
HOW... UNFORTUNATE.

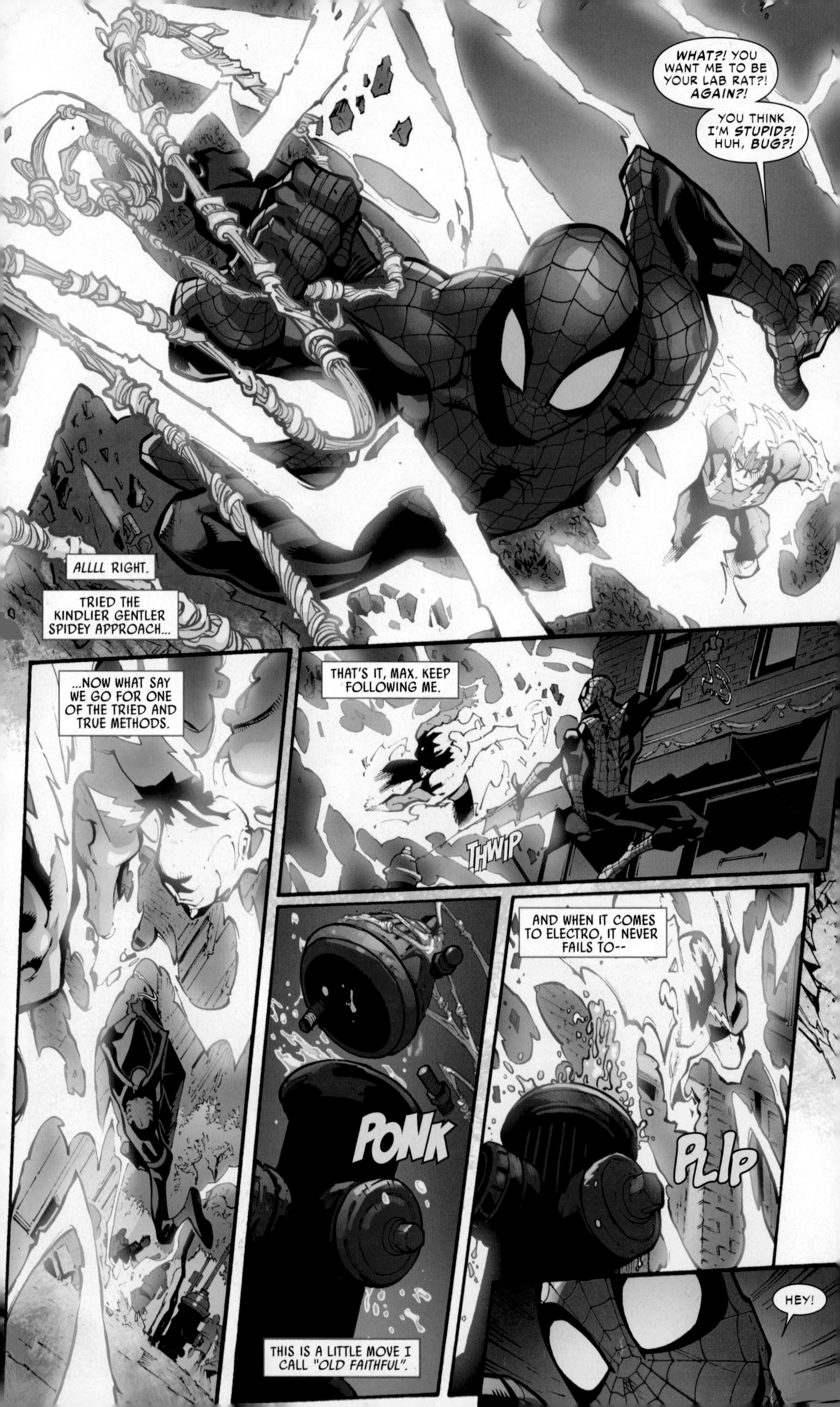
WHAT?! YOU WANT ME TO BE YOUR LAB RAT?! AGAIN?!
YOU THINK I'M STUPID?! HUH, BUG?!
ALLLL RIGHT.
TRIED THE KINDLIER GENTLER SPIDEY APPROACH...
...NOW WHAT SAY WE GO FOR ONE OF THE TRIED AND TRUE METHODS.
THAT'S IT, MAX. KEEP FOLLOWING ME.
THWIP
PONK
THIS IS A LITTLE MOVE I CALL "OLD FAITHFUL".
AND WHEN IT COMES TO ELECTRO, IT NEVER FAILS TO--
PLIP
HEY!

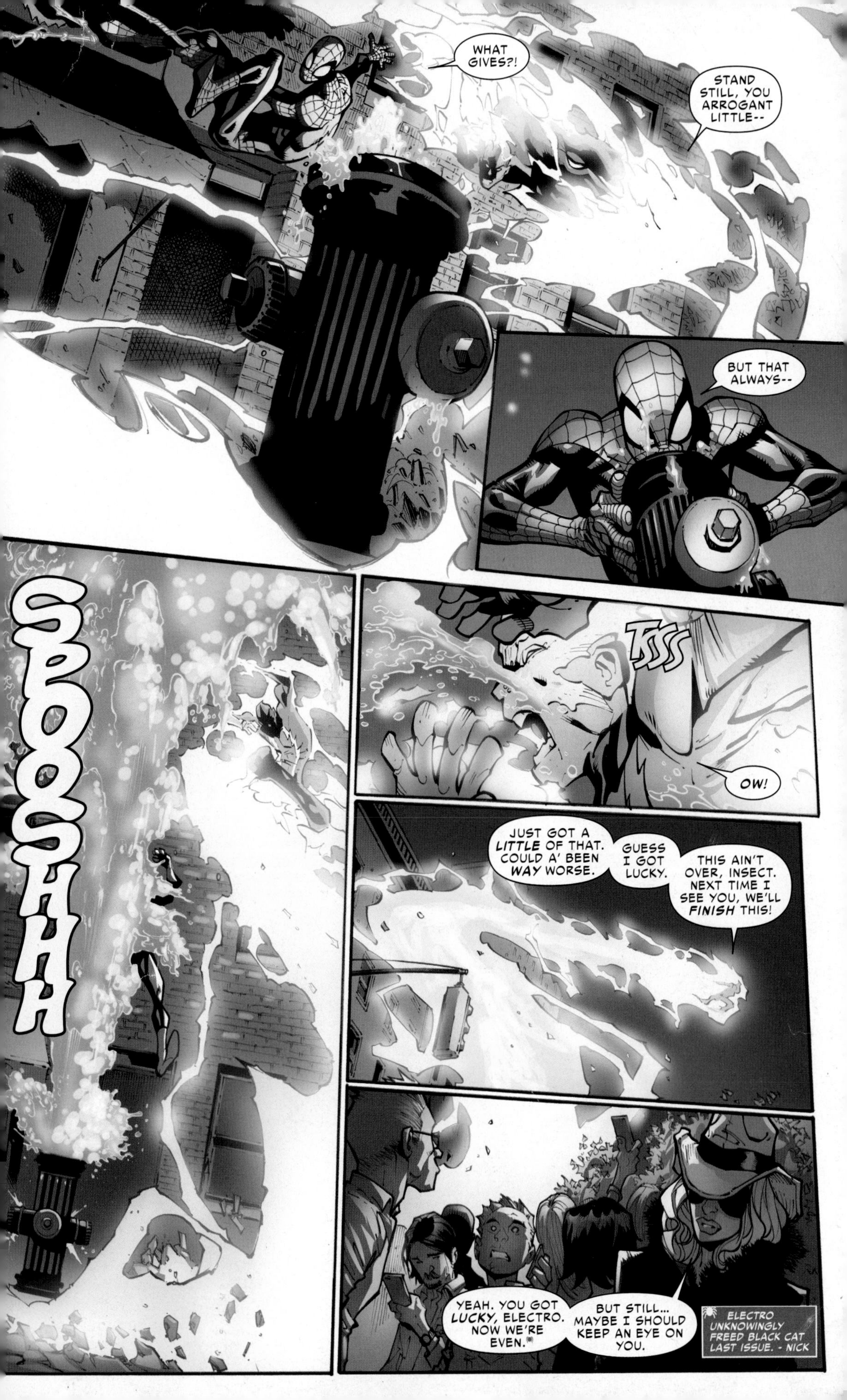
WHAT GIVES?!
STAND STILL, YOU ARROGANT LITTLE--
BUT THAT ALWAYS--
SPOOSHHH
TSSS
OW!
JUST GOT A LITTLE OF THAT. COULD A' BEEN WAY WORSE.
GUESS I GOT LUCKY.
THIS AIN'T OVER, INSECT. NEXT TIME I SEE YOU, WE'LL FINISH THIS!
YEAH. YOU GOT LUCKY, ELECTRO. NOW WE'RE EVEN.
BUT STILL... MAYBE I SHOULD KEEP AN EYE ON YOU.
ELECTRO UNKNOWINGLY FREED BLACK CAT LAST ISSUE. - NICK

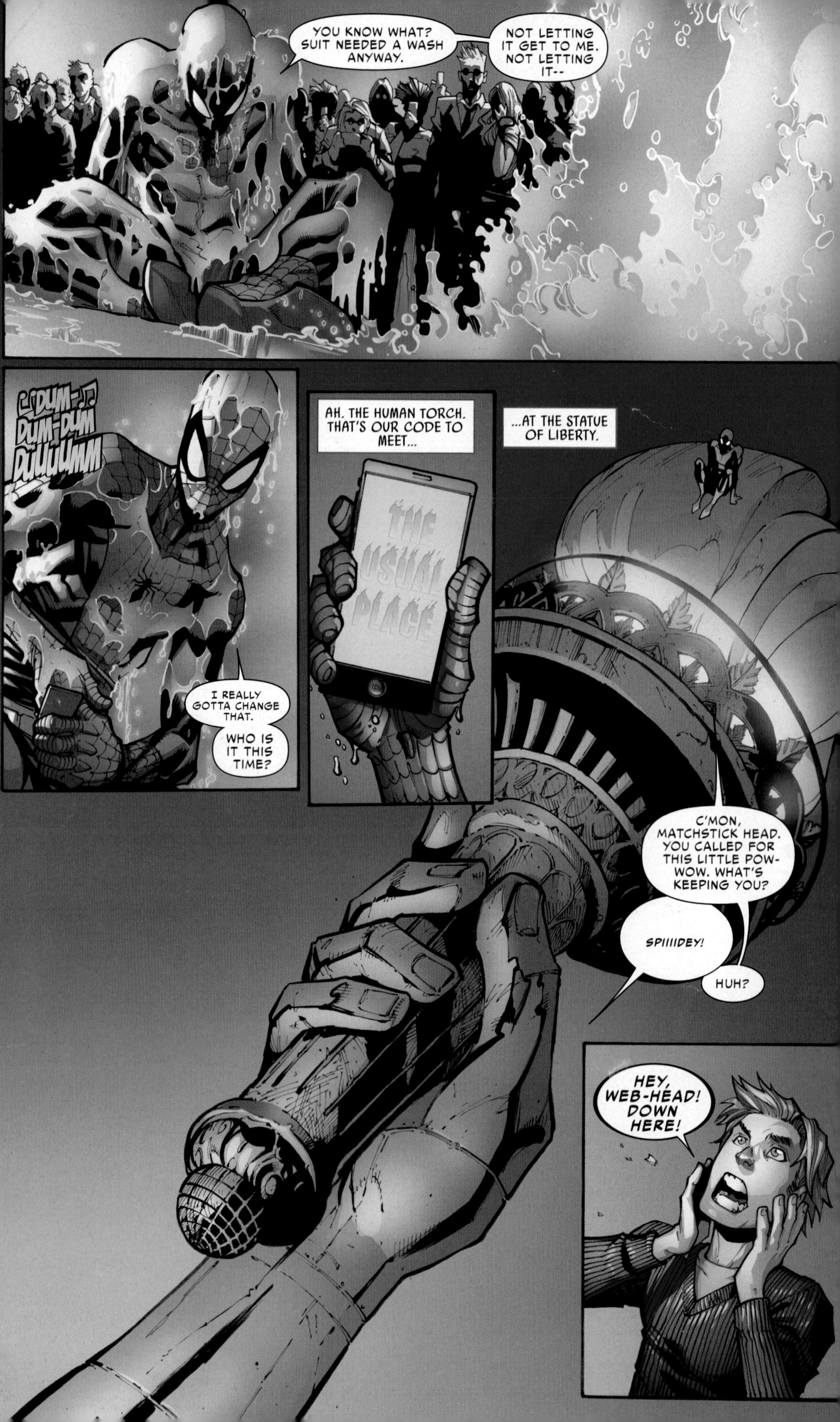
YOU KNOW WHAT? SUIT NEEDED A WASH ANYWAY.
NOT LETTING IT GET TO ME. NOT LETTING IT--
DUM-DUM-DUM DUUUUMM
I REALLY GOTTA CHANGE THAT.
WHO IS IT THIS TIME?
AH. THE HUMAN TORCH. THAT'S OUR CODE TO MEET...
THE USUAL PLACE
...AT THE STATUE OF LIBERTY.
C'MON, MATCHSTICK HEAD. YOU CALLED FOR THIS LITTLE POW-WOW. WHAT'S KEEPING YOU?
SPIIIIDEY!
HUH?
HEY, WEB-HEAD! DOWN HERE!

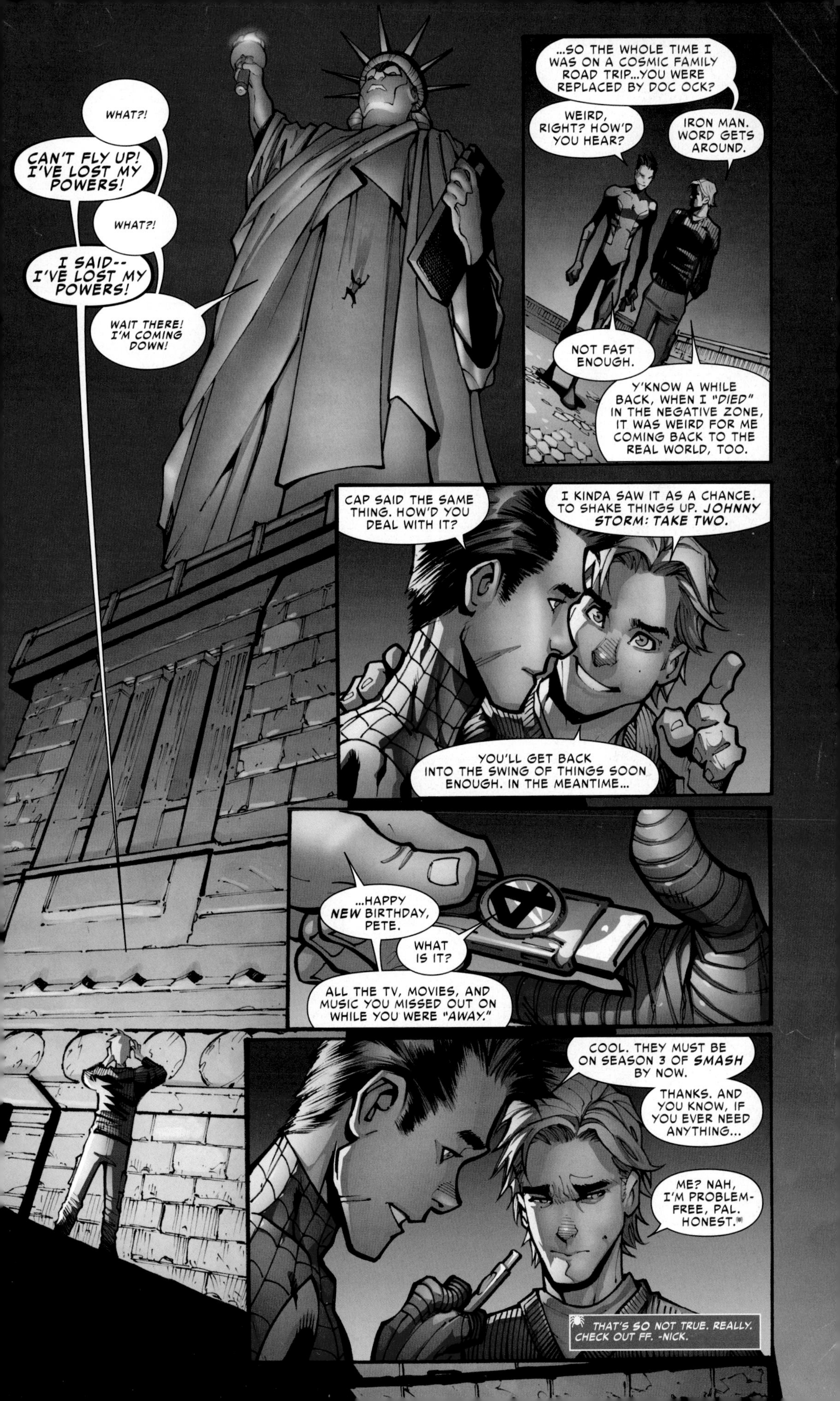
WHAT?!
CAN'T FLY UP! I'VE LOST MY POWERS!
WHAT?!
I SAID-- I'VE LOST MY POWERS!
WAIT THERE! I'M COMING DOWN!
...SO THE WHOLE TIME I WAS ON A COSMIC FAMILY ROAD TRIP...YOU WERE REPLACED BY DOC OCK?
WEIRD, RIGHT? HOW'D YOU HEAR?
IRON MAN. WORD GETS AROUND.
NOT FAST ENOUGH.
Y'KNOW A WHILE BACK, WHEN I "DIED" IN THE NEGATIVE ZONE, IT WAS WEIRD FOR ME COMING BACK TO THE REAL WORLD, TOO.
CAP SAID THE SAME THING. HOW'D YOU DEAL WITH IT?
I KINDA SAW IT AS A CHANCE. TO SHAKE THINGS UP. JOHNNY STORM: TAKE TWO.
YOU'LL GET BACK INTO THE SWING OF THINGS SOON ENOUGH. IN THE MEANTIME...
...HAPPY NEW BIRTHDAY, PETE.
WHAT IS IT?
ALL THE TV, MOVIES, AND MUSIC YOU MISSED OUT ON WHILE YOU WERE "AWAY."
COOL. THEY MUST BE ON SEASON 3 OF SMASH BY NOW.
THANKS. AND YOU KNOW, IF YOU EVER NEED ANYTHING...
ME? NAH, I'M PROBLEM-FREE, PAL. HONEST.
THAT'S SO NOT TRUE. REALLY. CHECK OUT FF. -NICK.

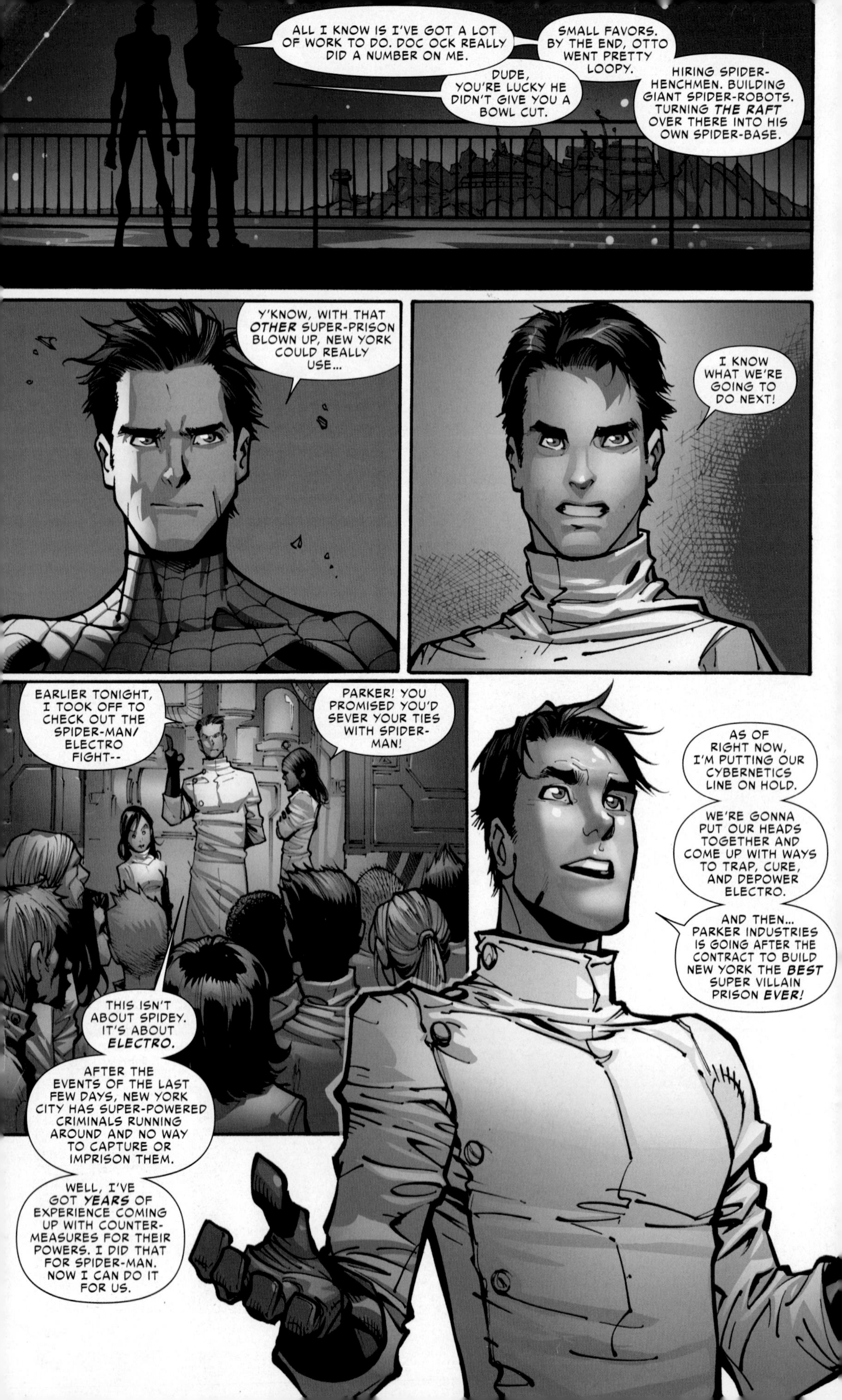
ALL I KNOW IS I'VE GOT A LOT OF WORK TO DO. DOC OCK REALLY DID A NUMBER ON ME.
SMALL FAVORS. BY THE END, OTTO WENT PRETTY LOOPY.
DUDE, YOU'RE LUCKY HE DIDN'T GIVE YOU A BOWL CUT.
HIRING SPIDER-HENCHMEN. BUILDING GIANT SPIDER-ROBOTS. TURNING THE RAFT OVER THERE INTO HIS OWN SPIDER-BASE.
Y'KNOW, WITH THAT OTHER SUPER-PRISON BLOWN UP, NEW YORK COULD REALLY USE...
I KNOW WHAT WE'RE GOING TO DO NEXT!
EARLIER TONIGHT, I TOOK OFF TO CHECK OUT THE SPIDER-MAN/ ELECTRO FIGHT--
PARKER! YOU PROMISED YOU'D SEVER YOUR TIES WITH SPIDER-MAN!
THIS ISN'T ABOUT SPIDEY. IT'S ABOUT ELECTRO.
AFTER THE EVENTS OF THE LAST FEW DAYS, NEW YORK CITY HAS SUPER-POWERED CRIMINALS RUNNING AROUND AND NO WAY TO CAPTURE OR IMPRISON THEM.
WELL, I'VE GOT YEARS OF EXPERIENCE COMING UP WITH COUNTER-MEASURES FOR THEIR POWERS. I DID THAT FOR SPIDER-MAN. NOW I CAN DO IT FOR US.
AS OF RIGHT NOW, I'M PUTTING OUR CYBERNETICS LINE ON HOLD.
WE'RE GONNA PUT OUR HEADS TOGETHER AND COME UP WITH WAYS TO TRAP, CURE, AND DEPOWER ELECTRO.
AND THEN... PARKER INDUSTRIES IS GOING AFTER THE CONTRACT TO BUILD NEW YORK THE BEST SUPER VILLAIN PRISON EVER!

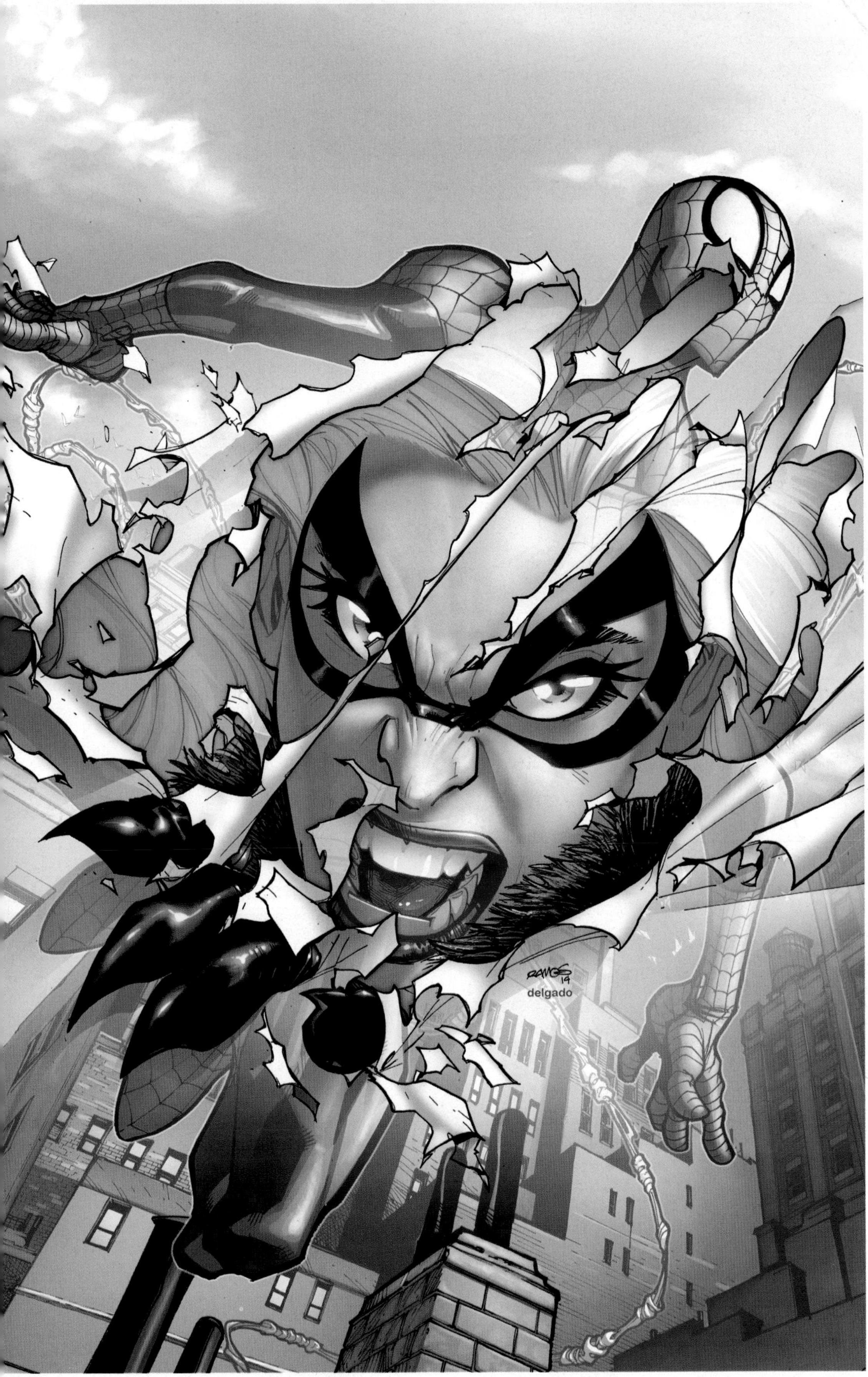
RAMOS
14
delgado

3

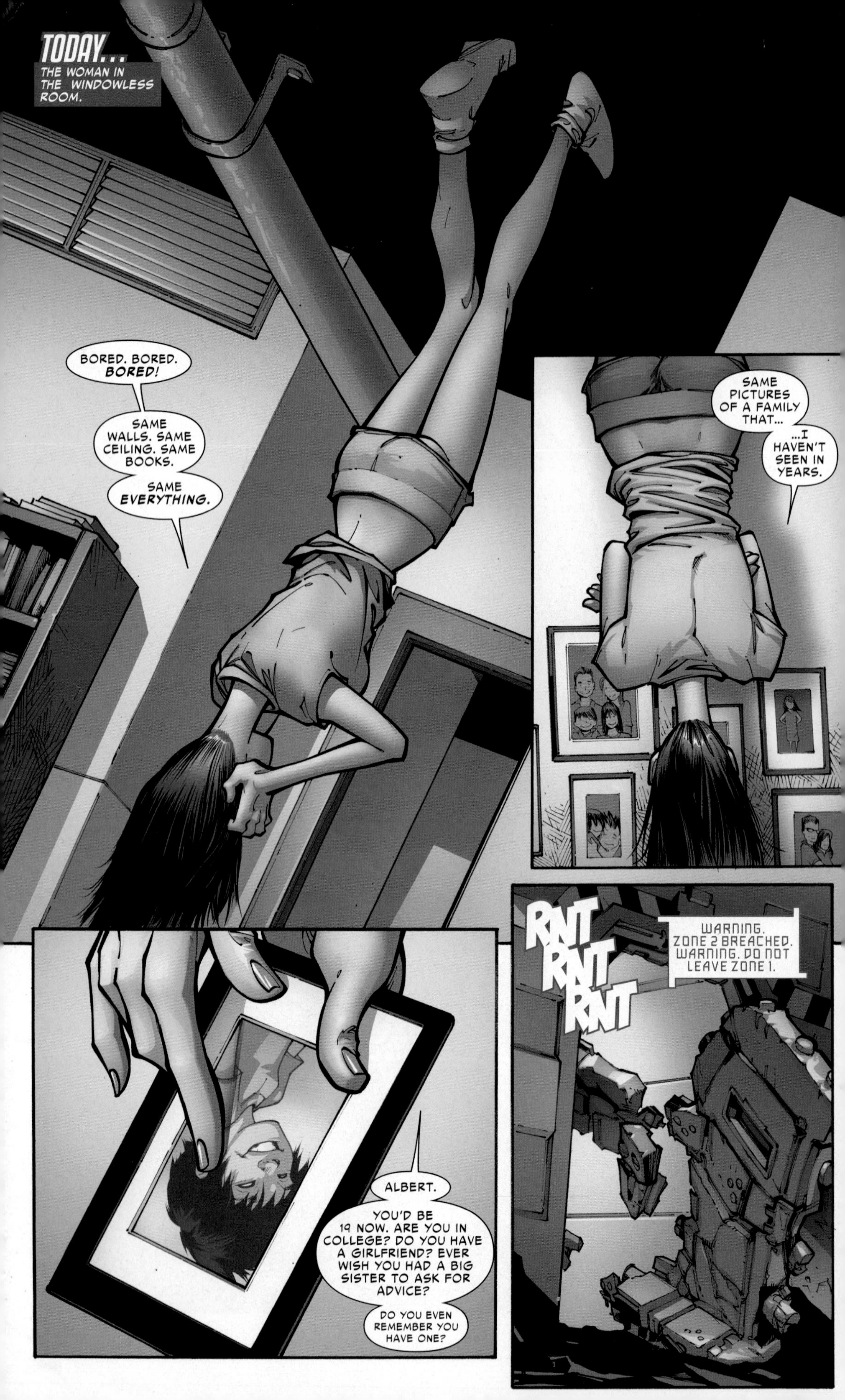
TODAY...
THE WOMAN IN THE WINDOWLESS ROOM.
BORED. BORED. BORED!
SAME WALLS. SAME CEILING. SAME BOOKS.
SAME EVERYTHING.
SAME PICTURES OF A FAMILY THAT...
...I HAVEN'T SEEN IN YEARS.
ALBERT.
YOU'D BE 19 NOW. ARE YOU IN COLLEGE? DO YOU HAVE A GIRLFRIEND? EVER WISH YOU HAD A BIG SISTER TO ASK FOR ADVICE?
DO YOU EVEN REMEMBER YOU HAVE ONE?
RNT RNT RNT
WARNING. ZONE 2 BREACHED. WARNING. DO NOT LEAVE ZONE 1.

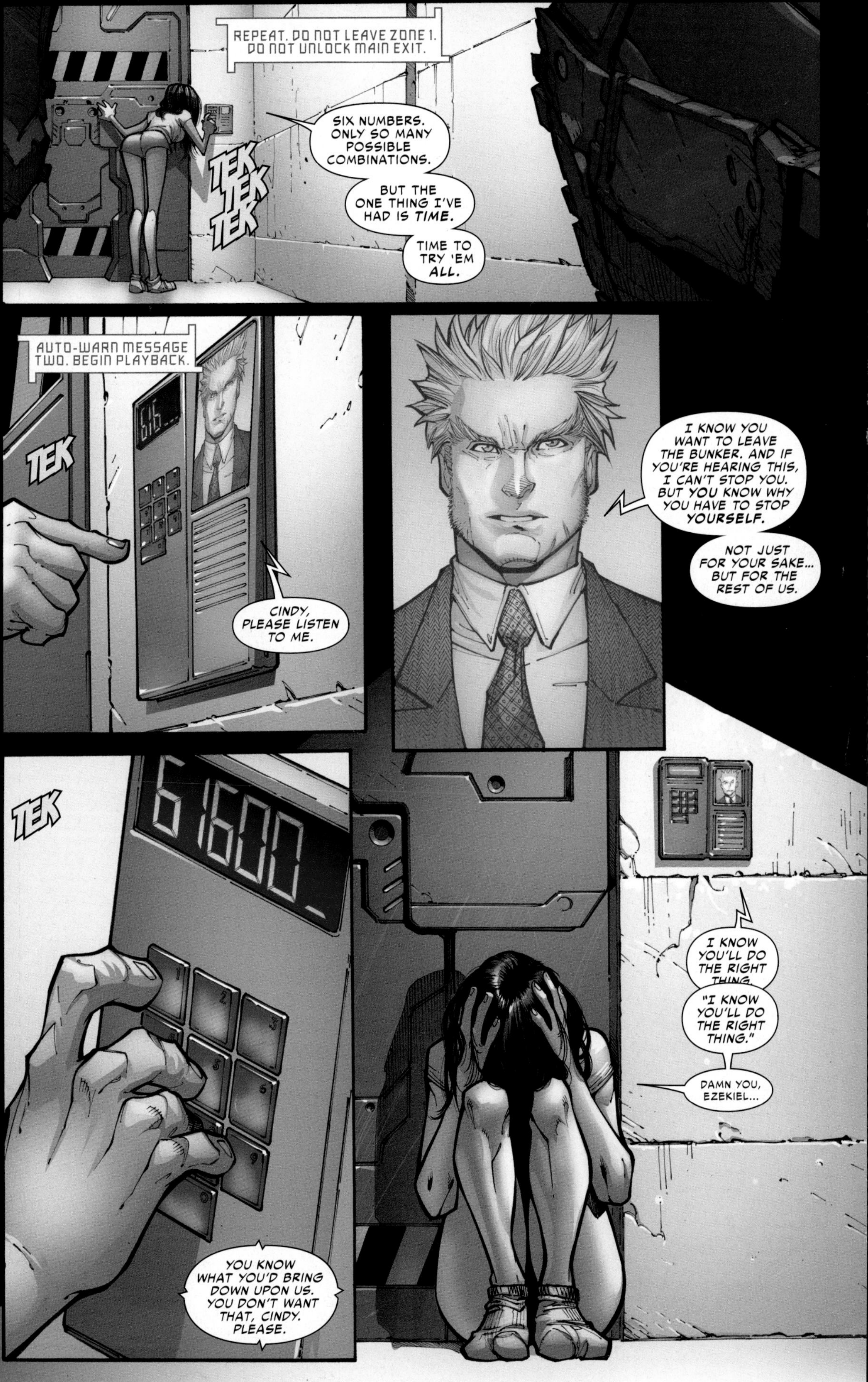

REPEAT. DO NOT LEAVE ZONE 1. DO NOT UNLOCK MAIN EXIT.
SIX NUMBERS. ONLY SO MANY POSSIBLE COMBINATIONS.
TEK TEK TEK
BUT THE ONE THING I'VE HAD IS TIME.
TIME TO TRY 'EM ALL.
AUTO-WARN MESSAGE TWO. BEGIN PLAYBACK.
TEK
CINDY, PLEASE LISTEN TO ME.
I KNOW YOU WANT TO LEAVE THE BUNKER. AND IF YOU'RE HEARING THIS, I CAN'T STOP YOU. BUT YOU KNOW WHY YOU HAVE TO STOP YOURSELF.
NOT JUST FOR YOUR SAKE... BUT FOR THE REST OF US.
TEK
61600_
YOU KNOW WHAT YOU'D BRING DOWN UPON US. YOU DON'T WANT THAT, CINDY. PLEASE.
I KNOW YOU'LL DO THE RIGHT THING.
"I KNOW YOU'LL DO THE RIGHT THING."
DAMN YOU, EZEKIEL...

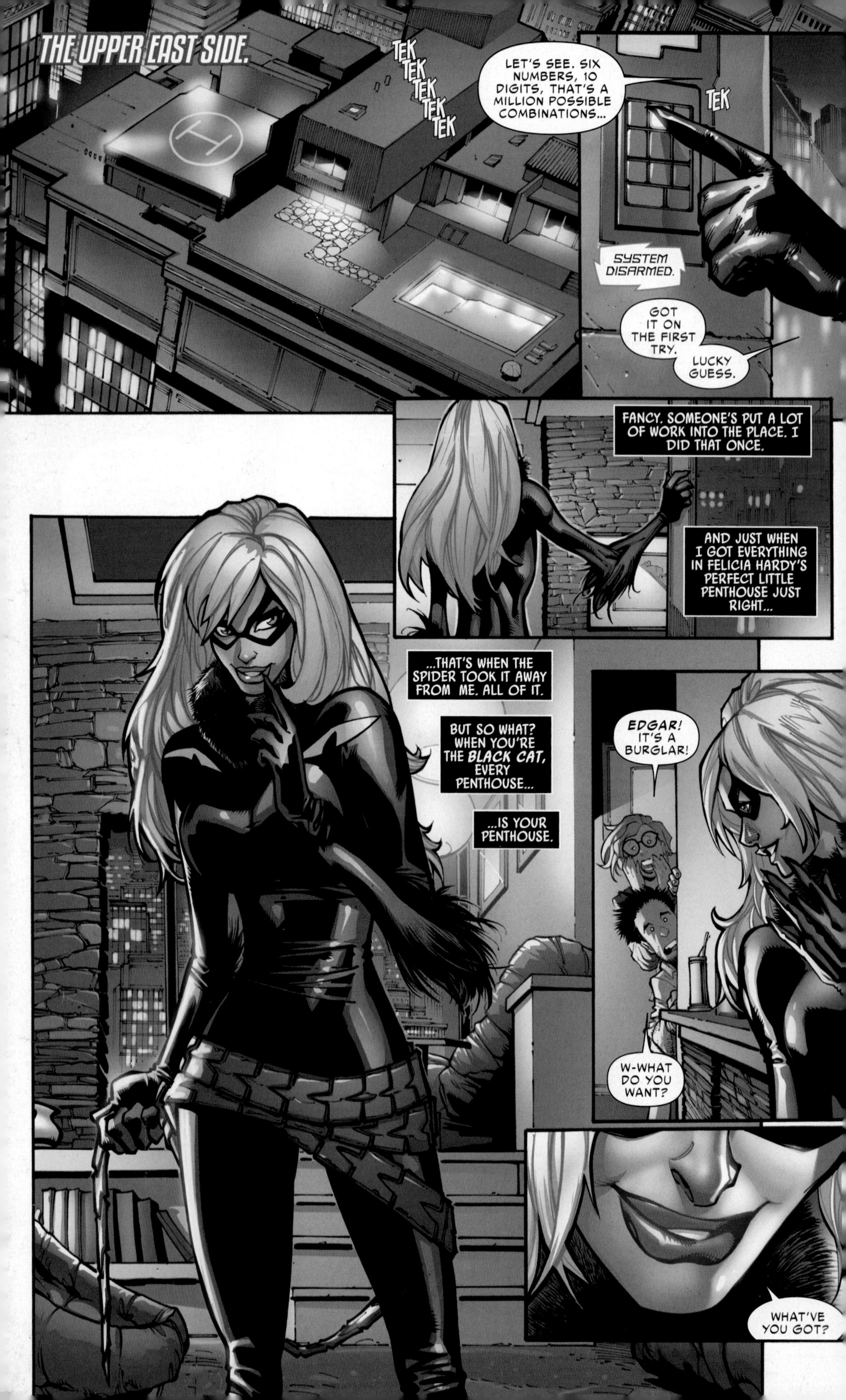
THE UPPER EAST SIDE.
TEK TEK TEK TEK TEK
LET'S SEE. SIX NUMBERS, 10 DIGITS, THAT'S A MILLION POSSIBLE COMBINATIONS...
TEK
SYSTEM DISARMED.
GOT IT ON THE FIRST TRY.
LUCKY GUESS.
FANCY. SOMEONE'S PUT A LOT OF WORK INTO THE PLACE. I DID THAT ONCE.
AND JUST WHEN I GOT EVERYTHING IN FELICIA HARDY'S PERFECT LITTLE PENTHOUSE JUST RIGHT...
...THAT'S WHEN THE SPIDER TOOK IT AWAY FROM ME. ALL OF IT.
BUT SO WHAT? WHEN YOU'RE THE BLACK CAT, EVERY PENTHOUSE...
...IS YOUR PENTHOUSE.
EDGAR! IT'S A BURGLAR!
W-WHAT DO YOU WANT?
WHAT'VE YOU GOT?

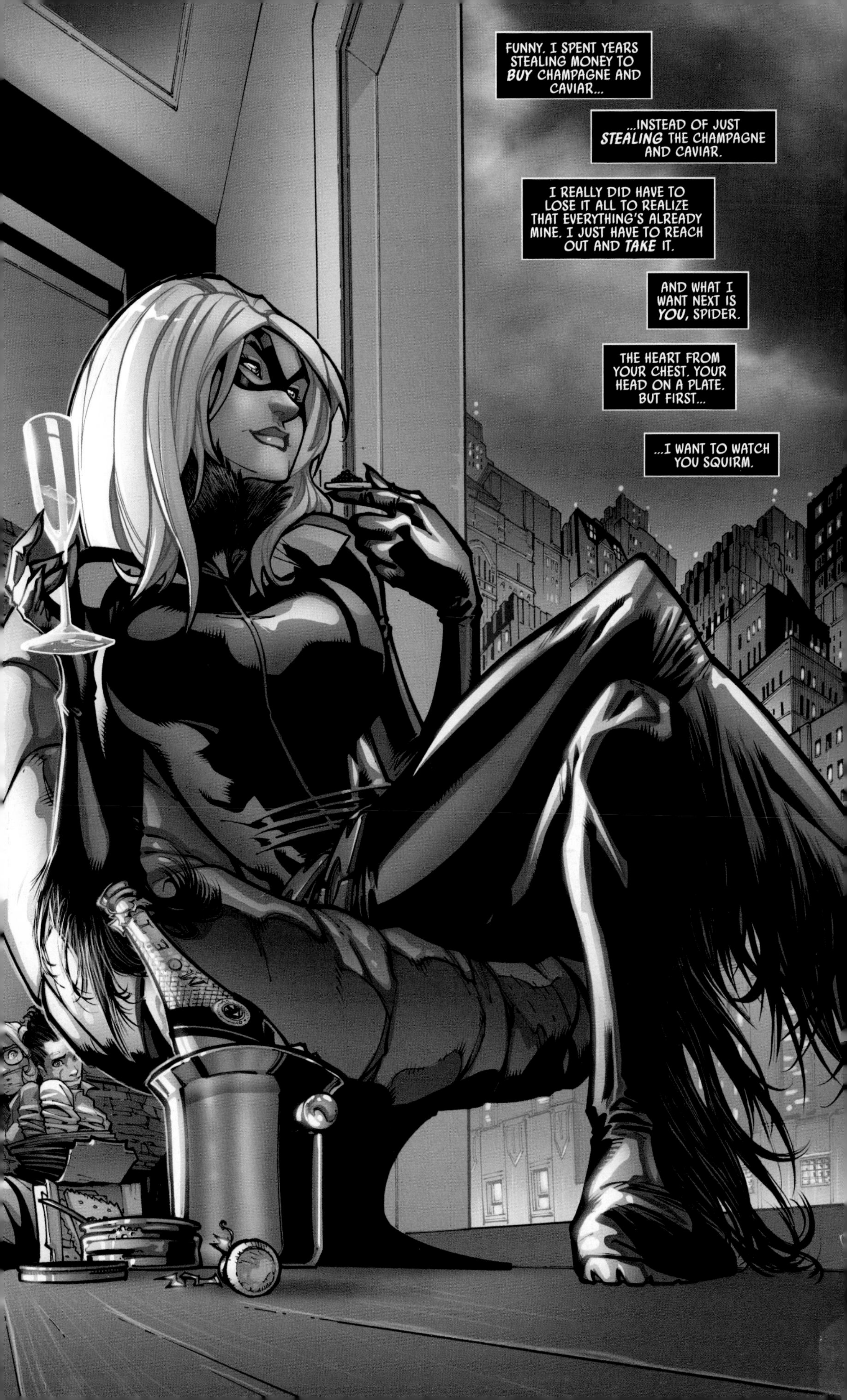
FUNNY. I SPENT YEARS STEALING MONEY TO BUY CHAMPAGNE AND CAVIAR...
...INSTEAD OF JUST STEALING THE CHAMPAGNE AND CAVIAR.
I REALLY DID HAVE TO LOSE IT ALL TO REALIZE THAT EVERYTHING'S ALREADY MINE. I JUST HAVE TO REACH OUT AND TAKE IT.
AND WHAT I WANT NEXT IS YOU, SPIDER.
THE HEART FROM YOUR CHEST. YOUR HEAD ON A PLATE. BUT FIRST...
...I WANT TO WATCH YOU SQUIRM.

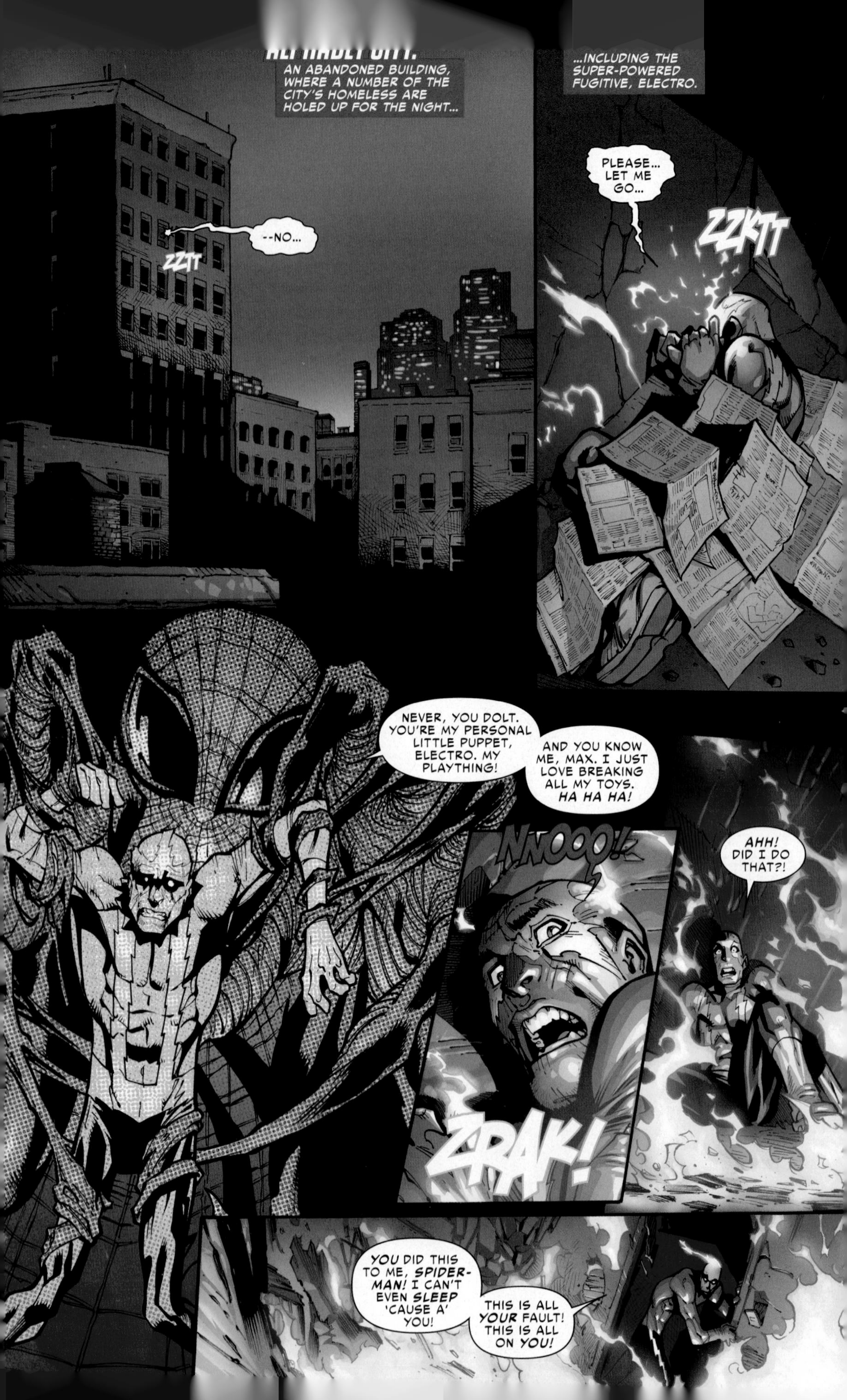
AN ABANDONED BUILDING, WHERE A NUMBER OF THE CITY'S HOMELESS ARE HOLED UP FOR THE NIGHT...
ZZTT
--NO...
...INCLUDING THE SUPER-POWERED FUGITIVE, ELECTRO.
PLEASE... LET ME GO...
ZZKTT
NEVER, YOU DOLT. YOU'RE MY PERSONAL LITTLE PUPPET, ELECTRO. MY PLAYTHING!
AND YOU KNOW ME, MAX. I JUST LOVE BREAKING ALL MY TOYS. HA HA HA!
NNOOOO!
ZRAK!
AHH! DID I DO THAT?!
YOU DID THIS TO ME, SPIDER-MAN! I CAN'T EVEN SLEEP 'CAUSE A' YOU!
THIS IS ALL YOUR FAULT! THIS IS ALL ON YOU!

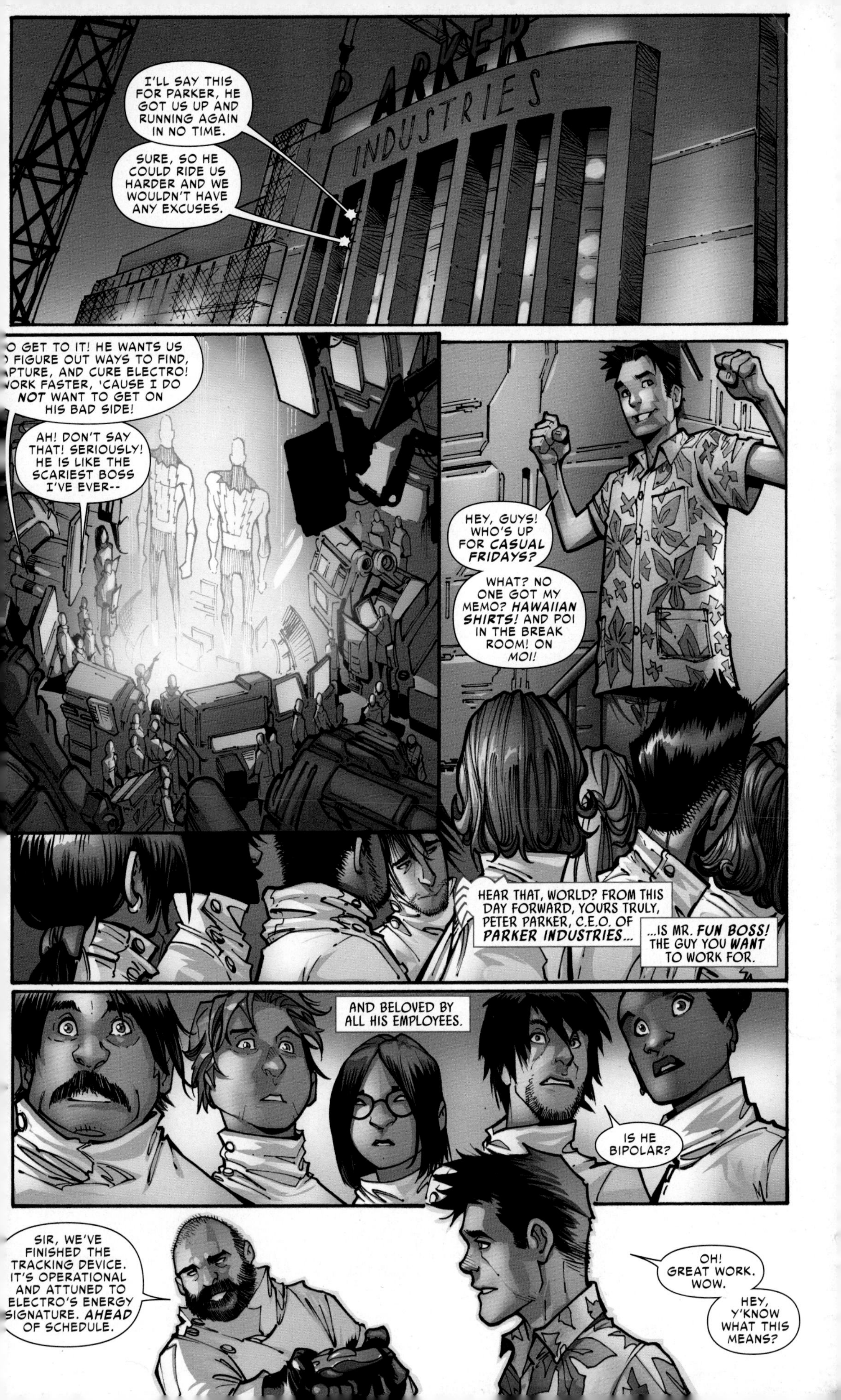

PARKER
INDUSTRIES
I'LL SAY THIS FOR PARKER, HE GOT US UP AND RUNNING AGAIN IN NO TIME.
SURE, SO HE COULD RIDE US HARDER AND WE WOULDN'T HAVE ANY EXCUSES.
O GET TO IT! HE WANTS US D FIGURE OUT WAYS TO FIND, APTURE, AND CURE ELECTRO! VORK FASTER, 'CAUSE I DO NOT WANT TO GET ON HIS BAD SIDE!
AH! DON'T SAY THAT! SERIOUSLY! HE IS LIKE THE SCARIEST BOSS I'VE EVER--
HEY, GUYS! WHO'S UP FOR CASUAL FRIDAYS?
WHAT? NO ONE GOT MY MEMO? HAWAIIAN SHIRTS! AND POI IN THE BREAK ROOM! ON MOI!
HEAR THAT, WORLD? FROM THIS DAY FORWARD, YOURS TRULY, PETER PARKER, C.E.O. OF PARKER INDUSTRIES...
...IS MR. FUN BOSS! THE GUY YOU WANT TO WORK FOR.
AND BELOVED BY ALL HIS EMPLOYEES.
IS HE BIPOLAR?
SIR, WE'VE FINISHED THE TRACKING DEVICE. IT'S OPERATIONAL AND ATTUNED TO ELECTRO'S ENERGY SIGNATURE. AHEAD OF SCHEDULE.
OH! GREAT WORK. WOW.
HEY, Y'KNOW WHAT THIS MEANS?

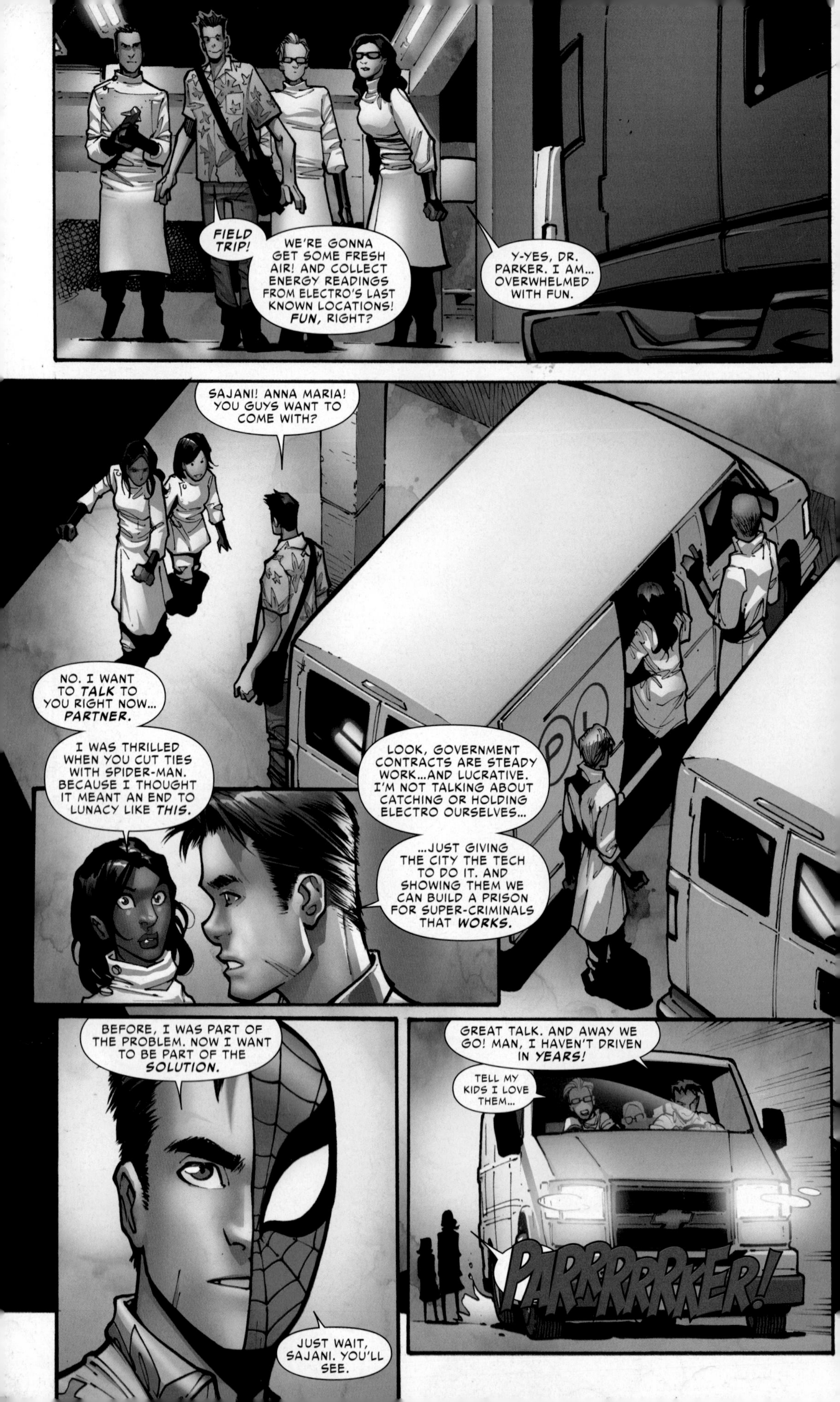
FIELD TRIP!
WE'RE GONNA GET SOME FRESH AIR! AND COLLECT ENERGY READINGS FROM ELECTRO'S LAST KNOWN LOCATIONS! FUN, RIGHT?
Y-YES, DR. PARKER. I AM... OVERWHELMED WITH FUN.
SAJANI! ANNA MARIA! YOU GUYS WANT TO COME WITH?
NO. I WANT TO TALK TO YOU RIGHT NOW... PARTNER.
I WAS THRILLED WHEN YOU CUT TIES WITH SPIDER-MAN. BECAUSE I THOUGHT IT MEANT AN END TO LUNACY LIKE THIS.
LOOK, GOVERNMENT CONTRACTS ARE STEADY WORK...AND LUCRATIVE. I'M NOT TALKING ABOUT CATCHING OR HOLDING ELECTRO OURSELVES...
...JUST GIVING THE CITY THE TECH TO DO IT. AND SHOWING THEM WE CAN BUILD A PRISON FOR SUPER-CRIMINALS THAT WORKS.
BEFORE, I WAS PART OF THE PROBLEM. NOW I WANT TO BE PART OF THE SOLUTION.
JUST WAIT, SAJANI. YOU'LL SEE.
GREAT TALK. AND AWAY WE GO! MAN, I HAVEN'T DRIVEN IN YEARS!
TELL MY KIDS I LOVE THEM...
PARRRRRKER!

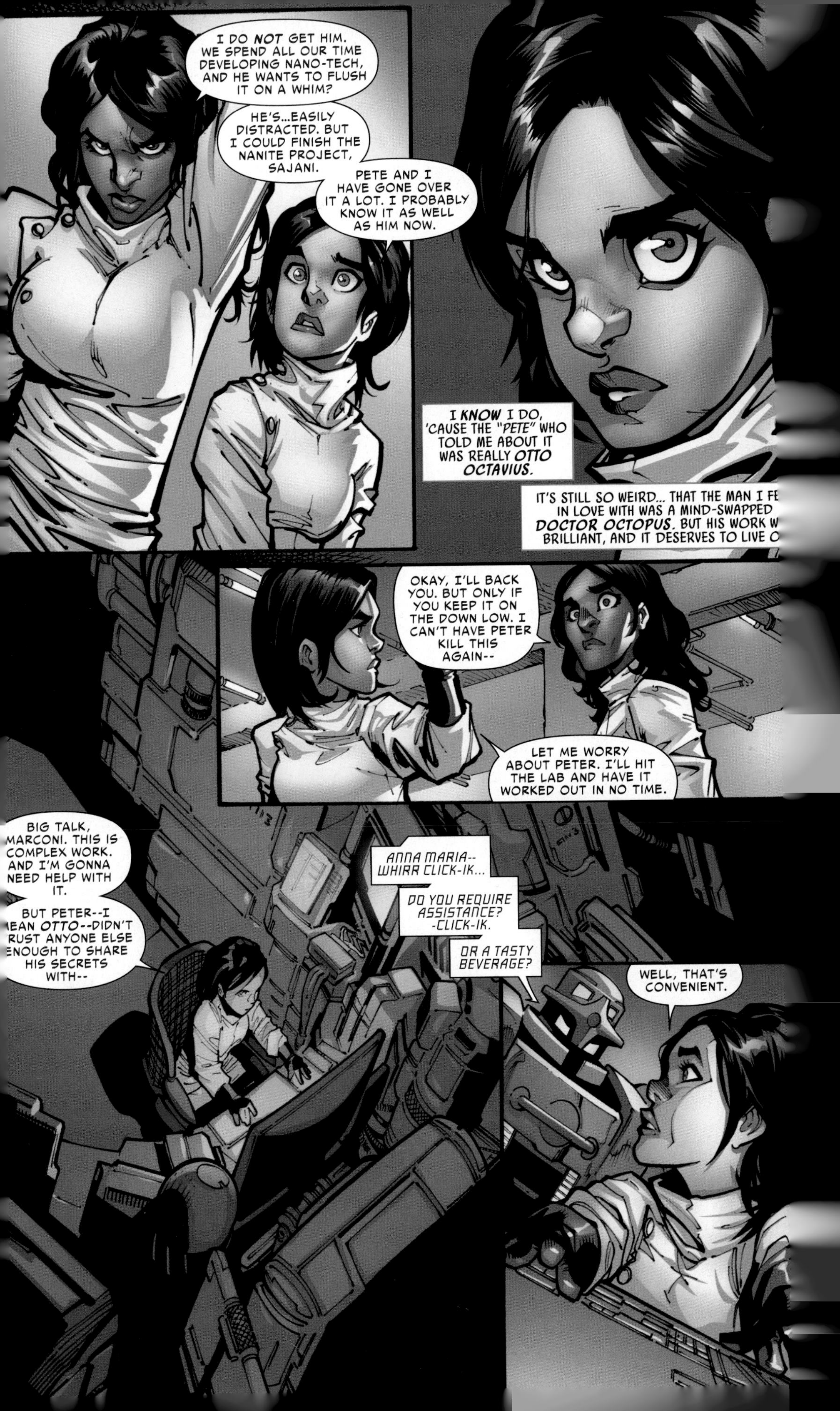
I DO NOT GET HIM. WE SPEND ALL OUR TIME DEVELOPING NANO-TECH, AND HE WANTS TO FLUSH IT ON A WHIM?
HE'S...EASILY DISTRACTED. BUT I COULD FINISH THE NANITE PROJECT, SAJANI.
PETE AND I HAVE GONE OVER IT A LOT. I PROBABLY KNOW IT AS WELL AS HIM NOW.
I KNOW I DO, 'CAUSE THE "PETE" WHO TOLD ME ABOUT IT WAS REALLY OTTO OCTAVIUS.
IT'S STILL SO WEIRD... THAT THE MAN I FE IN LOVE WITH WAS A MIND-SWAPPED DOCTOR OCTOPUS. BUT HIS WORK W BRILLIANT, AND IT DESERVES TO LIVE O
OKAY, I'LL BACK YOU. BUT ONLY IF YOU KEEP IT ON THE DOWN LOW. I CAN'T HAVE PETER KILL THIS AGAIN--
LET ME WORRY ABOUT PETER. I'LL HIT THE LAB AND HAVE IT WORKED OUT IN NO TIME.
BIG TALK, MARCONI. THIS IS COMPLEX WORK. AND I'M GONNA NEED HELP WITH IT.
BUT PETER--I EAN OTTO--DIDN'T RUST ANYONE ELSE ENOUGH TO SHARE HIS SECRETS WITH--
ANNA MARIA-- WHIRR CLICK-IK...
DO YOU REQUIRE ASSISTANCE? -CLICK-IK.
OR A TASTY BEVERAGE?
WELL, THAT'S CONVENIENT.

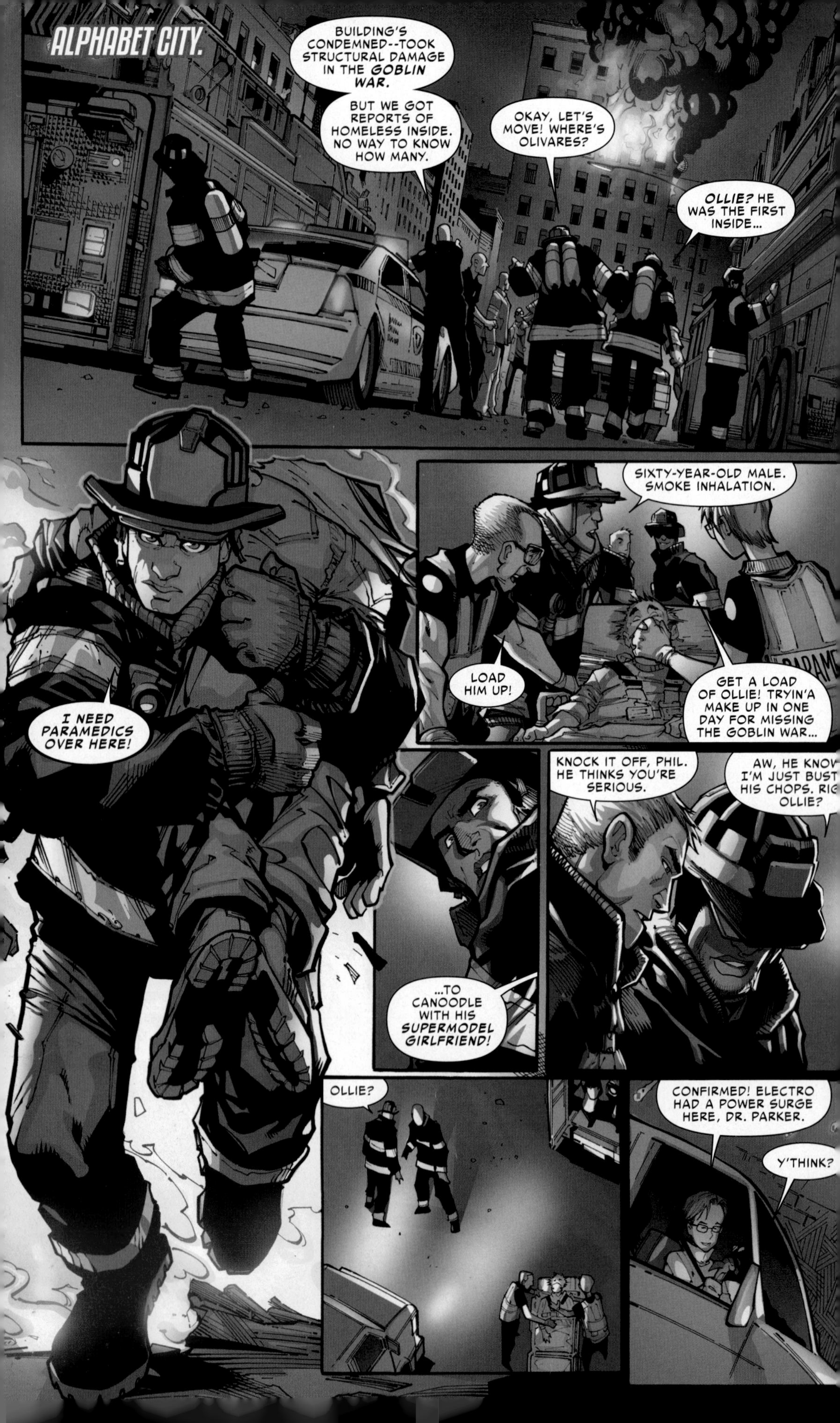
ALPHABET CITY.
BUILDING'S CONDEMNED--TOOK STRUCTURAL DAMAGE IN THE GOBLIN WAR.
BUT WE GOT REPORTS OF HOMELESS INSIDE. NO WAY TO KNOW HOW MANY.
OKAY, LET'S MOVE! WHERE'S OLIVARES?
OLLIE? HE WAS THE FIRST INSIDE...
I NEED PARAMEDICS OVER HERE!
SIXTY-YEAR-OLD MALE. SMOKE INHALATION.
LOAD HIM UP!
GET A LOAD OF OLLIE! TRYIN'A MAKE UP IN ONE DAY FOR MISSING THE GOBLIN WAR...
...TO CANOODLE WITH HIS SUPERMODEL GIRLFRIEND!
KNOCK IT OFF, PHIL. HE THINKS YOU'RE SERIOUS.
AW, HE KNOW I'M JUST BUST HIS CHOPS. RIG OLLIE?
OLLIE?
CONFIRMED! ELECTRO HAD A POWER SURGE HERE, DR. PARKER.
Y'THINK?

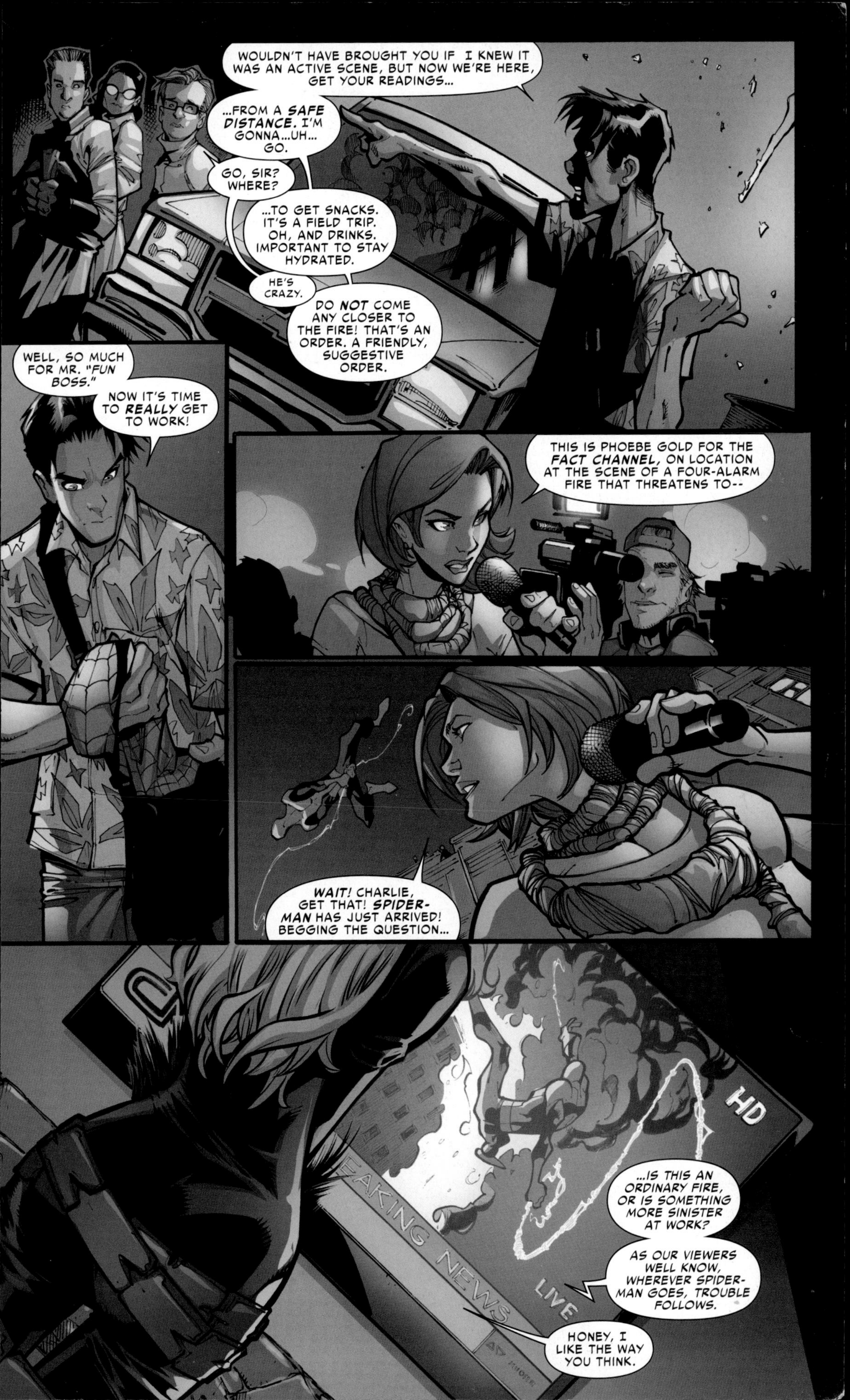

WOULDN'T HAVE BROUGHT YOU IF I KNEW IT WAS AN ACTIVE SCENE, BUT NOW WE'RE HERE, GET YOUR READINGS...
...FROM A SAFE DISTANCE. I'M GONNA...UH... GO.
GO, SIR? WHERE?
...TO GET SNACKS. IT'S A FIELD TRIP. OH, AND DRINKS. IMPORTANT TO STAY HYDRATED.
HE'S CRAZY.
DO NOT COME ANY CLOSER TO THE FIRE! THAT'S AN ORDER. A FRIENDLY, SUGGESTIVE ORDER.
WELL, SO MUCH FOR MR. "FUN BOSS."
NOW IT'S TIME TO REALLY GET TO WORK!
THIS IS PHOEBE GOLD FOR THE FACT CHANNEL, ON LOCATION AT THE SCENE OF A FOUR-ALARM FIRE THAT THREATENS TO--
WAIT! CHARLIE, GET THAT! SPIDER-MAN HAS JUST ARRIVED! BEGGING THE QUESTION...
HD
EAKING NEWS
LIVE
...IS THIS AN ORDINARY FIRE, OR IS SOMETHING MORE SINISTER AT WORK?
AS OUR VIEWERS WELL KNOW, WHEREVER SPIDER-MAN GOES, TROUBLE FOLLOWS.
HONEY, I LIKE THE WAY YOU THINK.

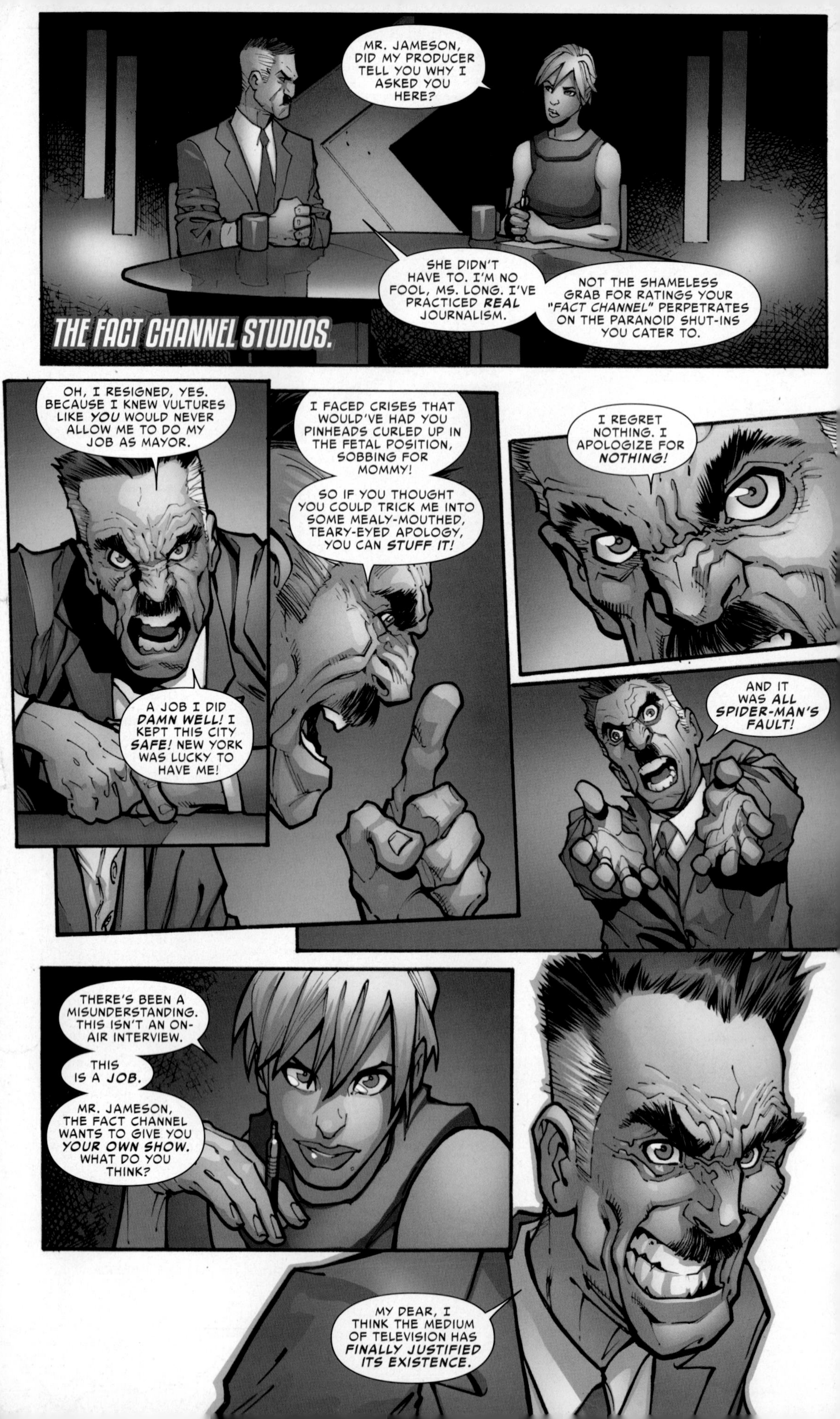

MR. JAMESON, DID MY PRODUCER TELL YOU WHY I ASKED YOU HERE?
SHE DIDN'T HAVE TO. I'M NO FOOL, MS. LONG. I'VE PRACTICED REAL JOURNALISM.
NOT THE SHAMELESS GRAB FOR RATINGS YOUR "FACT CHANNEL" PERPETRATES ON THE PARANOID SHUT-INS YOU CATER TO.
THE FACT CHANNEL STUDIOS.
OH, I RESIGNED, YES. BECAUSE I KNEW VULTURES LIKE YOU WOULD NEVER ALLOW ME TO DO MY JOB AS MAYOR.
A JOB I DID DAMN WELL! I KEPT THIS CITY SAFE! NEW YORK WAS LUCKY TO HAVE ME!
I FACED CRISES THAT WOULD'VE HAD YOU PINHEADS CURLED UP IN THE FETAL POSITION, SOBBING FOR MOMMY!
SO IF YOU THOUGHT YOU COULD TRICK ME INTO SOME MEALY-MOUTHED, TEARY-EYED APOLOGY, YOU CAN STUFF IT!
I REGRET NOTHING. I APOLOGIZE FOR NOTHING!
AND IT WAS ALL SPIDER-MAN'S FAULT!
THERE'S BEEN A MISUNDERSTANDING. THIS ISN'T AN ON-AIR INTERVIEW.
THIS IS A JOB.
MR. JAMESON, THE FACT CHANNEL WANTS TO GIVE YOU YOUR OWN SHOW. WHAT DO YOU THINK?
MY DEAR, I THINK THE MEDIUM OF TELEVISION HAS FINALLY JUSTIFIED ITS EXISTENCE.

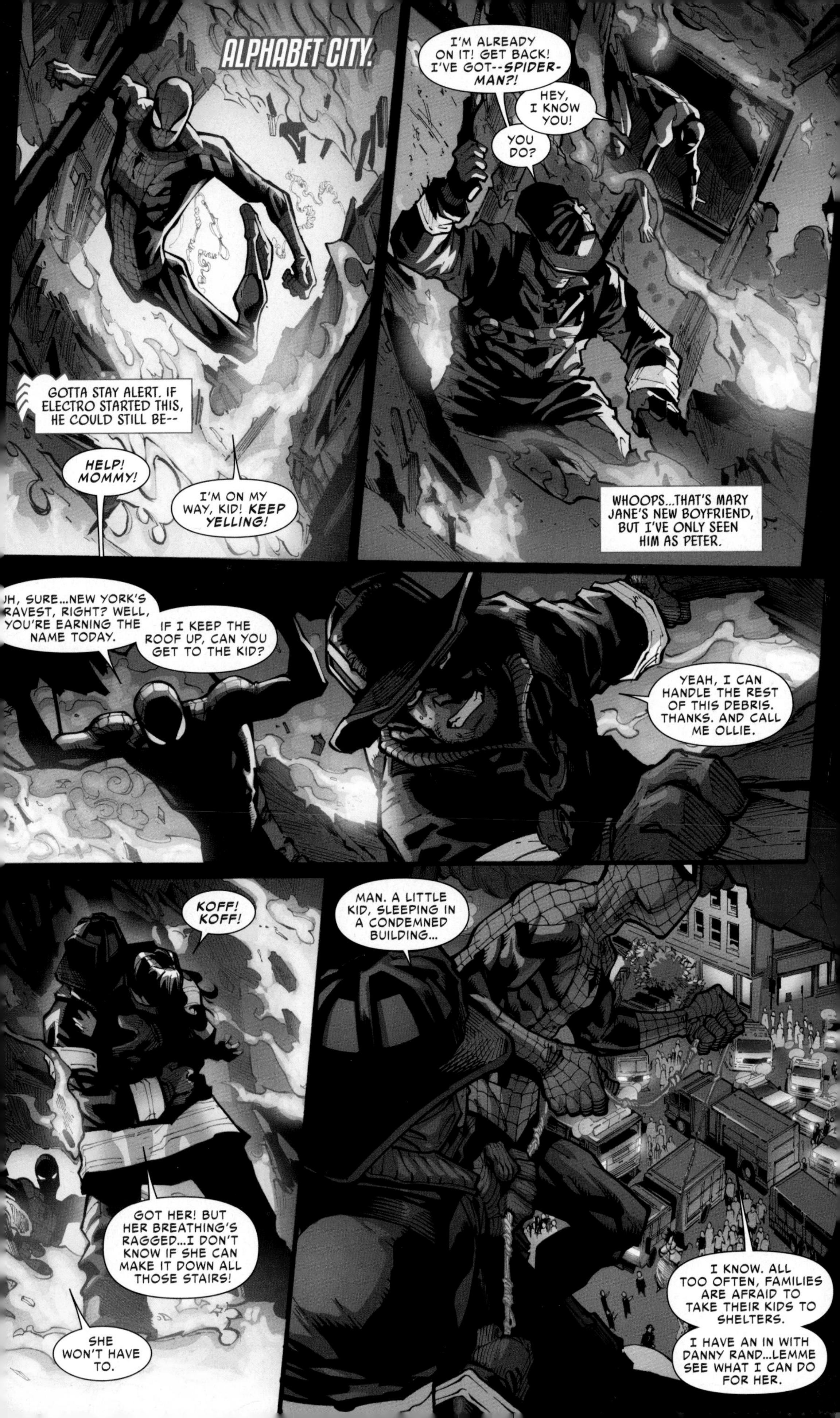

ALPHABET CITY.
GOTTA STAY ALERT. IF ELECTRO STARTED THIS, HE COULD STILL BE--
HELP! MOMMY!
I'M ON MY WAY, KID! KEEP YELLING!
I'M ALREADY ON IT! GET BACK! I'VE GOT--SPIDER-MAN?!
HEY, I KNOW YOU!
YOU DO?
WHOOPS...THAT'S MARY JANE'S NEW BOYFRIEND, BUT I'VE ONLY SEEN HIM AS PETER.
UH, SURE...NEW YORK'S BRAVEST, RIGHT? WELL, YOU'RE EARNING THE NAME TODAY.
IF I KEEP THE ROOF UP, CAN YOU GET TO THE KID?
YEAH, I CAN HANDLE THE REST OF THIS DEBRIS. THANKS. AND CALL ME OLLIE.
KOFF! KOFF!
GOT HER! BUT HER BREATHING'S RAGGED...I DON'T KNOW IF SHE CAN MAKE IT DOWN ALL THOSE STAIRS!
SHE WON'T HAVE TO.
MAN. A LITTLE KID, SLEEPING IN A CONDEMNED BUILDING...
I KNOW. ALL TOO OFTEN, FAMILIES ARE AFRAID TO TAKE THEIR KIDS TO SHELTERS.
I HAVE AN IN WITH DANNY RAND...LEMME SEE WHAT I CAN DO FOR HER.

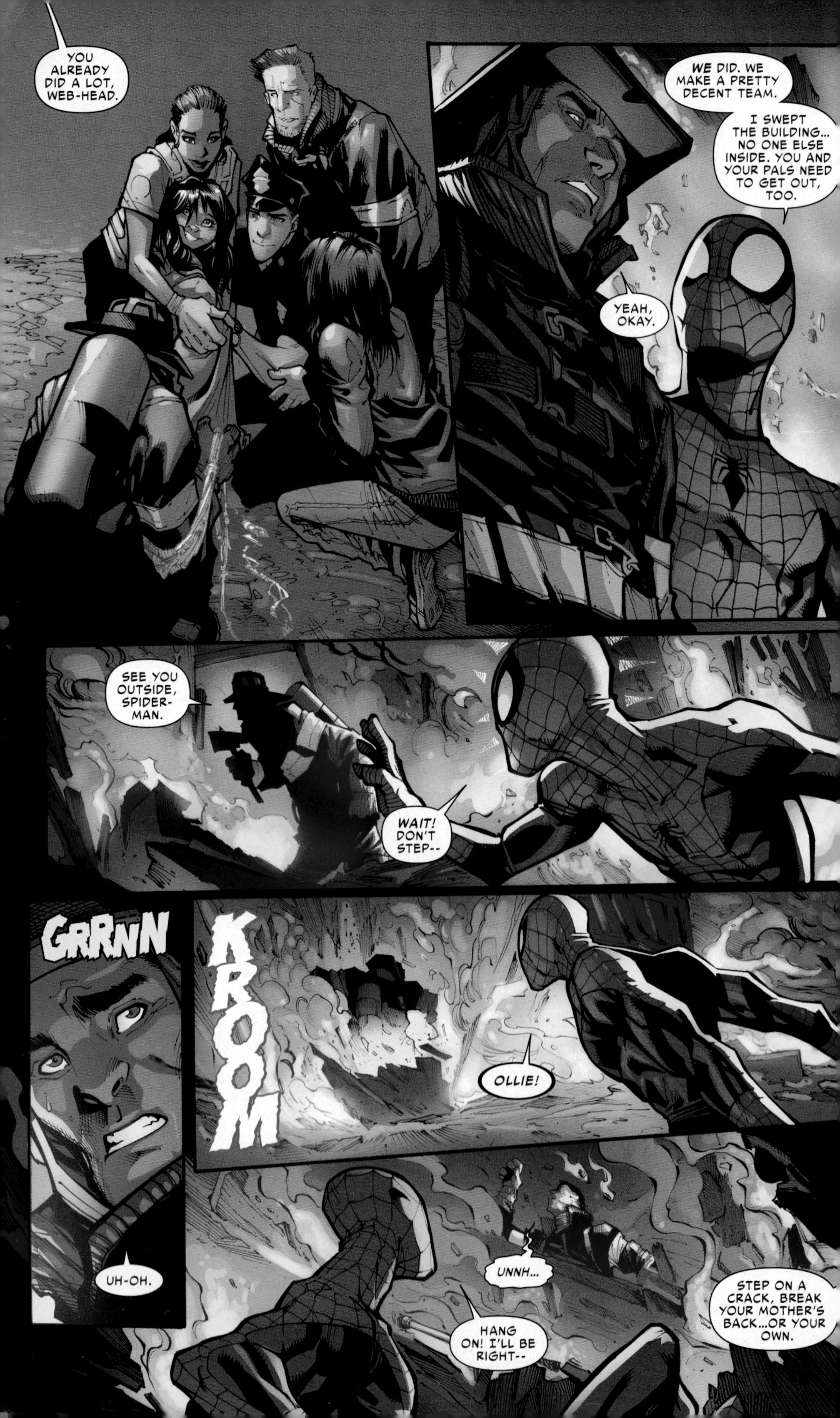
YOU ALREADY DID A LOT, WEB-HEAD.
WE DID. WE MAKE A PRETTY DECENT TEAM.
I SWEPT THE BUILDING... NO ONE ELSE INSIDE. YOU AND YOUR PALS NEED TO GET OUT, TOO.
YEAH, OKAY.
SEE YOU OUTSIDE, SPIDER-MAN.
WAIT! DON'T STEP--
GRRNN
UH-OH.
KROOM
OLLIE!
UNNH...
HANG ON! I'LL BE RIGHT--
STEP ON A CRACK, BREAK YOUR MOTHER'S BACK...OR YOUR OWN.

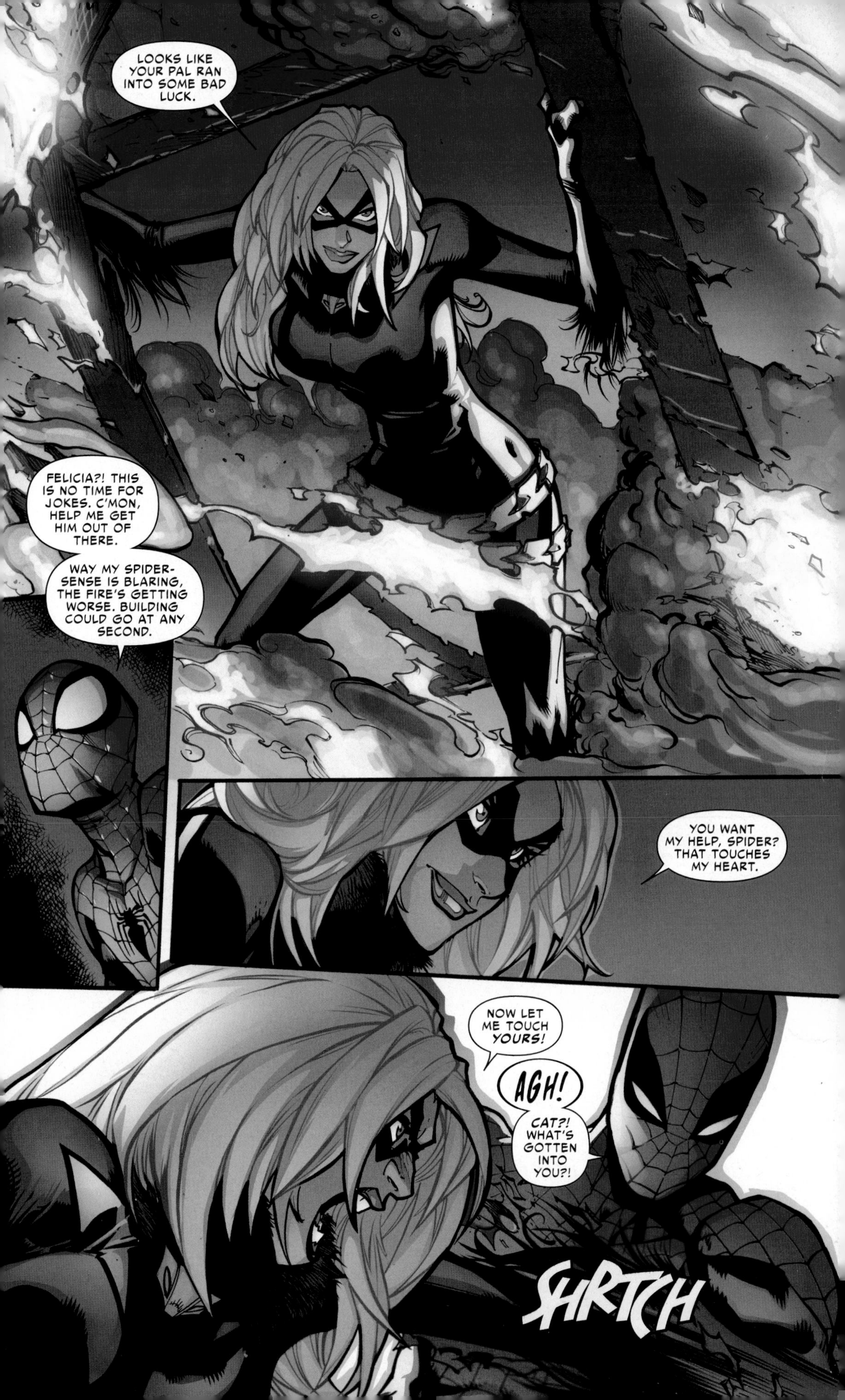
LOOKS LIKE YOUR PAL RAN INTO SOME BAD LUCK.
FELICIA?! THIS IS NO TIME FOR JOKES. C'MON, HELP ME GET HIM OUT OF THERE.
WAY MY SPIDER-SENSE IS BLARING, THE FIRE'S GETTING WORSE. BUILDING COULD GO AT ANY SECOND.
YOU WANT MY HELP, SPIDER? THAT TOUCHES MY HEART.
NOW LET ME TOUCH YOURS!
AGH!
CAT?! WHAT'S GOTTEN INTO YOU?!
SHRTCH

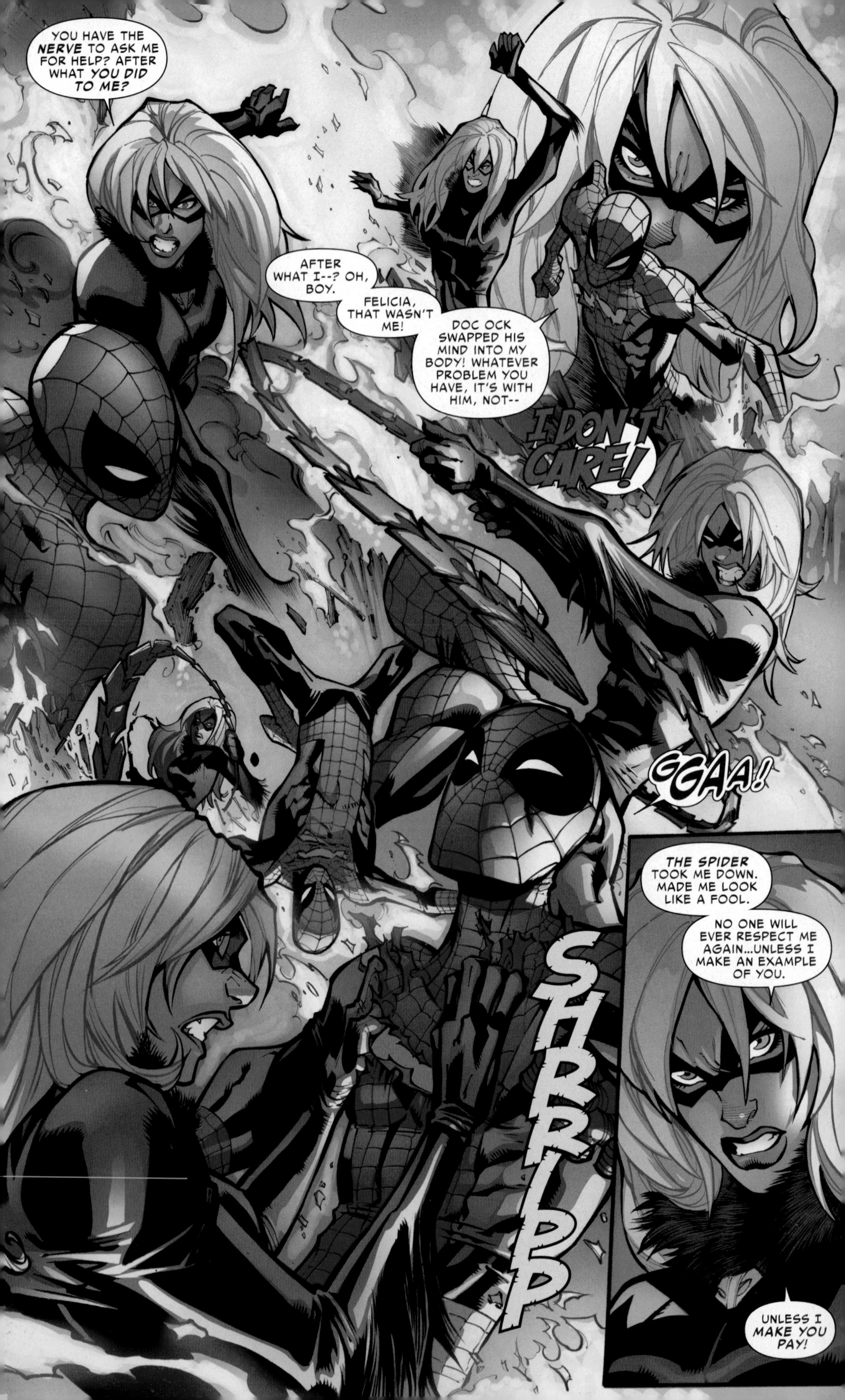
YOU HAVE THE NERVE TO ASK ME FOR HELP? AFTER WHAT YOU DID TO ME?
AFTER WHAT I--? OH, BOY.
FELICIA, THAT WASN'T ME!
DOC OCK SWAPPED HIS MIND INTO MY BODY! WHATEVER PROBLEM YOU HAVE, IT'S WITH HIM, NOT--
I DON'T CARE!
GGAA!
SHRIPP
THE SPIDER TOOK ME DOWN. MADE ME LOOK LIKE A FOOL.
NO ONE WILL EVER RESPECT ME AGAIN...UNLESS I MAKE AN EXAMPLE OF YOU.
UNLESS I MAKE YOU PAY!

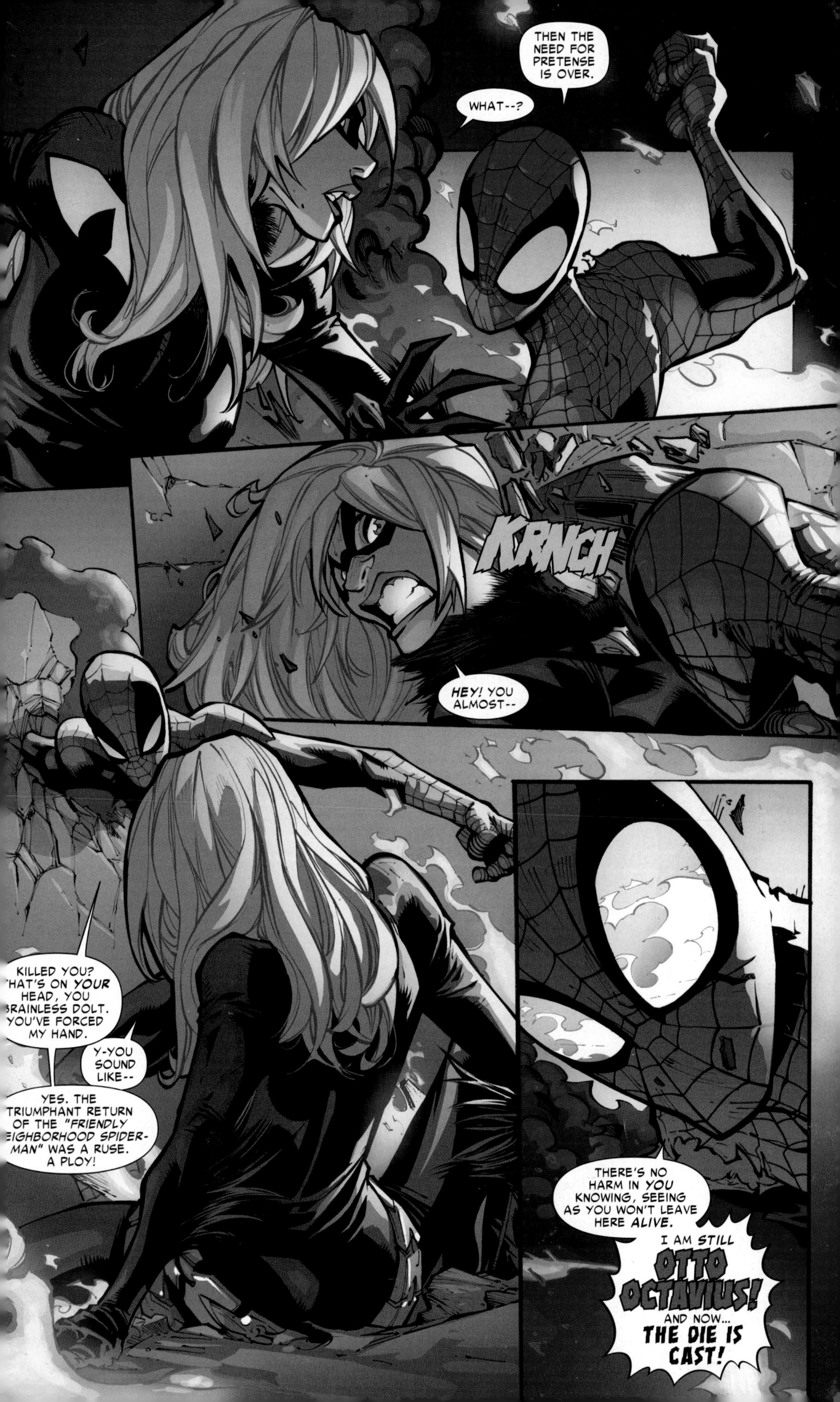
THEN THE NEED FOR PRETENSE IS OVER.
WHAT--?
KRNCH
HEY! YOU ALMOST--
KILLED YOU? THAT'S ON YOUR HEAD, YOU BRAINLESS DOLT. YOU'VE FORCED MY HAND.
Y-YOU SOUND LIKE--
YES. THE TRIUMPHANT RETURN OF THE "FRIENDLY NEIGHBORHOOD SPIDER-MAN" WAS A RUSE. A PLOY!
THERE'S NO HARM IN YOU KNOWING, SEEING AS YOU WON'T LEAVE HERE ALIVE.
I AM STILL OTTO OCTAVIUS! AND NOW... THE DIE IS CAST!

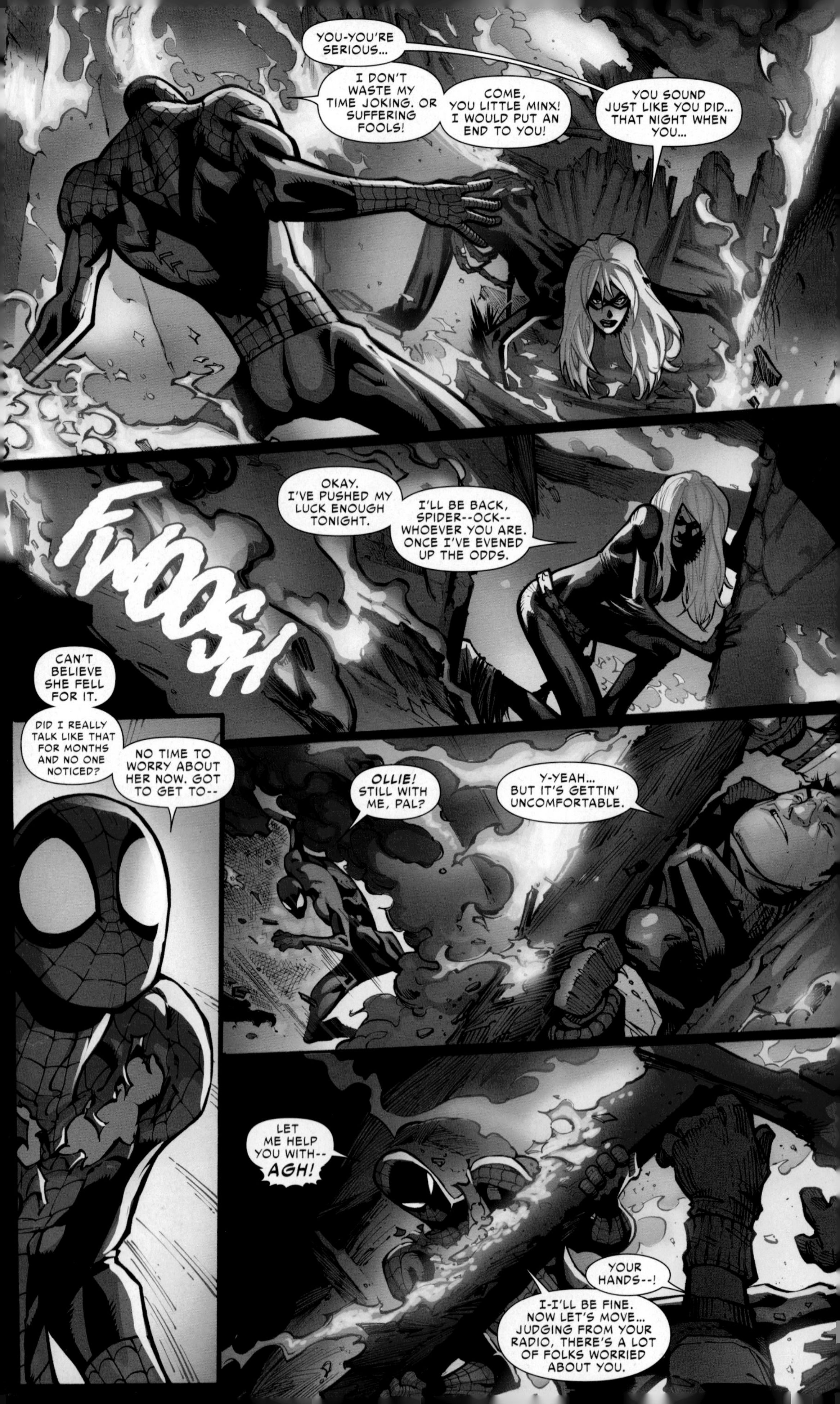
YOU-YOU'RE SERIOUS...
I DON'T WASTE MY TIME JOKING. OR SUFFERING FOOLS!
COME, YOU LITTLE MINX! I WOULD PUT AN END TO YOU!
YOU SOUND JUST LIKE YOU DID... THAT NIGHT WHEN YOU...
FWOOSH
OKAY. I'VE PUSHED MY LUCK ENOUGH TONIGHT.
I'LL BE BACK, SPIDER--OCK--WHOEVER YOU ARE. ONCE I'VE EVENED UP THE ODDS.
CAN'T BELIEVE SHE FELL FOR IT.
DID I REALLY TALK LIKE THAT FOR MONTHS AND NO ONE NOTICED?
NO TIME TO WORRY ABOUT HER NOW. GOT TO GET TO--
OLLIE! STILL WITH ME, PAL?
Y-YEAH... BUT IT'S GETTIN' UNCOMFORTABLE.
LET ME HELP YOU WITH-- AGH!
YOUR HANDS--!
I-I'LL BE FINE. NOW LET'S MOVE... JUDGING FROM YOUR RADIO, THERE'S A LOT OF FOLKS WORRIED ABOUT YOU.

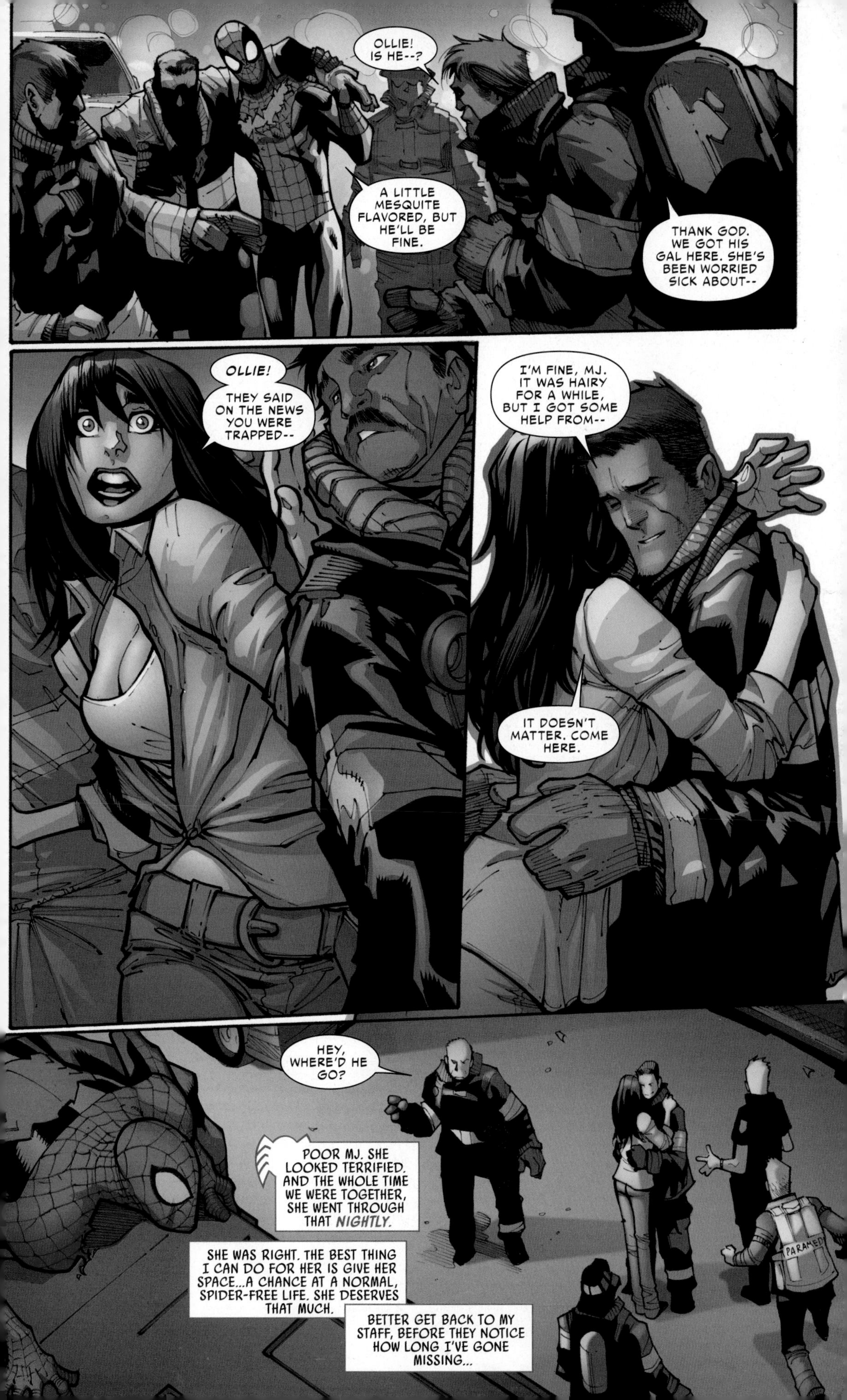
OLLIE! IS HE--?
A LITTLE MESQUITE FLAVORED, BUT HE'LL BE FINE.
THANK GOD. WE GOT HIS GAL HERE. SHE'S BEEN WORRIED SICK ABOUT--
OLLIE!
THEY SAID ON THE NEWS YOU WERE TRAPPED--
I'M FINE, MJ. IT WAS HAIRY FOR A WHILE, BUT I GOT SOME HELP FROM--
IT DOESN'T MATTER. COME HERE.
HEY, WHERE'D HE GO?
POOR MJ. SHE LOOKED TERRIFIED. AND THE WHOLE TIME WE WERE TOGETHER, SHE WENT THROUGH THAT NIGHTLY.
SHE WAS RIGHT. THE BEST THING I CAN DO FOR HER IS GIVE HER SPACE...A CHANCE AT A NORMAL, SPIDER-FREE LIFE. SHE DESERVES THAT MUCH.
BETTER GET BACK TO MY STAFF, BEFORE THEY NOTICE HOW LONG I'VE GONE MISSING...
PARAMED

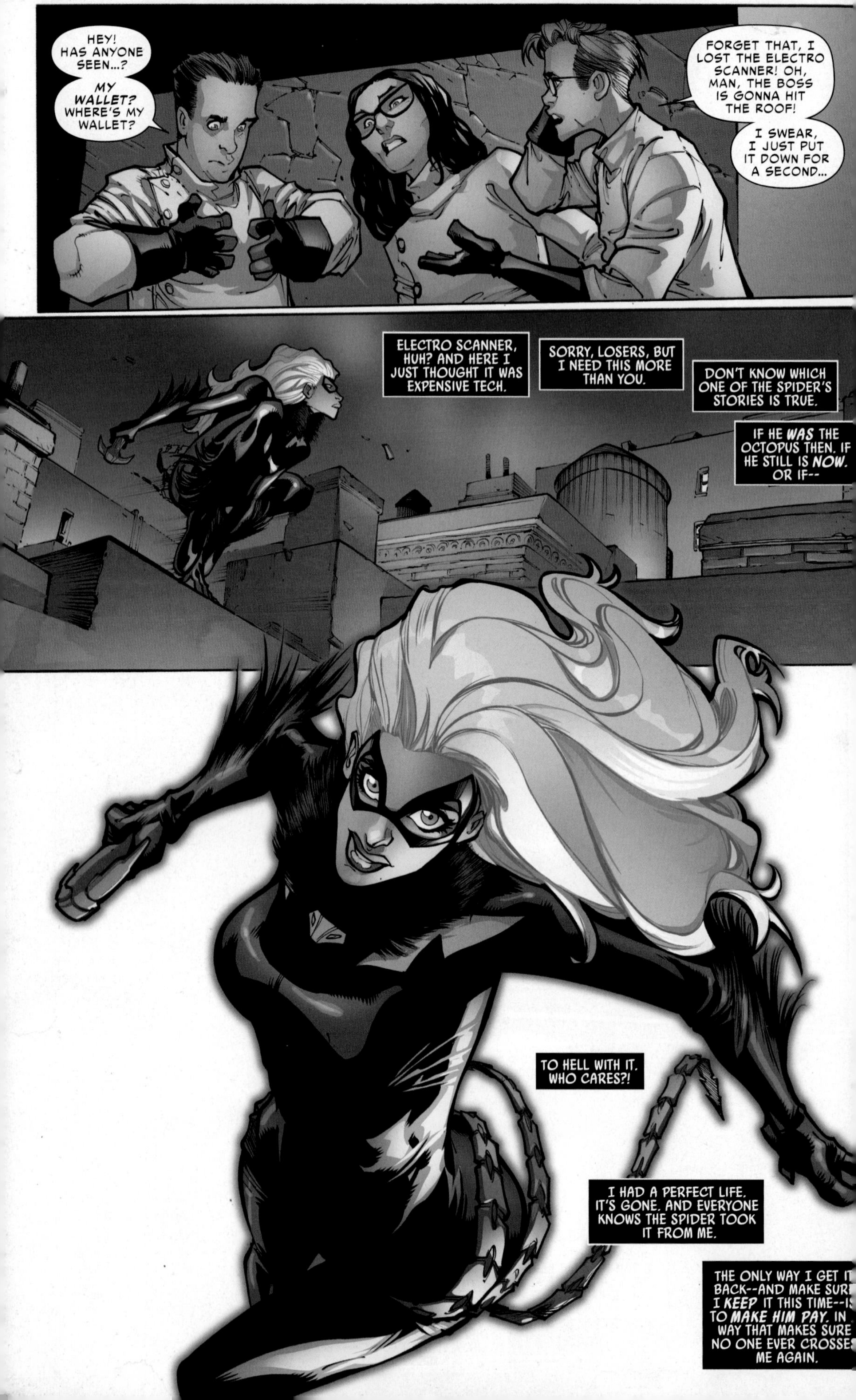
HEY! HAS ANYONE SEEN...?
MY WALLET? WHERE'S MY WALLET?
FORGET THAT, I LOST THE ELECTRO SCANNER! OH, MAN, THE BOSS IS GONNA HIT THE ROOF!
I SWEAR, I JUST PUT IT DOWN FOR A SECOND...
ELECTRO SCANNER, HUH? AND HERE I JUST THOUGHT IT WAS EXPENSIVE TECH.
SORRY, LOSERS, BUT I NEED THIS MORE THAN YOU.
DON'T KNOW WHICH ONE OF THE SPIDER'S STORIES IS TRUE.
IF HE WAS THE OCTOPUS THEN. IF HE STILL IS NOW. OR IF--
TO HELL WITH IT. WHO CARES?!
I HAD A PERFECT LIFE. IT'S GONE. AND EVERYONE KNOWS THE SPIDER TOOK IT FROM ME.
THE ONLY WAY I GET IT BACK--AND MAKE SURE I KEEP IT THIS TIME--IS TO MAKE HIM PAY. IN WAY THAT MAKES SURE NO ONE EVER CROSSES ME AGAIN.

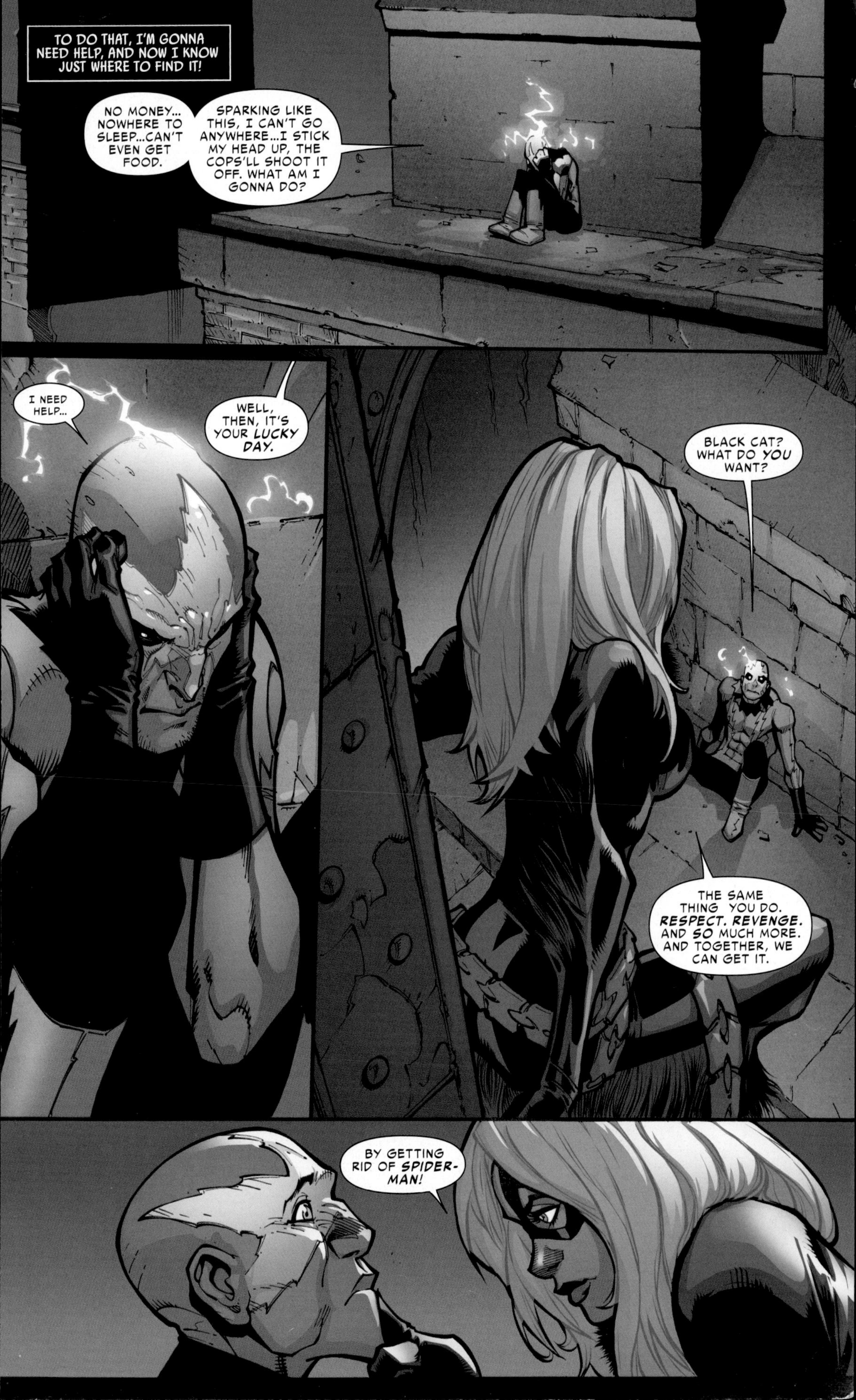
TO DO THAT, I'M GONNA NEED HELP, AND NOW I KNOW JUST WHERE TO FIND IT!
NO MONEY... NOWHERE TO SLEEP...CAN'T EVEN GET FOOD.
SPARKING LIKE THIS, I CAN'T GO ANYWHERE...I STICK MY HEAD UP, THE COPS'LL SHOOT IT OFF. WHAT AM I GONNA DO?
I NEED HELP...
WELL, THEN, IT'S YOUR LUCKY DAY.
BLACK CAT? WHAT DO YOU WANT?
THE SAME THING YOU DO. RESPECT. REVENGE. AND SO MUCH MORE. AND TOGETHER, WE CAN GET IT.
BY GETTING RID OF SPIDER-MAN!

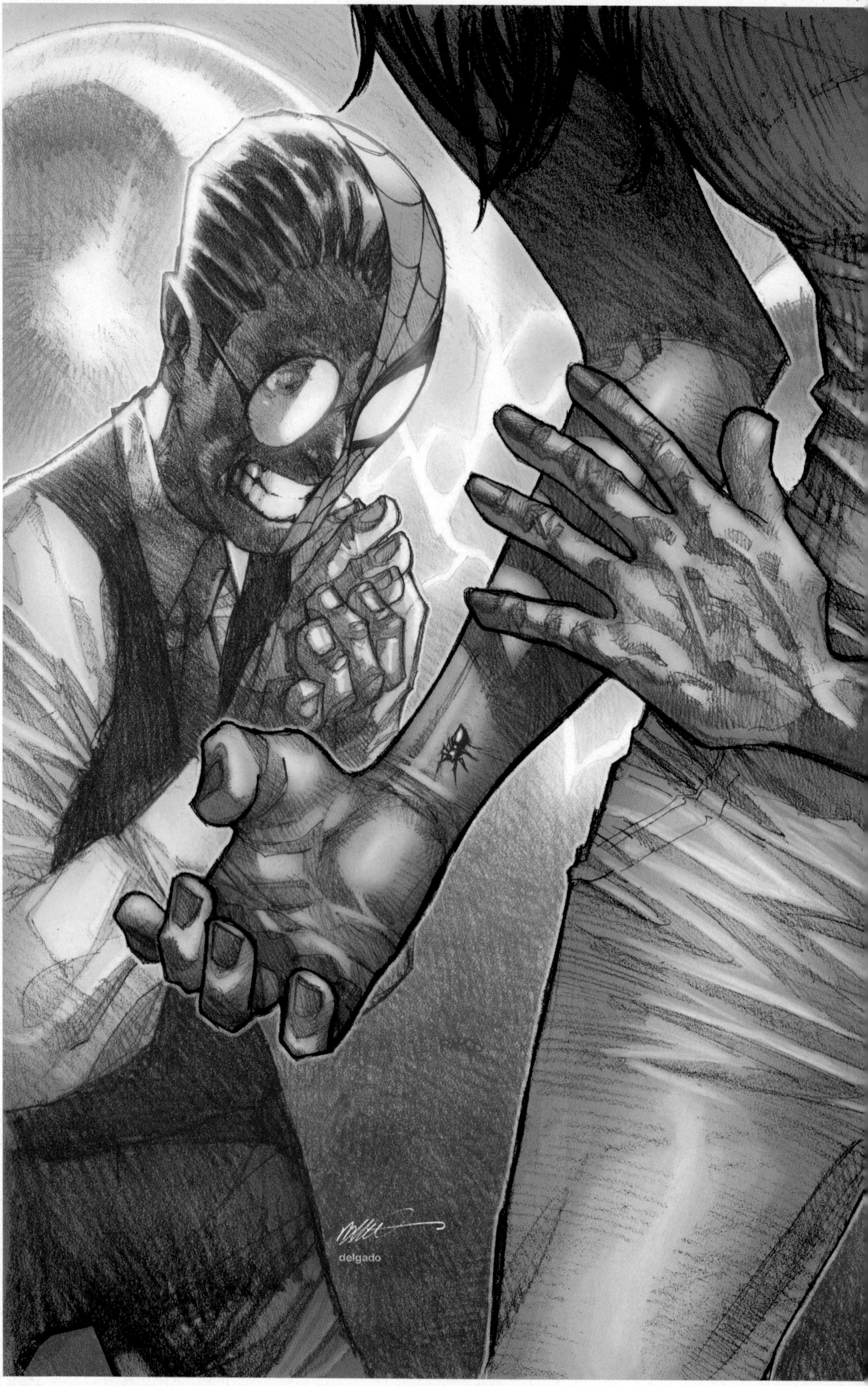
delgado

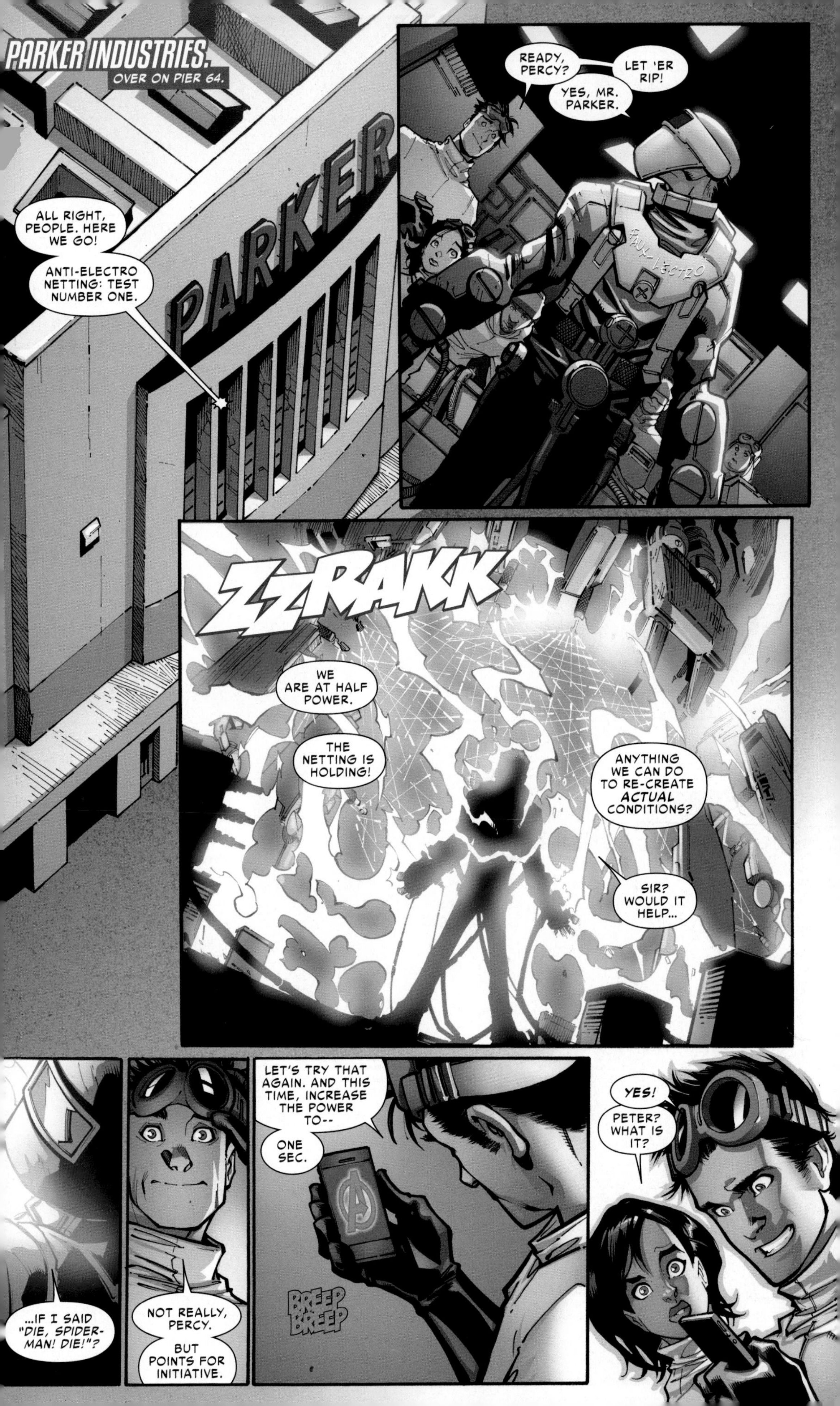
PARKER INDUSTRIES.
OVER ON PIER 64.
PARKER
ALL RIGHT, PEOPLE. HERE WE GO!
ANTI-ELECTRO NETTING: TEST NUMBER ONE.
READY, PERCY?
YES, MR. PARKER.
LET 'ER RIP!
FAUX-LECTRO
ZZRAKK
WE ARE AT HALF POWER.
THE NETTING IS HOLDING!
ANYTHING WE CAN DO TO RE-CREATE *ACTUAL* CONDITIONS?
SIR? WOULD IT HELP...
...IF I SAID "DIE, SPIDER-MAN! DIE!"?
NOT REALLY, PERCY.
BUT POINTS FOR INITIATIVE.
LET'S TRY THAT AGAIN. AND THIS TIME, INCREASE THE POWER TO--
ONE SEC.
BREEP BREEP
YES!
PETER? WHAT IS IT?

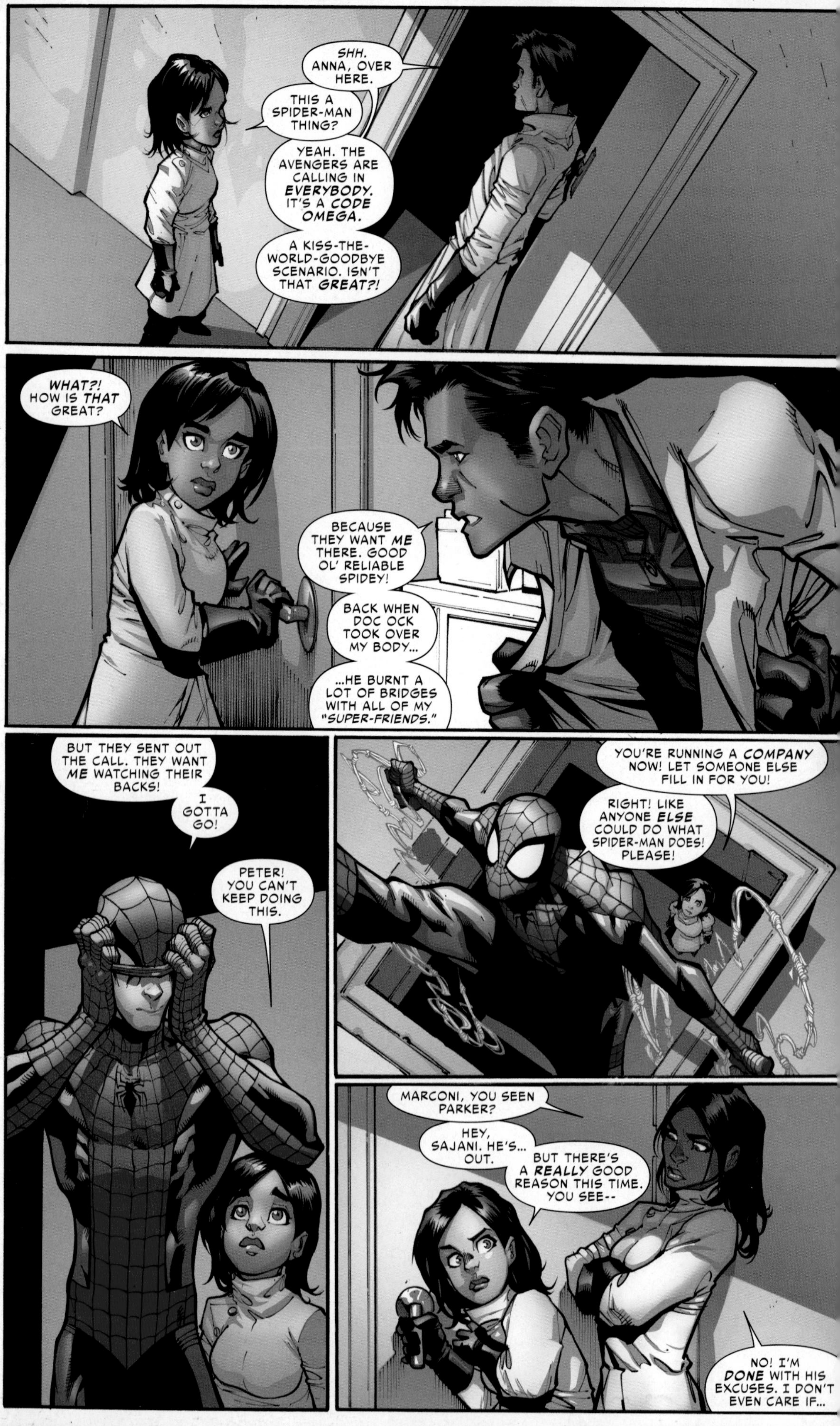
SHH. ANNA, OVER HERE.
THIS A SPIDER-MAN THING?
YEAH. THE AVENGERS ARE CALLING IN EVERYBODY. IT'S A CODE OMEGA.
A KISS-THE-WORLD-GOODBYE SCENARIO. ISN'T THAT GREAT?!
WHAT?! HOW IS THAT GREAT?
BECAUSE THEY WANT ME THERE. GOOD OL' RELIABLE SPIDEY!
BACK WHEN DOC OCK TOOK OVER MY BODY...
...HE BURNT A LOT OF BRIDGES WITH ALL OF MY "SUPER-FRIENDS."
BUT THEY SENT OUT THE CALL. THEY WANT ME WATCHING THEIR BACKS!
I GOTTA GO!
PETER! YOU CAN'T KEEP DOING THIS.
YOU'RE RUNNING A COMPANY NOW! LET SOMEONE ELSE FILL IN FOR YOU!
RIGHT! LIKE ANYONE ELSE COULD DO WHAT SPIDER-MAN DOES! PLEASE!
MARCONI, YOU SEEN PARKER?
HEY, SAJANI. HE'S... OUT.
BUT THERE'S A REALLY GOOD REASON THIS TIME. YOU SEE--
NO! I'M DONE WITH HIS EXCUSES. I DON'T EVEN CARE IF...

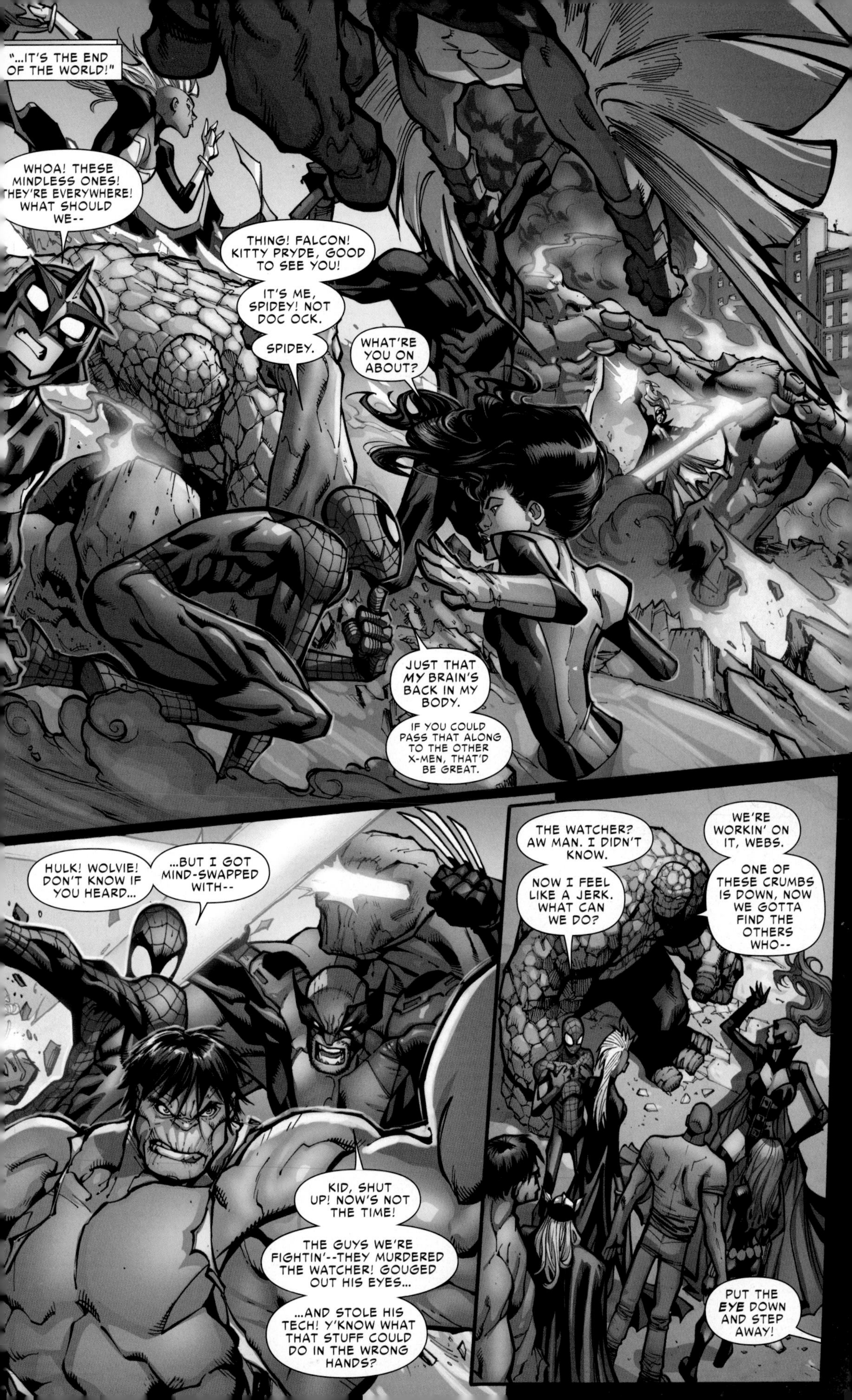
"...IT'S THE END OF THE WORLD!"
WHOA! THESE MINDLESS ONES! THEY'RE EVERYWHERE! WHAT SHOULD WE--
THING! FALCON! KITTY PRYDE, GOOD TO SEE YOU!
IT'S ME, SPIDEY! NOT DOC OCK.
SPIDEY.
WHAT'RE YOU ON ABOUT?
JUST THAT MY BRAIN'S BACK IN MY BODY.
IF YOU COULD PASS THAT ALONG TO THE OTHER X-MEN, THAT'D BE GREAT.
HULK! WOLVIE! DON'T KNOW IF YOU HEARD...
...BUT I GOT MIND-SWAPPED WITH--
KID, SHUT UP! NOW'S NOT THE TIME!
THE GUYS WE'RE FIGHTIN'--THEY MURDERED THE WATCHER! GOUGED OUT HIS EYES...
...AND STOLE HIS TECH! Y'KNOW WHAT THAT STUFF COULD DO IN THE WRONG HANDS?
THE WATCHER? AW MAN. I DIDN'T KNOW.
NOW I FEEL LIKE A JERK. WHAT CAN WE DO?
WE'RE WORKIN' ON IT, WEBS.
ONE OF THESE CRUMBS IS DOWN, NOW WE GOTTA FIND THE OTHERS WHO--
PUT THE EYE DOWN AND STEP AWAY!

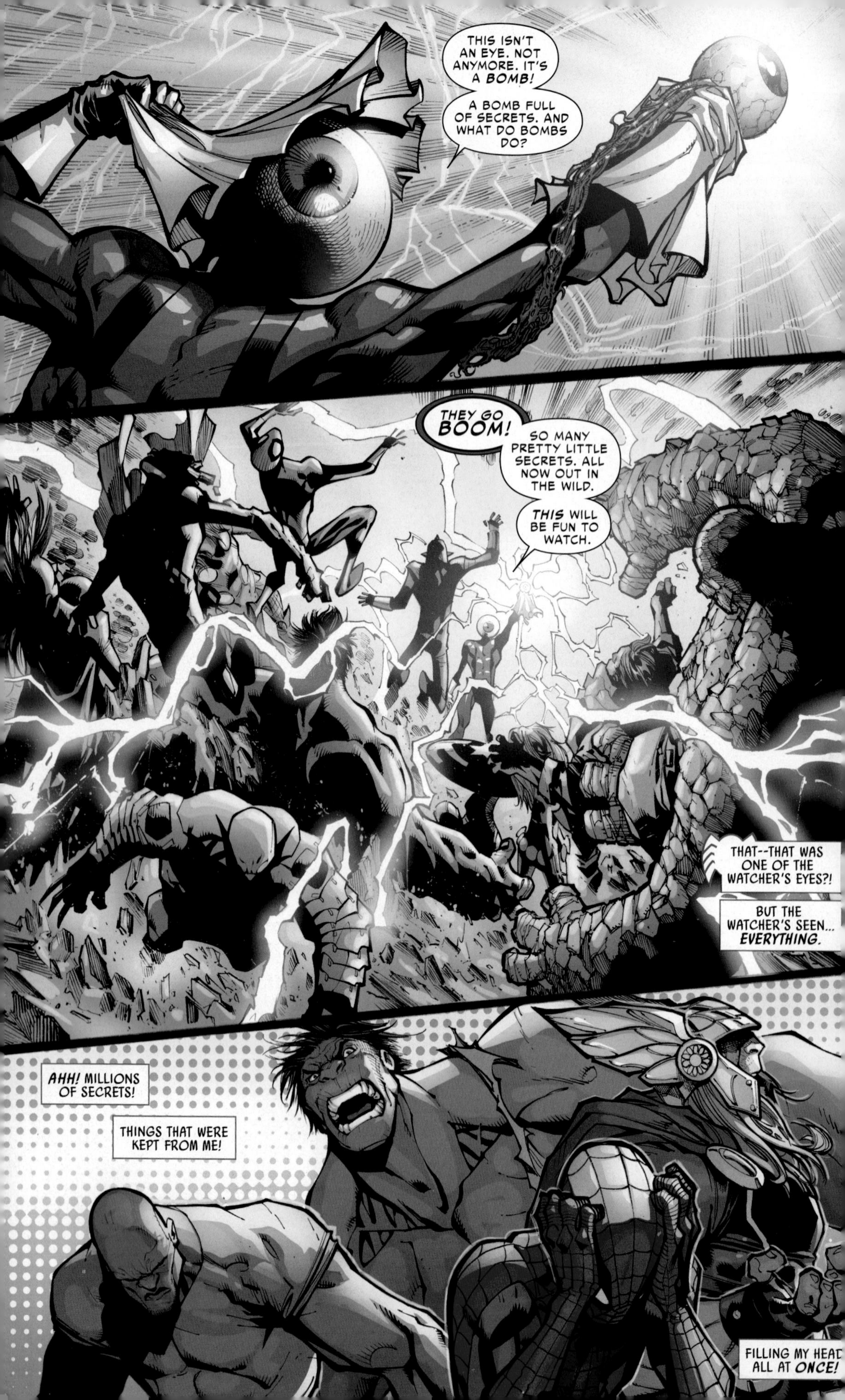
THIS ISN'T AN EYE. NOT ANYMORE. IT'S A *BOMB!*
A BOMB FULL OF SECRETS. AND WHAT DO BOMBS DO?
THEY GO **BOOM!**
SO MANY PRETTY LITTLE SECRETS. ALL NOW OUT IN THE WILD.
THIS WILL BE FUN TO WATCH.
THAT--THAT WAS ONE OF THE WATCHER'S EYES?!
BUT THE WATCHER'S SEEN... ***EVERYTHING.***
AHH! MILLIONS OF SECRETS!
THINGS THAT WERE KEPT FROM ME!
FILLING MY HEAD ALL AT *ONCE!*

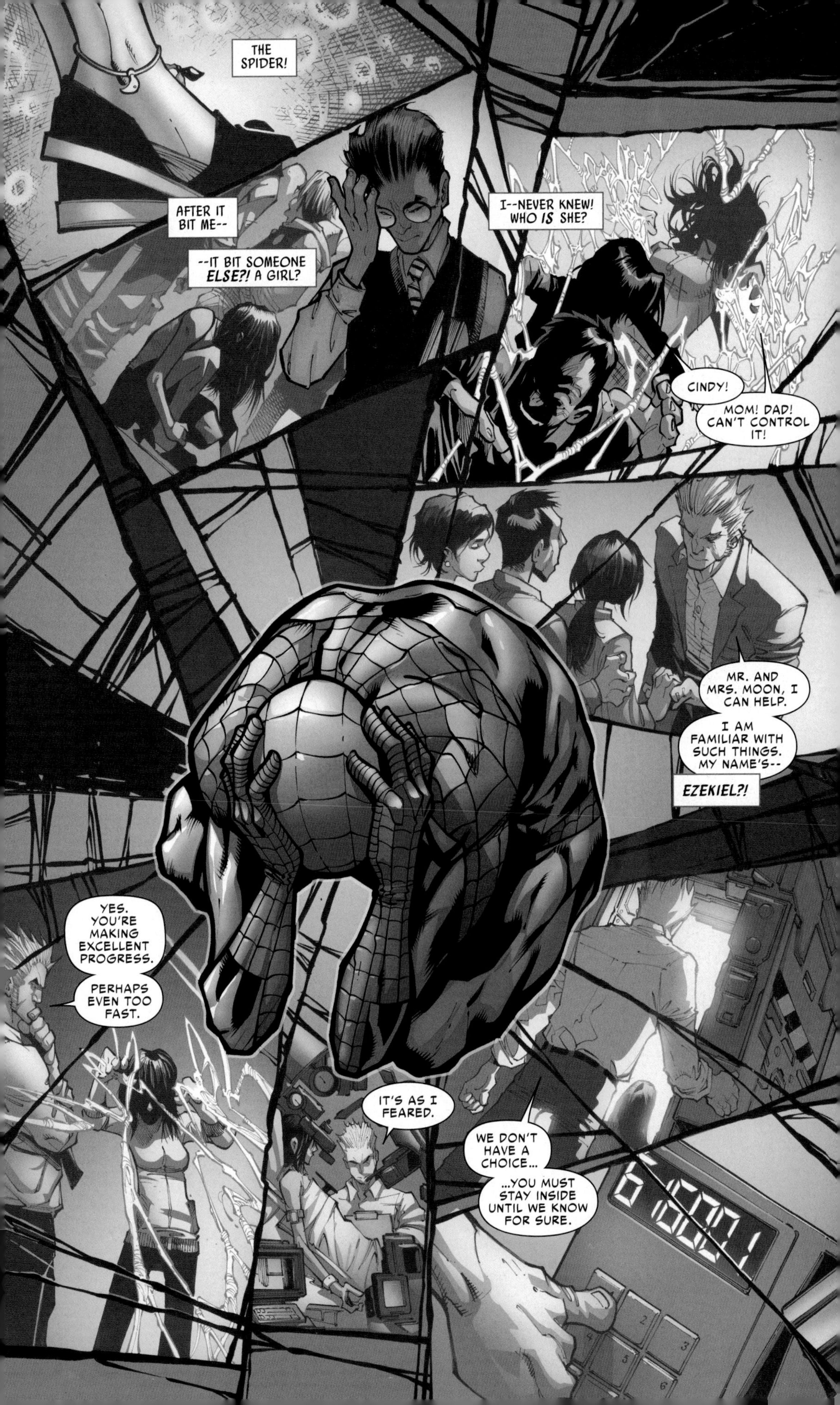
THE SPIDER!
AFTER IT BIT ME--
--IT BIT SOMEONE ELSE?! A GIRL?
I--NEVER KNEW! WHO IS SHE?
CINDY!
MOM! DAD! CAN'T CONTROL IT!
MR. AND MRS. MOON, I CAN HELP.
I AM FAMILIAR WITH SUCH THINGS. MY NAME'S--
EZEKIEL?!
YES. YOU'RE MAKING EXCELLENT PROGRESS.
PERHAPS EVEN TOO FAST.
IT'S AS I FEARED.
WE DON'T HAVE A CHOICE...
...YOU MUST STAY INSIDE UNTIL WE KNOW FOR SURE.

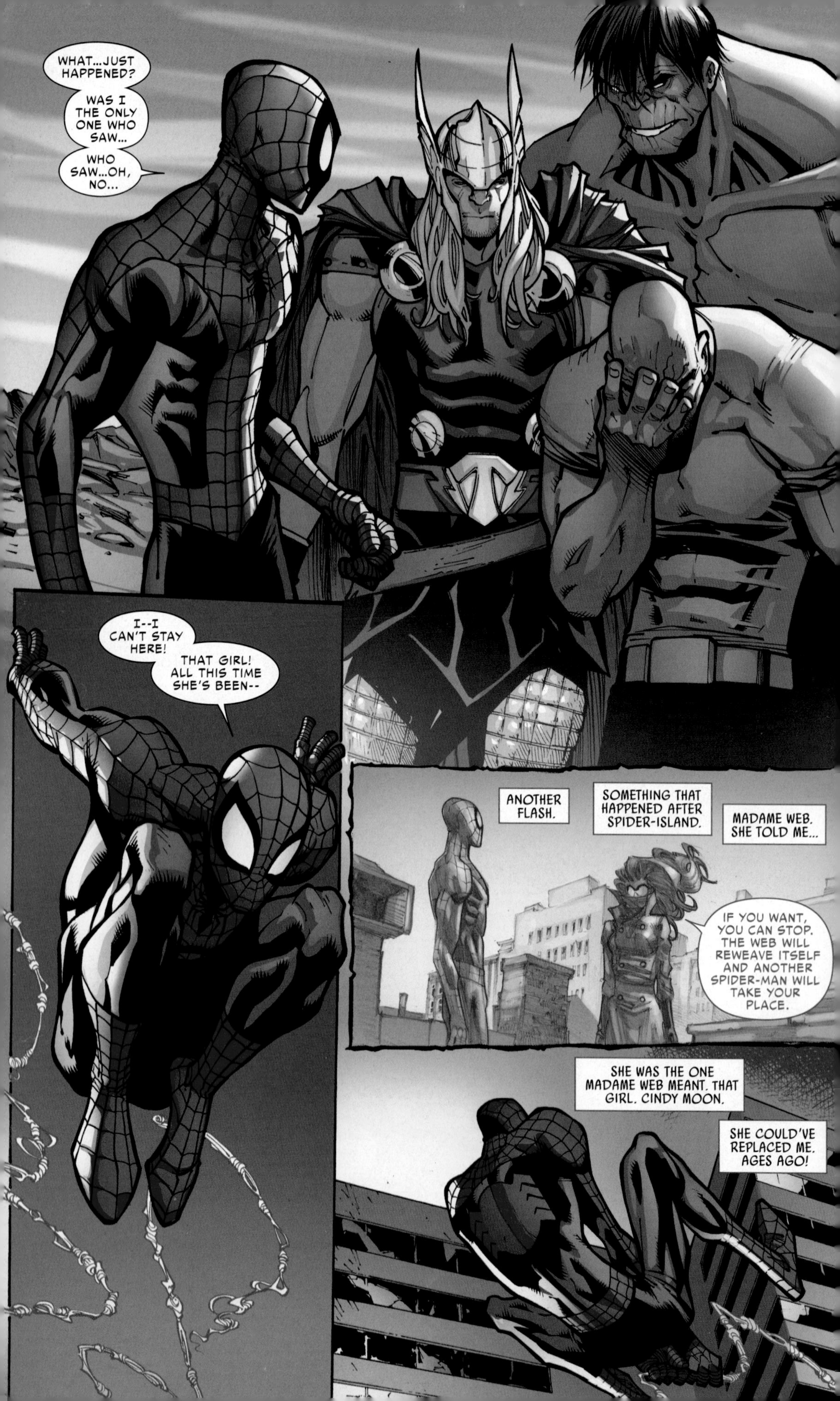

WHAT...JUST HAPPENED?
WAS I THE ONLY ONE WHO SAW...
WHO SAW...OH, NO...
I--I CAN'T STAY HERE!
THAT GIRL! ALL THIS TIME SHE'S BEEN--
ANOTHER FLASH.
SOMETHING THAT HAPPENED AFTER SPIDER-ISLAND.
MADAME WEB. SHE TOLD ME...
IF YOU WANT, YOU CAN STOP. THE WEB WILL REWEAVE ITSELF AND ANOTHER SPIDER-MAN WILL TAKE YOUR PLACE.
SHE WAS THE ONE MADAME WEB MEANT. THAT GIRL. CINDY MOON.
SHE COULD'VE REPLACED ME. AGES AGO!

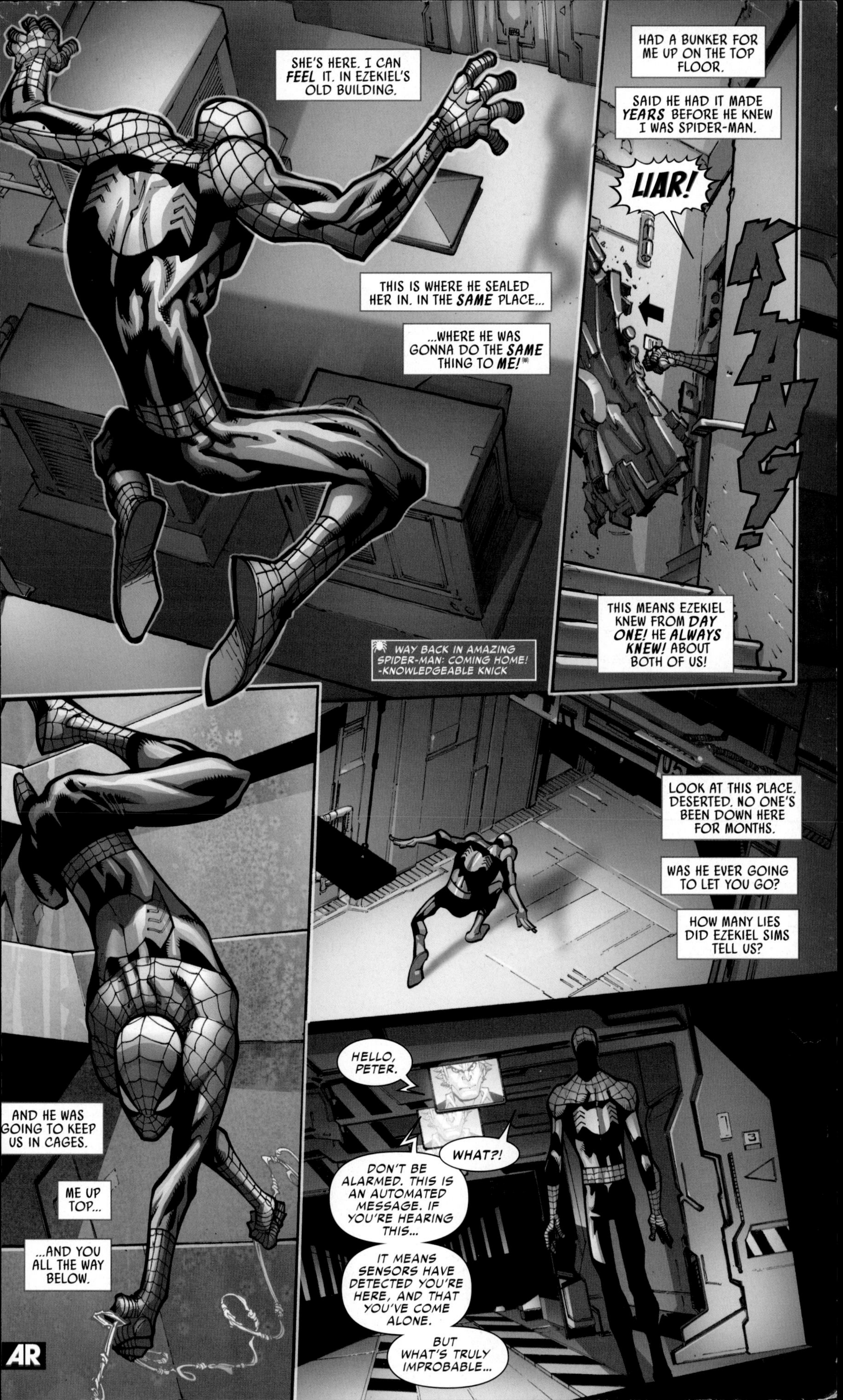

SHE'S HERE. I CAN FEEL IT. IN EZEKIEL'S OLD BUILDING.
THIS IS WHERE HE SEALED HER IN. IN THE SAME PLACE...
...WHERE HE WAS GONNA DO THE SAME THING TO ME!*
*WAY BACK IN AMAZING SPIDER-MAN: COMING HOME! -KNOWLEDGEABLE KNICK
HAD A BUNKER FOR ME UP ON THE TOP FLOOR.
SAID HE HAD IT MADE YEARS BEFORE HE KNEW I WAS SPIDER-MAN.
LIAR!
KLANG!
THIS MEANS EZEKIEL KNEW FROM DAY ONE! HE ALWAYS KNEW! ABOUT BOTH OF US!
AND HE WAS GOING TO KEEP US IN CAGES.
ME UP TOP...
...AND YOU ALL THE WAY BELOW.
LOOK AT THIS PLACE. DESERTED. NO ONE'S BEEN DOWN HERE FOR MONTHS.
WAS HE EVER GOING TO LET YOU GO?
HOW MANY LIES DID EZEKIEL SIMS TELL US?
HELLO, PETER.
WHAT?!
DON'T BE ALARMED. THIS IS AN AUTOMATED MESSAGE. IF YOU'RE HEARING THIS...
IT MEANS SENSORS HAVE DETECTED YOU'RE HERE, AND THAT YOU'VE COME ALONE.
BUT WHAT'S TRULY IMPROBABLE...

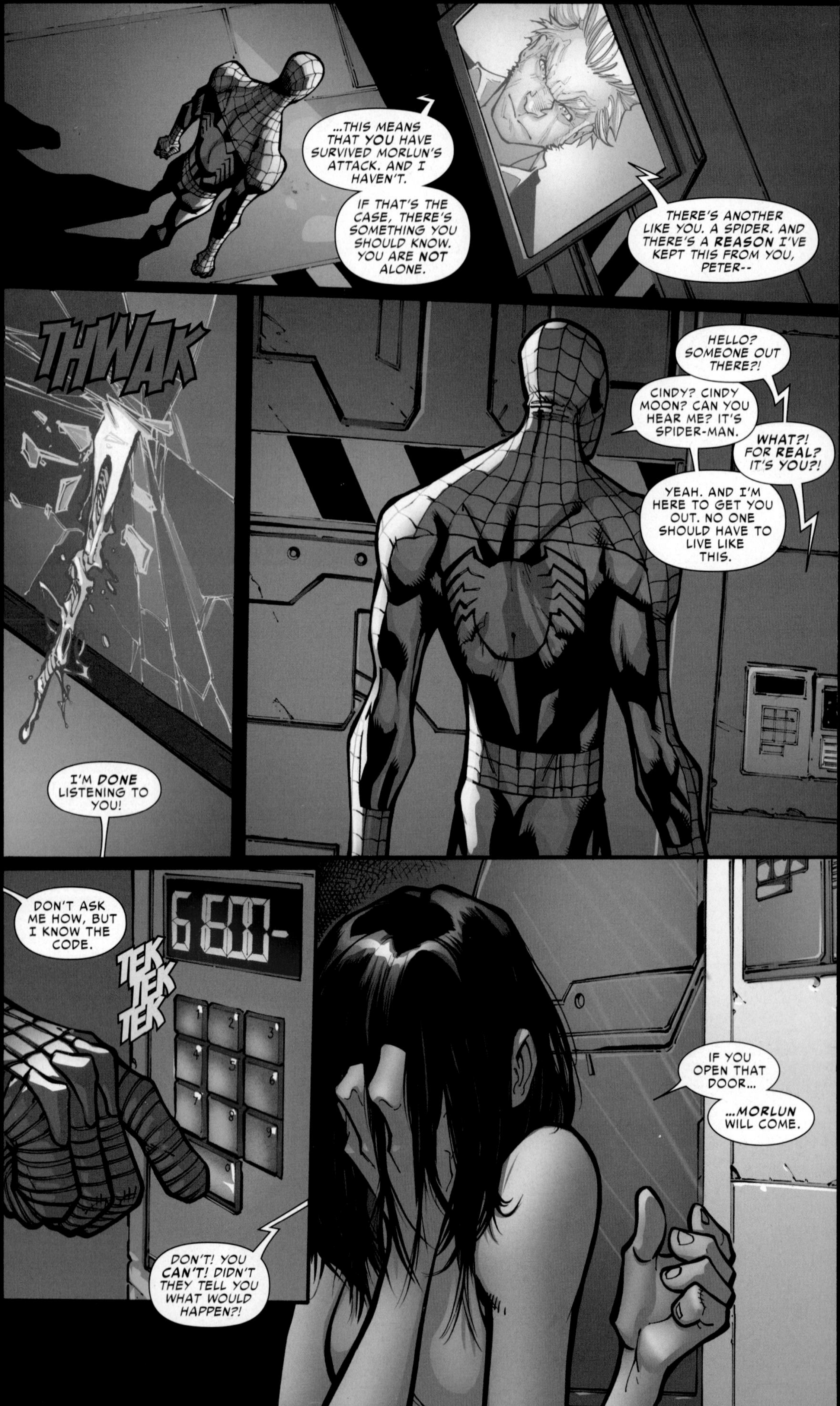
...THIS MEANS THAT YOU HAVE SURVIVED MORLUN'S ATTACK. AND I HAVEN'T.
IF THAT'S THE CASE, THERE'S SOMETHING YOU SHOULD KNOW. YOU ARE **NOT** ALONE.
THERE'S ANOTHER LIKE YOU. A SPIDER. AND THERE'S A **REASON** I'VE KEPT THIS FROM YOU, PETER--
THWAK
I'M **DONE** LISTENING TO YOU!
HELLO? SOMEONE OUT THERE?!
CINDY? CINDY MOON? CAN YOU HEAR ME? IT'S SPIDER-MAN.
WHAT?! FOR **REAL?** IT'S **YOU?!**
YEAH. AND I'M HERE TO GET YOU OUT. NO ONE SHOULD HAVE TO LIVE LIKE THIS.
DON'T ASK ME HOW, BUT I KNOW THE CODE.
TEK TEK TEK
DON'T! YOU **CAN'T!** DIDN'T THEY TELL YOU WHAT WOULD HAPPEN?!
IF YOU OPEN THAT DOOR...
...**MORLUN** WILL COME.

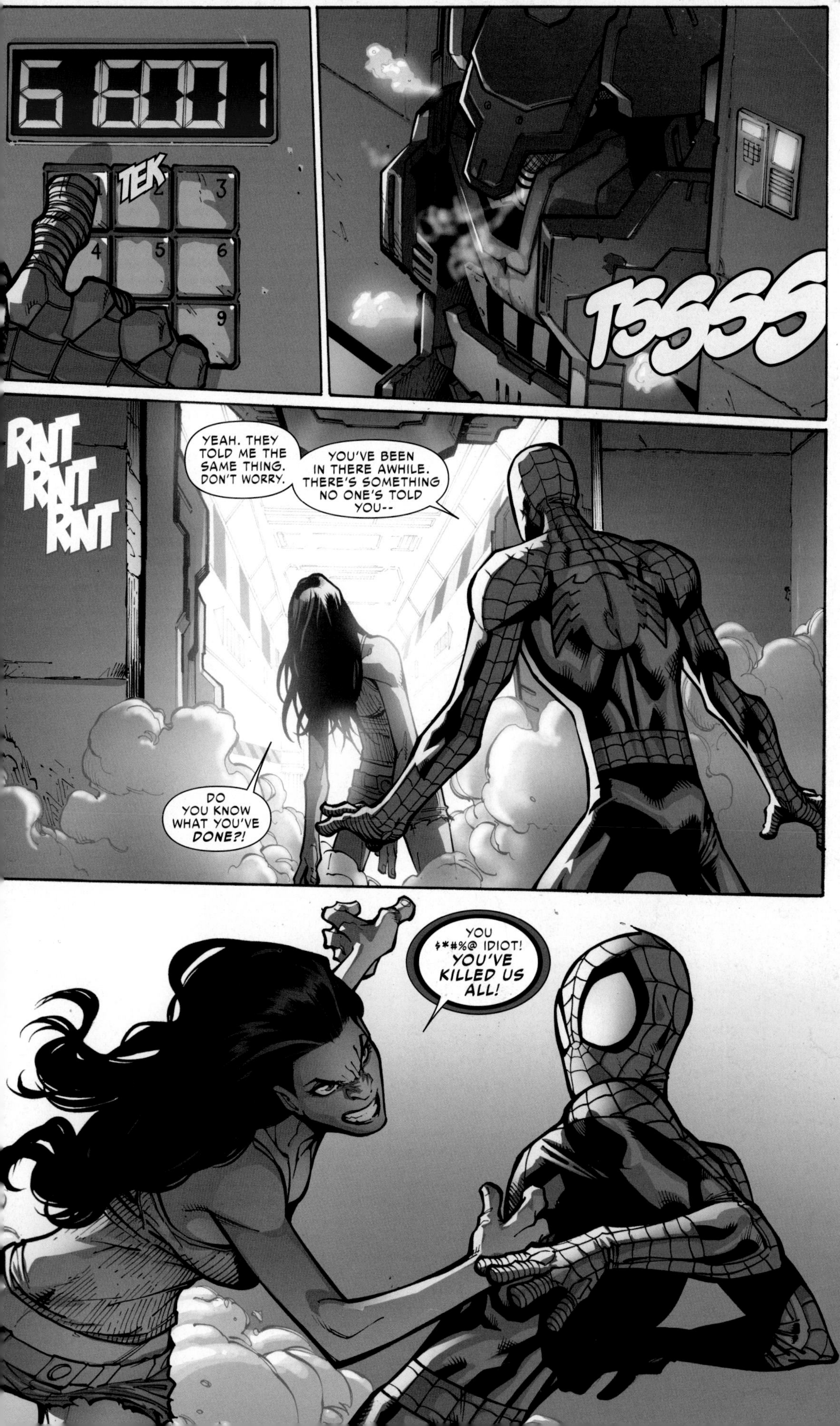
TEK
TSSSS
RNT RNT RNT
YEAH. THEY TOLD ME THE SAME THING. DON'T WORRY.
YOU'VE BEEN IN THERE AWHILE. THERE'S SOMETHING NO ONE'S TOLD YOU--
DO YOU KNOW WHAT YOU'VE DONE?!
YOU $*#%@ IDIOT! YOU'VE KILLED US ALL!

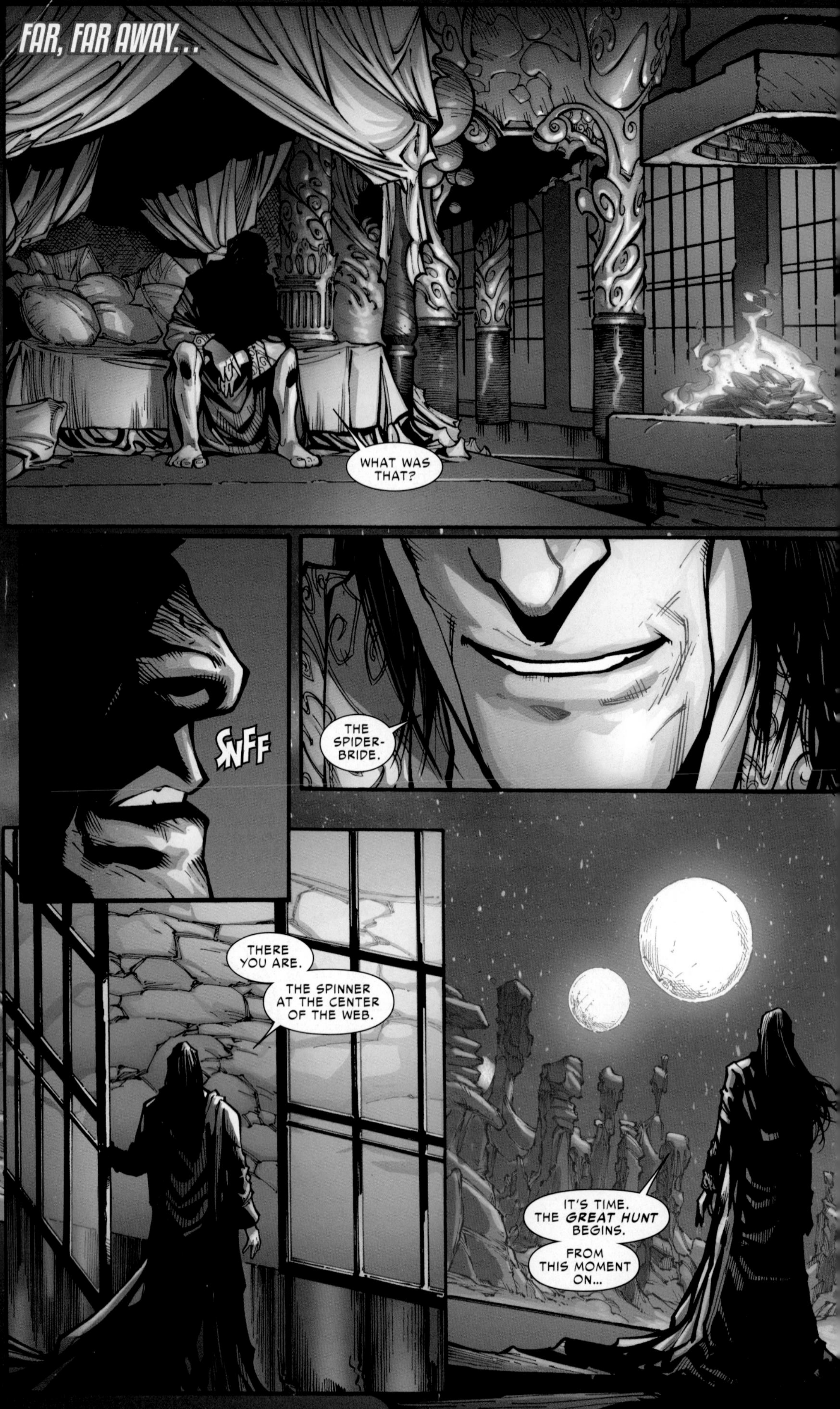

FAR, FAR AWAY...
WHAT WAS THAT?
SNFF
THE SPIDER-BRIDE.
THERE YOU ARE.
THE SPINNER AT THE CENTER OF THE WEB.
IT'S TIME. THE GREAT HUNT BEGINS.
FROM THIS MOMENT ON...

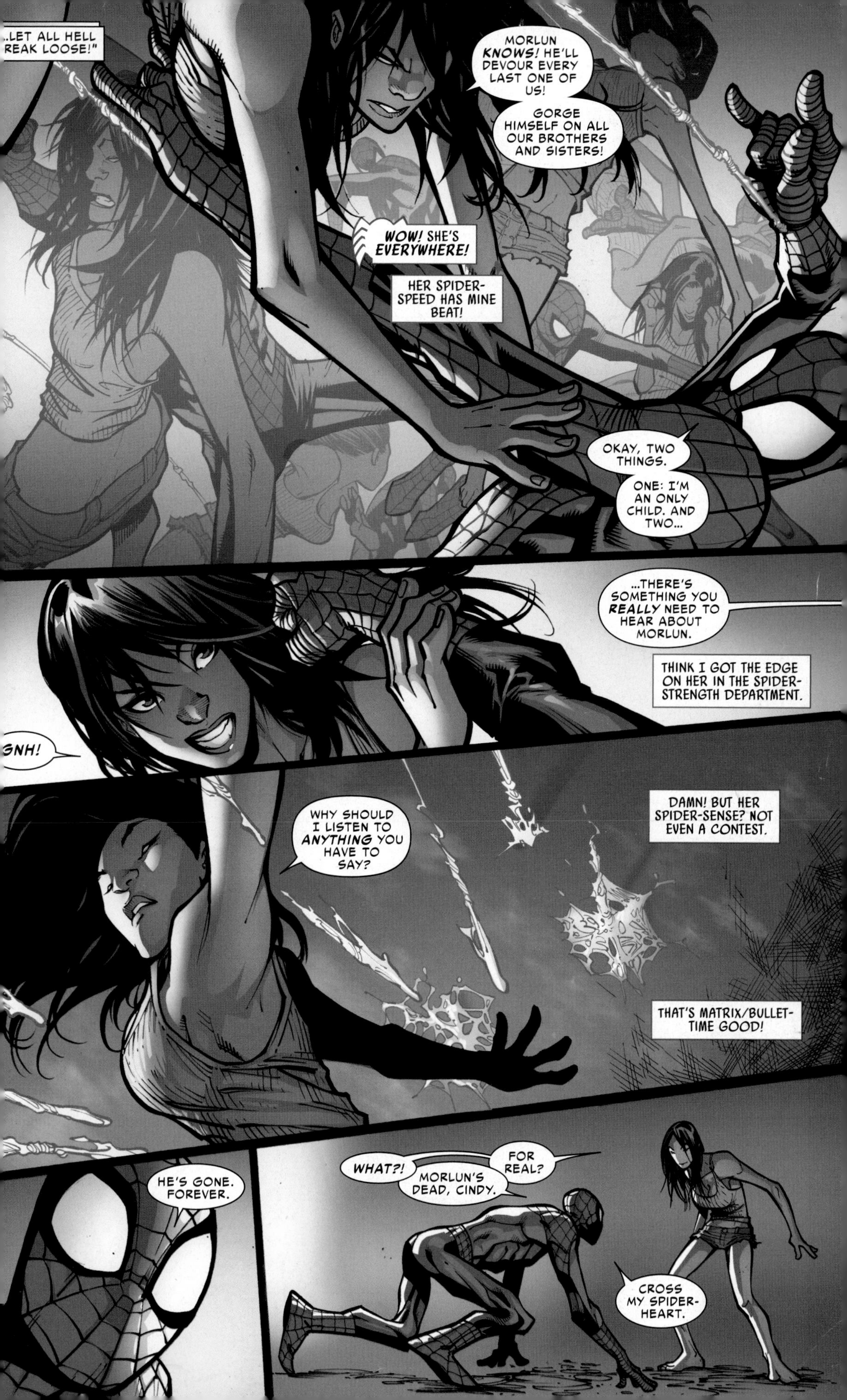
..LET ALL HELL
REAK LOOSE!"
MORLUN KNOWS! HE'LL DEVOUR EVERY LAST ONE OF US!
GORGE HIMSELF ON ALL OUR BROTHERS AND SISTERS!
WOW! SHE'S EVERYWHERE!
HER SPIDER-SPEED HAS MINE BEAT!
OKAY, TWO THINGS.
ONE: I'M AN ONLY CHILD. AND TWO...
...THERE'S SOMETHING YOU REALLY NEED TO HEAR ABOUT MORLUN.
THINK I GOT THE EDGE ON HER IN THE SPIDER-STRENGTH DEPARTMENT.
GNH!
WHY SHOULD I LISTEN TO ANYTHING YOU HAVE TO SAY?
DAMN! BUT HER SPIDER-SENSE? NOT EVEN A CONTEST.
THAT'S MATRIX/BULLET-TIME GOOD!
HE'S GONE. FOREVER.
WHAT?!
FOR REAL?
MORLUN'S DEAD, CINDY.
CROSS MY SPIDER-HEART.

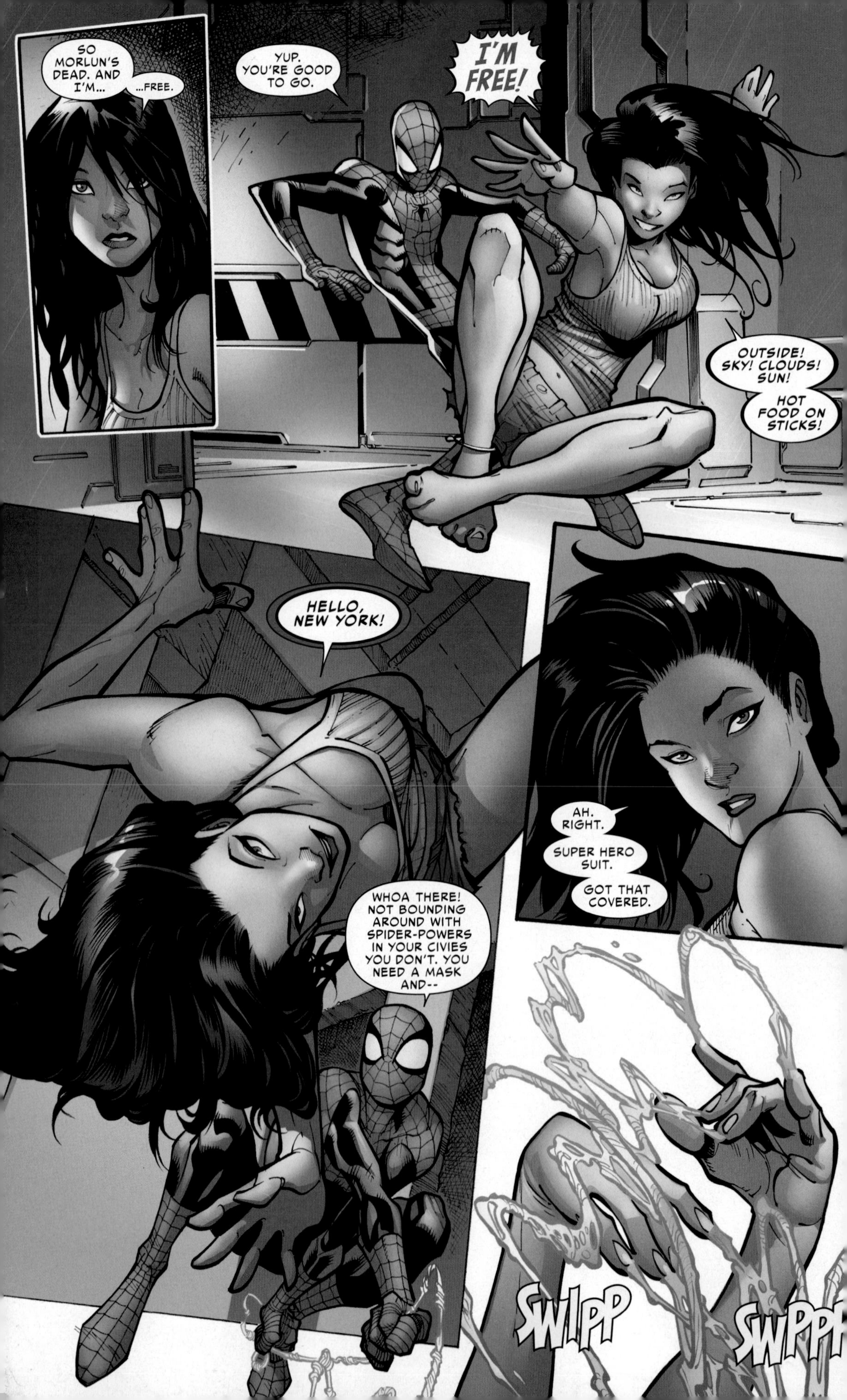
SO MORLUN'S DEAD. AND I'M...
...FREE.
YUP. YOU'RE GOOD TO GO.
I'M FREE!
OUTSIDE! SKY! CLOUDS! SUN!
HOT FOOD ON STICKS!
HELLO, NEW YORK!
WHOA THERE! NOT BOUNDING AROUND WITH SPIDER-POWERS IN YOUR CIVIES YOU DON'T. YOU NEED A MASK AND--
AH. RIGHT.
SUPER HERO SUIT.
GOT THAT COVERED.
SWIPP

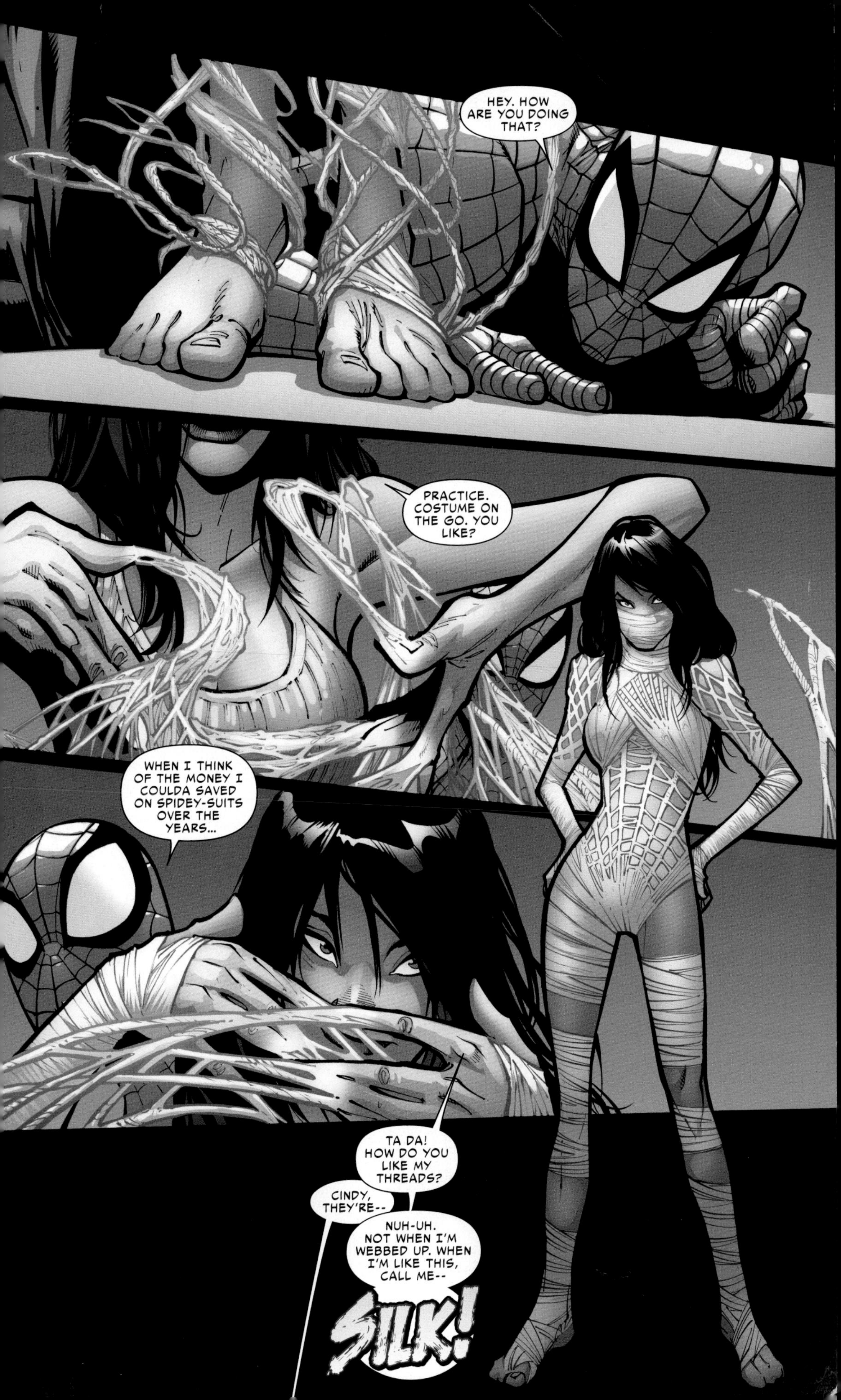
HEY. HOW ARE YOU DOING THAT?
PRACTICE. COSTUME ON THE GO. YOU LIKE?
WHEN I THINK OF THE MONEY I COULDA SAVED ON SPIDEY-SUITS OVER THE YEARS...
TA DA! HOW DO YOU LIKE MY THREADS?
CINDY, THEY'RE--
NUH-UH. NOT WHEN I'M WEBBED UP. WHEN I'M LIKE THIS, CALL ME--
SILK!

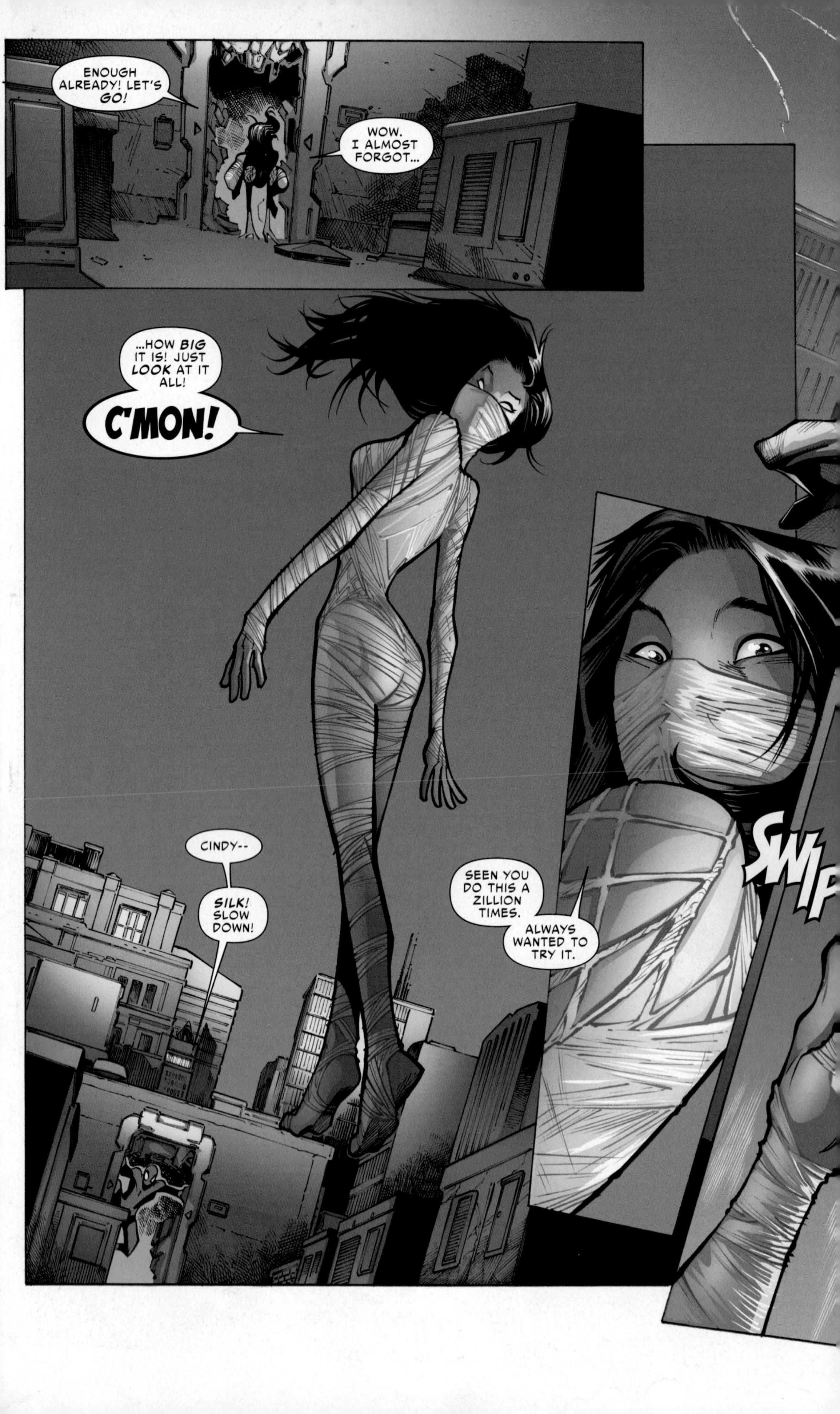
ENOUGH ALREADY! LET'S GO!
WOW. I ALMOST FORGOT...
...HOW BIG IT IS! JUST LOOK AT IT ALL!
C'MON!
CINDY--
SILK! SLOW DOWN!
SEEN YOU DO THIS A ZILLION TIMES.
ALWAYS WANTED TO TRY IT.
SWIF

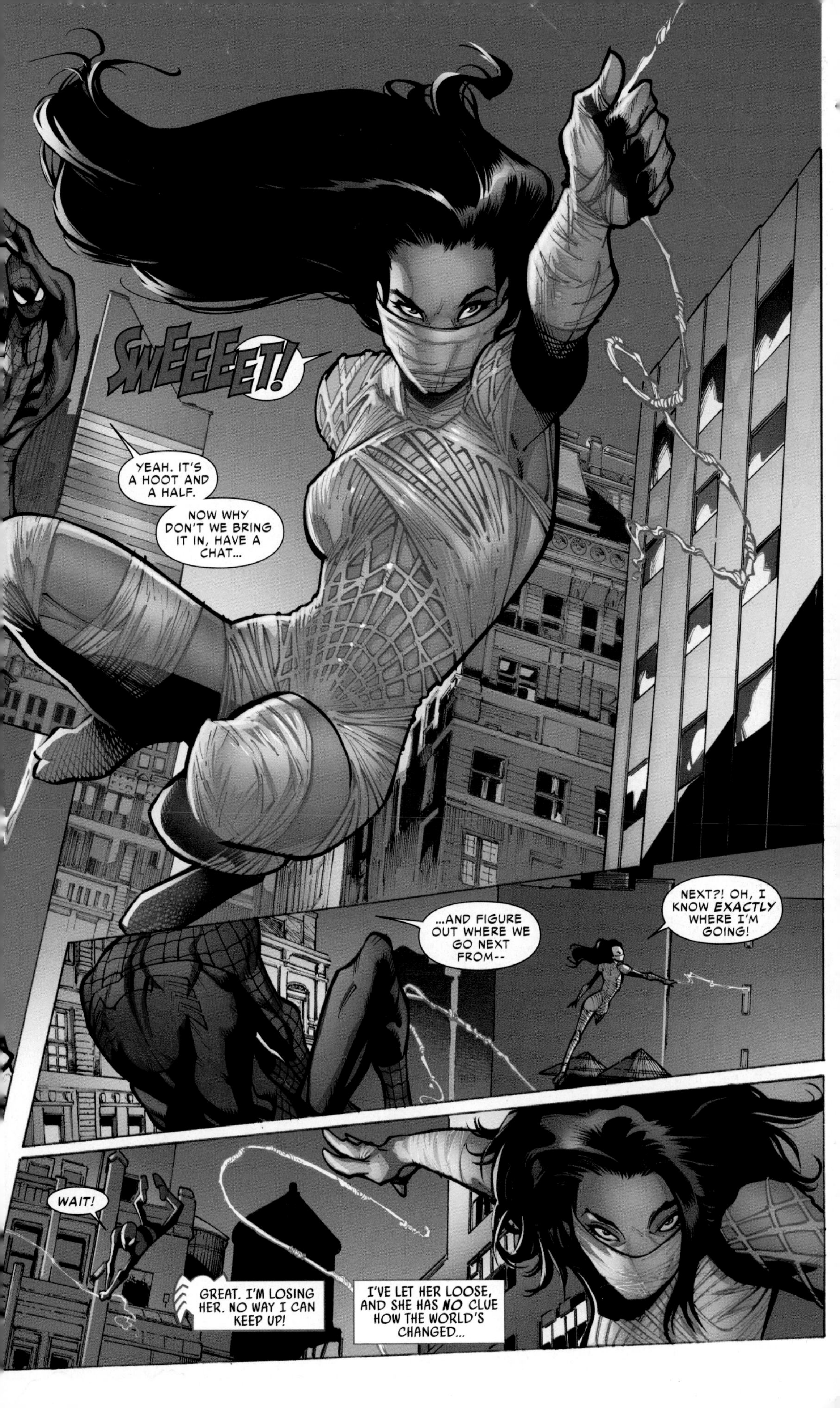
SWEEEET!
YEAH. IT'S A HOOT AND A HALF.
NOW WHY DON'T WE BRING IT IN, HAVE A CHAT...
...AND FIGURE OUT WHERE WE GO NEXT FROM--
NEXT?! OH, I KNOW EXACTLY WHERE I'M GOING!
WAIT!
GREAT. I'M LOSING HER. NO WAY I CAN KEEP UP!
I'VE LET HER LOOSE, AND SHE HAS NO CLUE HOW THE WORLD'S CHANGED...

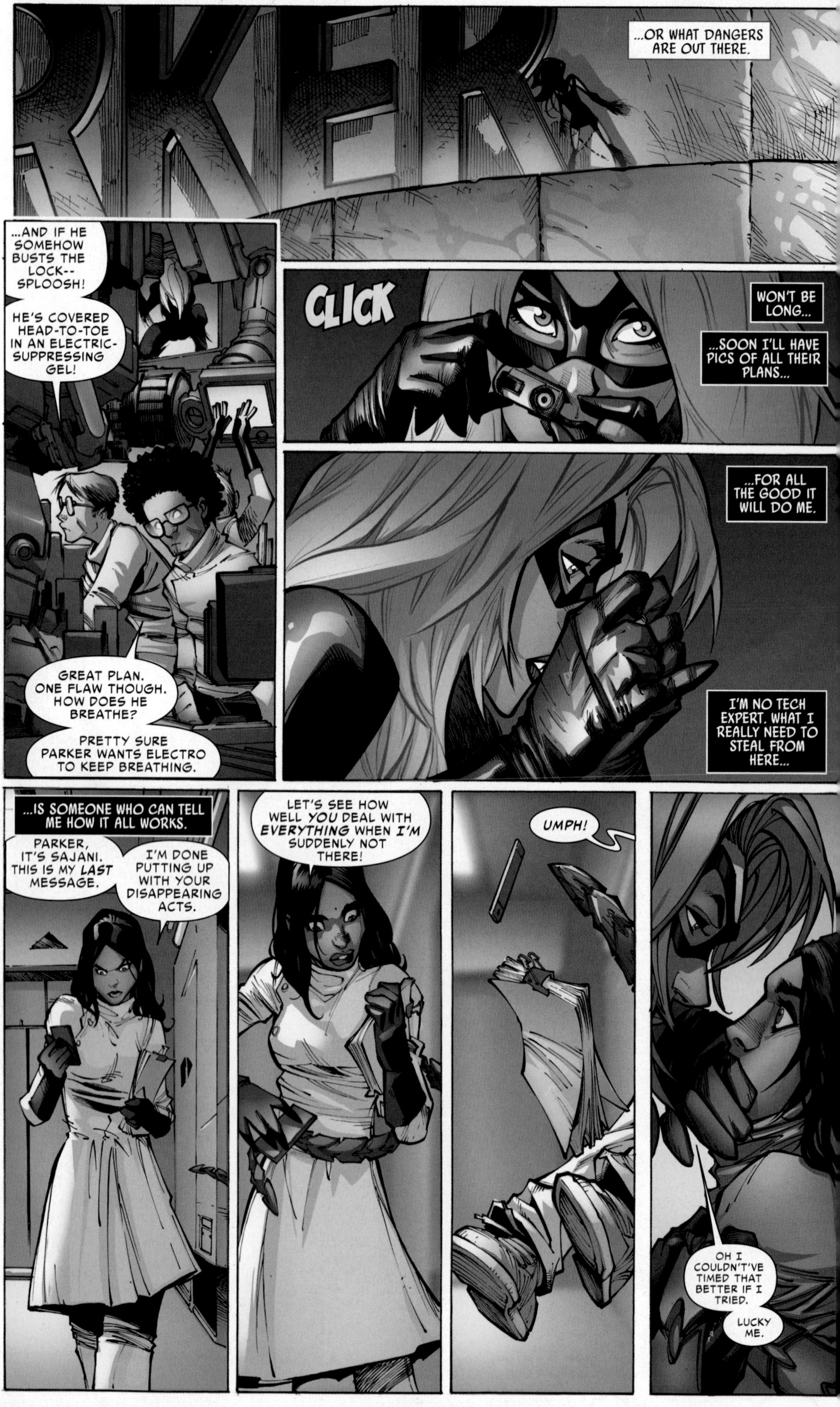

...OR WHAT DANGERS ARE OUT THERE.
...AND IF HE SOMEHOW BUSTS THE LOCK-- SPLOOSH!
HE'S COVERED HEAD-TO-TOE IN AN ELECTRIC-SUPPRESSING GEL!
GREAT PLAN. ONE FLAW THOUGH. HOW DOES HE BREATHE?
PRETTY SURE PARKER WANTS ELECTRO TO KEEP BREATHING.
CLICK
WON'T BE LONG...
...SOON I'LL HAVE PICS OF ALL THEIR PLANS...
...FOR ALL THE GOOD IT WILL DO ME.
I'M NO TECH EXPERT. WHAT I REALLY NEED TO STEAL FROM HERE...
...IS SOMEONE WHO CAN TELL ME HOW IT ALL WORKS.
PARKER, IT'S SAJANI. THIS IS MY LAST MESSAGE.
I'M DONE PUTTING UP WITH YOUR DISAPPEARING ACTS.
LET'S SEE HOW WELL YOU DEAL WITH EVERYTHING WHEN I'M SUDDENLY NOT THERE!
UMPH!
OH I COULDN'T'VE TIMED THAT BETTER IF I TRIED.
LUCKY ME.

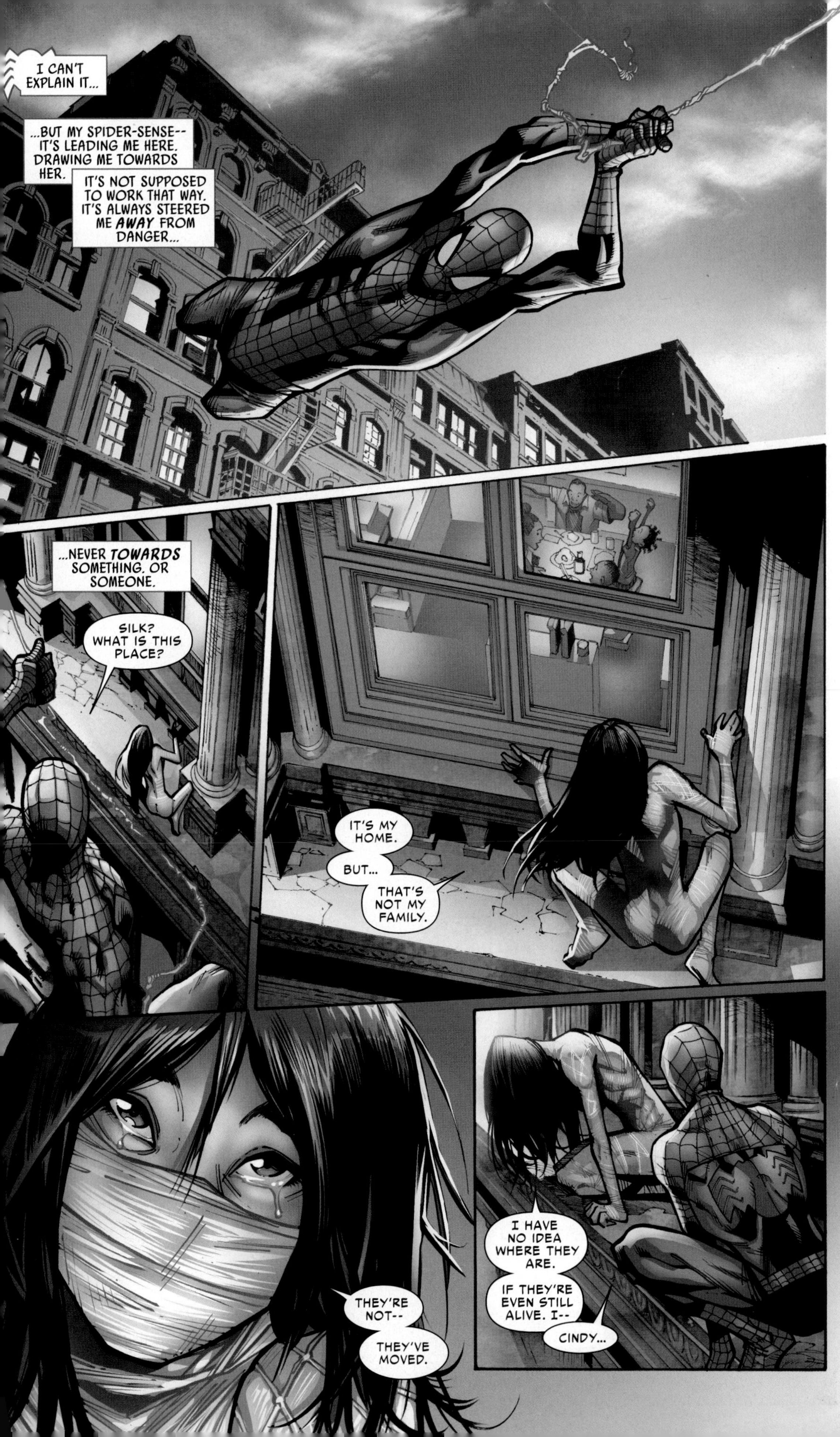

I CAN'T EXPLAIN IT...
...BUT MY SPIDER-SENSE-- IT'S LEADING ME HERE. DRAWING ME TOWARDS HER.
IT'S NOT SUPPOSED TO WORK THAT WAY. IT'S ALWAYS STEERED ME *AWAY* FROM DANGER...
...NEVER ***TOWARDS*** SOMETHING. OR SOMEONE.
SILK? WHAT IS THIS PLACE?
IT'S MY HOME.
BUT...
THAT'S NOT MY FAMILY.
THEY'RE NOT--
THEY'VE MOVED.
I HAVE NO IDEA WHERE THEY ARE.
IF THEY'RE EVEN STILL ALIVE. I--
CINDY...

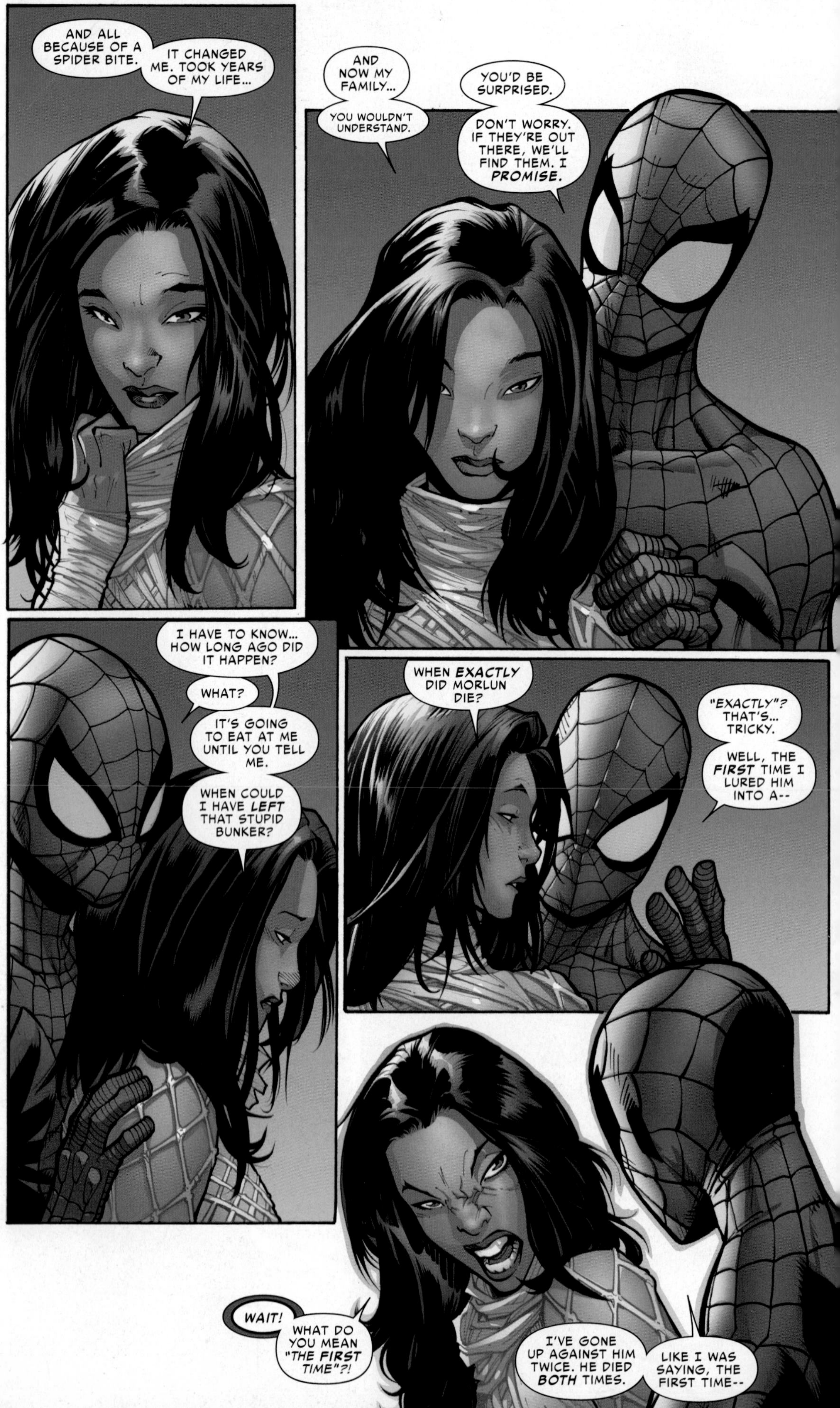
AND ALL BECAUSE OF A SPIDER BITE.
IT CHANGED ME. TOOK YEARS OF MY LIFE...
AND NOW MY FAMILY...
YOU WOULDN'T UNDERSTAND.
YOU'D BE SURPRISED.
DON'T WORRY. IF THEY'RE OUT THERE, WE'LL FIND THEM. I *PROMISE.*
I HAVE TO KNOW... HOW LONG AGO DID IT HAPPEN?
WHAT?
IT'S GOING TO EAT AT ME UNTIL YOU TELL ME.
WHEN COULD I HAVE *LEFT* THAT STUPID BUNKER?
WHEN *EXACTLY* DID MORLUN DIE?
"EXACTLY"? THAT'S... TRICKY.
WELL, THE *FIRST* TIME I LURED HIM INTO A--
WAIT!
WHAT DO YOU MEAN *"THE FIRST TIME"*?!
I'VE GONE UP AGAINST HIM TWICE. HE DIED *BOTH* TIMES.
LIKE I WAS SAYING, THE FIRST TIME--

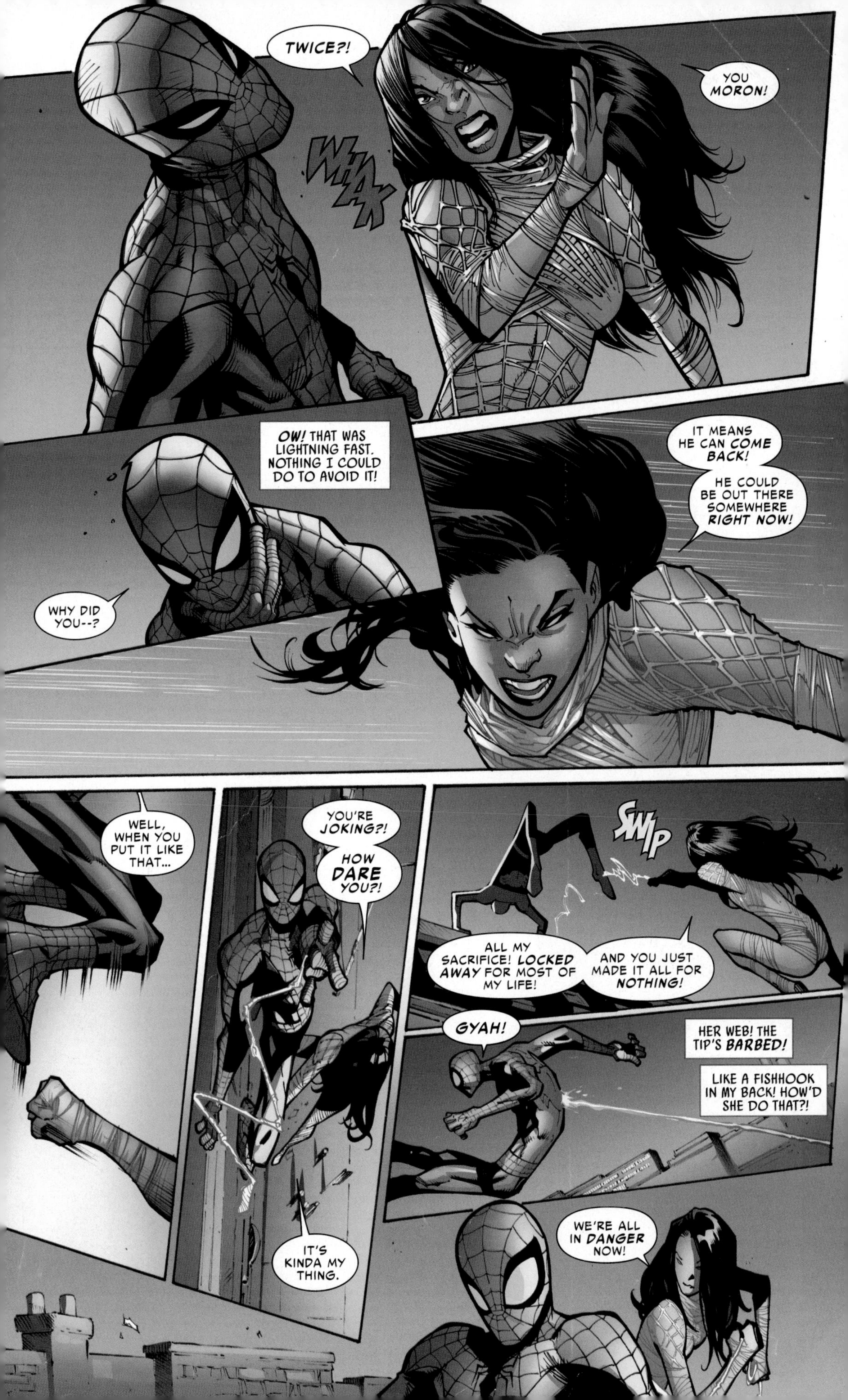

TWICE?!
WHAK
YOU MORON!
OW! THAT WAS LIGHTNING FAST. NOTHING I COULD DO TO AVOID IT!
WHY DID YOU--?
IT MEANS HE CAN COME BACK!
HE COULD BE OUT THERE SOMEWHERE RIGHT NOW!
WELL, WHEN YOU PUT IT LIKE THAT...
YOU'RE JOKING?!
HOW DARE YOU?!
IT'S KINDA MY THING.
SWIP
ALL MY SACRIFICE! LOCKED AWAY FOR MOST OF MY LIFE!
AND YOU JUST MADE IT ALL FOR NOTHING!
GYAH!
HER WEB! THE TIP'S BARBED!
LIKE A FISHHOOK IN MY BACK! HOW'D SHE DO THAT?!
WE'RE ALL IN DANGER NOW!

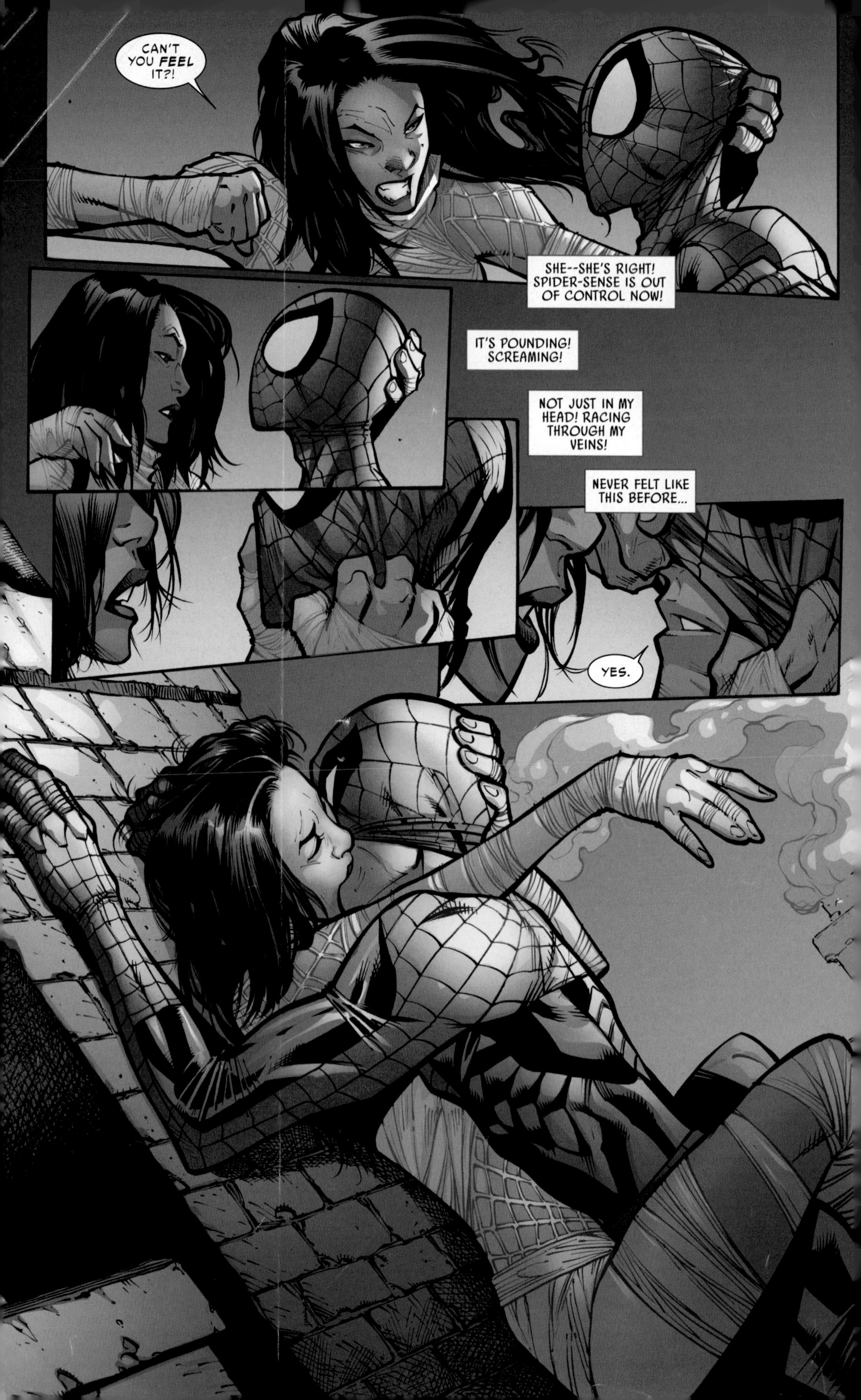
CAN'T YOU FEEL IT?!
SHE--SHE'S RIGHT! SPIDER-SENSE IS OUT OF CONTROL NOW!
IT'S POUNDING! SCREAMING!
NOT JUST IN MY HEAD! RACING THROUGH MY VEINS!
NEVER FELT LIKE THIS BEFORE...
YES.

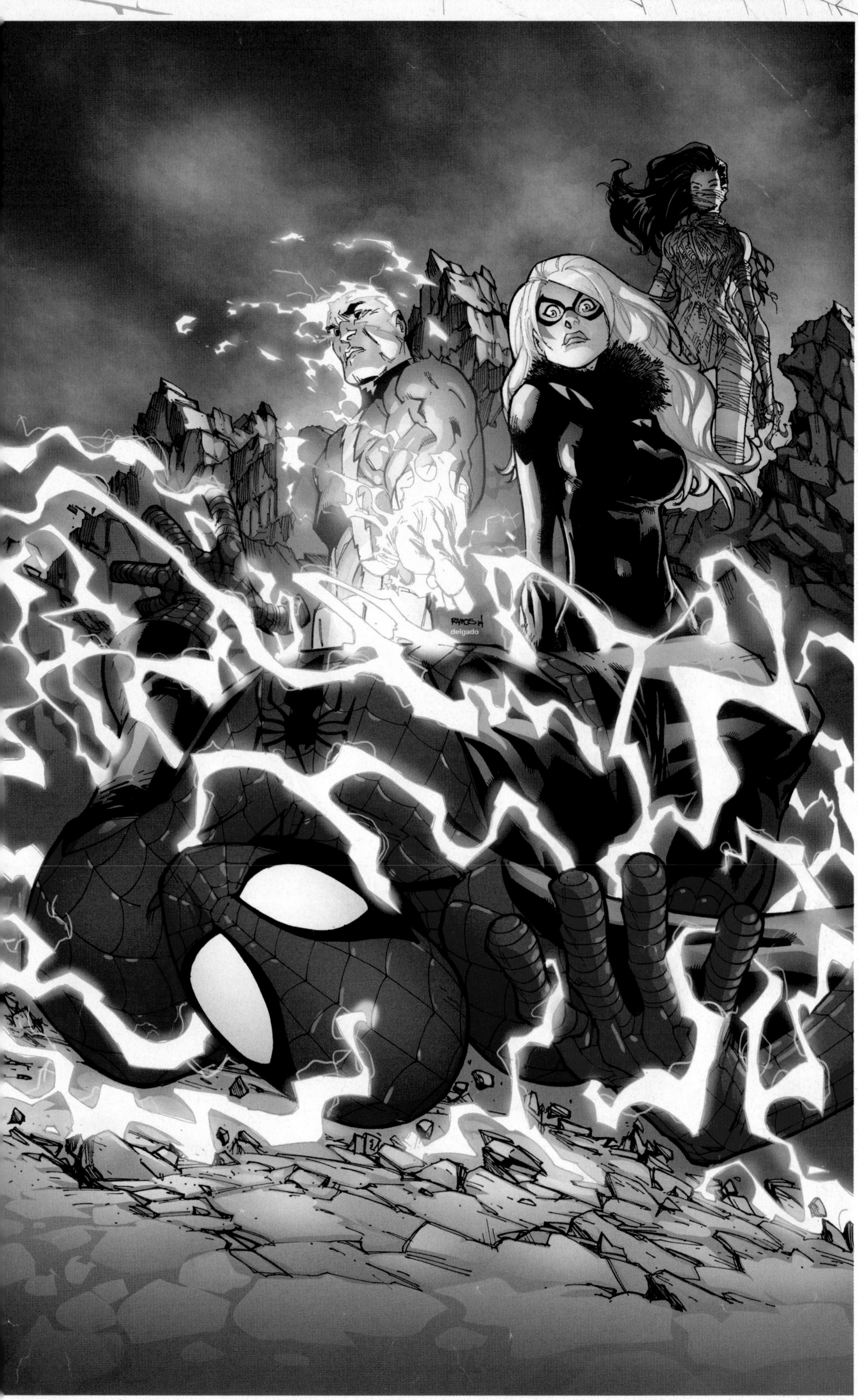
delgado

5

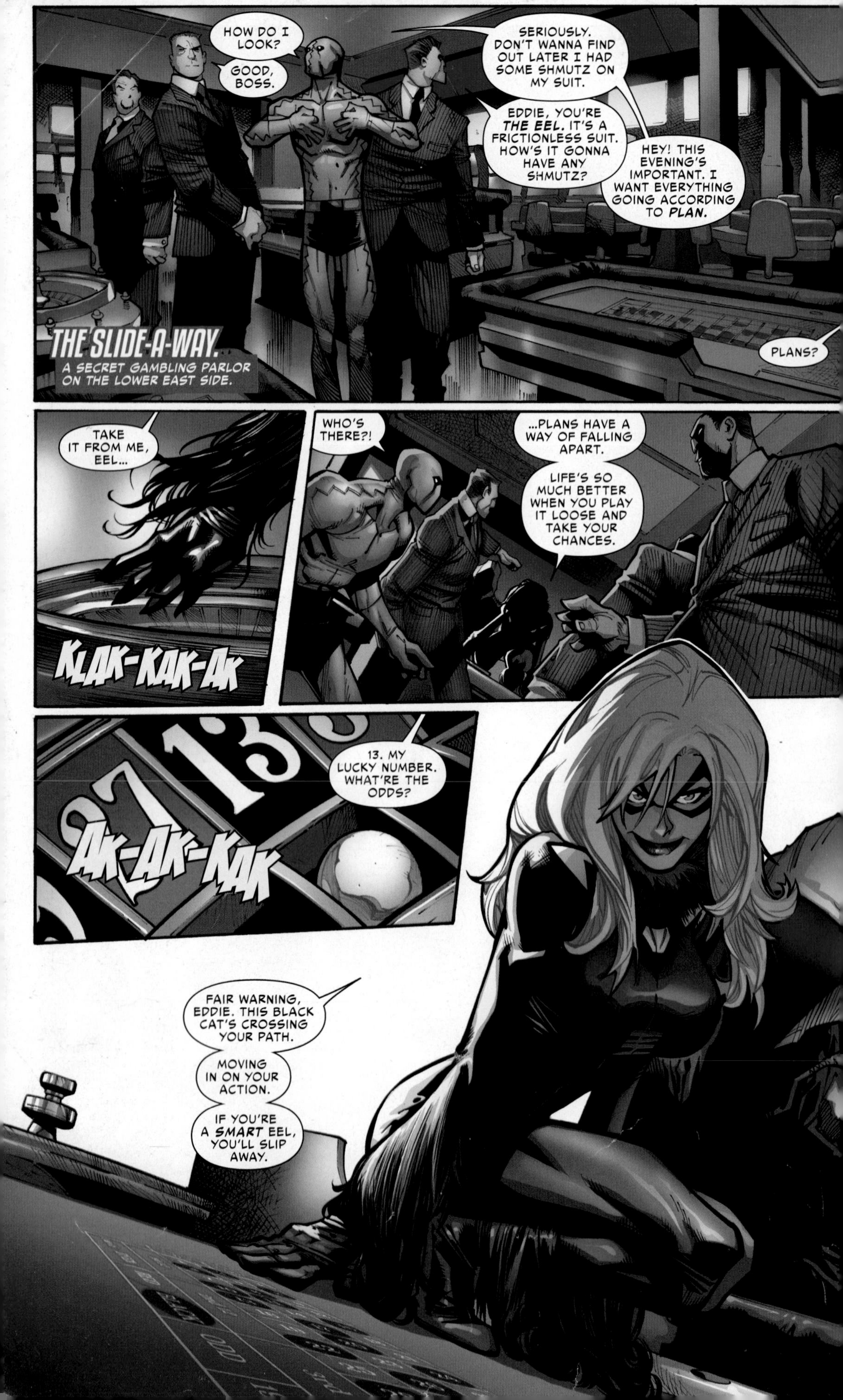
HOW DO I LOOK?
GOOD, BOSS.
SERIOUSLY. DON'T WANNA FIND OUT LATER I HAD SOME SHMUTZ ON MY SUIT.
EDDIE, YOU'RE THE EEL. IT'S A FRICTIONLESS SUIT. HOW'S IT GONNA HAVE ANY SHMUTZ?
HEY! THIS EVENING'S IMPORTANT. I WANT EVERYTHING GOING ACCORDING TO PLAN.
THE SLIDE-A-WAY.
A SECRET GAMBLING PARLOR ON THE LOWER EAST SIDE.
PLANS?
TAKE IT FROM ME, EEL...
KLAK-KAK-AK
WHO'S THERE?!
...PLANS HAVE A WAY OF FALLING APART.
LIFE'S SO MUCH BETTER WHEN YOU PLAY IT LOOSE AND TAKE YOUR CHANCES.
13. MY LUCKY NUMBER. WHAT'RE THE ODDS?
AK-AK-KAK
FAIR WARNING, EDDIE. THIS BLACK CAT'S CROSSING YOUR PATH.
MOVING IN ON YOUR ACTION.
IF YOU'RE A SMART EEL, YOU'LL SLIP AWAY.

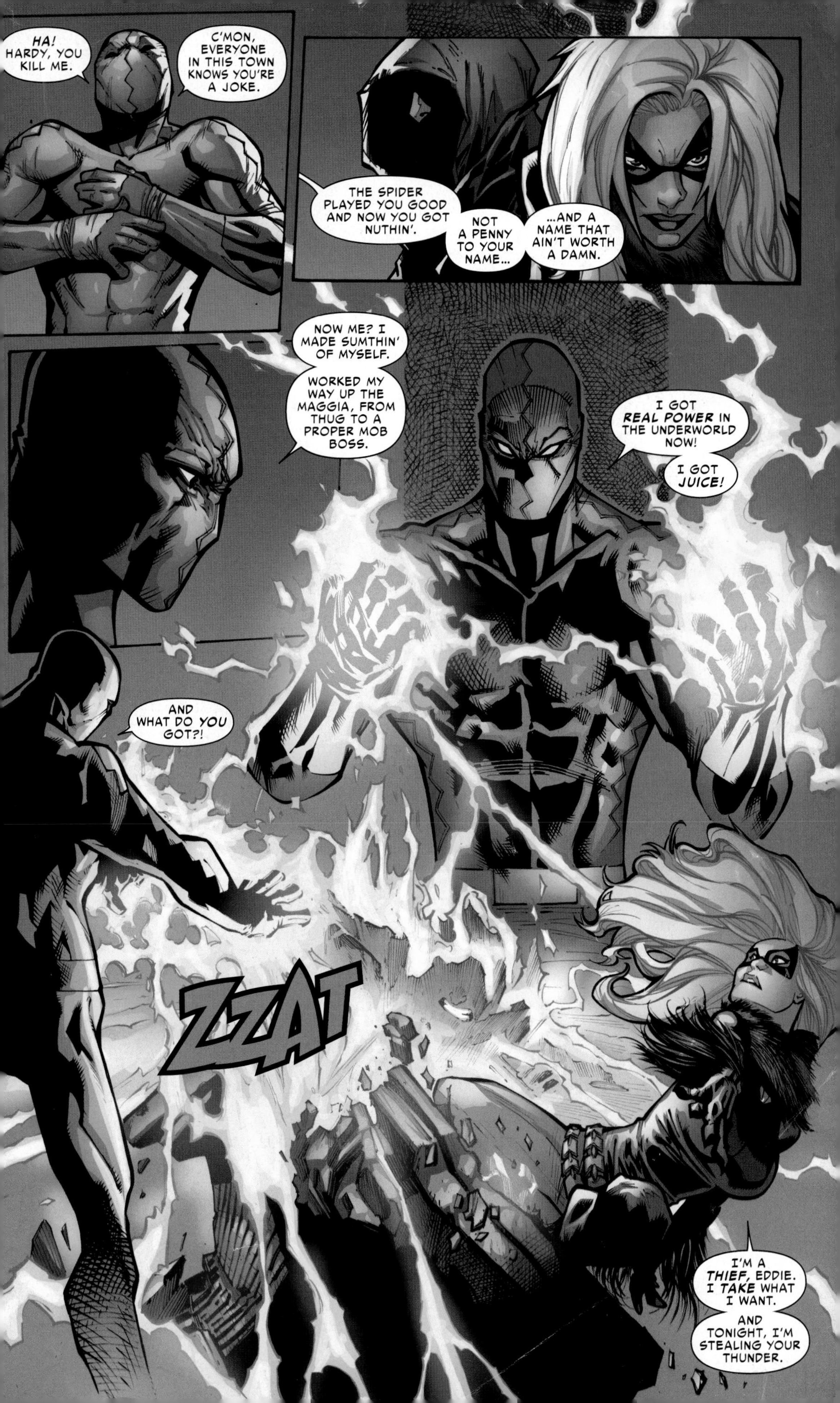
HA! HARDY, YOU KILL ME.
C'MON, EVERYONE IN THIS TOWN KNOWS YOU'RE A JOKE.
THE SPIDER PLAYED YOU GOOD AND NOW YOU GOT NUTHIN'.
NOT A PENNY TO YOUR NAME...
...AND A NAME THAT AIN'T WORTH A DAMN.
NOW ME? I MADE SUMTHIN' OF MYSELF.
WORKED MY WAY UP THE MAGGIA, FROM THUG TO A PROPER MOB BOSS.
I GOT REAL POWER IN THE UNDERWORLD NOW!
I GOT JUICE!
AND WHAT DO YOU GOT?!
ZZAT
I'M A THIEF, EDDIE. I TAKE WHAT I WANT.
AND TONIGHT, I'M STEALING YOUR THUNDER.

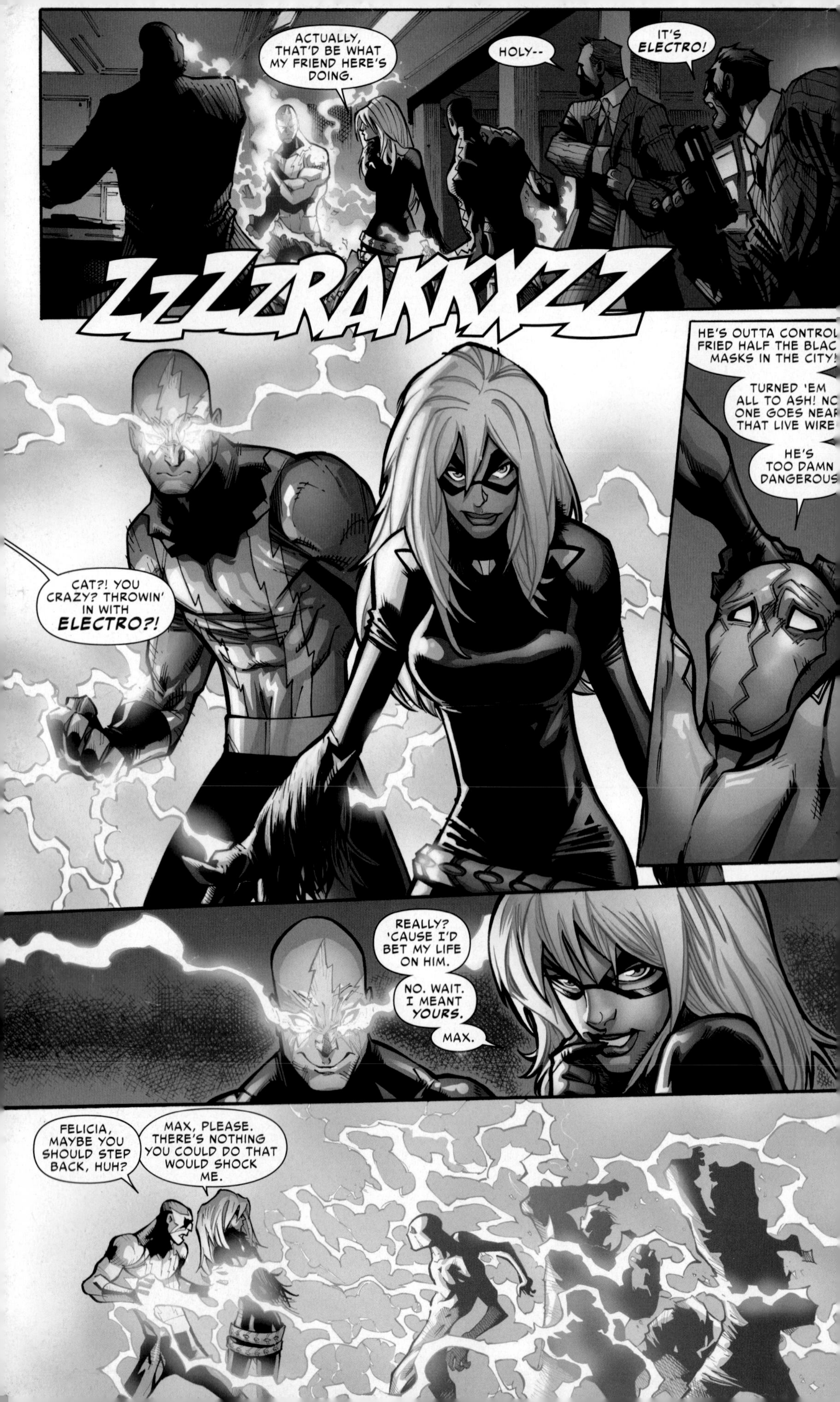
ACTUALLY, THAT'D BE WHAT MY FRIEND HERE'S DOING.
HOLY--
IT'S ELECTRO!
ZZZZRAKKXZZ
HE'S OUTTA CONTROL FRIED HALF THE BLAC MASKS IN THE CITY!
TURNED 'EM ALL TO ASH! NO ONE GOES NEAR THAT LIVE WIRE
HE'S TOO DAMN DANGEROUS
CAT?! YOU CRAZY? THROWIN' IN WITH ELECTRO?!
REALLY? 'CAUSE I'D BET MY LIFE ON HIM.
NO. WAIT. I MEANT YOURS.
MAX.
FELICIA, MAYBE YOU SHOULD STEP BACK, HUH?
MAX, PLEASE. THERE'S NOTHING YOU COULD DO THAT WOULD SHOCK ME.

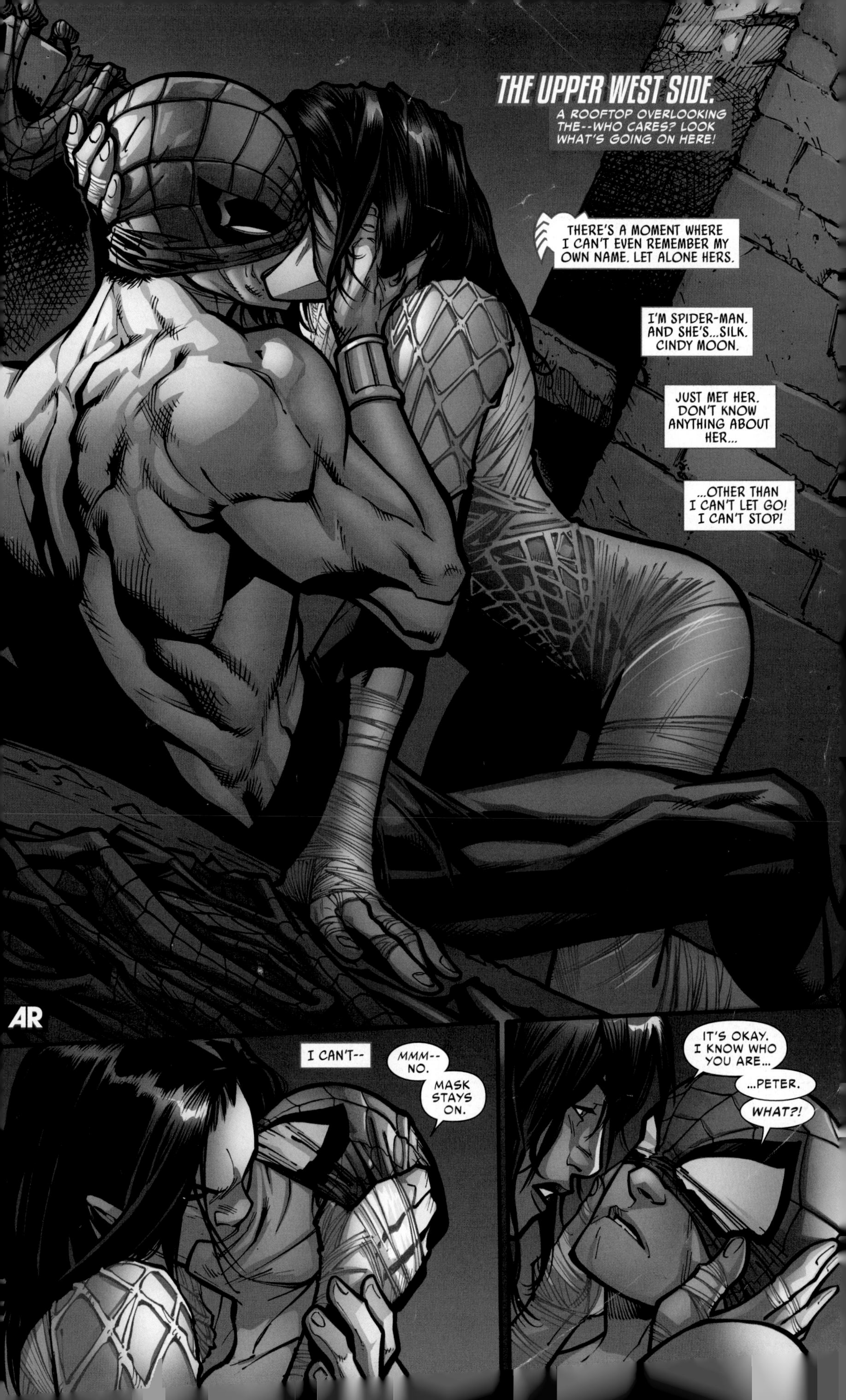
THE UPPER WEST SIDE.
A ROOFTOP OVERLOOKING THE--WHO CARES? LOOK WHAT'S GOING ON HERE!
THERE'S A MOMENT WHERE I CAN'T EVEN REMEMBER MY OWN NAME. LET ALONE HERS.
I'M SPIDER-MAN. AND SHE'S...SILK. CINDY MOON.
JUST MET HER. DON'T KNOW ANYTHING ABOUT HER...
...OTHER THAN I CAN'T LET GO! I CAN'T STOP!
AR
I CAN'T--
MMM-- NO.
MASK STAYS ON.
IT'S OKAY. I KNOW WHO YOU ARE...
...PETER.
WHAT?!

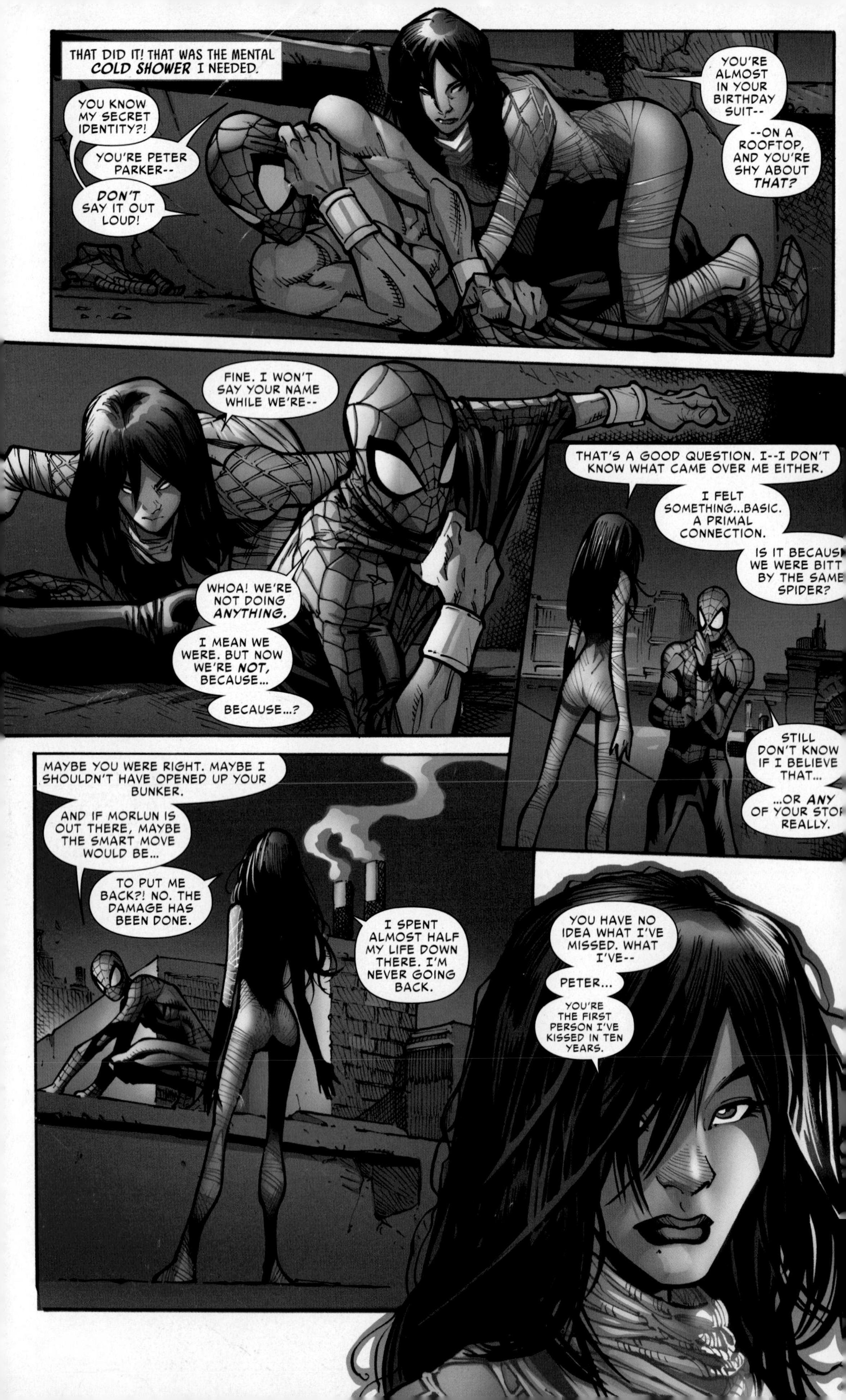
THAT DID IT! THAT WAS THE MENTAL COLD SHOWER I NEEDED.
YOU KNOW MY SECRET IDENTITY?!
YOU'RE PETER PARKER--
DON'T SAY IT OUT LOUD!
YOU'RE ALMOST IN YOUR BIRTHDAY SUIT--
--ON A ROOFTOP, AND YOU'RE SHY ABOUT THAT?
FINE. I WON'T SAY YOUR NAME WHILE WE'RE--
WHOA! WE'RE NOT DOING ANYTHING.
I MEAN WE WERE. BUT NOW WE'RE NOT, BECAUSE...
BECAUSE...?
THAT'S A GOOD QUESTION. I--I DON'T KNOW WHAT CAME OVER ME EITHER.
I FELT SOMETHING...BASIC. A PRIMAL CONNECTION.
IS IT BECAUS WE WERE BITT BY THE SAME SPIDER?
STILL DON'T KNOW IF I BELIEVE THAT...
...OR ANY OF YOUR STOR REALLY.
MAYBE YOU WERE RIGHT. MAYBE I SHOULDN'T HAVE OPENED UP YOUR BUNKER.
AND IF MORLUN IS OUT THERE, MAYBE THE SMART MOVE WOULD BE...
TO PUT ME BACK?! NO. THE DAMAGE HAS BEEN DONE.
I SPENT ALMOST HALF MY LIFE DOWN THERE. I'M NEVER GOING BACK.
YOU HAVE NO IDEA WHAT I'VE MISSED. WHAT I'VE--
PETER...
YOU'RE THE FIRST PERSON I'VE KISSED IN TEN YEARS.

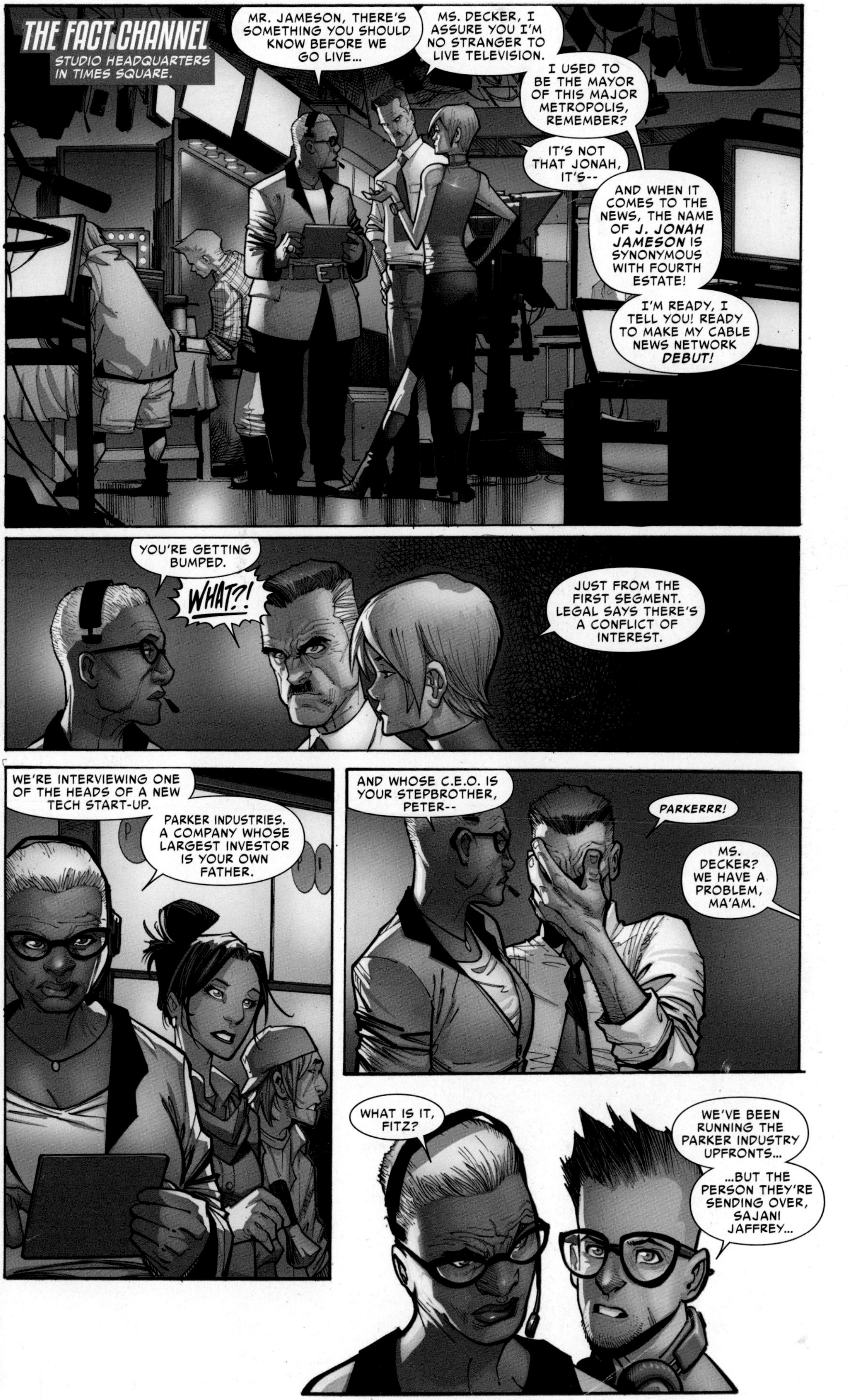
THE FACT CHANNEL
STUDIO HEADQUARTERS IN TIMES SQUARE.
MR. JAMESON, THERE'S SOMETHING YOU SHOULD KNOW BEFORE WE GO LIVE...
MS. DECKER, I ASSURE YOU I'M NO STRANGER TO LIVE TELEVISION.
I USED TO BE THE MAYOR OF THIS MAJOR METROPOLIS, REMEMBER?
IT'S NOT THAT JONAH, IT'S--
AND WHEN IT COMES TO THE NEWS, THE NAME OF J. JONAH JAMESON IS SYNONYMOUS WITH FOURTH ESTATE!
I'M READY, I TELL YOU! READY TO MAKE MY CABLE NEWS NETWORK DEBUT!
YOU'RE GETTING BUMPED.
WHAT?!
JUST FROM THE FIRST SEGMENT. LEGAL SAYS THERE'S A CONFLICT OF INTEREST.
WE'RE INTERVIEWING ONE OF THE HEADS OF A NEW TECH START-UP.
PARKER INDUSTRIES. A COMPANY WHOSE LARGEST INVESTOR IS YOUR OWN FATHER.
AND WHOSE C.E.O. IS YOUR STEPBROTHER, PETER--
PARKERRR!
MS. DECKER? WE HAVE A PROBLEM, MA'AM.
WHAT IS IT, FITZ?
WE'VE BEEN RUNNING THE PARKER INDUSTRY UPFRONTS...
...BUT THE PERSON THEY'RE SENDING OVER, SAJANI JAFFREY...

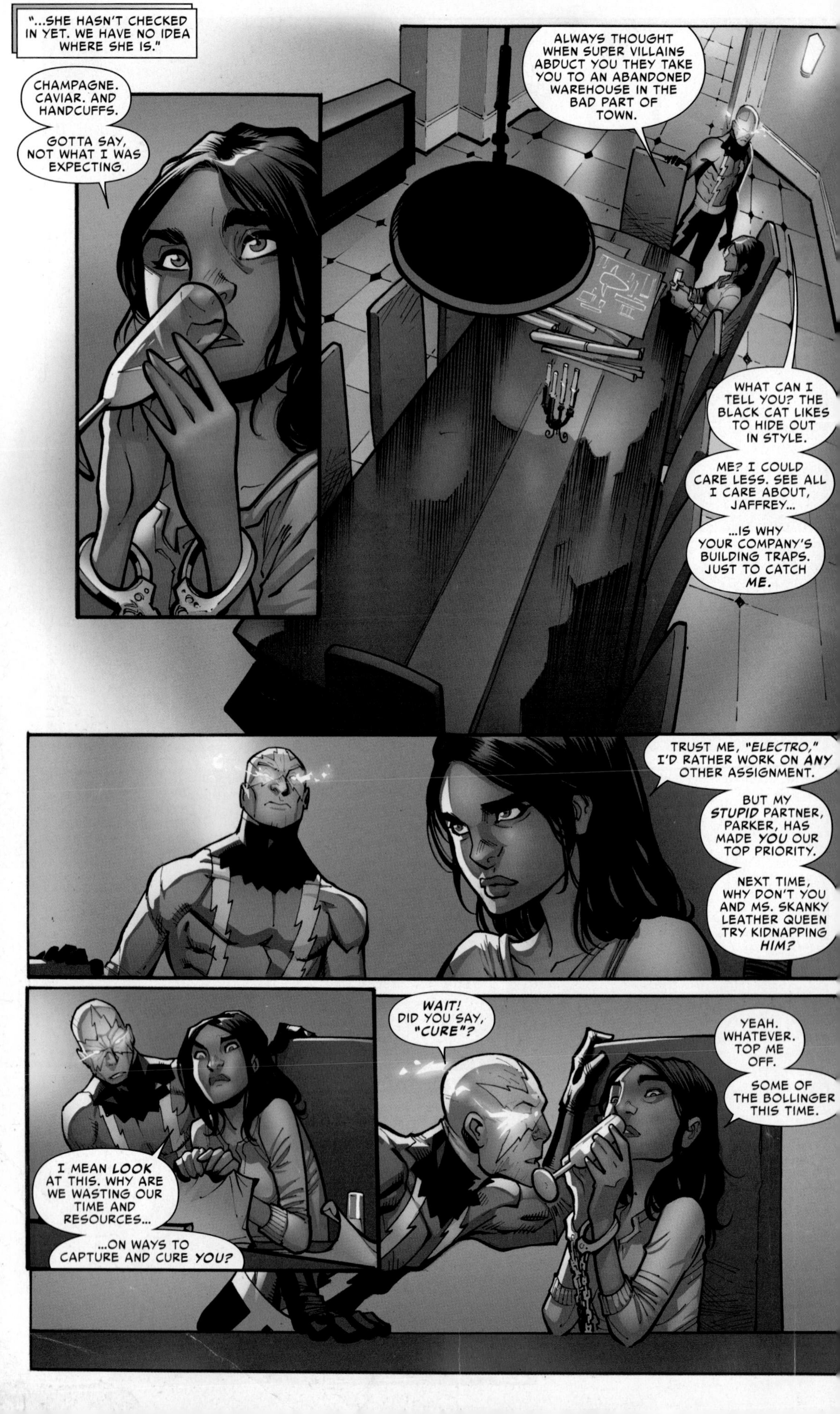
"...SHE HASN'T CHECKED IN YET. WE HAVE NO IDEA WHERE SHE IS."
CHAMPAGNE. CAVIAR. AND HANDCUFFS.
GOTTA SAY, NOT WHAT I WAS EXPECTING.
ALWAYS THOUGHT WHEN SUPER VILLAINS ABDUCT YOU THEY TAKE YOU TO AN ABANDONED WAREHOUSE IN THE BAD PART OF TOWN.
WHAT CAN I TELL YOU? THE BLACK CAT LIKES TO HIDE OUT IN STYLE.
ME? I COULD CARE LESS. SEE ALL I CARE ABOUT, JAFFREY...
...IS WHY YOUR COMPANY'S BUILDING TRAPS. JUST TO CATCH ME.
TRUST ME, "ELECTRO," I'D RATHER WORK ON ANY OTHER ASSIGNMENT.
BUT MY STUPID PARTNER, PARKER, HAS MADE YOU OUR TOP PRIORITY.
NEXT TIME, WHY DON'T YOU AND MS. SKANKY LEATHER QUEEN TRY KIDNAPPING HIM?
I MEAN LOOK AT THIS. WHY ARE WE WASTING OUR TIME AND RESOURCES...
...ON WAYS TO CAPTURE AND CURE YOU?
WAIT! DID YOU SAY, "CURE"?
YEAH. WHATEVER. TOP ME OFF.
SOME OF THE BOLLINGER THIS TIME.

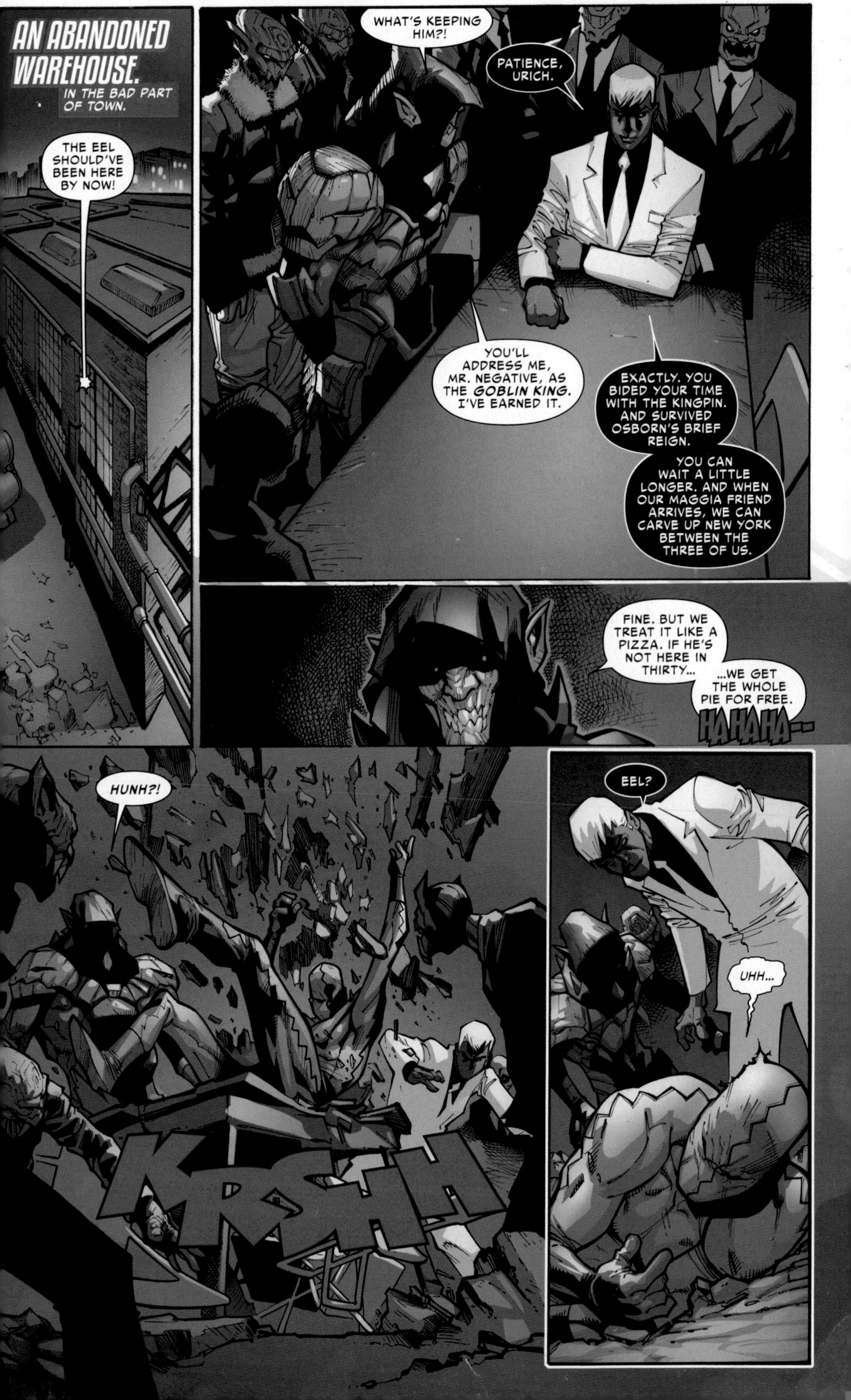

AN ABANDONED WAREHOUSE.
IN THE BAD PART OF TOWN.
THE EEL SHOULD'VE BEEN HERE BY NOW!
WHAT'S KEEPING HIM?!
PATIENCE, URICH.
YOU'LL ADDRESS ME, MR. NEGATIVE, AS THE GOBLIN KING. I'VE EARNED IT.
EXACTLY. YOU BIDED YOUR TIME WITH THE KINGPIN. AND SURVIVED OSBORN'S BRIEF REIGN.
YOU CAN WAIT A LITTLE LONGER. AND WHEN OUR MAGGIA FRIEND ARRIVES, WE CAN CARVE UP NEW YORK BETWEEN THE THREE OF US.
FINE. BUT WE TREAT IT LIKE A PIZZA. IF HE'S NOT HERE IN THIRTY...
...WE GET THE WHOLE PIE FOR FREE.
HAHAHA--
HUNH?!
KRSHH
EEL?
UHH...

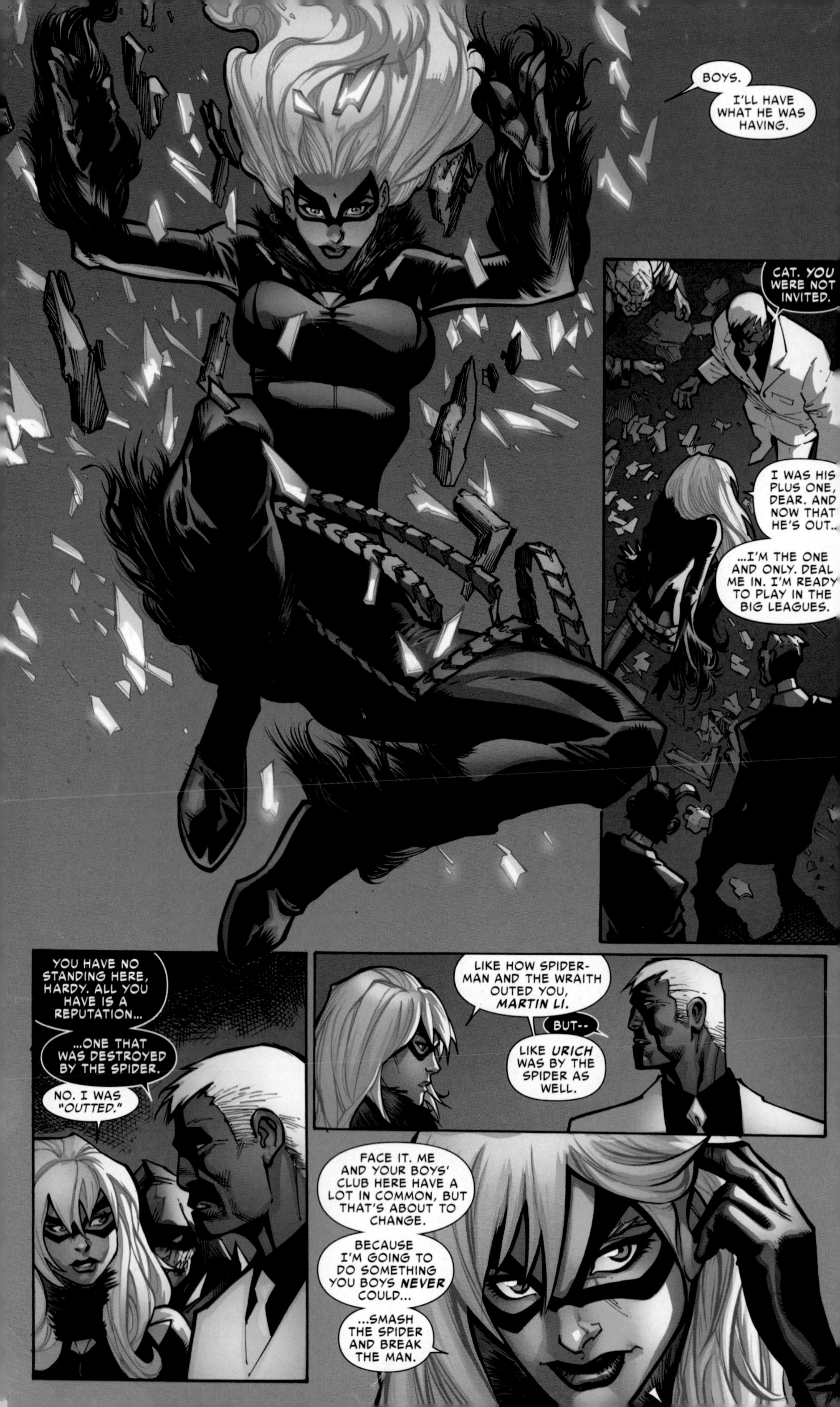
BOYS.
I'LL HAVE WHAT HE WAS HAVING.
CAT. YOU WERE NOT INVITED.
I WAS HIS PLUS ONE, DEAR. AND NOW THAT HE'S OUT..
...I'M THE ONE AND ONLY. DEAL ME IN. I'M READY TO PLAY IN THE BIG LEAGUES.
YOU HAVE NO STANDING HERE, HARDY. ALL YOU HAVE IS A REPUTATION...
...ONE THAT WAS DESTROYED BY THE SPIDER.
NO. I WAS "OUTTED."
LIKE HOW SPIDER-MAN AND THE WRAITH OUTED YOU, MARTIN LI.
BUT--
LIKE URICH WAS BY THE SPIDER AS WELL.
FACE IT. ME AND YOUR BOYS' CLUB HERE HAVE A LOT IN COMMON, BUT THAT'S ABOUT TO CHANGE.
BECAUSE I'M GOING TO DO SOMETHING YOU BOYS NEVER COULD...
...SMASH THE SPIDER AND BREAK THE MAN.

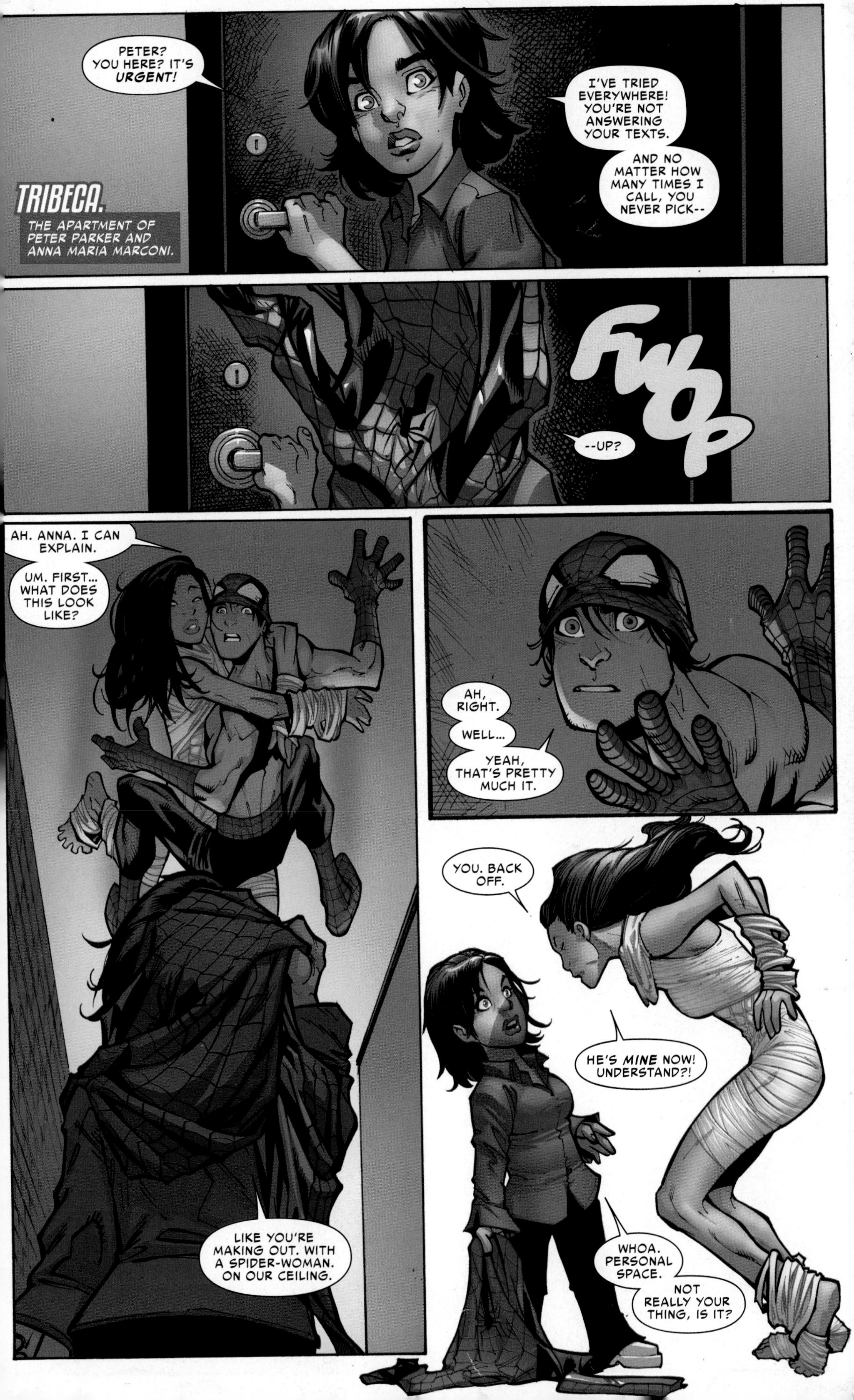
PETER? YOU HERE? IT'S URGENT!
I'VE TRIED EVERYWHERE! YOU'RE NOT ANSWERING YOUR TEXTS.
AND NO MATTER HOW MANY TIMES I CALL, YOU NEVER PICK--
TRIBECA.
THE APARTMENT OF PETER PARKER AND ANNA MARIA MARCONI.
FWOP
--UP?
AH. ANNA. I CAN EXPLAIN.
UM. FIRST... WHAT DOES THIS LOOK LIKE?
AH, RIGHT.
WELL...
YEAH, THAT'S PRETTY MUCH IT.
LIKE YOU'RE MAKING OUT. WITH A SPIDER-WOMAN. ON OUR CEILING.
YOU. BACK OFF.
HE'S MINE NOW! UNDERSTAND?!
WHOA. PERSONAL SPACE.
NOT REALLY YOUR THING, IS IT?

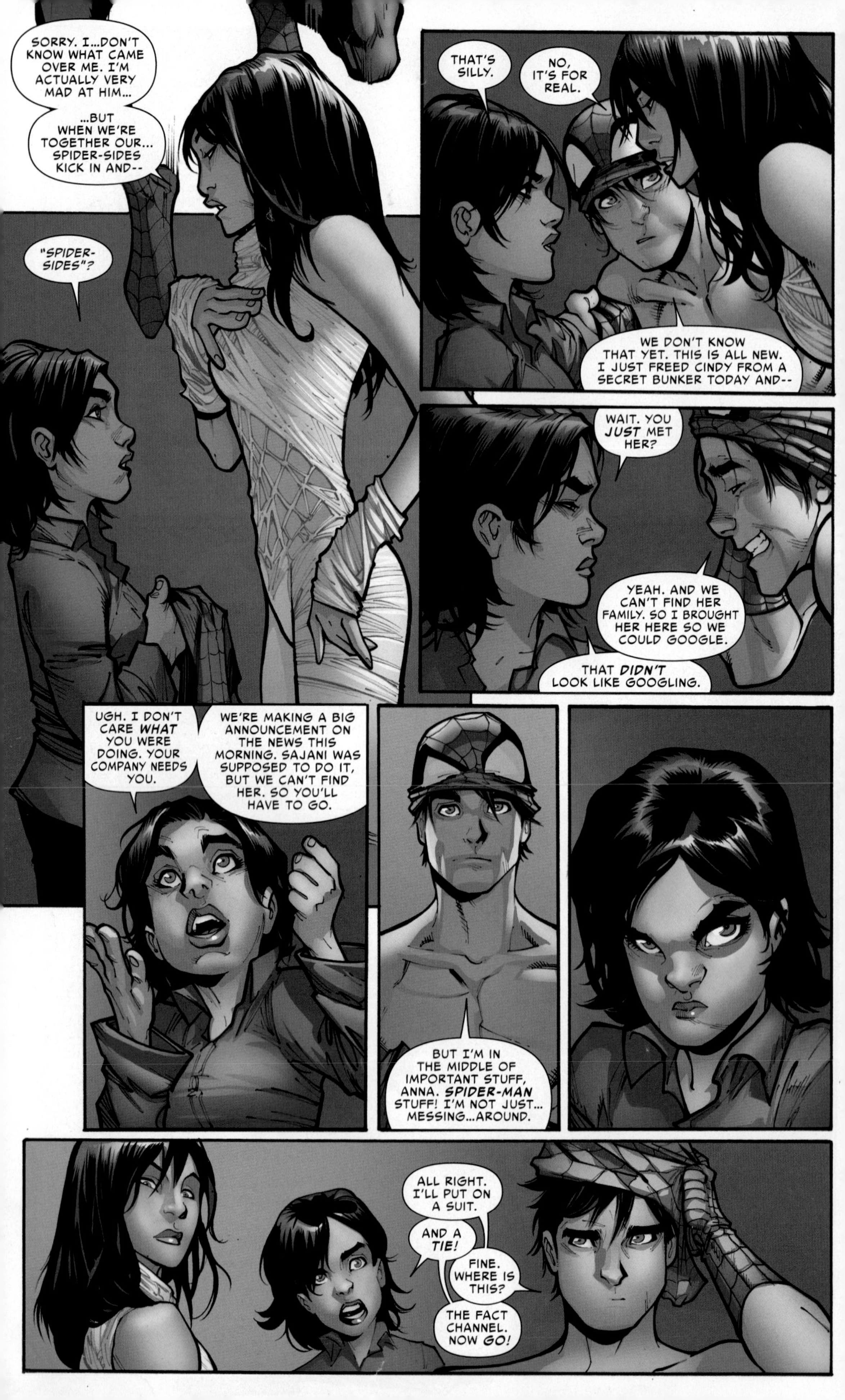
SORRY. I...DON'T KNOW WHAT CAME OVER ME. I'M ACTUALLY VERY MAD AT HIM...
...BUT WHEN WE'RE TOGETHER OUR... SPIDER-SIDES KICK IN AND--
"SPIDER-SIDES"?
THAT'S SILLY.
NO, IT'S FOR REAL.
WE DON'T KNOW THAT YET. THIS IS ALL NEW. I JUST FREED CINDY FROM A SECRET BUNKER TODAY AND--
WAIT. YOU JUST MET HER?
YEAH. AND WE CAN'T FIND HER FAMILY. SO I BROUGHT HER HERE SO WE COULD GOOGLE.
THAT DIDN'T LOOK LIKE GOOGLING.
UGH. I DON'T CARE WHAT YOU WERE DOING. YOUR COMPANY NEEDS YOU.
WE'RE MAKING A BIG ANNOUNCEMENT ON THE NEWS THIS MORNING. SAJANI WAS SUPPOSED TO DO IT, BUT WE CAN'T FIND HER. SO YOU'LL HAVE TO GO.
BUT I'M IN THE MIDDLE OF IMPORTANT STUFF, ANNA. SPIDER-MAN STUFF! I'M NOT JUST... MESSING...AROUND.
ALL RIGHT. I'LL PUT ON A SUIT.
AND A TIE!
FINE. WHERE IS THIS?
THE FACT CHANNEL. NOW GO!

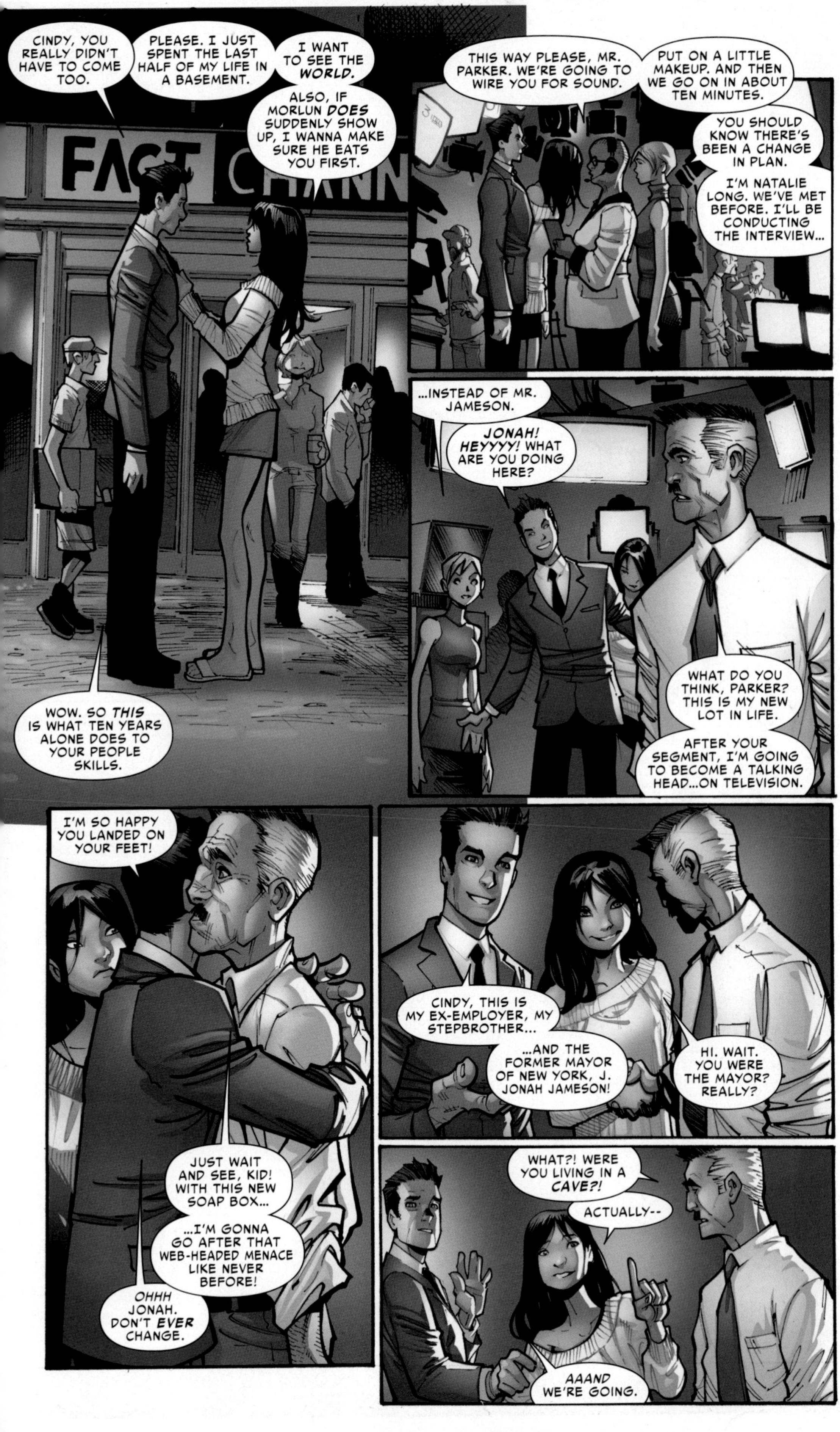

CINDY, YOU REALLY DIDN'T HAVE TO COME TOO.
PLEASE. I JUST SPENT THE LAST HALF OF MY LIFE IN A BASEMENT.
I WANT TO SEE THE WORLD.
ALSO, IF MORLUN DOES SUDDENLY SHOW UP, I WANNA MAKE SURE HE EATS YOU FIRST.
FACT CHANN
WOW. SO THIS IS WHAT TEN YEARS ALONE DOES TO YOUR PEOPLE SKILLS.
THIS WAY PLEASE, MR. PARKER. WE'RE GOING TO WIRE YOU FOR SOUND.
PUT ON A LITTLE MAKEUP. AND THEN WE GO ON IN ABOUT TEN MINUTES.
YOU SHOULD KNOW THERE'S BEEN A CHANGE IN PLAN.
I'M NATALIE LONG. WE'VE MET BEFORE. I'LL BE CONDUCTING THE INTERVIEW...
...INSTEAD OF MR. JAMESON.
JONAH! HEYYYY! WHAT ARE YOU DOING HERE?
WHAT DO YOU THINK, PARKER? THIS IS MY NEW LOT IN LIFE.
AFTER YOUR SEGMENT, I'M GOING TO BECOME A TALKING HEAD...ON TELEVISION.
I'M SO HAPPY YOU LANDED ON YOUR FEET!
JUST WAIT AND SEE, KID! WITH THIS NEW SOAP BOX...
...I'M GONNA GO AFTER THAT WEB-HEADED MENACE LIKE NEVER BEFORE!
OHHH JONAH. DON'T EVER CHANGE.
CINDY, THIS IS MY EX-EMPLOYER, MY STEPBROTHER...
...AND THE FORMER MAYOR OF NEW YORK, J. JONAH JAMESON!
HI. WAIT. YOU WERE THE MAYOR? REALLY?
WHAT?! WERE YOU LIVING IN A CAVE?!
ACTUALLY--
AAAND WE'RE GOING.

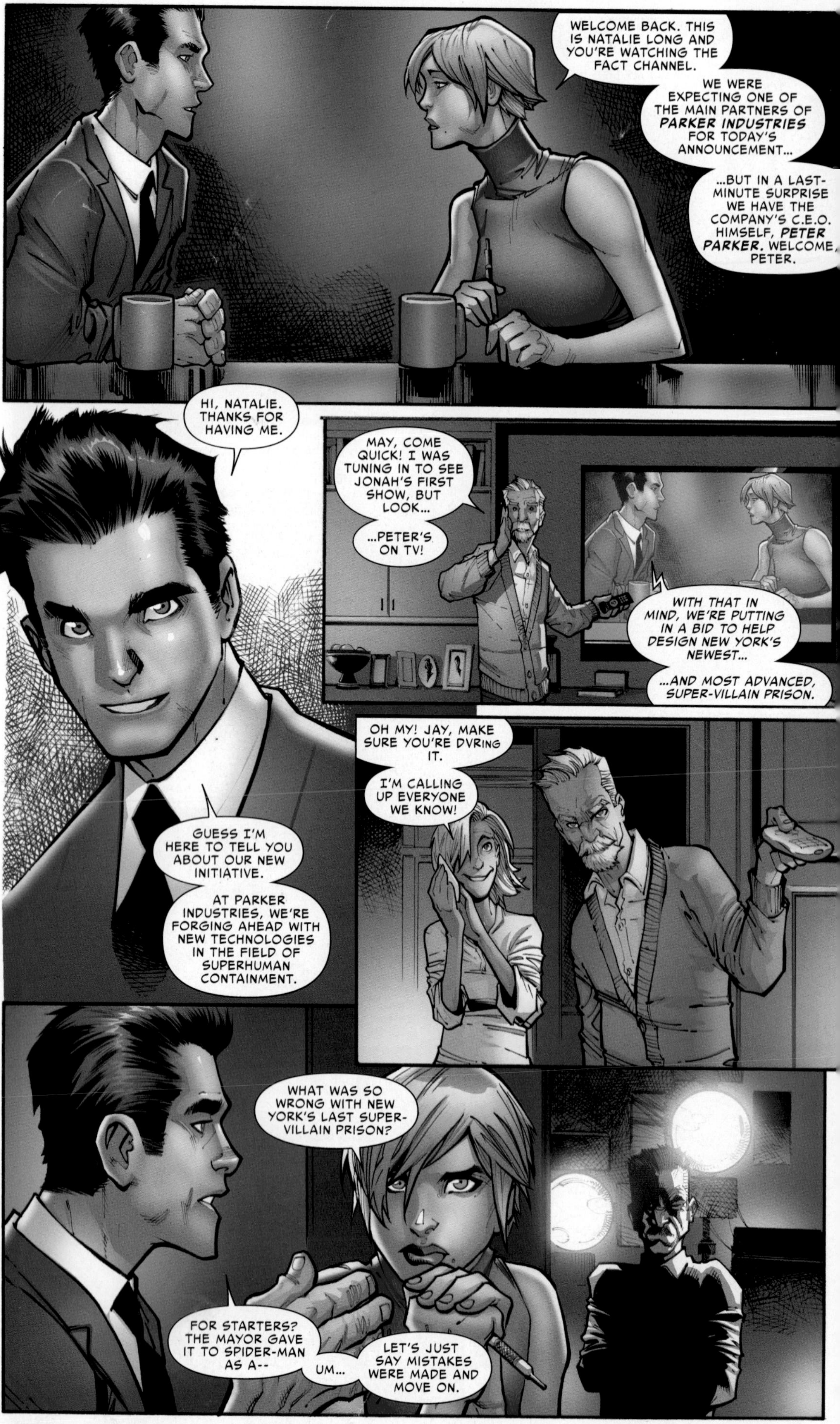
WELCOME BACK. THIS IS NATALIE LONG AND YOU'RE WATCHING THE FACT CHANNEL.
WE WERE EXPECTING ONE OF THE MAIN PARTNERS OF PARKER INDUSTRIES FOR TODAY'S ANNOUNCEMENT...
...BUT IN A LAST-MINUTE SURPRISE WE HAVE THE COMPANY'S C.E.O. HIMSELF, PETER PARKER. WELCOME, PETER.
HI, NATALIE. THANKS FOR HAVING ME.
MAY, COME QUICK! I WAS TUNING IN TO SEE JONAH'S FIRST SHOW, BUT LOOK...
...PETER'S ON TV!
WITH THAT IN MIND, WE'RE PUTTING IN A BID TO HELP DESIGN NEW YORK'S NEWEST...
...AND MOST ADVANCED, SUPER-VILLAIN PRISON.
GUESS I'M HERE TO TELL YOU ABOUT OUR NEW INITIATIVE.
AT PARKER INDUSTRIES, WE'RE FORGING AHEAD WITH NEW TECHNOLOGIES IN THE FIELD OF SUPERHUMAN CONTAINMENT.
OH MY! JAY, MAKE SURE YOU'RE DVRING IT.
I'M CALLING UP EVERYONE WE KNOW!
WHAT WAS SO WRONG WITH NEW YORK'S LAST SUPER-VILLAIN PRISON?
FOR STARTERS? THE MAYOR GAVE IT TO SPIDER-MAN AS A--
UM...
LET'S JUST SAY MISTAKES WERE MADE AND MOVE ON.

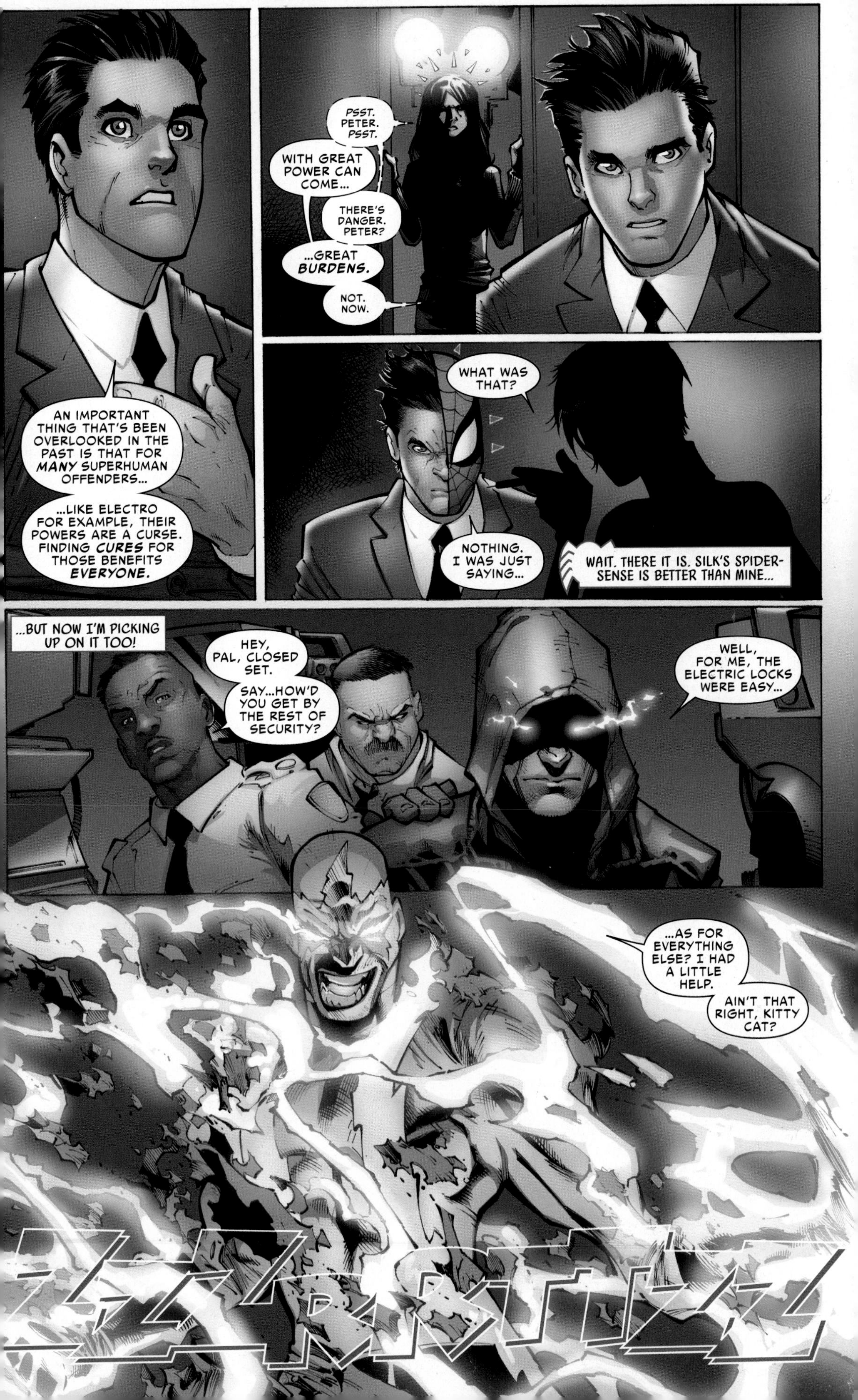
AN IMPORTANT THING THAT'S BEEN OVERLOOKED IN THE PAST IS THAT FOR *MANY* SUPERHUMAN OFFENDERS...
...LIKE ELECTRO FOR EXAMPLE, THEIR POWERS ARE A CURSE. FINDING *CURES* FOR THOSE BENEFITS *EVERYONE.*
PSST. PETER. PSST.
WITH GREAT POWER CAN COME...
THERE'S DANGER. PETER?
...GREAT *BURDENS.*
NOT. NOW.
WHAT WAS THAT?
NOTHING. I WAS JUST SAYING...
WAIT. THERE IT IS. SILK'S SPIDER-SENSE IS BETTER THAN MINE...
...BUT NOW I'M PICKING UP ON IT TOO!
HEY, PAL, CLOSED SET.
SAY...HOW'D YOU GET BY THE REST OF SECURITY?
WELL, FOR ME, THE ELECTRIC LOCKS WERE EASY...
...AS FOR EVERYTHING ELSE? I HAD A LITTLE HELP.
AIN'T THAT RIGHT, KITTY CAT?

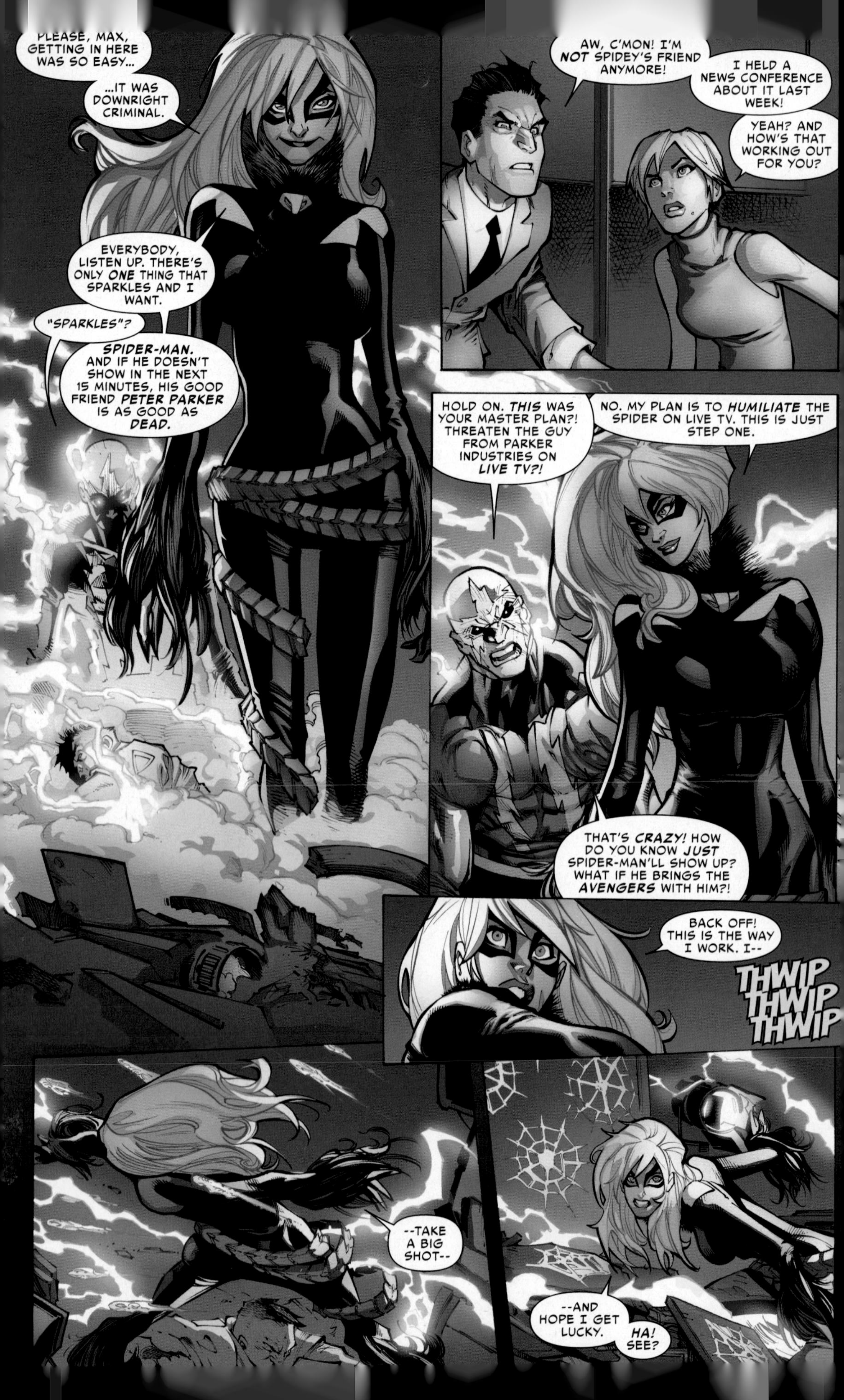
PLEASE, MAX, GETTING IN HERE WAS SO EASY...
...IT WAS DOWNRIGHT CRIMINAL.
EVERYBODY, LISTEN UP. THERE'S ONLY ONE THING THAT SPARKLES AND I WANT.
"SPARKLES"?
SPIDER-MAN. AND IF HE DOESN'T SHOW IN THE NEXT 15 MINUTES, HIS GOOD FRIEND PETER PARKER IS AS GOOD AS DEAD.
AW, C'MON! I'M NOT SPIDEY'S FRIEND ANYMORE!
I HELD A NEWS CONFERENCE ABOUT IT LAST WEEK!
YEAH? AND HOW'S THAT WORKING OUT FOR YOU?
HOLD ON. THIS WAS YOUR MASTER PLAN?! THREATEN THE GUY FROM PARKER INDUSTRIES ON LIVE TV?!
NO. MY PLAN IS TO HUMILIATE THE SPIDER ON LIVE TV. THIS IS JUST STEP ONE.
THAT'S CRAZY! HOW DO YOU KNOW JUST SPIDER-MAN'LL SHOW UP? WHAT IF HE BRINGS THE AVENGERS WITH HIM?!
BACK OFF! THIS IS THE WAY I WORK. I--
THWIP THWIP THWIP
--TAKE A BIG SHOT--
--AND HOPE I GET LUCKY.
HA! SEE?

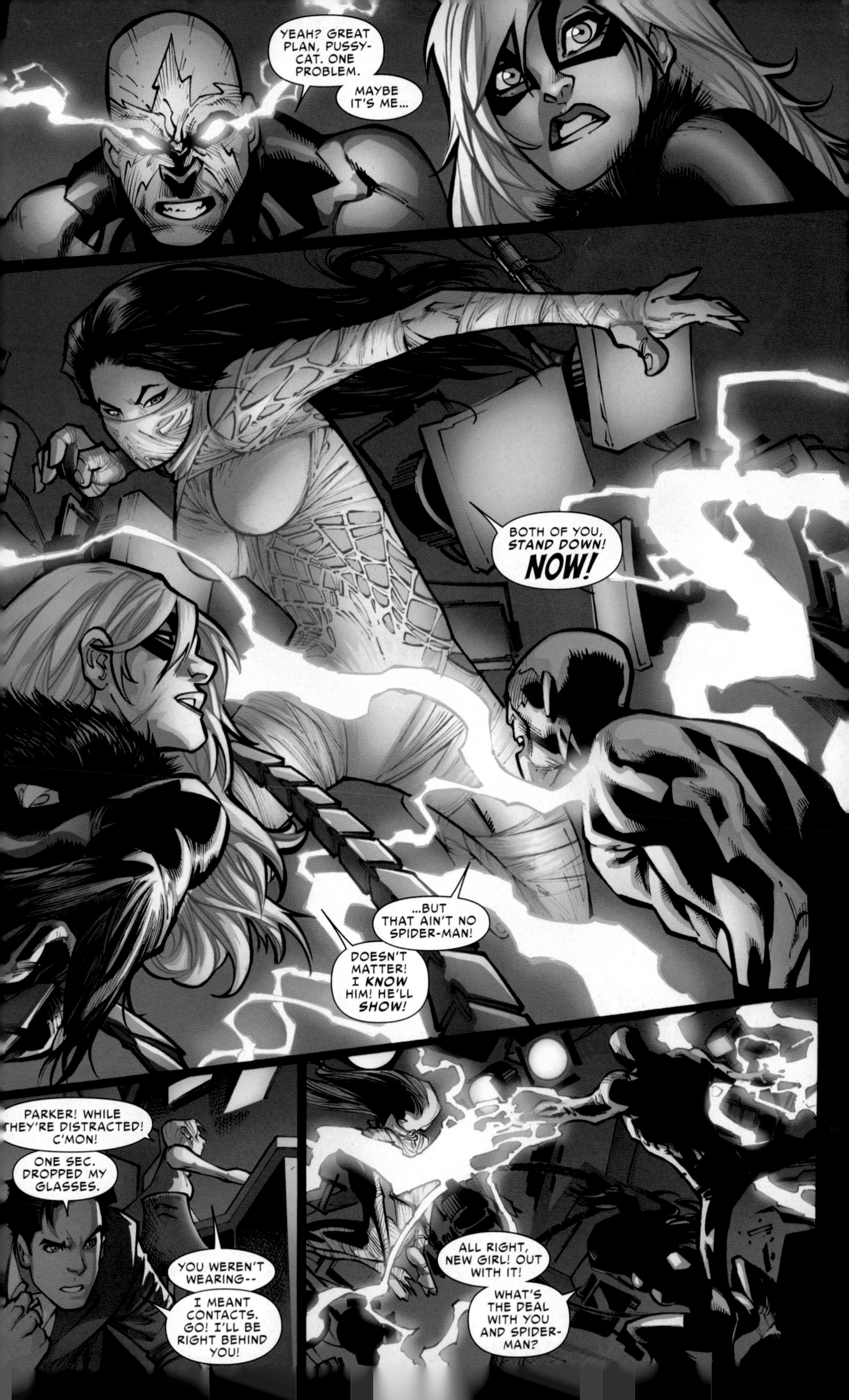
YEAH? GREAT PLAN, PUSSY-CAT. ONE PROBLEM.
MAYBE IT'S ME...
BOTH OF YOU, STAND DOWN! NOW!
...BUT THAT AIN'T NO SPIDER-MAN!
DOESN'T MATTER! I KNOW HIM! HE'LL SHOW!
PARKER! WHILE THEY'RE DISTRACTED! C'MON!
ONE SEC. DROPPED MY GLASSES.
YOU WEREN'T WEARING--
I MEANT CONTACTS. GO! I'LL BE RIGHT BEHIND YOU!
ALL RIGHT, NEW GIRL! OUT WITH IT!
WHAT'S THE DEAL WITH YOU AND SPIDER-MAN?

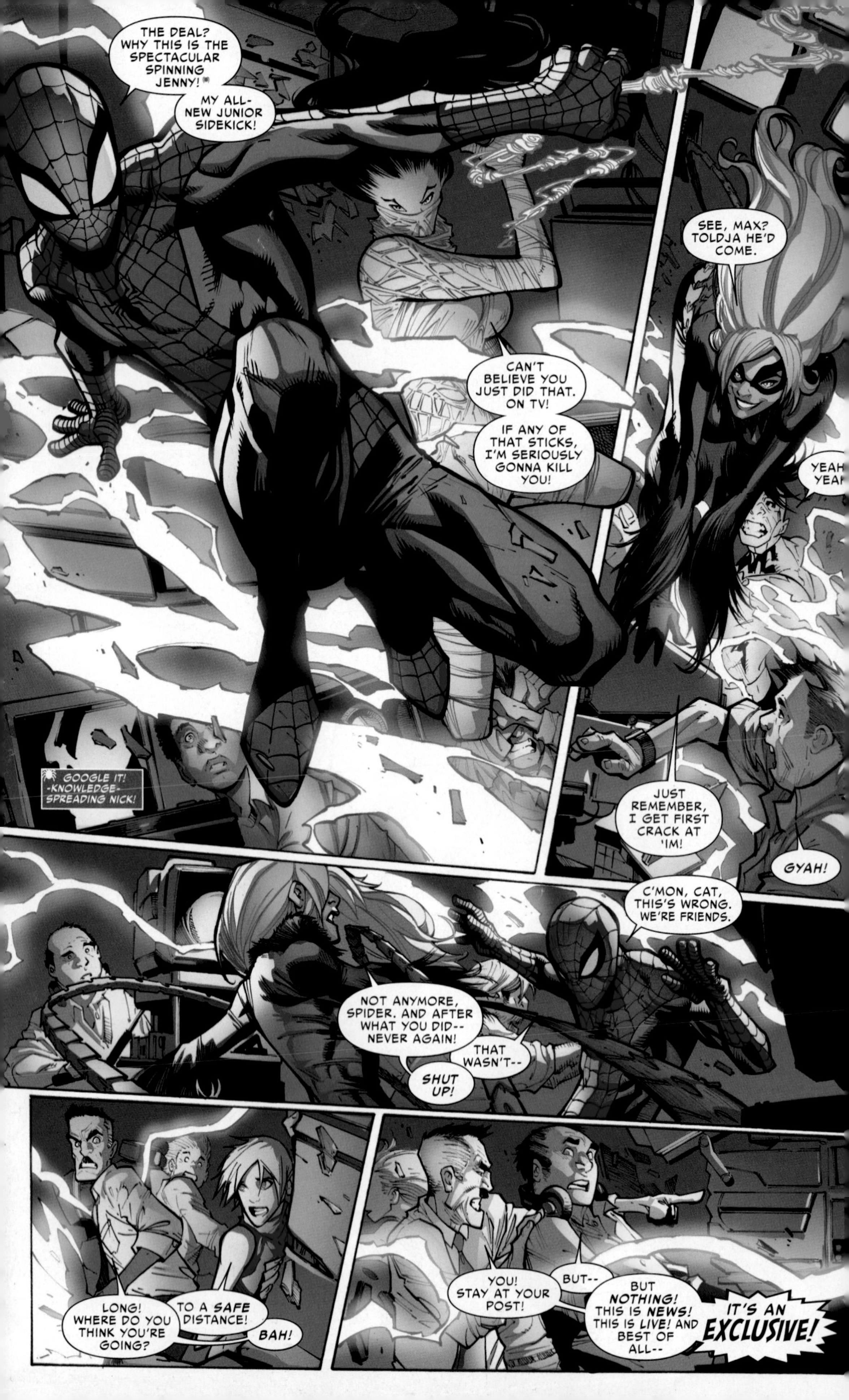
THE DEAL? WHY THIS IS THE SPECTACULAR SPINNING JENNY!
MY ALL-NEW JUNIOR SIDEKICK!
SEE, MAX? TOLDJA HE'D COME.
CAN'T BELIEVE YOU JUST DID THAT. ON TV!
IF ANY OF THAT STICKS, I'M SERIOUSLY GONNA KILL YOU!
GOOGLE IT! -KNOWLEDGE-SPREADING NICK!
JUST REMEMBER, I GET FIRST CRACK AT 'IM!
GYAH!
C'MON, CAT, THIS'S WRONG. WE'RE FRIENDS.
NOT ANYMORE, SPIDER. AND AFTER WHAT YOU DID-- NEVER AGAIN!
THAT WASN'T--
SHUT UP!
LONG! WHERE DO YOU THINK YOU'RE GOING?
TO A SAFE DISTANCE!
BAH!
YOU! STAY AT YOUR POST!
BUT--
BUT NOTHING! THIS IS NEWS! THIS IS LIVE! AND BEST OF ALL--
IT'S AN EXCLUSIVE!

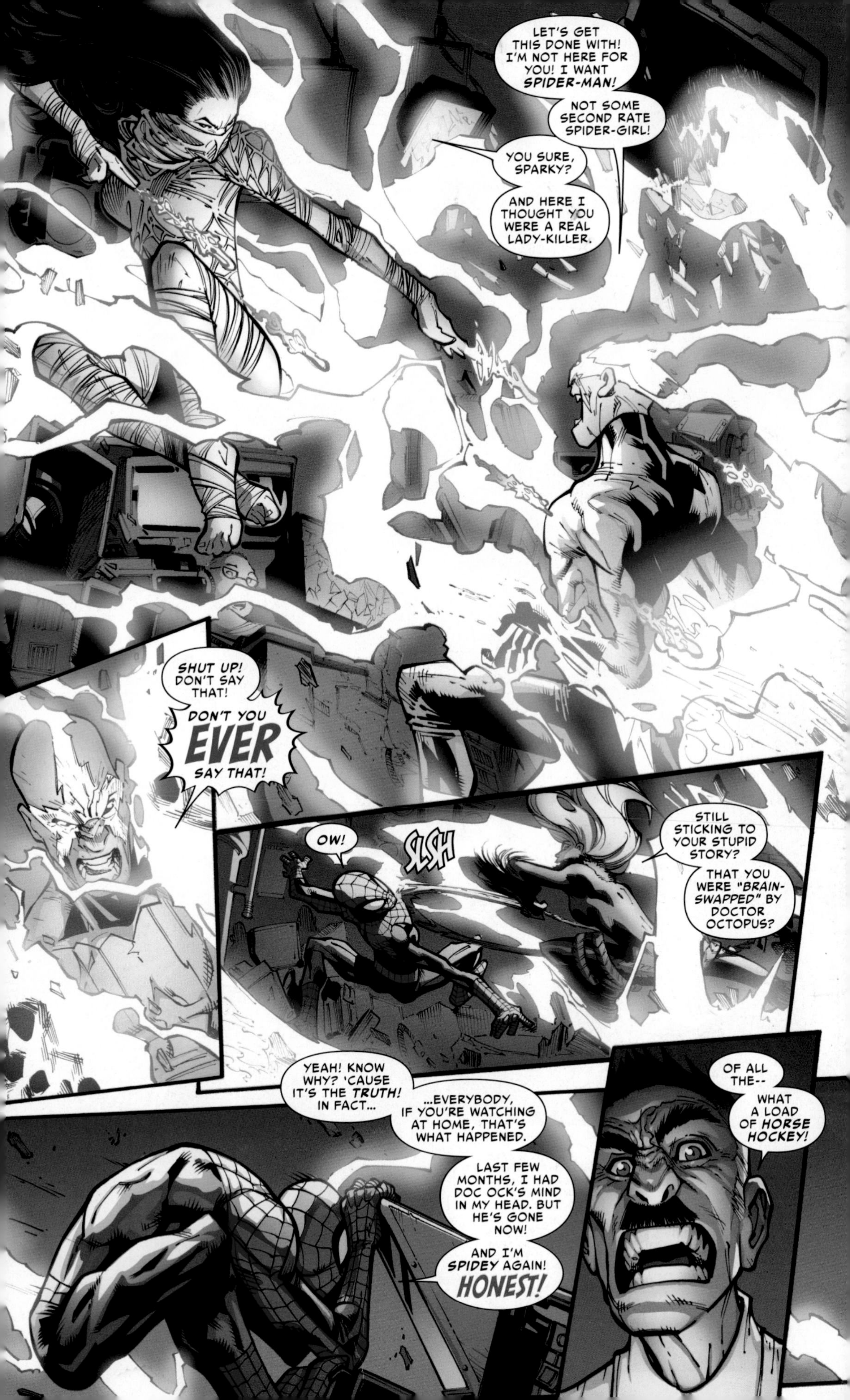
LET'S GET THIS DONE WITH! I'M NOT HERE FOR YOU! I WANT SPIDER-MAN!
NOT SOME SECOND RATE SPIDER-GIRL!
YOU SURE, SPARKY?
AND HERE I THOUGHT YOU WERE A REAL LADY-KILLER.
SHUT UP! DON'T SAY THAT!
DON'T YOU EVER SAY THAT!
OW!
SLSH
STILL STICKING TO YOUR STUPID STORY?
THAT YOU WERE "BRAIN-SWAPPED" BY DOCTOR OCTOPUS?
YEAH! KNOW WHY? 'CAUSE IT'S THE TRUTH! IN FACT...
...EVERYBODY, IF YOU'RE WATCHING AT HOME, THAT'S WHAT HAPPENED.
LAST FEW MONTHS, I HAD DOC OCK'S MIND IN MY HEAD. BUT HE'S GONE NOW!
AND I'M SPIDEY AGAIN! HONEST!
OF ALL THE--
WHAT A LOAD OF HORSE HOCKEY!

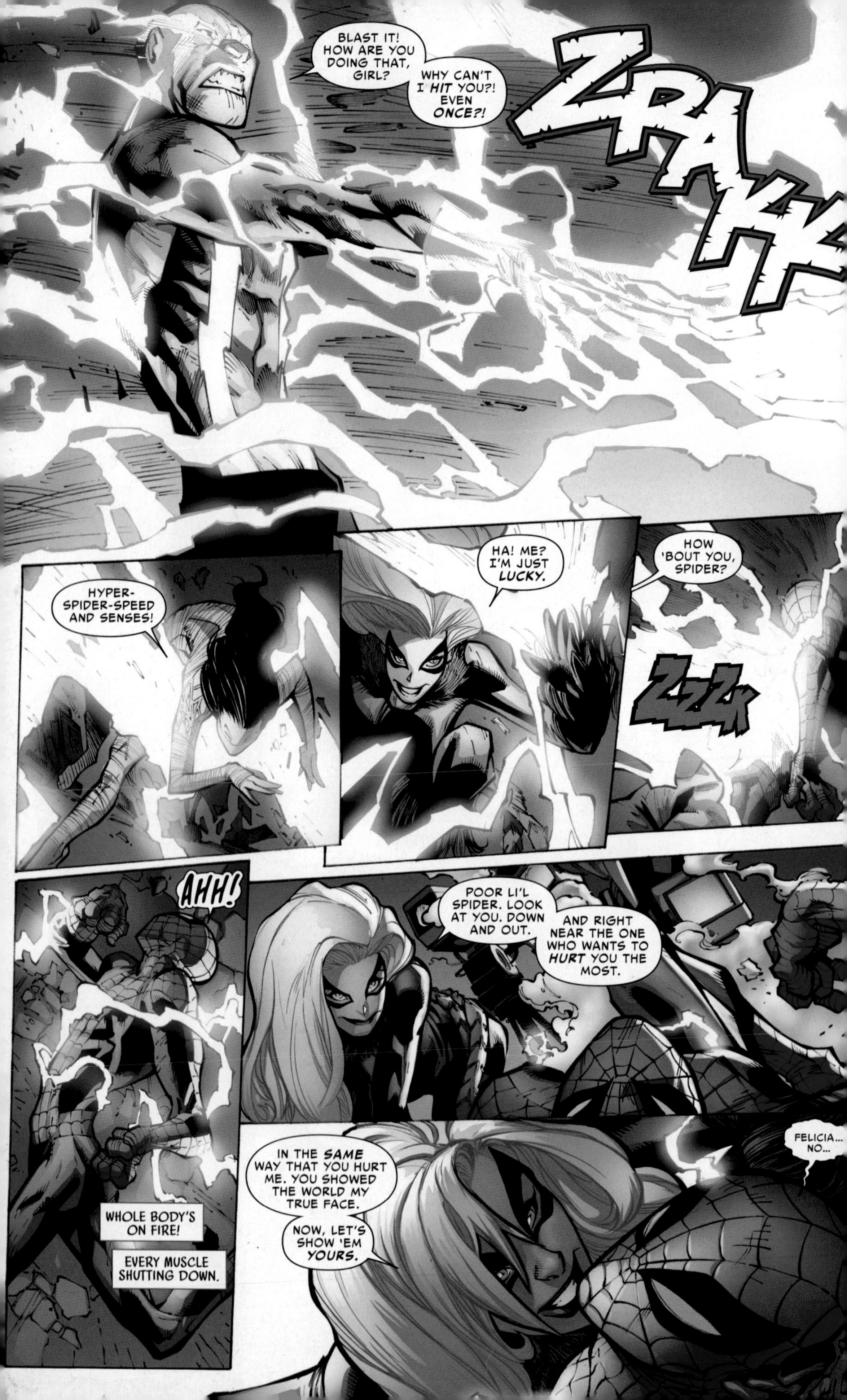

BLAST IT! HOW ARE YOU DOING THAT, GIRL?
WHY CAN'T I *HIT* YOU?! EVEN *ONCE?!*
ZRAKK
HYPER-SPIDER-SPEED AND SENSES!
HA! ME? I'M JUST *LUCKY.*
HOW 'BOUT YOU, SPIDER?
ZZZK
AHH!
POOR LI'L SPIDER. LOOK AT YOU. DOWN AND OUT.
AND RIGHT NEAR THE ONE WHO WANTS TO *HURT* YOU THE MOST.
WHOLE BODY'S ON FIRE!
EVERY MUSCLE SHUTTING DOWN.
IN THE *SAME* WAY THAT YOU HURT ME. YOU SHOWED THE WORLD MY TRUE FACE.
NOW, LET'S SHOW 'EM *YOURS.*
FELICIA... NO...

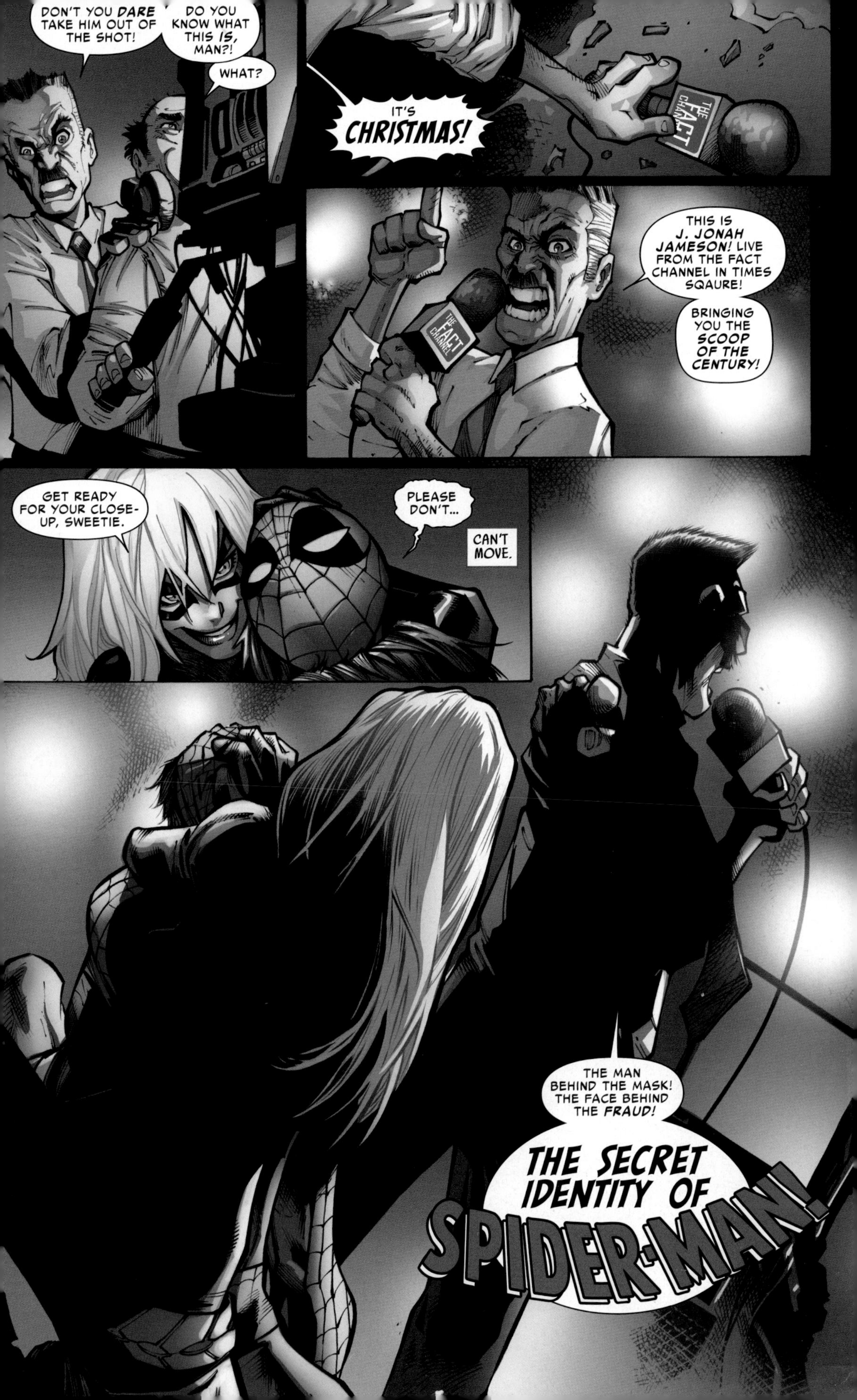
DON'T YOU DARE TAKE HIM OUT OF THE SHOT!
DO YOU KNOW WHAT THIS IS, MAN?!
WHAT?
IT'S CHRISTMAS!
THE FACT CHANNEL
THIS IS J. JONAH JAMESON! LIVE FROM THE FACT CHANNEL IN TIMES SQAURE!
BRINGING YOU THE SCOOP OF THE CENTURY!
THE FACT CHANNEL
GET READY FOR YOUR CLOSE-UP, SWEETIE.
PLEASE DON'T...
CAN'T MOVE.
THE MAN BEHIND THE MASK! THE FACE BEHIND THE FRAUD!
THE SECRET IDENTITY OF SPIDER-MAN!

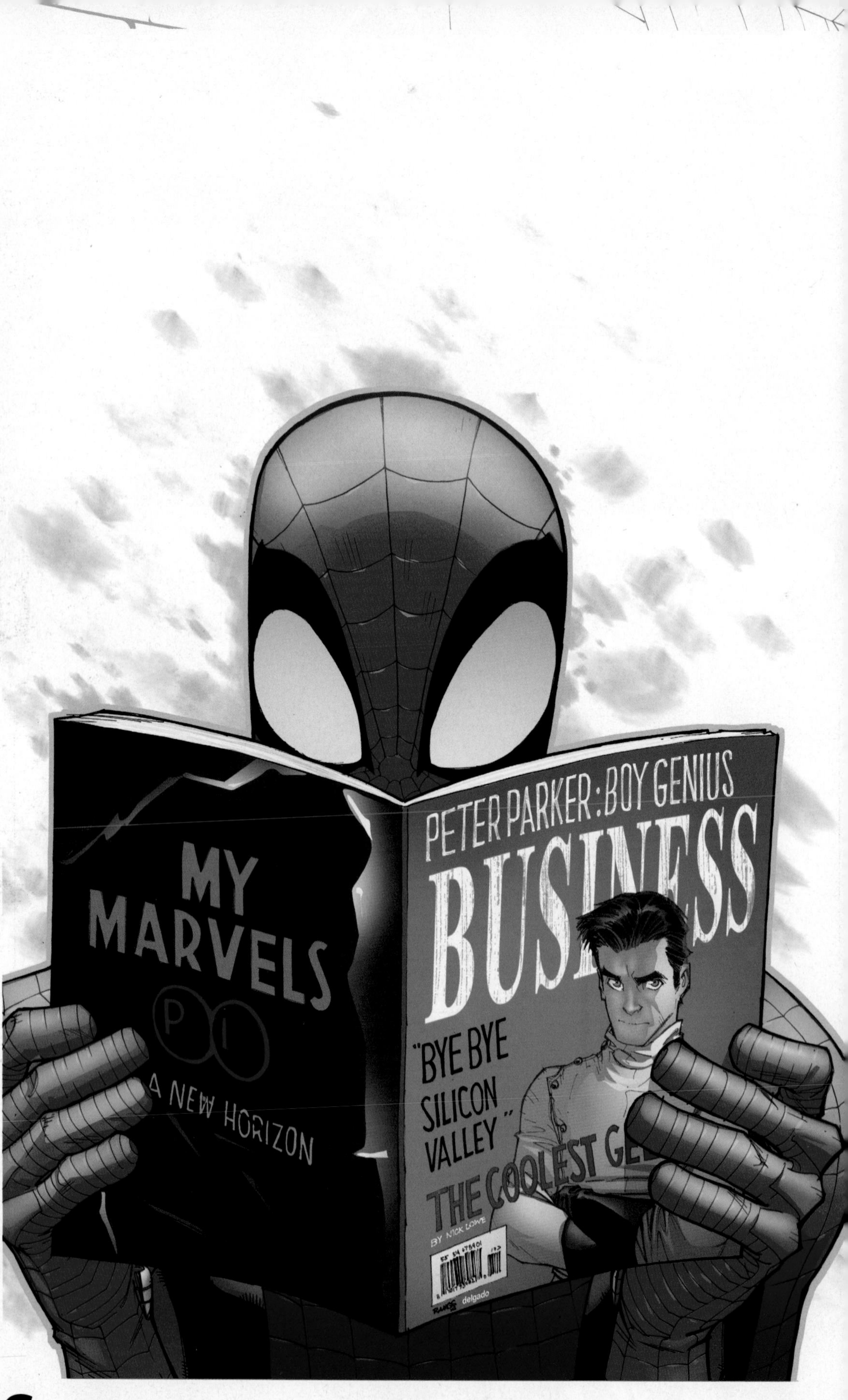

MY
MARVELS
PI
A NEW HORIZON
PETER PARKER : BOY GENIUS
BUSINESS
"BYE BYE
SILICON
VALLEY"
THE COOLEST GE
BY NICK LOWE
delgado

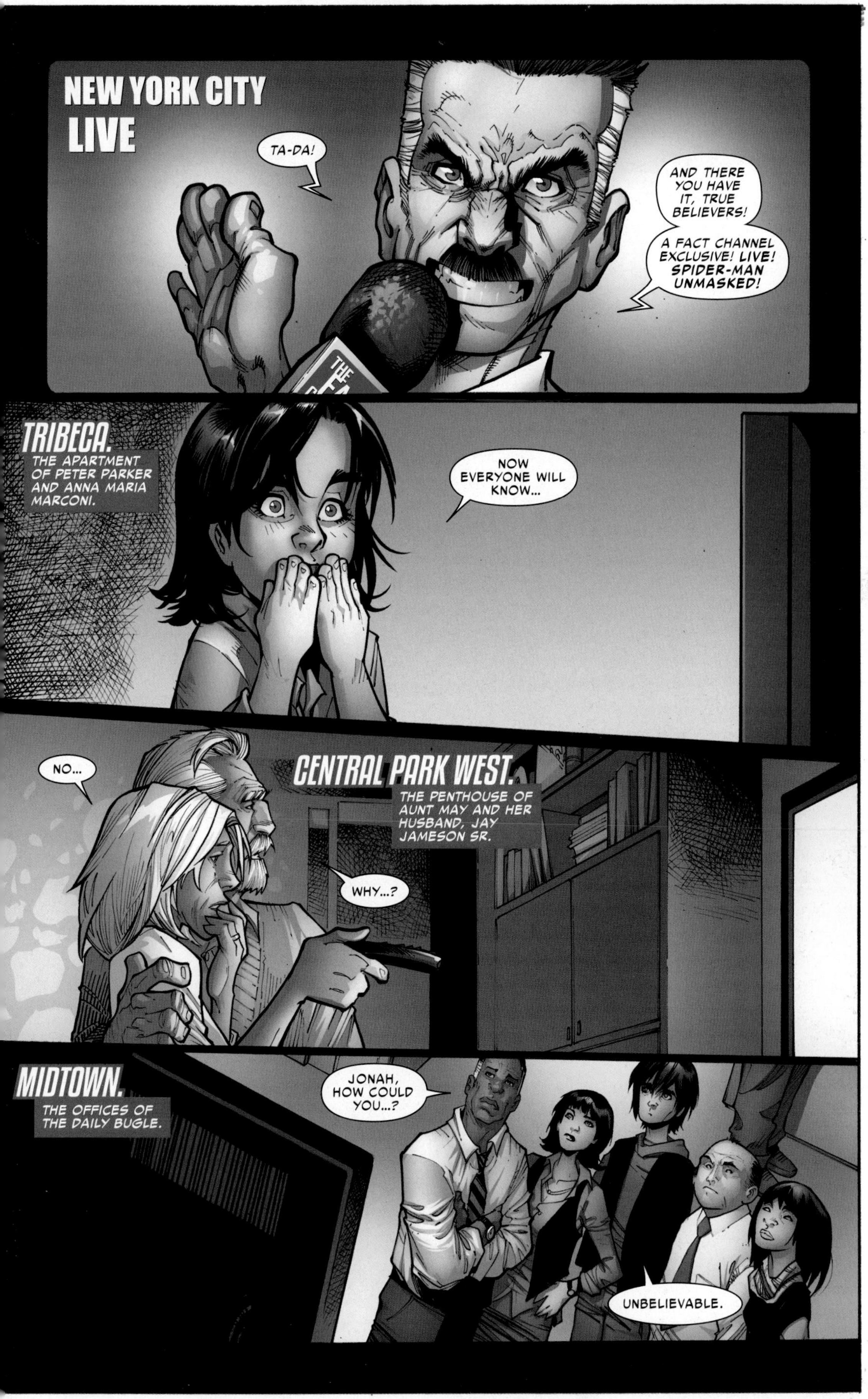

NEW YORK CITY
LIVE
TA-DA!
AND THERE YOU HAVE IT, TRUE BELIEVERS!
A FACT CHANNEL EXCLUSIVE! LIVE! SPIDER-MAN UNMASKED!
TRIBECA.
THE APARTMENT OF PETER PARKER AND ANNA MARIA MARCONI.
NOW EVERYONE WILL KNOW...
NO...
CENTRAL PARK WEST.
THE PENTHOUSE OF AUNT MAY AND HER HUSBAND, JAY JAMESON SR.
WHY...?
MIDTOWN.
THE OFFICES OF THE DAILY BUGLE.
JONAH, HOW COULD YOU...?
UNBELIEVABLE.

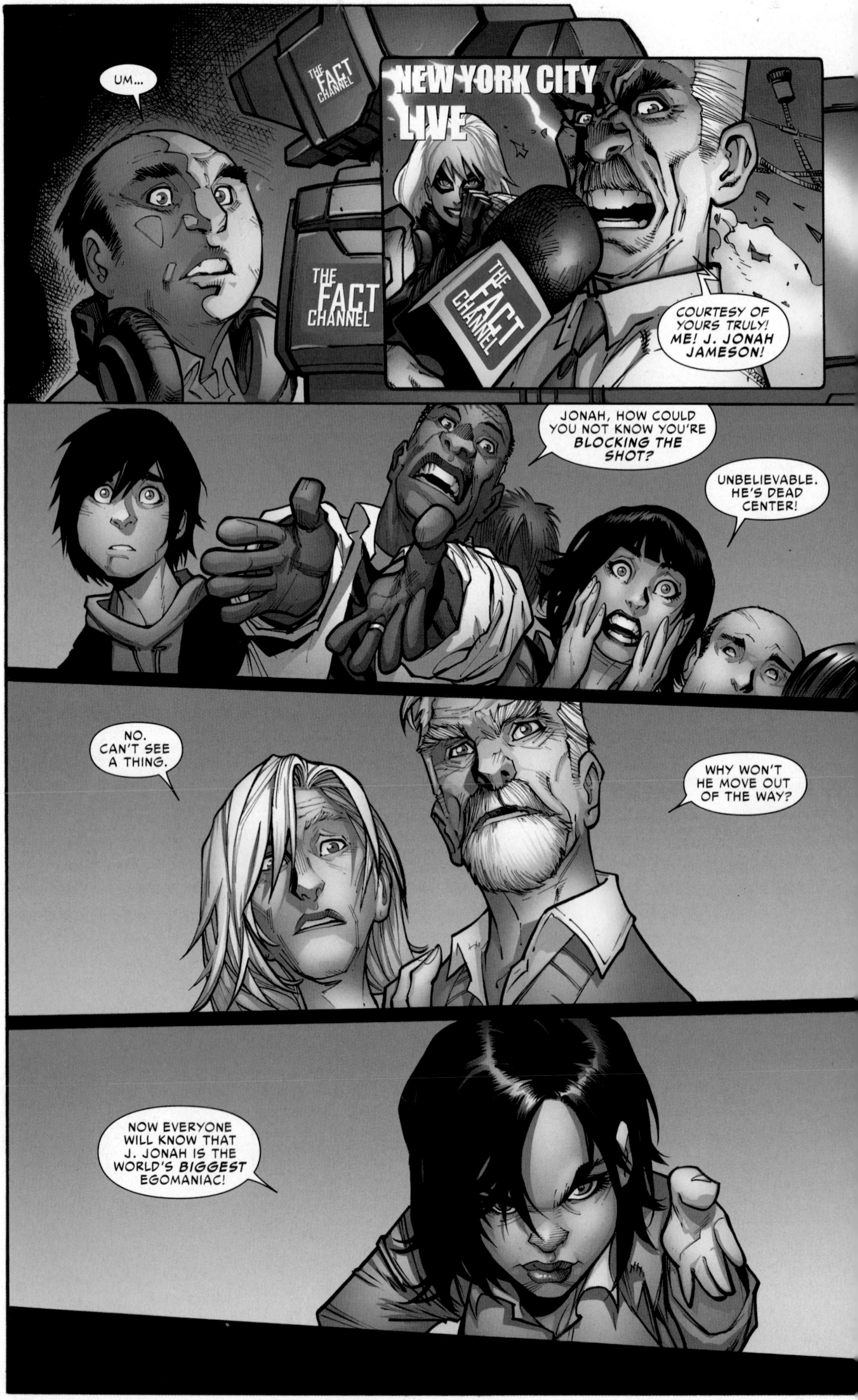
UM...
NEW YORK CITY
LIVE
THE FACT CHANNEL
THE FACT CHANNEL
THE FACT CHANNEL
COURTESY OF YOURS TRULY! ME! J. JONAH JAMESON!
JONAH, HOW COULD YOU NOT KNOW YOU'RE BLOCKING THE SHOT?
UNBELIEVABLE. HE'S DEAD CENTER!
NO. CAN'T SEE A THING.
WHY WON'T HE MOVE OUT OF THE WAY?
NOW EVERYONE WILL KNOW THAT J. JONAH IS THE WORLD'S BIGGEST EGOMANIAC!

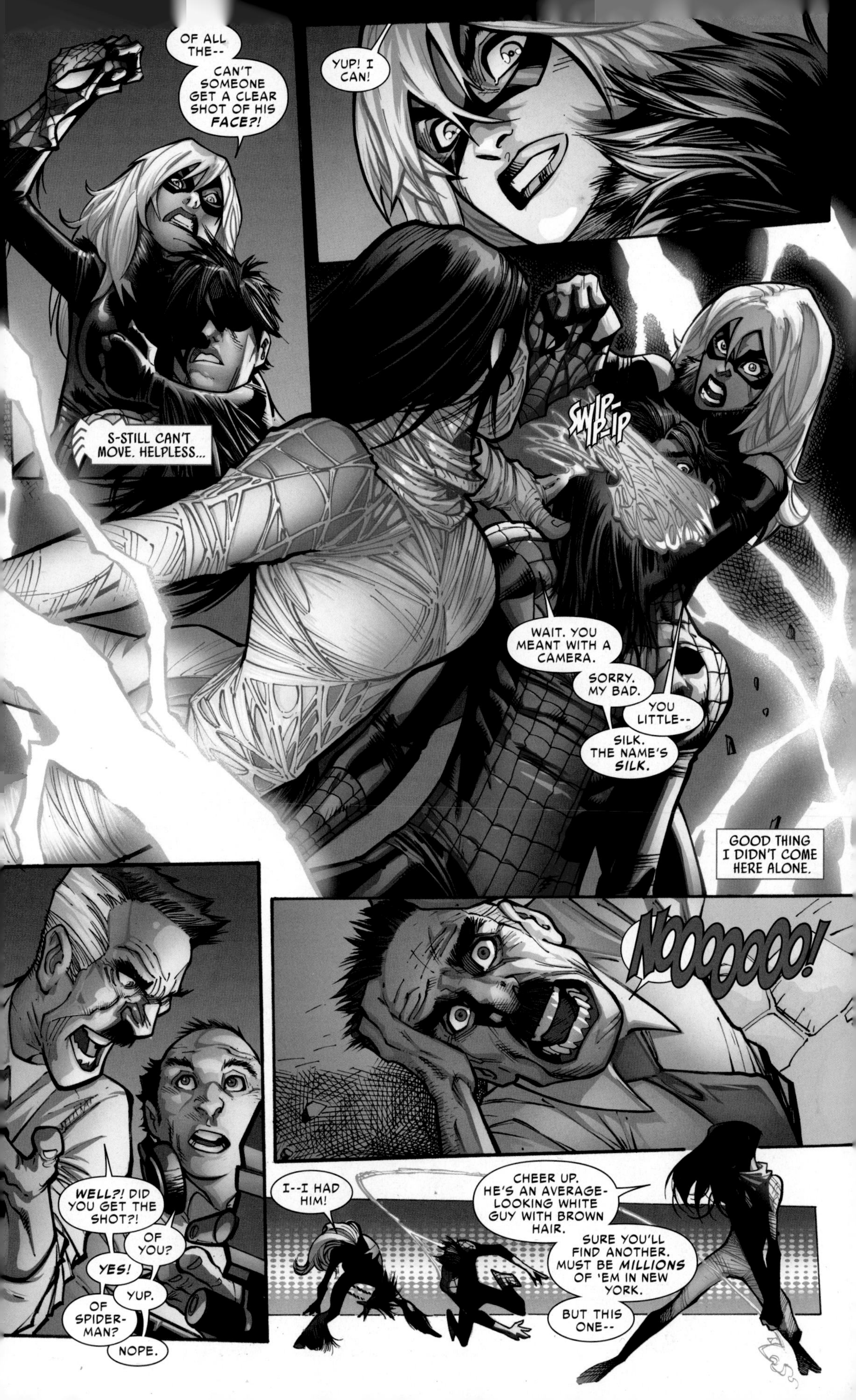
OF ALL THE--
CAN'T SOMEONE GET A CLEAR SHOT OF HIS FACE?!
YUP! I CAN!
S-STILL CAN'T MOVE. HELPLESS...
SWIP-IP-IP
WAIT. YOU MEANT WITH A CAMERA.
SORRY. MY BAD.
YOU LITTLE--
SILK. THE NAME'S SILK.
GOOD THING I DIDN'T COME HERE ALONE.
WELL?! DID YOU GET THE SHOT?!
OF YOU?
YES!
YUP.
OF SPIDER-MAN?
NOPE.
NOOOOOOO!
I--I HAD HIM!
CHEER UP. HE'S AN AVERAGE-LOOKING WHITE GUY WITH BROWN HAIR.
SURE YOU'LL FIND ANOTHER. MUST BE MILLIONS OF 'EM IN NEW YORK.
BUT THIS ONE--

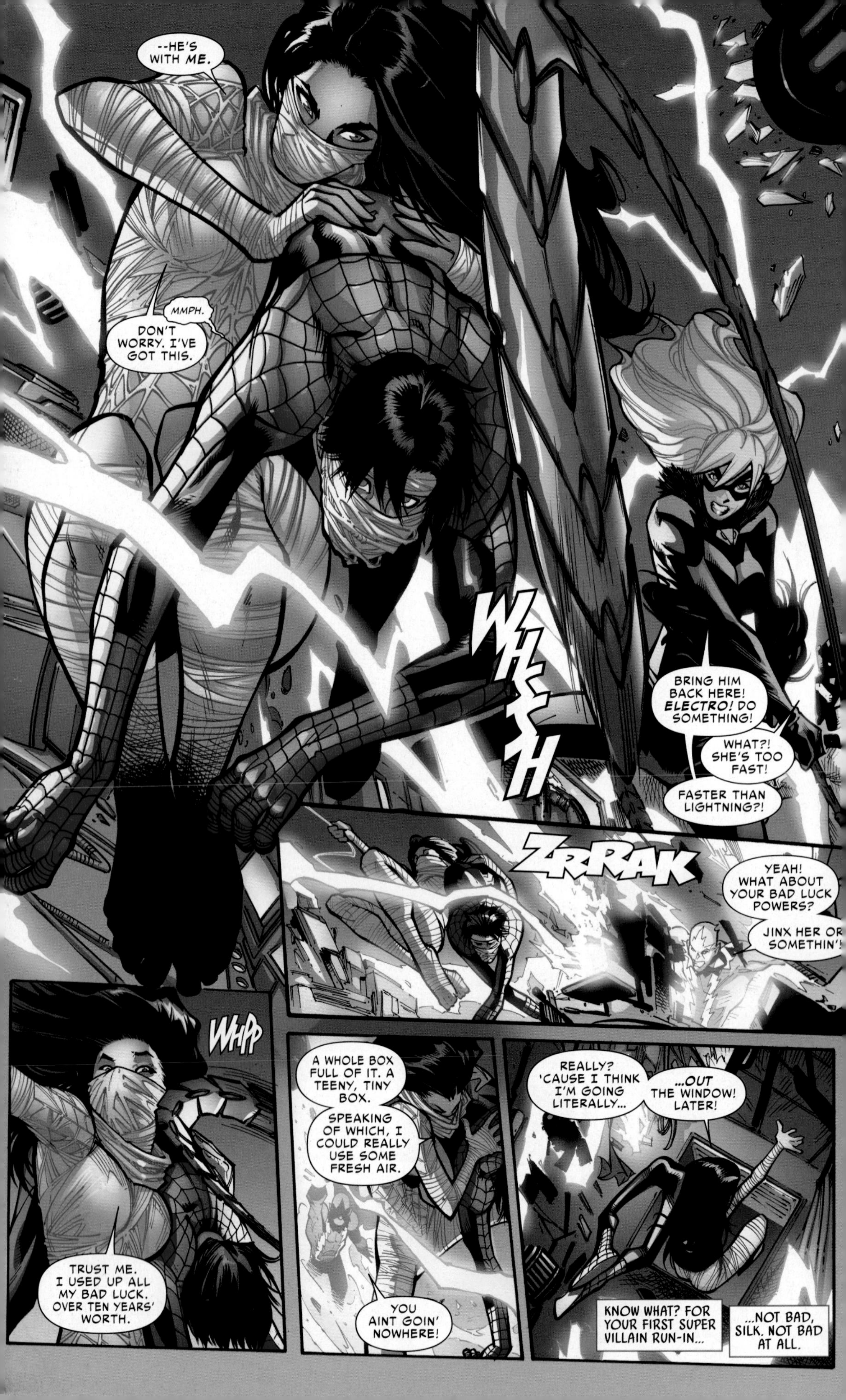

--HE'S WITH ME.
MMPH.
DON'T WORRY. I'VE GOT THIS.
WHSHH
BRING HIM BACK HERE! ELECTRO! DO SOMETHING!
WHAT?! SHE'S TOO FAST!
FASTER THAN LIGHTNING?!
ZRRAK
YEAH! WHAT ABOUT YOUR BAD LUCK POWERS?
JINX HER OR SOMETHIN'!
WHPP
TRUST ME. I USED UP ALL MY BAD LUCK. OVER TEN YEARS' WORTH.
A WHOLE BOX FULL OF IT. A TEENY, TINY BOX.
SPEAKING OF WHICH, I COULD REALLY USE SOME FRESH AIR.
YOU AINT GOIN' NOWHERE!
REALLY? 'CAUSE I THINK I'M GOING LITERALLY...
...OUT THE WINDOW! LATER!
KNOW WHAT? FOR YOUR FIRST SUPER VILLAIN RUN-IN...
...NOT BAD, SILK. NOT BAD AT ALL.

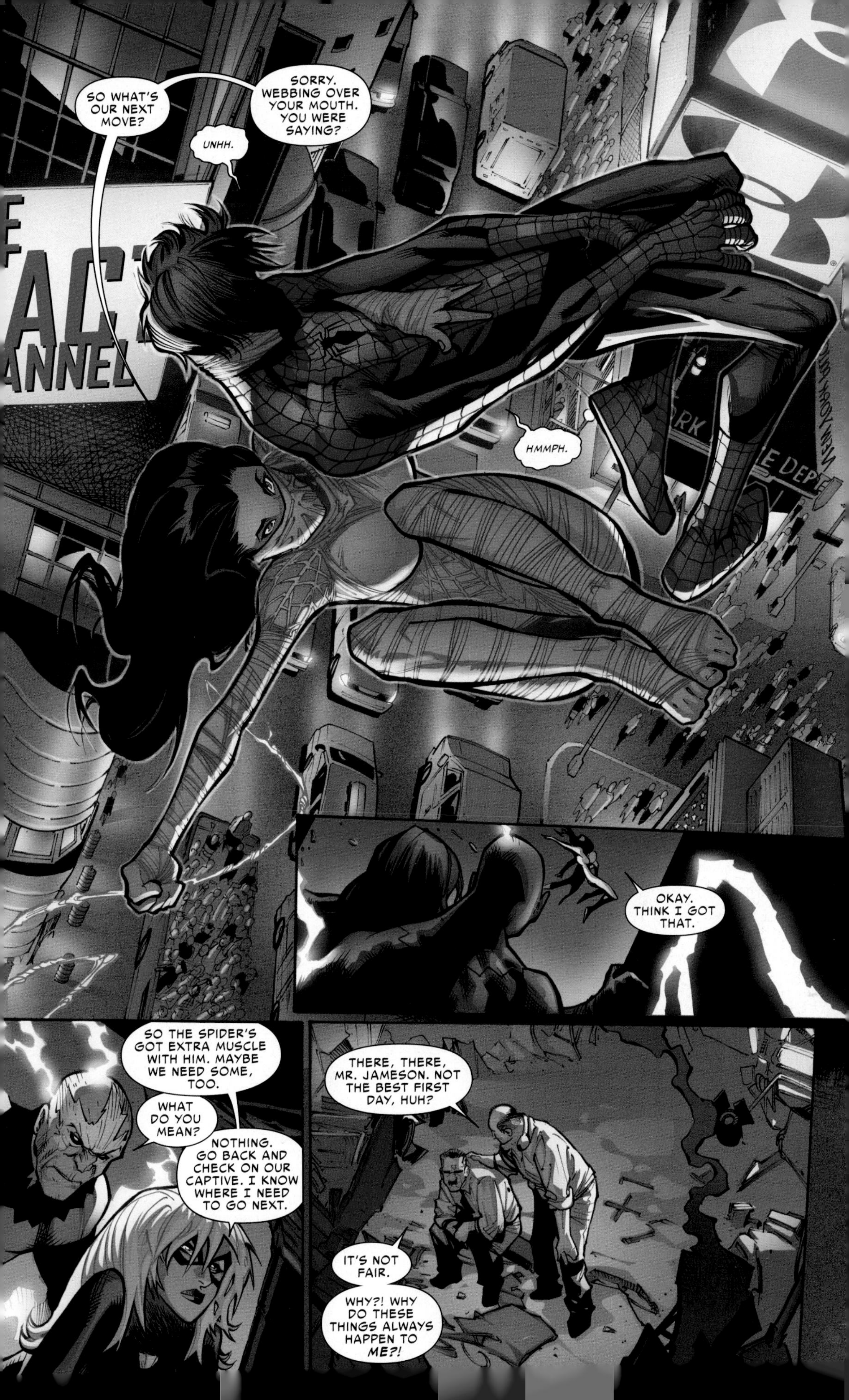
SO WHAT'S OUR NEXT MOVE?
UNHH.
SORRY. WEBBING OVER YOUR MOUTH. YOU WERE SAYING?
HMMPH.
OKAY. THINK I GOT THAT.
SO THE SPIDER'S GOT EXTRA MUSCLE WITH HIM. MAYBE WE NEED SOME, TOO.
WHAT DO YOU MEAN?
NOTHING. GO BACK AND CHECK ON OUR CAPTIVE. I KNOW WHERE I NEED TO GO NEXT.
THERE, THERE, MR. JAMESON. NOT THE BEST FIRST DAY, HUH?
IT'S NOT FAIR.
WHY?! WHY DO THESE THINGS ALWAYS HAPPEN TO ME?!

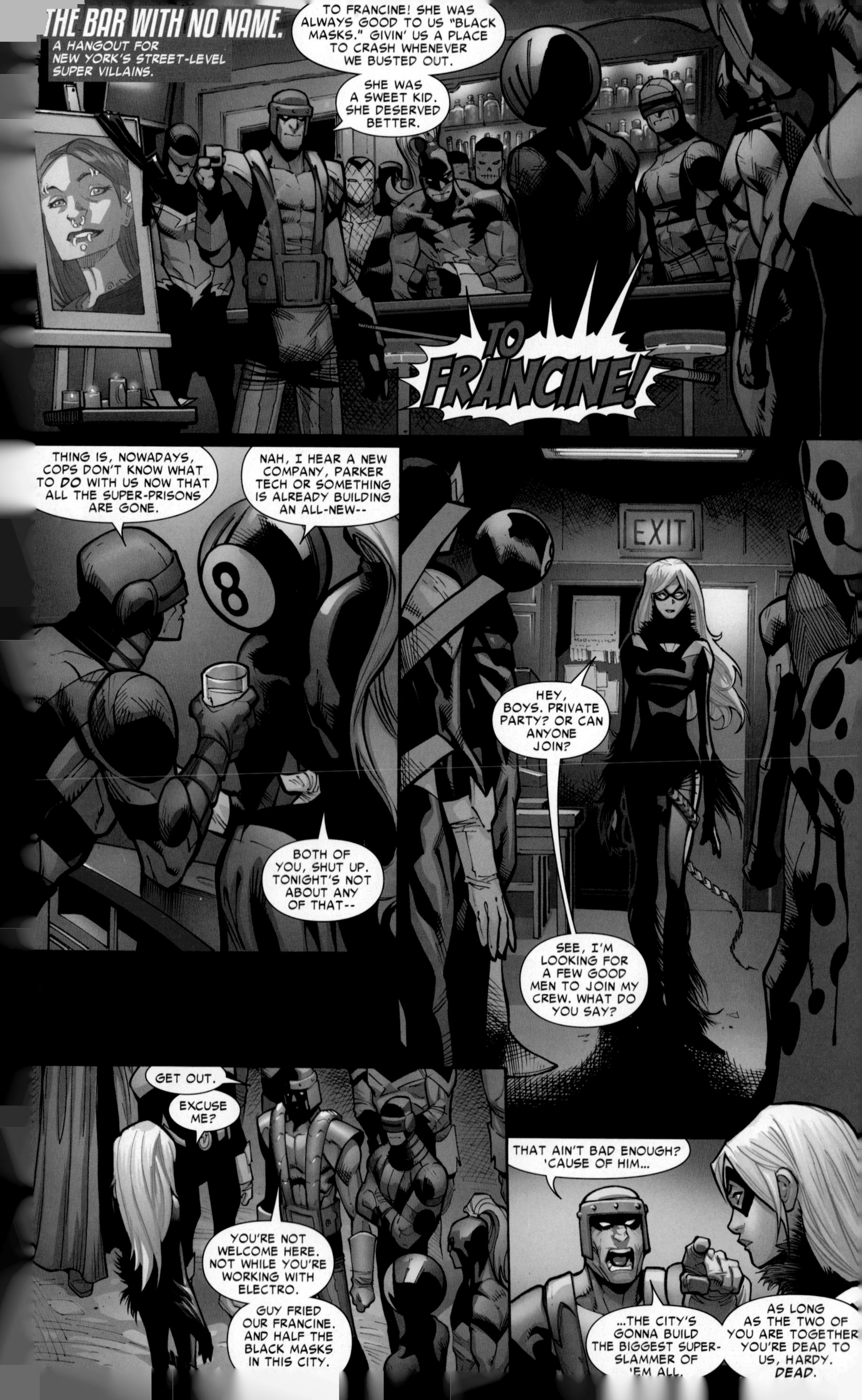
THE BAR WITH NO NAME.
A HANGOUT FOR NEW YORK'S STREET-LEVEL SUPER VILLAINS.
TO FRANCINE! SHE WAS ALWAYS GOOD TO US "BLACK MASKS." GIVIN' US A PLACE TO CRASH WHENEVER WE BUSTED OUT.
SHE WAS A SWEET KID. SHE DESERVED BETTER.
TO FRANCINE!
THING IS, NOWADAYS, COPS DON'T KNOW WHAT TO DO WITH US NOW THAT ALL THE SUPER-PRISONS ARE GONE.
NAH, I HEAR A NEW COMPANY, PARKER TECH OR SOMETHING IS ALREADY BUILDING AN ALL-NEW--
BOTH OF YOU, SHUT UP. TONIGHT'S NOT ABOUT ANY OF THAT--
EXIT
HEY, BOYS. PRIVATE PARTY? OR CAN ANYONE JOIN?
SEE, I'M LOOKING FOR A FEW GOOD MEN TO JOIN MY CREW. WHAT DO YOU SAY?
GET OUT.
EXCUSE ME?
YOU'RE NOT WELCOME HERE. NOT WHILE YOU'RE WORKING WITH ELECTRO.
GUY FRIED OUR FRANCINE. AND HALF THE BLACK MASKS IN THIS CITY.
THAT AIN'T BAD ENOUGH? 'CAUSE OF HIM...
...THE CITY'S GONNA BUILD THE BIGGEST SUPER-SLAMMER OF 'EM ALL.
AS LONG AS THE TWO OF YOU ARE TOGETHER YOU'RE DEAD TO US, HARDY. DEAD.

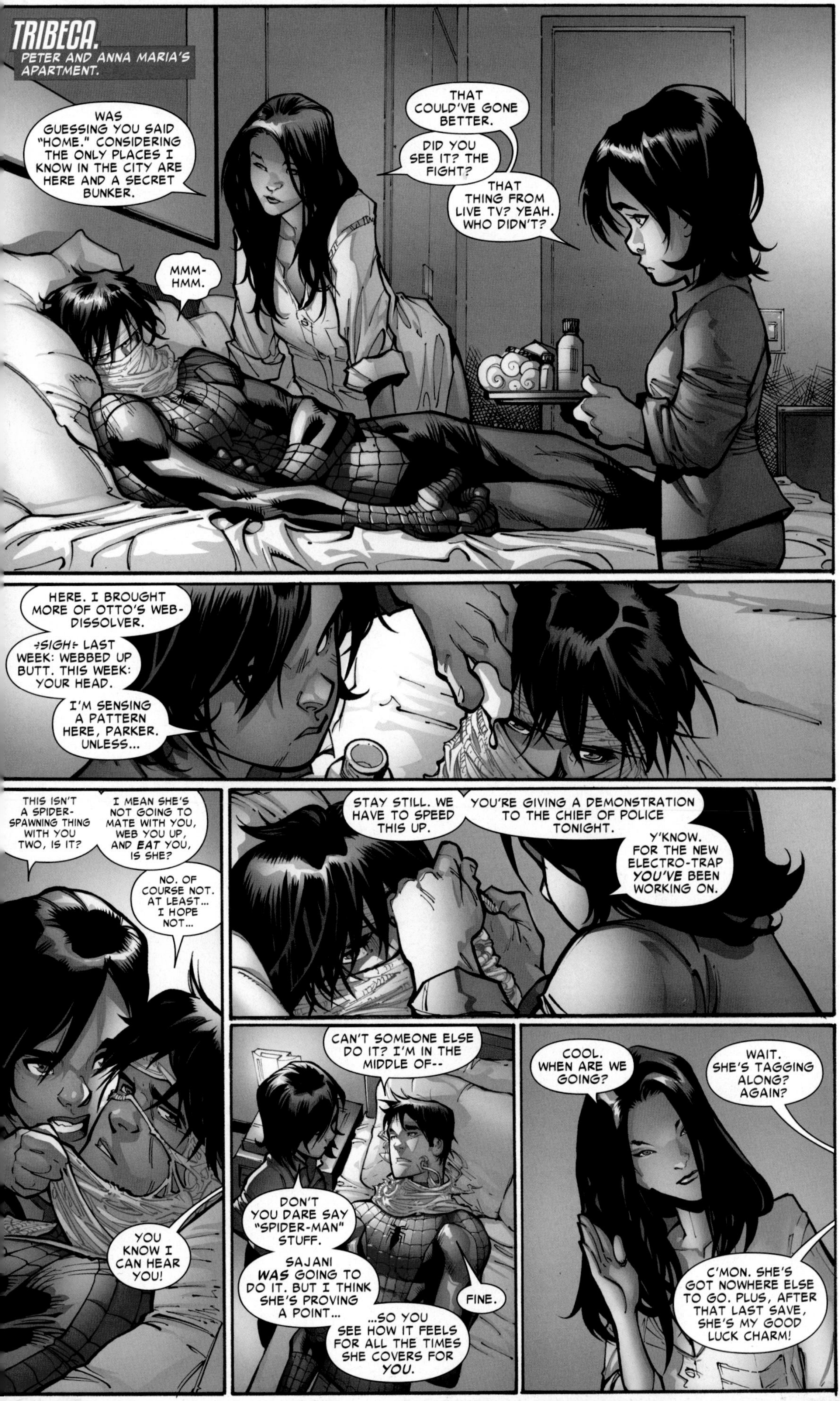
TRIBECA.
PETER AND ANNA MARIA'S APARTMENT.
WAS GUESSING YOU SAID "HOME." CONSIDERING THE ONLY PLACES I KNOW IN THE CITY ARE HERE AND A SECRET BUNKER.
MMM-HMM.
THAT COULD'VE GONE BETTER.
DID YOU SEE IT? THE FIGHT?
THAT THING FROM LIVE TV? YEAH. WHO DIDN'T?
HERE. I BROUGHT MORE OF OTTO'S WEB-DISSOLVER.
SIGH LAST WEEK: WEBBED UP BUTT. THIS WEEK: YOUR HEAD.
I'M SENSING A PATTERN HERE, PARKER. UNLESS...
THIS ISN'T A SPIDER-SPAWNING THING WITH YOU TWO, IS IT?
I MEAN SHE'S NOT GOING TO MATE WITH YOU, WEB YOU UP, AND EAT YOU, IS SHE?
NO. OF COURSE NOT. AT LEAST... I HOPE NOT...
YOU KNOW I CAN HEAR YOU!
STAY STILL. WE HAVE TO SPEED THIS UP.
YOU'RE GIVING A DEMONSTRATION TO THE CHIEF OF POLICE TONIGHT.
Y'KNOW. FOR THE NEW ELECTRO-TRAP YOU'VE BEEN WORKING ON.
CAN'T SOMEONE ELSE DO IT? I'M IN THE MIDDLE OF--
DON'T YOU DARE SAY "SPIDER-MAN" STUFF.
SAJANI WAS GOING TO DO IT. BUT I THINK SHE'S PROVING A POINT...
...SO YOU SEE HOW IT FEELS FOR ALL THE TIMES SHE COVERS FOR YOU.
FINE.
COOL. WHEN ARE WE GOING?
WAIT. SHE'S TAGGING ALONG? AGAIN?
C'MON. SHE'S GOT NOWHERE ELSE TO GO. PLUS, AFTER THAT LAST SAVE, SHE'S MY GOOD LUCK CHARM!

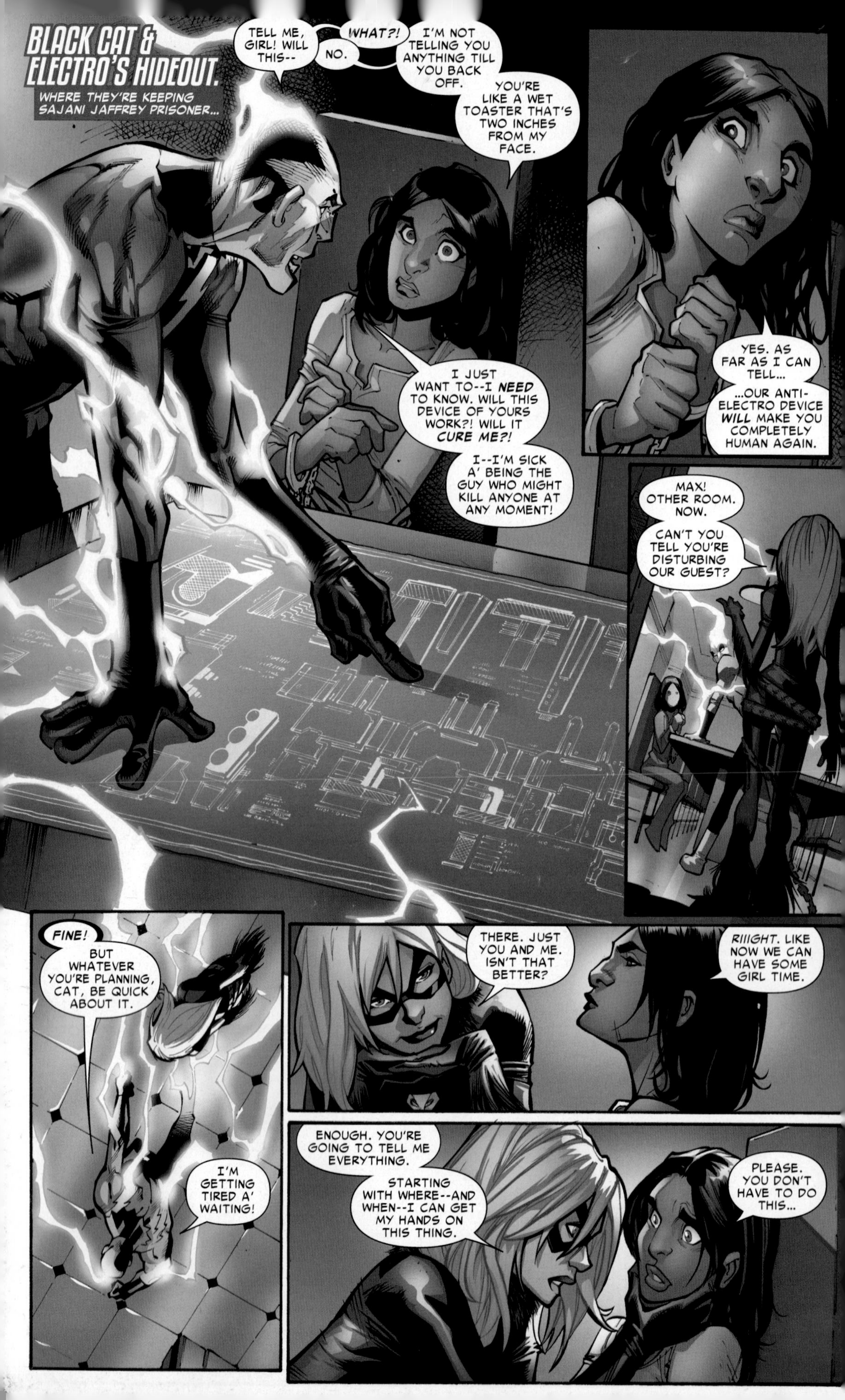
BLACK CAT & ELECTRO'S HIDEOUT.
WHERE THEY'RE KEEPING SAJANI JAFFREY PRISONER...
TELL ME, GIRL! WILL THIS--
NO.
WHAT?!
I'M NOT TELLING YOU ANYTHING TILL YOU BACK OFF.
YOU'RE LIKE A WET TOASTER THAT'S TWO INCHES FROM MY FACE.
I JUST WANT TO--I NEED TO KNOW. WILL THIS DEVICE OF YOURS WORK?! WILL IT CURE ME?!
I--I'M SICK A' BEING THE GUY WHO MIGHT KILL ANYONE AT ANY MOMENT!
YES. AS FAR AS I CAN TELL...
...OUR ANTI-ELECTRO DEVICE WILL MAKE YOU COMPLETELY HUMAN AGAIN.
MAX! OTHER ROOM. NOW.
CAN'T YOU TELL YOU'RE DISTURBING OUR GUEST?
FINE! BUT WHATEVER YOU'RE PLANNING, CAT, BE QUICK ABOUT IT.
I'M GETTING TIRED A' WAITING!
THERE. JUST YOU AND ME. ISN'T THAT BETTER?
RIIIGHT. LIKE NOW WE CAN HAVE SOME GIRL TIME.
ENOUGH. YOU'RE GOING TO TELL ME EVERYTHING.
STARTING WITH WHERE--AND WHEN--I CAN GET MY HANDS ON THIS THING.
PLEASE. YOU DON'T HAVE TO DO THIS...

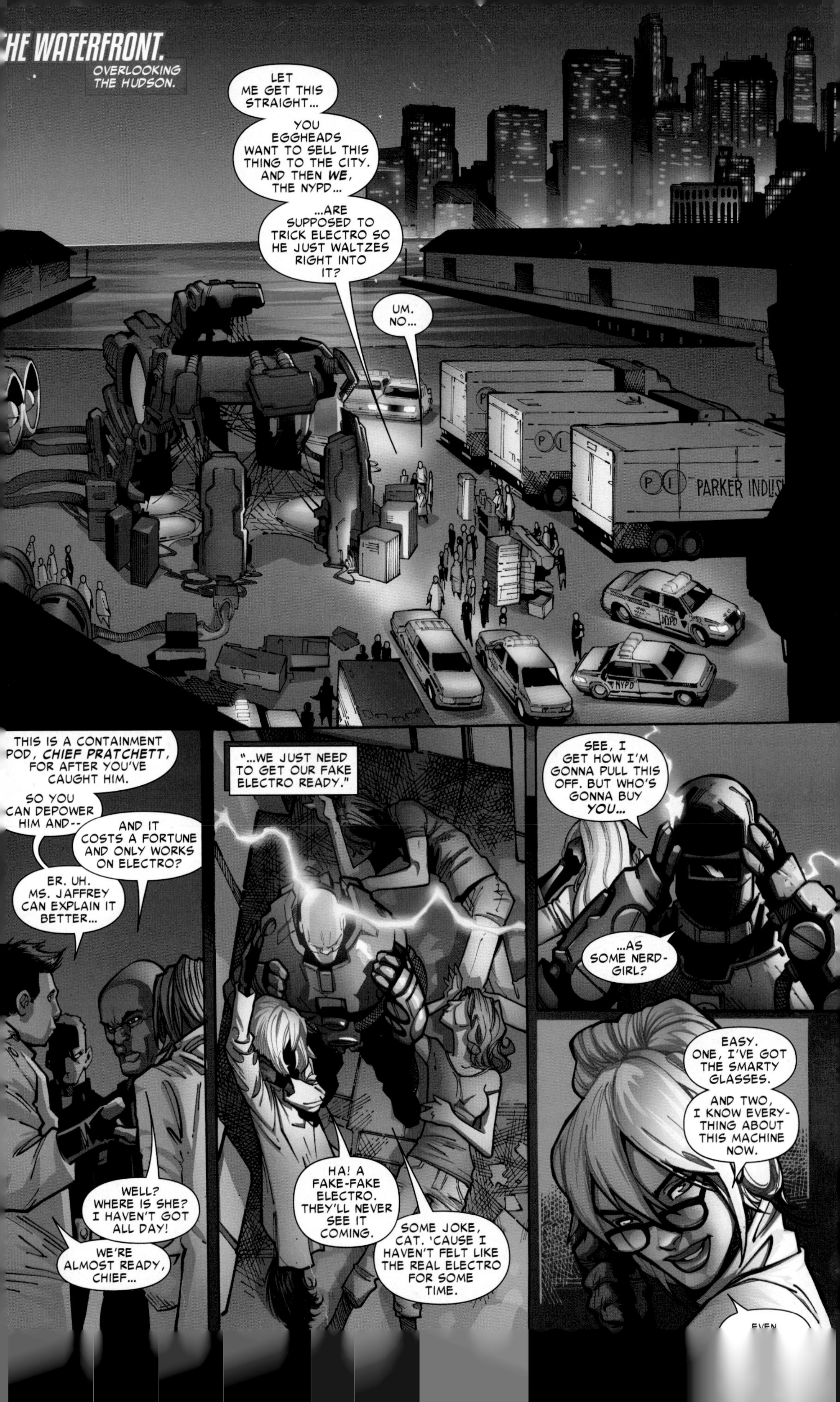

THE WATERFRONT.
OVERLOOKING THE HUDSON.
LET ME GET THIS STRAIGHT...
YOU EGGHEADS WANT TO SELL THIS THING TO THE CITY. AND THEN WE, THE NYPD...
...ARE SUPPOSED TO TRICK ELECTRO SO HE JUST WALTZES RIGHT INTO IT?
UM. NO...
PARKER INDUS
NYPD
THIS IS A CONTAINMENT POD, CHIEF PRATCHETT, FOR AFTER YOU'VE CAUGHT HIM.
SO YOU CAN DEPOWER HIM AND--
AND IT COSTS A FORTUNE AND ONLY WORKS ON ELECTRO?
ER. UH. MS. JAFFREY CAN EXPLAIN IT BETTER...
WELL? WHERE IS SHE? I HAVEN'T GOT ALL DAY!
WE'RE ALMOST READY, CHIEF...
"...WE JUST NEED TO GET OUR FAKE ELECTRO READY."
HA! A FAKE-FAKE ELECTRO. THEY'LL NEVER SEE IT COMING.
SOME JOKE, CAT. 'CAUSE I HAVEN'T FELT LIKE THE REAL ELECTRO FOR SOME TIME.
SEE, I GET HOW I'M GONNA PULL THIS OFF. BUT WHO'S GONNA BUY YOU...
...AS SOME NERD-GIRL?
EASY. ONE, I'VE GOT THE SMARTY GLASSES.
AND TWO, I KNOW EVERYTHING ABOUT THIS MACHINE NOW.
EVEN

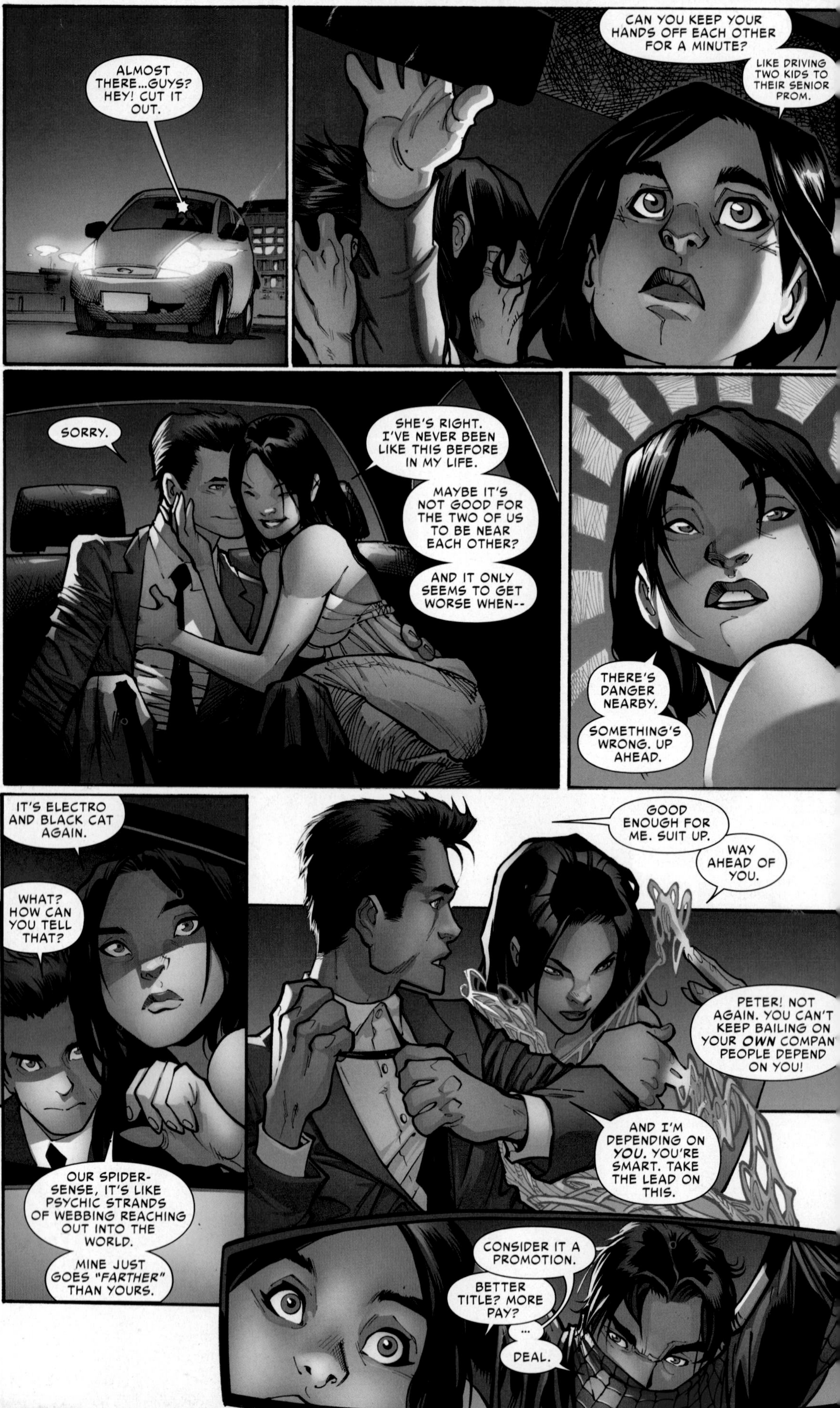

ALMOST THERE...GUYS? HEY! CUT IT OUT.
CAN YOU KEEP YOUR HANDS OFF EACH OTHER FOR A MINUTE?
LIKE DRIVING TWO KIDS TO THEIR SENIOR PROM.
SORRY.
SHE'S RIGHT. I'VE NEVER BEEN LIKE THIS BEFORE IN MY LIFE.
MAYBE IT'S NOT GOOD FOR THE TWO OF US TO BE NEAR EACH OTHER?
AND IT ONLY SEEMS TO GET WORSE WHEN--
THERE'S DANGER NEARBY.
SOMETHING'S WRONG. UP AHEAD.
IT'S ELECTRO AND BLACK CAT AGAIN.
WHAT? HOW CAN YOU TELL THAT?
OUR SPIDER-SENSE, IT'S LIKE PSYCHIC STRANDS OF WEBBING REACHING OUT INTO THE WORLD.
MINE JUST GOES "FARTHER" THAN YOURS.
GOOD ENOUGH FOR ME. SUIT UP.
WAY AHEAD OF YOU.
PETER! NOT AGAIN. YOU CAN'T KEEP BAILING ON YOUR OWN COMPAN PEOPLE DEPEND ON YOU!
AND I'M DEPENDING ON YOU. YOU'RE SMART. TAKE THE LEAD ON THIS.
CONSIDER IT A PROMOTION.
BETTER TITLE? MORE PAY?
...
DEAL.

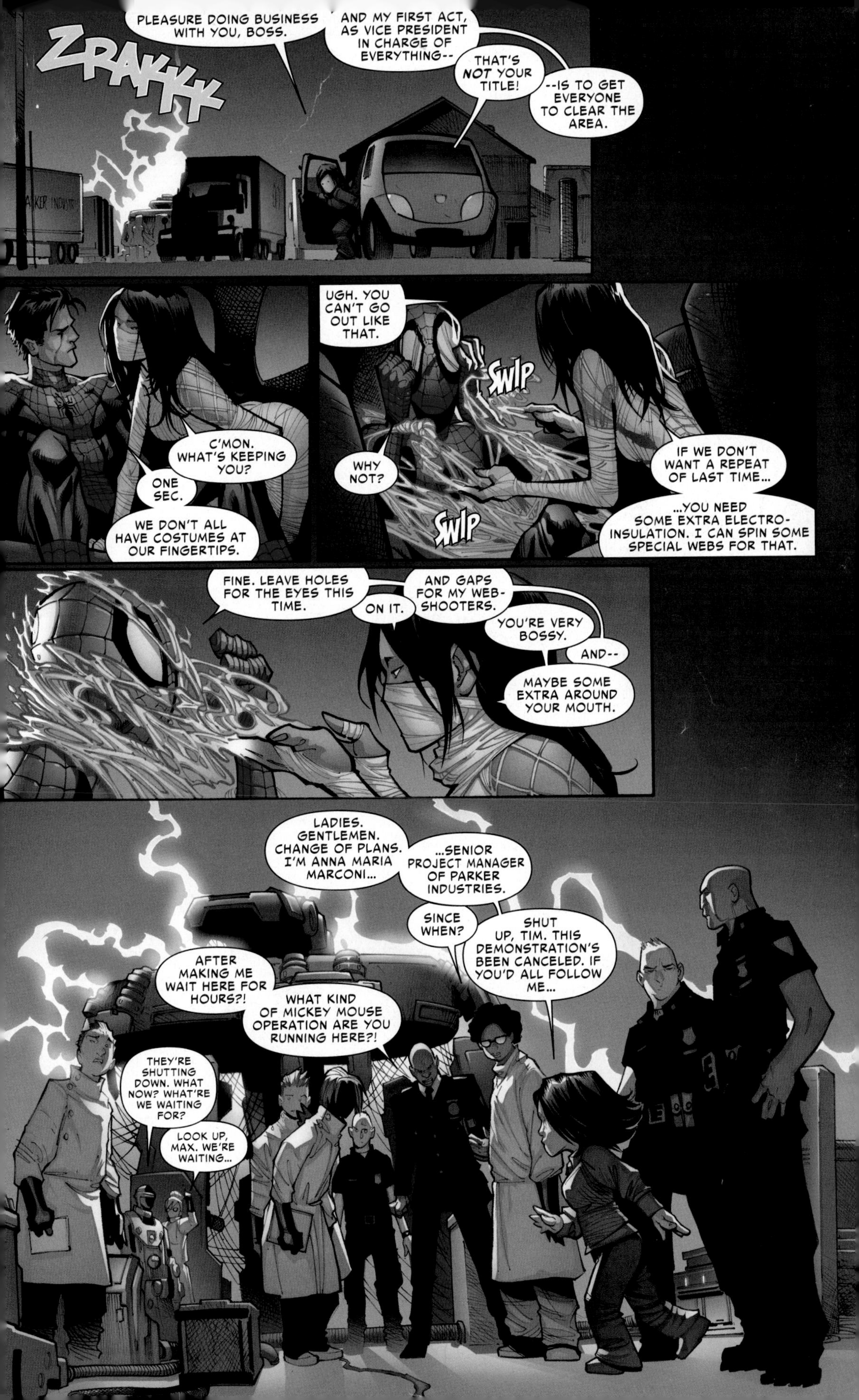

ZRAKKK
PLEASURE DOING BUSINESS WITH YOU, BOSS.
AND MY FIRST ACT, AS VICE PRESIDENT IN CHARGE OF EVERYTHING--
THAT'S NOT YOUR TITLE!
--IS TO GET EVERYONE TO CLEAR THE AREA.
C'MON. WHAT'S KEEPING YOU?
ONE SEC.
WE DON'T ALL HAVE COSTUMES AT OUR FINGERTIPS.
UGH. YOU CAN'T GO OUT LIKE THAT.
SWIP
WHY NOT?
SWIP
IF WE DON'T WANT A REPEAT OF LAST TIME...
...YOU NEED SOME EXTRA ELECTRO-INSULATION. I CAN SPIN SOME SPECIAL WEBS FOR THAT.
FINE. LEAVE HOLES FOR THE EYES THIS TIME.
ON IT.
AND GAPS FOR MY WEB-SHOOTERS.
YOU'RE VERY BOSSY.
AND--
MAYBE SOME EXTRA AROUND YOUR MOUTH.
LADIES. GENTLEMEN. CHANGE OF PLANS. I'M ANNA MARIA MARCONI...
...SENIOR PROJECT MANAGER OF PARKER INDUSTRIES.
SINCE WHEN?
SHUT UP, TIM. THIS DEMONSTRATION'S BEEN CANCELED. IF YOU'D ALL FOLLOW ME...
AFTER MAKING ME WAIT HERE FOR HOURS?!
WHAT KIND OF MICKEY MOUSE OPERATION ARE YOU RUNNING HERE?!
THEY'RE SHUTTING DOWN. WHAT NOW? WHAT'RE WE WAITING FOR?
LOOK UP, MAX. WE'RE WAITING...

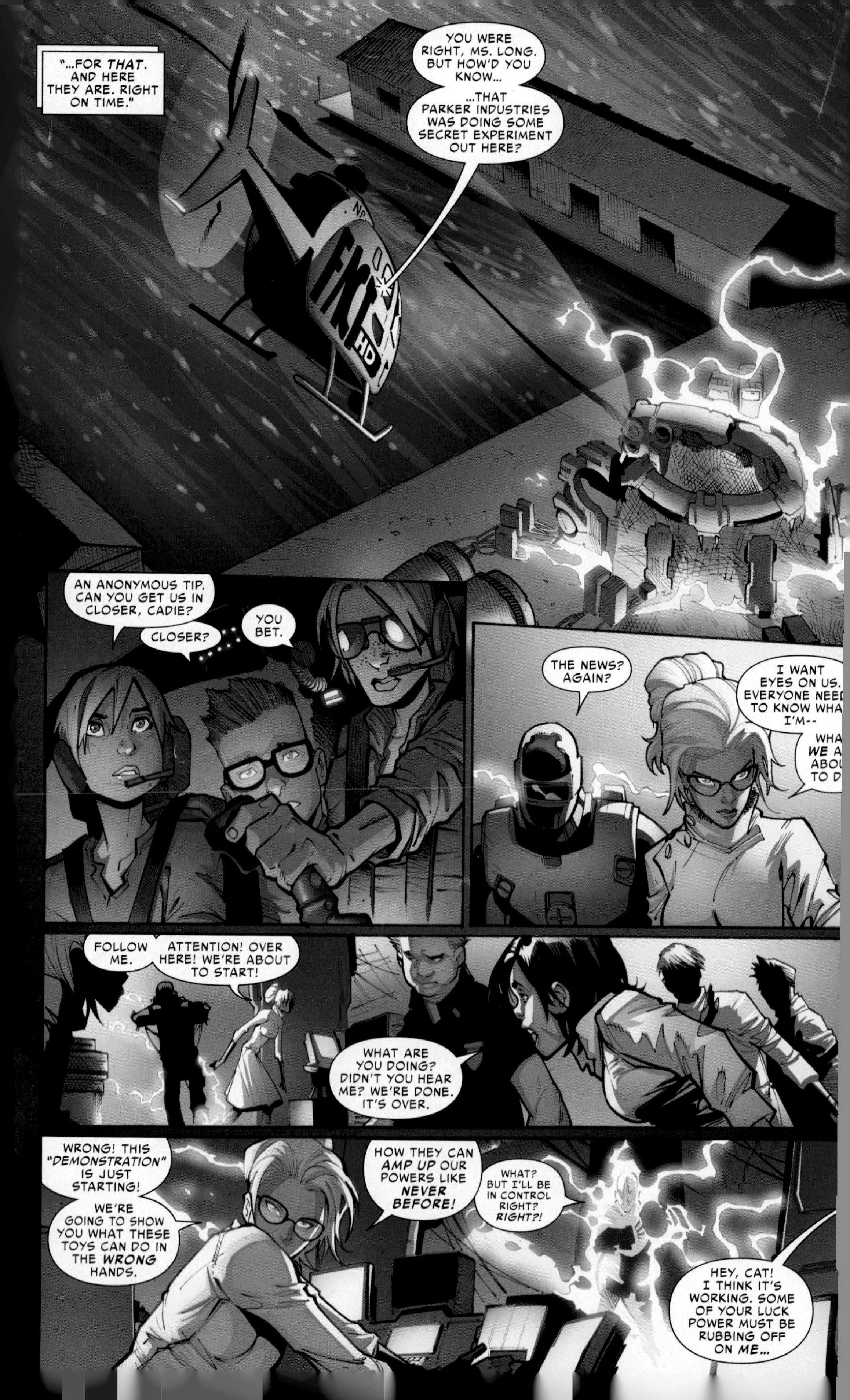
"...FOR *THAT*. AND HERE THEY ARE. RIGHT ON TIME."
YOU WERE RIGHT, MS. LONG. BUT HOW'D YOU KNOW...
...THAT PARKER INDUSTRIES WAS DOING SOME SECRET EXPERIMENT OUT HERE?
AN ANONYMOUS TIP. CAN YOU GET US IN CLOSER, CADIE?
CLOSER?
YOU BET.
THE NEWS? AGAIN?
I WANT EYES ON US. EVERYONE NEED TO KNOW WHA I'M--
WHA *WE* A ABOU TO D
FOLLOW ME.
ATTENTION! OVER HERE! WE'RE ABOUT TO START!
WHAT ARE YOU DOING? DIDN'T YOU HEAR ME? WE'RE DONE. IT'S OVER.
WRONG! THIS "*DEMONSTRATION*" IS JUST STARTING!
WE'RE GOING TO SHOW YOU WHAT THESE TOYS CAN DO IN THE *WRONG* HANDS.
HOW THEY CAN *AMP UP* OUR POWERS LIKE *NEVER BEFORE*!
WHAT? BUT I'LL BE IN CONTROL RIGHT? *RIGHT?!*
HEY, CAT! I THINK IT'S WORKING. SOME OF YOUR LUCK POWER MUST BE RUBBING OFF ON *ME*...

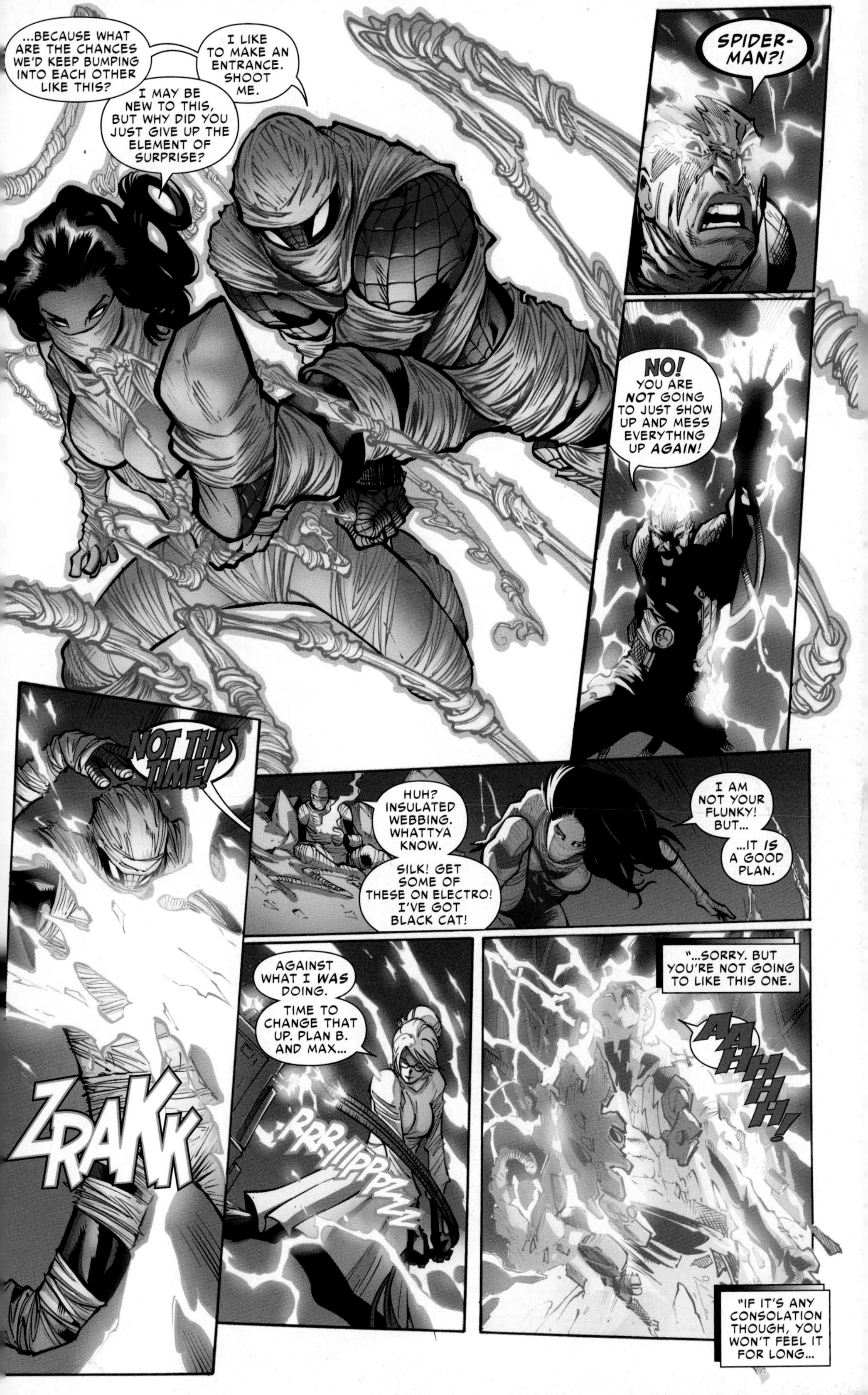
...BECAUSE WHAT ARE THE CHANCES WE'D KEEP BUMPING INTO EACH OTHER LIKE THIS?
I LIKE TO MAKE AN ENTRANCE. SHOOT ME.
I MAY BE NEW TO THIS, BUT WHY DID YOU JUST GIVE UP THE ELEMENT OF SURPRISE?
SPIDER-MAN?!
NO! YOU ARE NOT GOING TO JUST SHOW UP AND MESS EVERYTHING UP AGAIN!
NOT THIS TIME!
ZRAKK
HUH? INSULATED WEBBING. WHATTYA KNOW.
SILK! GET SOME OF THESE ON ELECTRO! I'VE GOT BLACK CAT!
I AM NOT YOUR FLUNKY! BUT...
...IT IS A GOOD PLAN.
AGAINST WHAT I WAS DOING.
TIME TO CHANGE THAT UP. PLAN B. AND MAX...
RRRIIIPPPZZZ
"...SORRY. BUT YOU'RE NOT GOING TO LIKE THIS ONE.
AAHHHH!
"IF IT'S ANY CONSOLATION THOUGH, YOU WON'T FEEL IT FOR LONG...

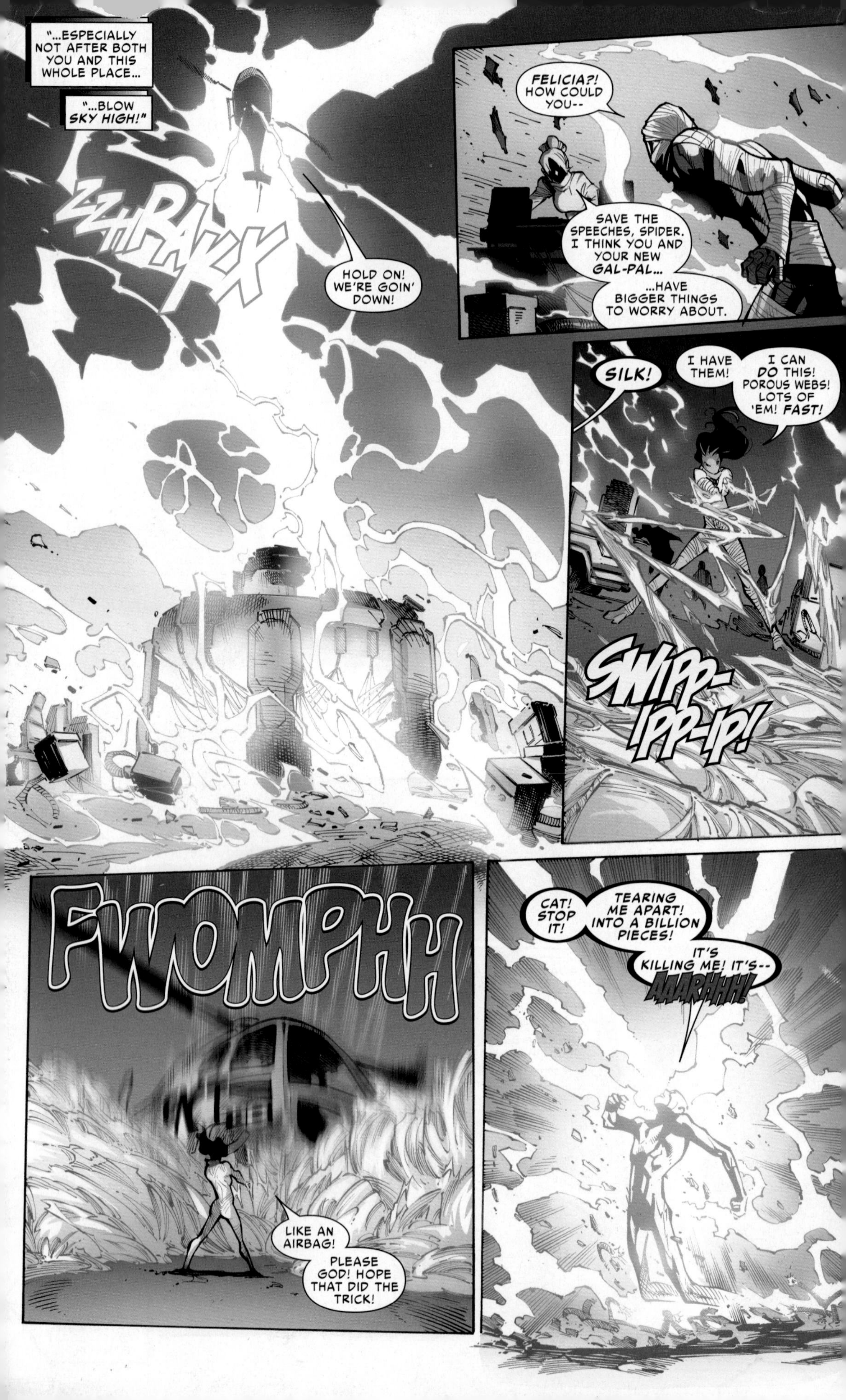
"...ESPECIALLY NOT AFTER BOTH YOU AND THIS WHOLE PLACE...
"...BLOW SKY HIGH!"
ZZHRAKK
HOLD ON! WE'RE GOIN' DOWN!
FELICIA?! HOW COULD YOU--
SAVE THE SPEECHES, SPIDER. I THINK YOU AND YOUR NEW GAL-PAL...
...HAVE BIGGER THINGS TO WORRY ABOUT.
SILK!
I HAVE THEM!
I CAN DO THIS! POROUS WEBS! LOTS OF 'EM! FAST!
SWIPP-IPP-IP!
FWOMPHH
LIKE AN AIRBAG!
PLEASE GOD! HOPE THAT DID THE TRICK!
CAT! STOP IT!
TEARING ME APART! INTO A BILLION PIECES!
IT'S KILLING ME! IT'S--
AAARHHH!

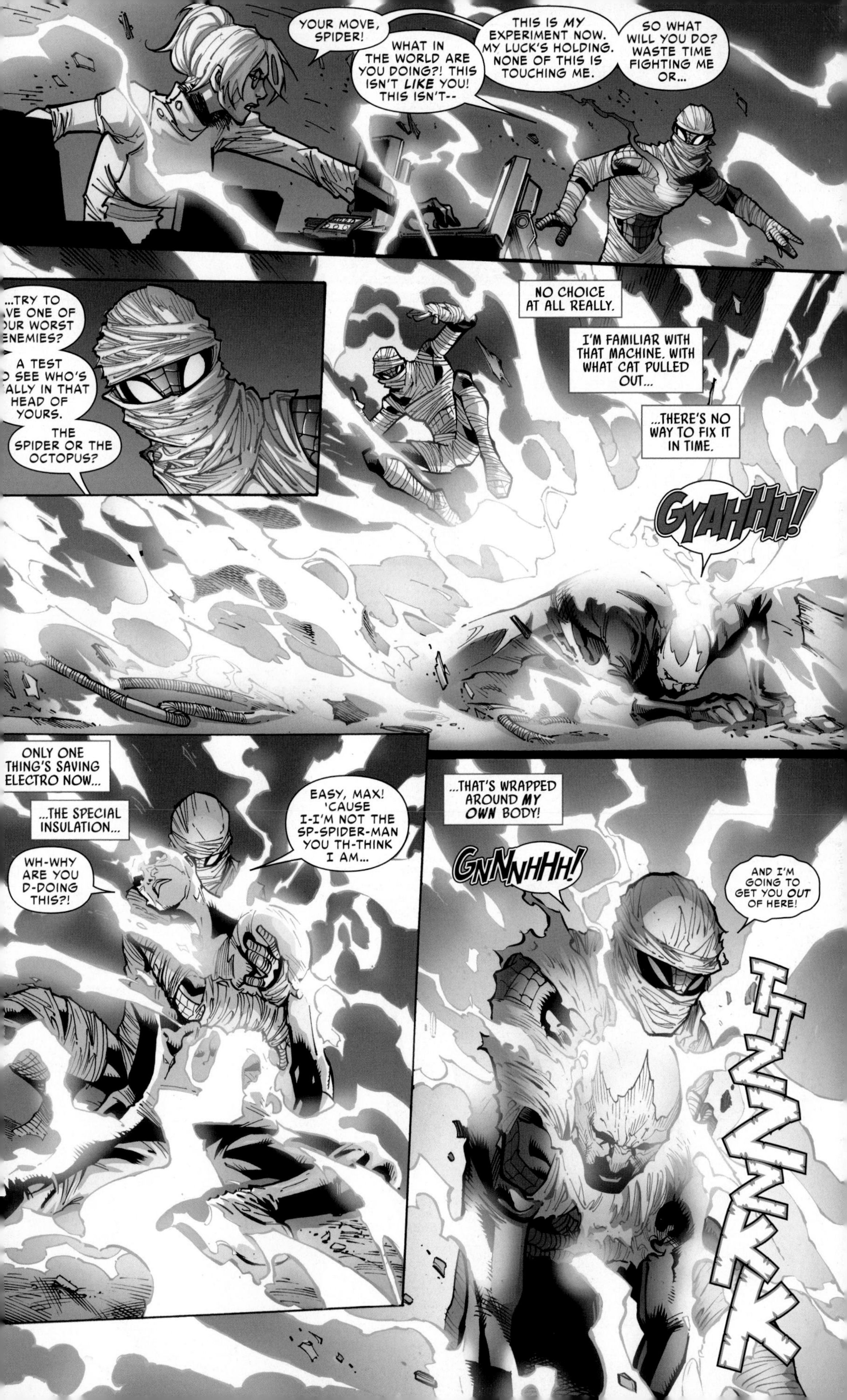
YOUR MOVE, SPIDER!
WHAT IN THE WORLD ARE YOU DOING?! THIS ISN'T LIKE YOU! THIS ISN'T--
THIS IS MY EXPERIMENT NOW. MY LUCK'S HOLDING. NONE OF THIS IS TOUCHING ME.
SO WHAT WILL YOU DO? WASTE TIME FIGHTING ME OR...
...TRY TO VE ONE OF UR WORST ENEMIES?
A TEST D SEE WHO'S ALLY IN THAT HEAD OF YOURS.
THE SPIDER OR THE OCTOPUS?
NO CHOICE AT ALL REALLY.
I'M FAMILIAR WITH THAT MACHINE. WITH WHAT CAT PULLED OUT...
...THERE'S NO WAY TO FIX IT IN TIME.
GYAHHH!
ONLY ONE THING'S SAVING ELECTRO NOW...
...THE SPECIAL INSULATION...
WH-WHY ARE YOU D-DOING THIS?!
EASY, MAX! 'CAUSE I-I'M NOT THE SP-SPIDER-MAN YOU TH-THINK I AM...
...THAT'S WRAPPED AROUND MY OWN BODY!
GNNHHH!
AND I'M GOING TO GET YOU OUT OF HERE!
THWNKK

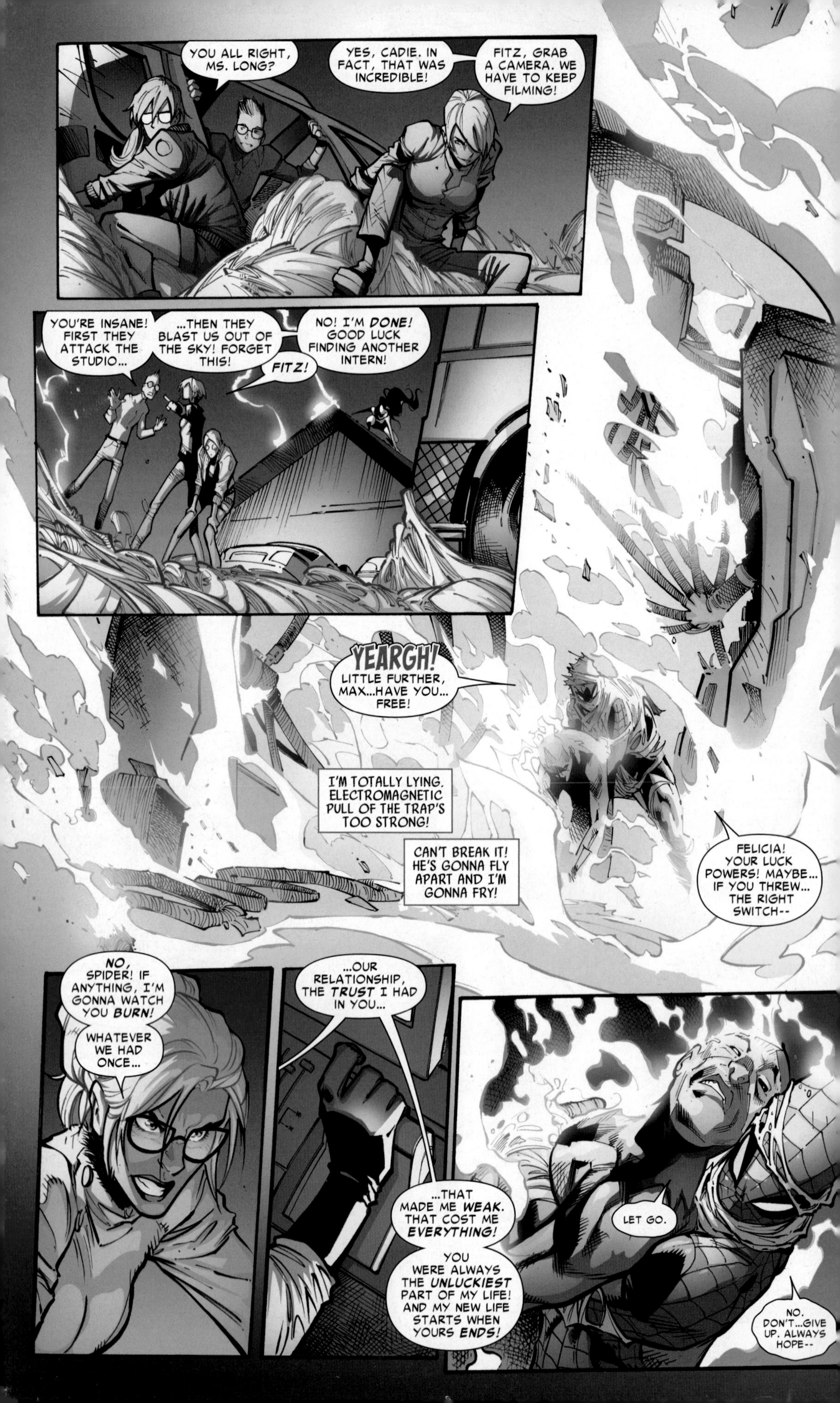
YOU ALL RIGHT, MS. LONG?
YES, CADIE. IN FACT, THAT WAS INCREDIBLE!
FITZ, GRAB A CAMERA. WE HAVE TO KEEP FILMING!
YOU'RE INSANE! FIRST THEY ATTACK THE STUDIO...
...THEN THEY BLAST US OUT OF THE SKY! FORGET THIS!
NO! I'M DONE! GOOD LUCK FINDING ANOTHER INTERN!
FITZ!
YEARGH!
LITTLE FURTHER, MAX...HAVE YOU... FREE!
I'M TOTALLY LYING. ELECTROMAGNETIC PULL OF THE TRAP'S TOO STRONG!
CAN'T BREAK IT! HE'S GONNA FLY APART AND I'M GONNA FRY!
FELICIA! YOUR LUCK POWERS! MAYBE... IF YOU THREW... THE RIGHT SWITCH--
NO, SPIDER! IF ANYTHING, I'M GONNA WATCH YOU BURN!
WHATEVER WE HAD ONCE...
...OUR RELATIONSHIP, THE TRUST I HAD IN YOU...
...THAT MADE ME WEAK. THAT COST ME EVERYTHING!
YOU WERE ALWAYS THE UNLUCKIEST PART OF MY LIFE! AND MY NEW LIFE STARTS WHEN YOURS ENDS!
LET GO.
NO. DON'T...GIVE UP. ALWAYS HOPE--

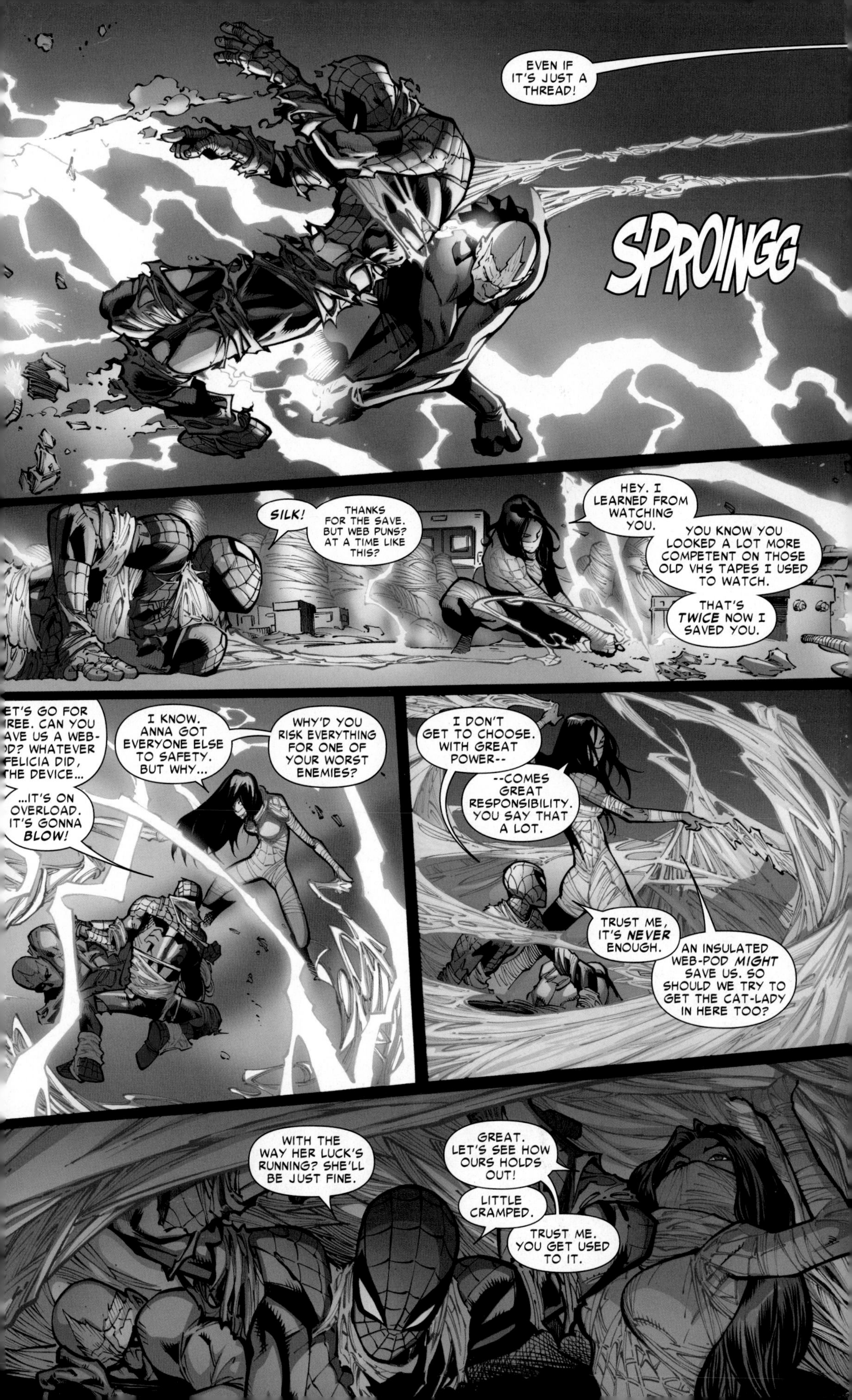

EVEN IF IT'S JUST A THREAD!
SPROINGG
SILK!
THANKS FOR THE SAVE. BUT WEB PUNS? AT A TIME LIKE THIS?
HEY. I LEARNED FROM WATCHING YOU.
YOU KNOW YOU LOOKED A LOT MORE COMPETENT ON THOSE OLD VHS TAPES I USED TO WATCH.
THAT'S TWICE NOW I SAVED YOU.
ET'S GO FOR REE. CAN YOU AVE US A WEB-OD? WHATEVER FELICIA DID, THE DEVICE...
...IT'S ON OVERLOAD. IT'S GONNA BLOW!
I KNOW. ANNA GOT EVERYONE ELSE TO SAFETY. BUT WHY...
WHY'D YOU RISK EVERYTHING FOR ONE OF YOUR WORST ENEMIES?
I DON'T GET TO CHOOSE. WITH GREAT POWER--
--COMES GREAT RESPONSIBILITY. YOU SAY THAT A LOT.
TRUST ME, IT'S NEVER ENOUGH.
AN INSULATED WEB-POD MIGHT SAVE US. SO SHOULD WE TRY TO GET THE CAT-LADY IN HERE TOO?
WITH THE WAY HER LUCK'S RUNNING? SHE'LL BE JUST FINE.
GREAT. LET'S SEE HOW OURS HOLDS OUT!
LITTLE CRAMPED.
TRUST ME. YOU GET USED TO IT.

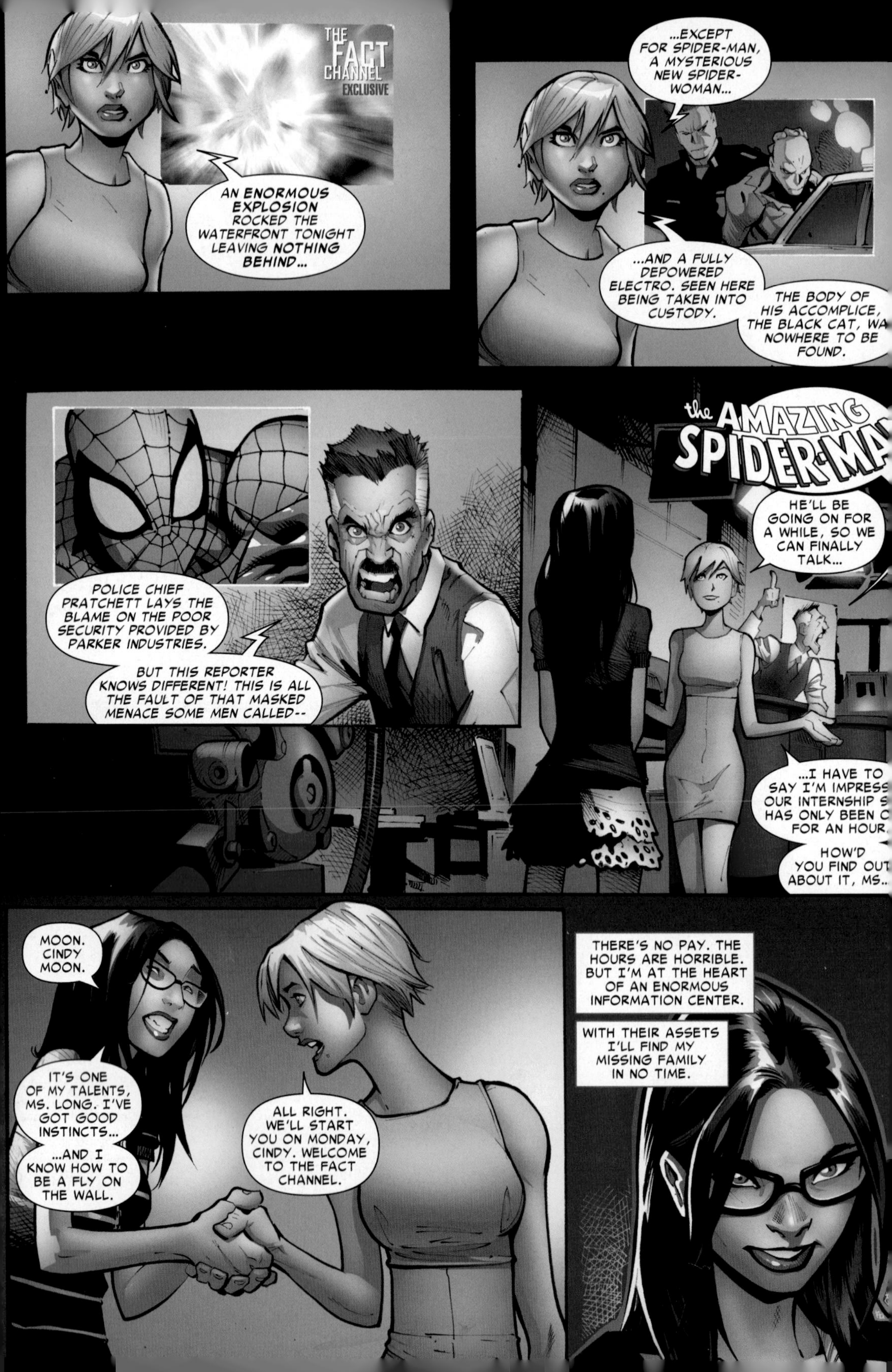
THE FACT CHANNEL EXCLUSIVE
AN ENORMOUS EXPLOSION ROCKED THE WATERFRONT TONIGHT LEAVING NOTHING BEHIND...
...EXCEPT FOR SPIDER-MAN, A MYSTERIOUS NEW SPIDER-WOMAN...
...AND A FULLY DEPOWERED ELECTRO. SEEN HERE BEING TAKEN INTO CUSTODY.
THE BODY OF HIS ACCOMPLICE, THE BLACK CAT, WA NOWHERE TO BE FOUND.
POLICE CHIEF PRATCHETT LAYS THE BLAME ON THE POOR SECURITY PROVIDED BY PARKER INDUSTRIES.
BUT THIS REPORTER KNOWS DIFFERENT! THIS IS ALL THE FAULT OF THAT MASKED MENACE SOME MEN CALLED--
the AMAZING SPIDER-MA
HE'LL BE GOING ON FOR A WHILE, SO WE CAN FINALLY TALK...
...I HAVE TO SAY I'M IMPRESS OUR INTERNSHIP S HAS ONLY BEEN C FOR AN HOUR.
HOW'D YOU FIND OUT ABOUT IT, MS...
MOON. CINDY MOON.
IT'S ONE OF MY TALENTS, MS. LONG. I'VE GOT GOOD INSTINCTS...
...AND I KNOW HOW TO BE A FLY ON THE WALL.
ALL RIGHT. WE'LL START YOU ON MONDAY, CINDY. WELCOME TO THE FACT CHANNEL.
THERE'S NO PAY. THE HOURS ARE HORRIBLE. BUT I'M AT THE HEART OF AN ENORMOUS INFORMATION CENTER.
WITH THEIR ASSETS I'LL FIND MY MISSING FAMILY IN NO TIME.

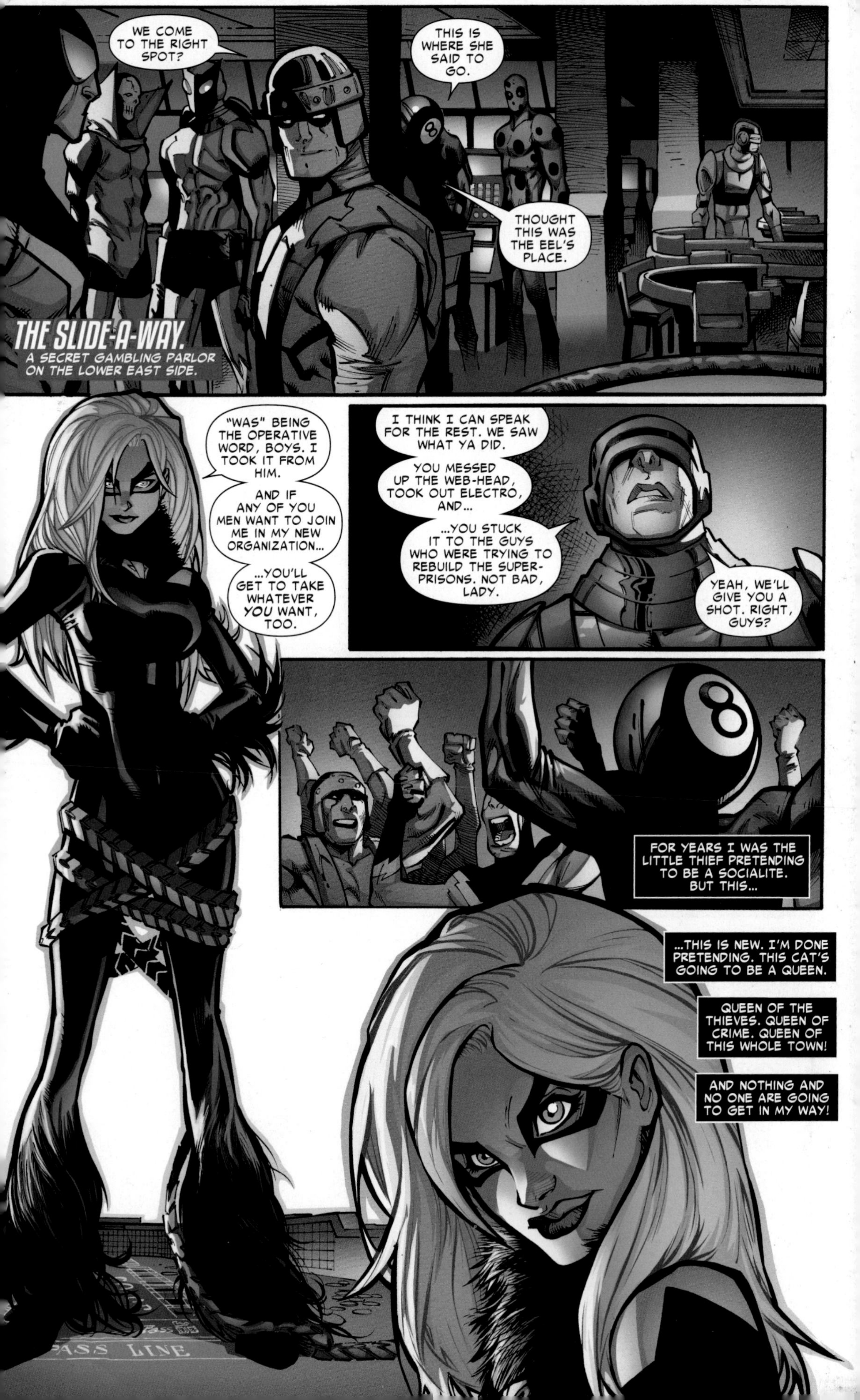
WE COME TO THE RIGHT SPOT?
THIS IS WHERE SHE SAID TO GO.
THOUGHT THIS WAS THE EEL'S PLACE.
THE SLIDE-A-WAY.
A SECRET GAMBLING PARLOR ON THE LOWER EAST SIDE.
"WAS" BEING THE OPERATIVE WORD, BOYS. I TOOK IT FROM HIM.
AND IF ANY OF YOU MEN WANT TO JOIN ME IN MY NEW ORGANIZATION...
...YOU'LL GET TO TAKE WHATEVER YOU WANT, TOO.
I THINK I CAN SPEAK FOR THE REST. WE SAW WHAT YA DID.
YOU MESSED UP THE WEB-HEAD, TOOK OUT ELECTRO, AND...
...YOU STUCK IT TO THE GUYS WHO WERE TRYING TO REBUILD THE SUPER-PRISONS. NOT BAD, LADY.
YEAH, WE'LL GIVE YOU A SHOT. RIGHT, GUYS?
FOR YEARS I WAS THE LITTLE THIEF PRETENDING TO BE A SOCIALITE. BUT THIS...
...THIS IS NEW. I'M DONE PRETENDING. THIS CAT'S GOING TO BE A QUEEN.
QUEEN OF THE THIEVES. QUEEN OF CRIME. QUEEN OF THIS WHOLE TOWN!
AND NOTHING AND NO ONE ARE GOING TO GET IN MY WAY!
PASS LINE

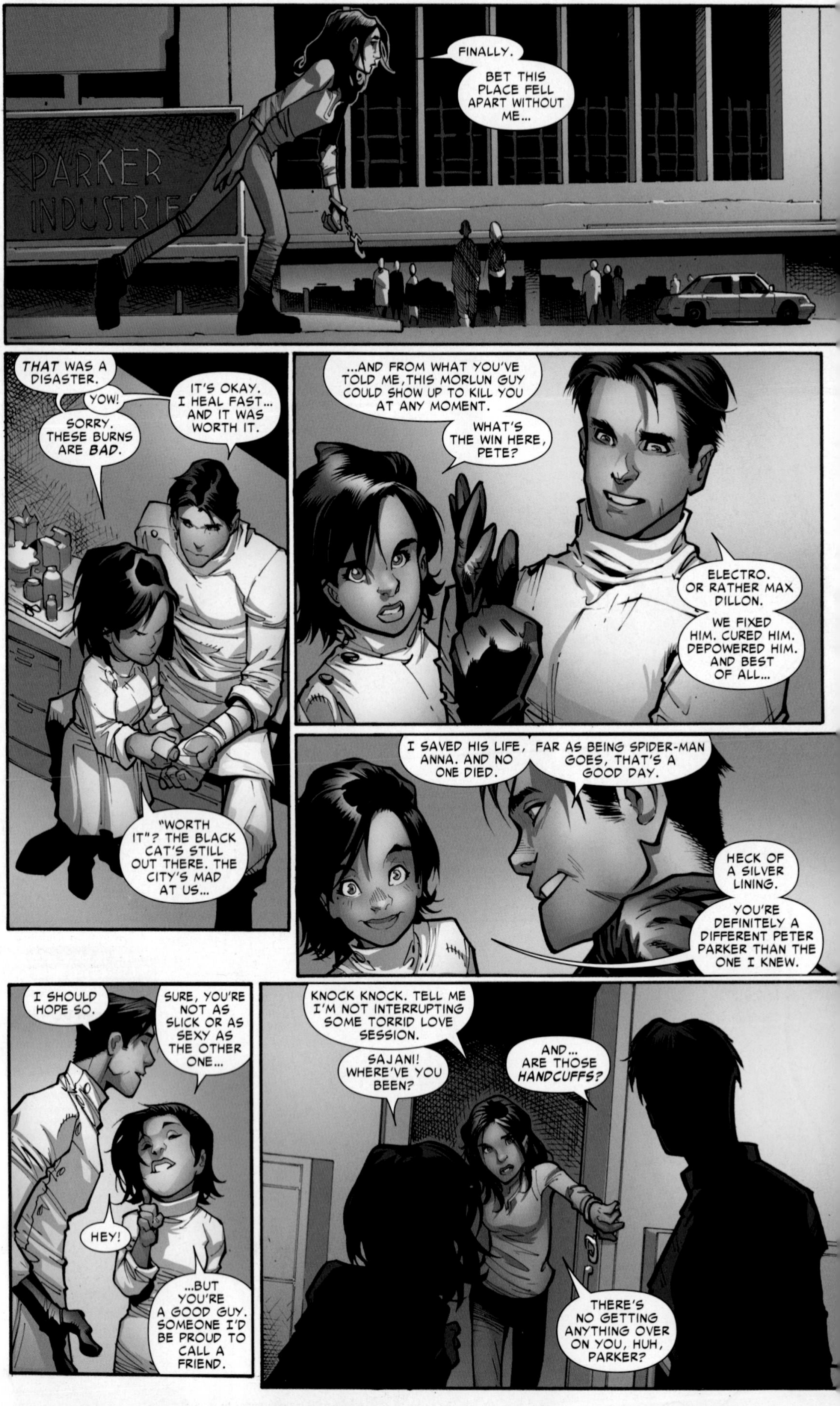
FINALLY.
BET THIS PLACE FELL APART WITHOUT ME...
PARKER INDUSTRIES
THAT WAS A DISASTER.
YOW!
SORRY. THESE BURNS ARE BAD.
IT'S OKAY. I HEAL FAST... AND IT WAS WORTH IT.
"WORTH IT"? THE BLACK CAT'S STILL OUT THERE. THE CITY'S MAD AT US...
...AND FROM WHAT YOU'VE TOLD ME, THIS MORLUN GUY COULD SHOW UP TO KILL YOU AT ANY MOMENT.
WHAT'S THE WIN HERE, PETE?
ELECTRO. OR RATHER MAX DILLON.
WE FIXED HIM. CURED HIM. DEPOWERED HIM. AND BEST OF ALL...
I SAVED HIS LIFE, ANNA. AND NO ONE DIED.
FAR AS BEING SPIDER-MAN GOES, THAT'S A GOOD DAY.
HECK OF A SILVER LINING.
YOU'RE DEFINITELY A DIFFERENT PETER PARKER THAN THE ONE I KNEW.
I SHOULD HOPE SO.
SURE, YOU'RE NOT AS SLICK OR AS SEXY AS THE OTHER ONE...
HEY!
...BUT YOU'RE A GOOD GUY. SOMEONE I'D BE PROUD TO CALL A FRIEND.
KNOCK KNOCK. TELL ME I'M NOT INTERRUPTING SOME TORRID LOVE SESSION.
SAJANI! WHERE'VE YOU BEEN?
AND... ARE THOSE HANDCUFFS?
THERE'S NO GETTING ANYTHING OVER ON YOU, HUH, PARKER?

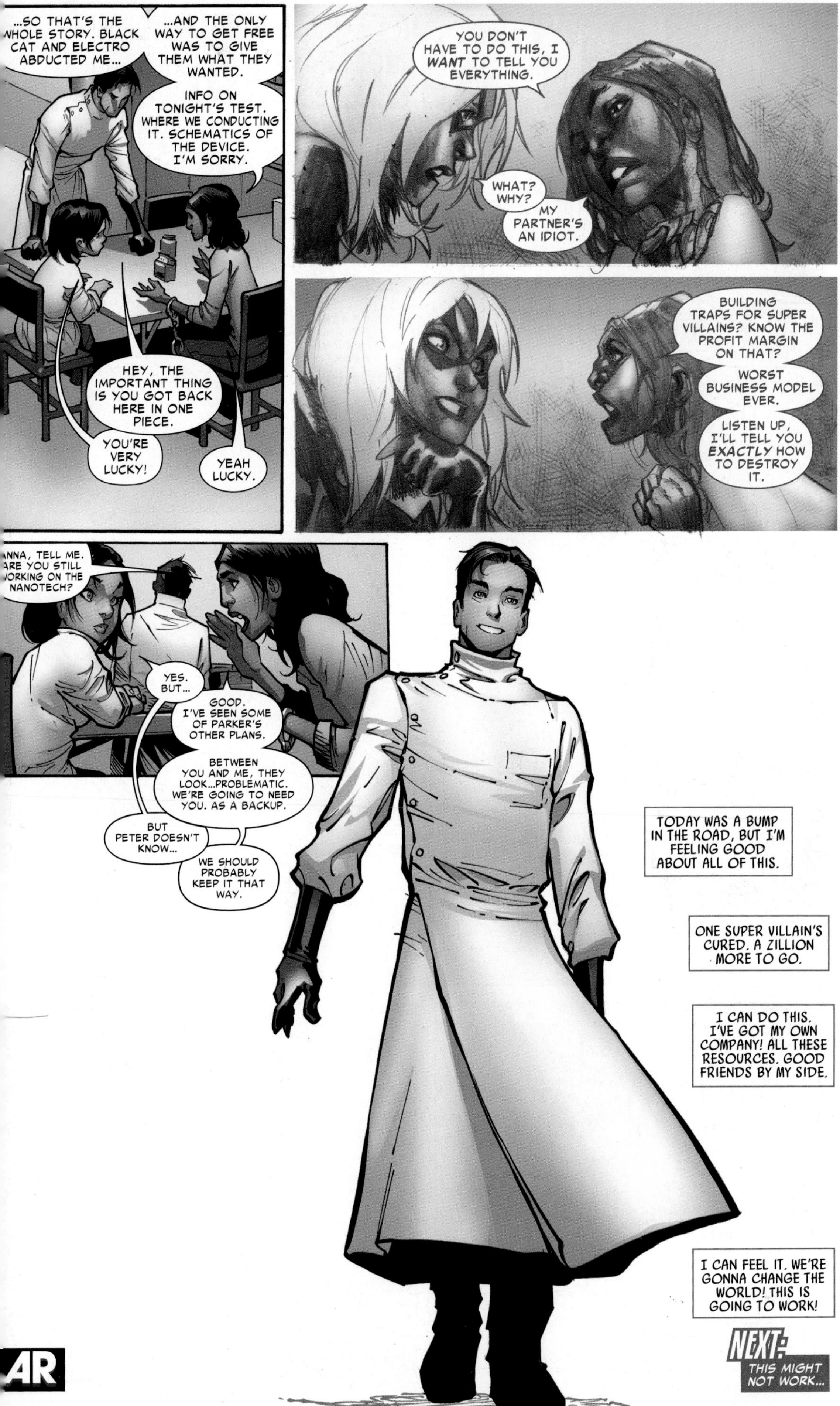
...SO THAT'S THE WHOLE STORY. BLACK CAT AND ELECTRO ABDUCTED ME...
...AND THE ONLY WAY TO GET FREE WAS TO GIVE THEM WHAT THEY WANTED.
INFO ON TONIGHT'S TEST. WHERE WE CONDUCTING IT. SCHEMATICS OF THE DEVICE. I'M SORRY.
HEY, THE IMPORTANT THING IS YOU GOT BACK HERE IN ONE PIECE.
YOU'RE VERY LUCKY!
YEAH LUCKY.
YOU DON'T HAVE TO DO THIS, I WANT TO TELL YOU EVERYTHING.
WHAT? WHY?
MY PARTNER'S AN IDIOT.
BUILDING TRAPS FOR SUPER VILLAINS? KNOW THE PROFIT MARGIN ON THAT?
WORST BUSINESS MODEL EVER.
LISTEN UP, I'LL TELL YOU EXACTLY HOW TO DESTROY IT.
ANNA, TELL ME. ARE YOU STILL WORKING ON THE NANOTECH?
YES. BUT...
GOOD. I'VE SEEN SOME OF PARKER'S OTHER PLANS.
BETWEEN YOU AND ME, THEY LOOK...PROBLEMATIC. WE'RE GOING TO NEED YOU. AS A BACKUP.
BUT PETER DOESN'T KNOW...
WE SHOULD PROBABLY KEEP IT THAT WAY.
TODAY WAS A BUMP IN THE ROAD, BUT I'M FEELING GOOD ABOUT ALL OF THIS.
ONE SUPER VILLAIN'S CURED. A ZILLION MORE TO GO.
I CAN DO THIS. I'VE GOT MY OWN COMPANY! ALL THESE RESOURCES. GOOD FRIENDS BY MY SIDE.
I CAN FEEL IT. WE'RE GONNA CHANGE THE WORLD! THIS IS GOING TO WORK!
NEXT: THIS MIGHT NOT WORK...

HOW MY STUFF WORKS

JOE CARAMAGNA
WRITER

CHRIS ELIOPOULOS
ARTIST

JIM CHARALAMPIDIS
COLORS

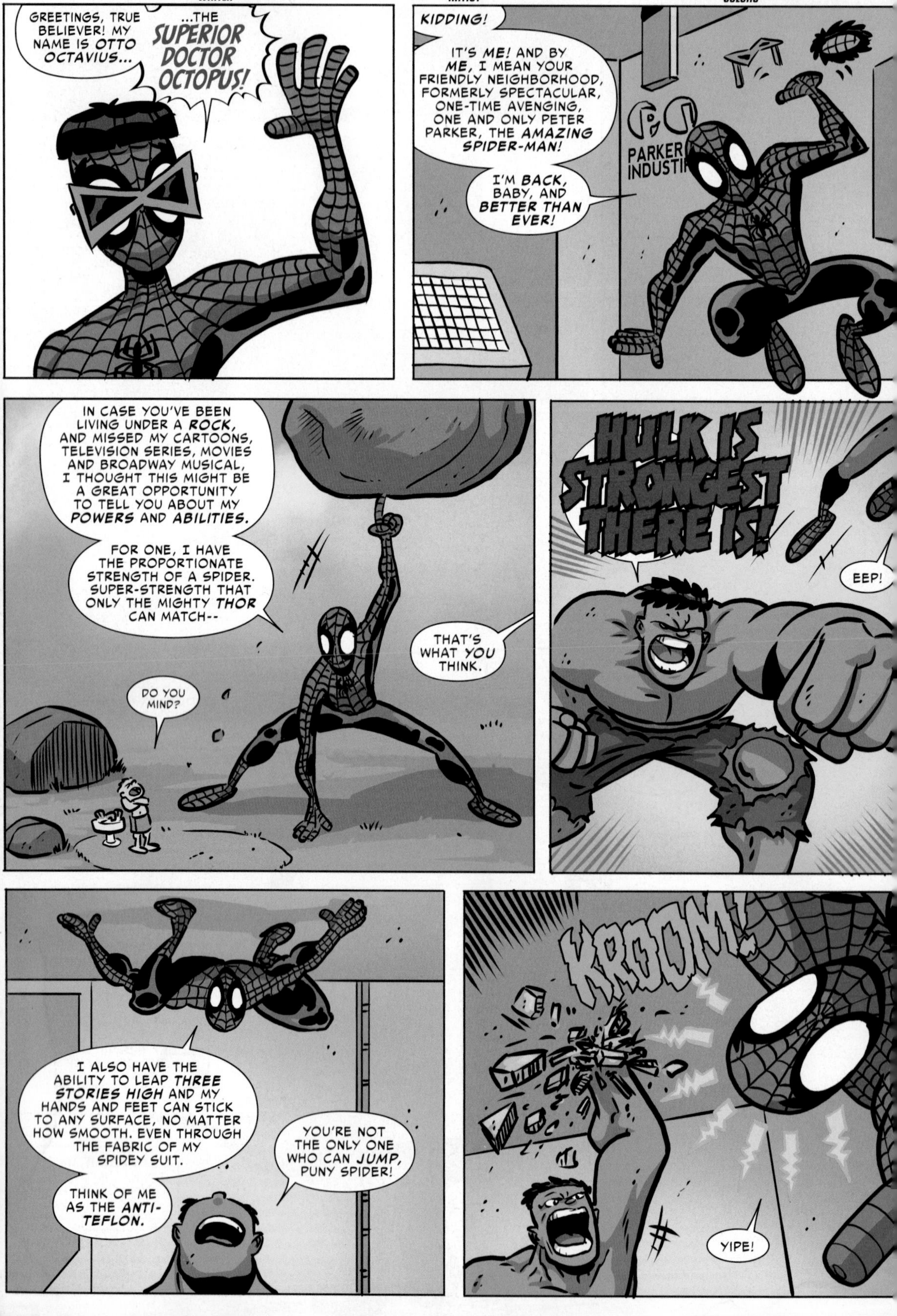
GREETINGS, TRUE BELIEVER! MY NAME IS OTTO OCTAVIUS...
...THE SUPERIOR DOCTOR OCTOPUS!
KIDDING!
IT'S ME! AND BY ME, I MEAN YOUR FRIENDLY NEIGHBORHOOD, FORMERLY SPECTACULAR, ONE-TIME AVENGING, ONE AND ONLY PETER PARKER, THE AMAZING SPIDER-MAN!
I'M BACK, BABY, AND BETTER THAN EVER!
PARKER INDUSTI
IN CASE YOU'VE BEEN LIVING UNDER A ROCK, AND MISSED MY CARTOONS, TELEVISION SERIES, MOVIES AND BROADWAY MUSICAL, I THOUGHT THIS MIGHT BE A GREAT OPPORTUNITY TO TELL YOU ABOUT MY POWERS AND ABILITIES.
FOR ONE, I HAVE THE PROPORTIONATE STRENGTH OF A SPIDER. SUPER-STRENGTH THAT ONLY THE MIGHTY THOR CAN MATCH--
THAT'S WHAT YOU THINK.
DO YOU MIND?
HULK IS STRONGEST THERE IS!
EEP!
I ALSO HAVE THE ABILITY TO LEAP THREE STORIES HIGH AND MY HANDS AND FEET CAN STICK TO ANY SURFACE, NO MATTER HOW SMOOTH. EVEN THROUGH THE FABRIC OF MY SPIDEY SUIT.
THINK OF ME AS THE ANTI-TEFLON.
YOU'RE NOT THE ONLY ONE WHO CAN JUMP, PUNY SPIDER!
KROOM!
YIPE!

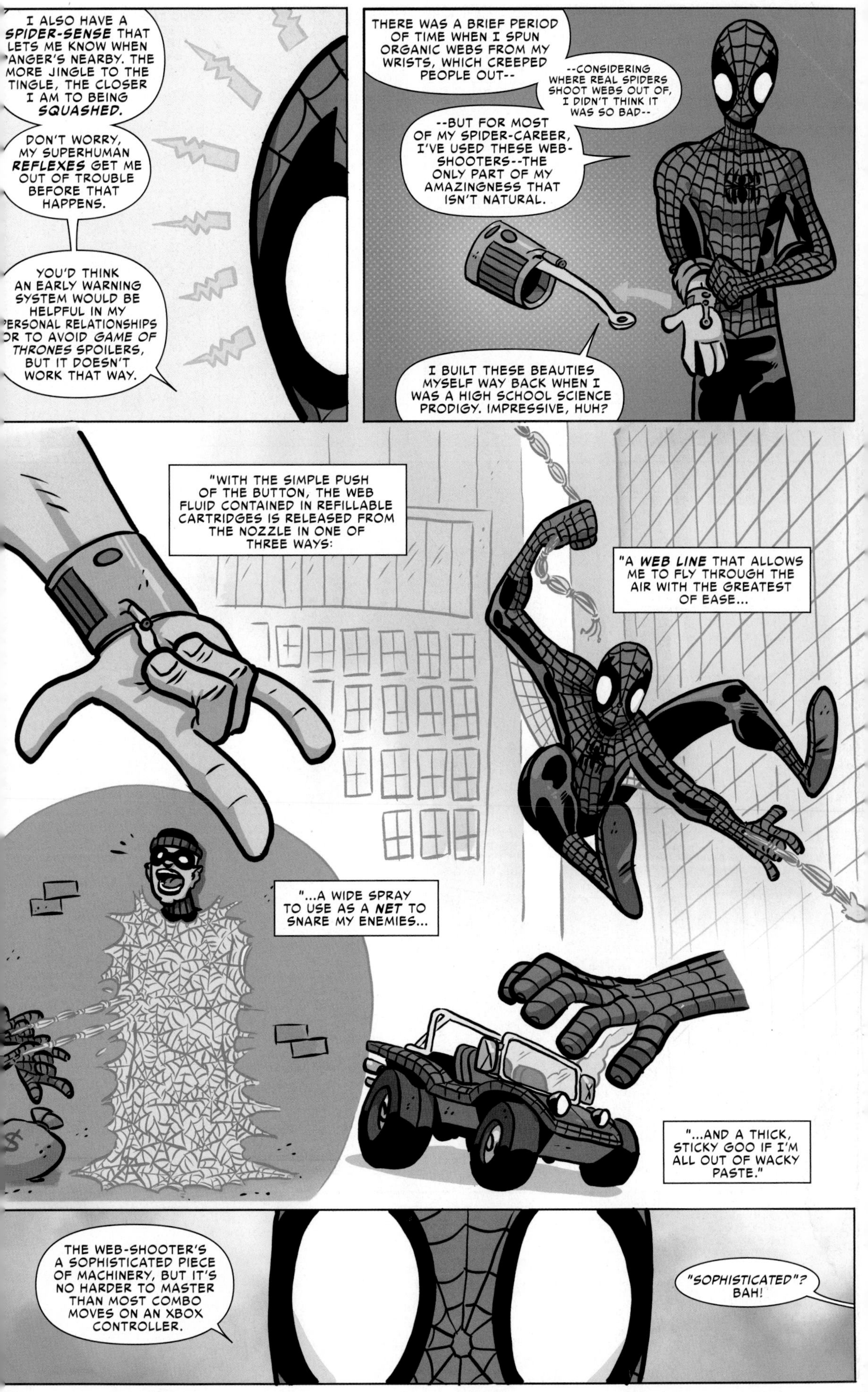
I ALSO HAVE A SPIDER-SENSE THAT LETS ME KNOW WHEN DANGER'S NEARBY. THE MORE JINGLE TO THE TINGLE, THE CLOSER I AM TO BEING SQUASHED.
DON'T WORRY, MY SUPERHUMAN REFLEXES GET ME OUT OF TROUBLE BEFORE THAT HAPPENS.
YOU'D THINK AN EARLY WARNING SYSTEM WOULD BE HELPFUL IN MY PERSONAL RELATIONSHIPS OR TO AVOID GAME OF THRONES SPOILERS, BUT IT DOESN'T WORK THAT WAY.
THERE WAS A BRIEF PERIOD OF TIME WHEN I SPUN ORGANIC WEBS FROM MY WRISTS, WHICH CREEPED PEOPLE OUT--
--CONSIDERING WHERE REAL SPIDERS SHOOT WEBS OUT OF, I DIDN'T THINK IT WAS SO BAD--
--BUT FOR MOST OF MY SPIDER-CAREER, I'VE USED THESE WEB-SHOOTERS--THE ONLY PART OF MY AMAZINGNESS THAT ISN'T NATURAL.
I BUILT THESE BEAUTIES MYSELF WAY BACK WHEN I WAS A HIGH SCHOOL SCIENCE PRODIGY. IMPRESSIVE, HUH?
"WITH THE SIMPLE PUSH OF THE BUTTON, THE WEB FLUID CONTAINED IN REFILLABLE CARTRIDGES IS RELEASED FROM THE NOZZLE IN ONE OF THREE WAYS:
"A WEB LINE THAT ALLOWS ME TO FLY THROUGH THE AIR WITH THE GREATEST OF EASE...
"...A WIDE SPRAY TO USE AS A NET TO SNARE MY ENEMIES...
"...AND A THICK, STICKY GOO IF I'M ALL OUT OF WACKY PASTE."
THE WEB-SHOOTER'S A SOPHISTICATED PIECE OF MACHINERY, BUT IT'S NO HARDER TO MASTER THAN MOST COMBO MOVES ON AN XBOX CONTROLLER.
"SOPHISTICATED"? BAH!

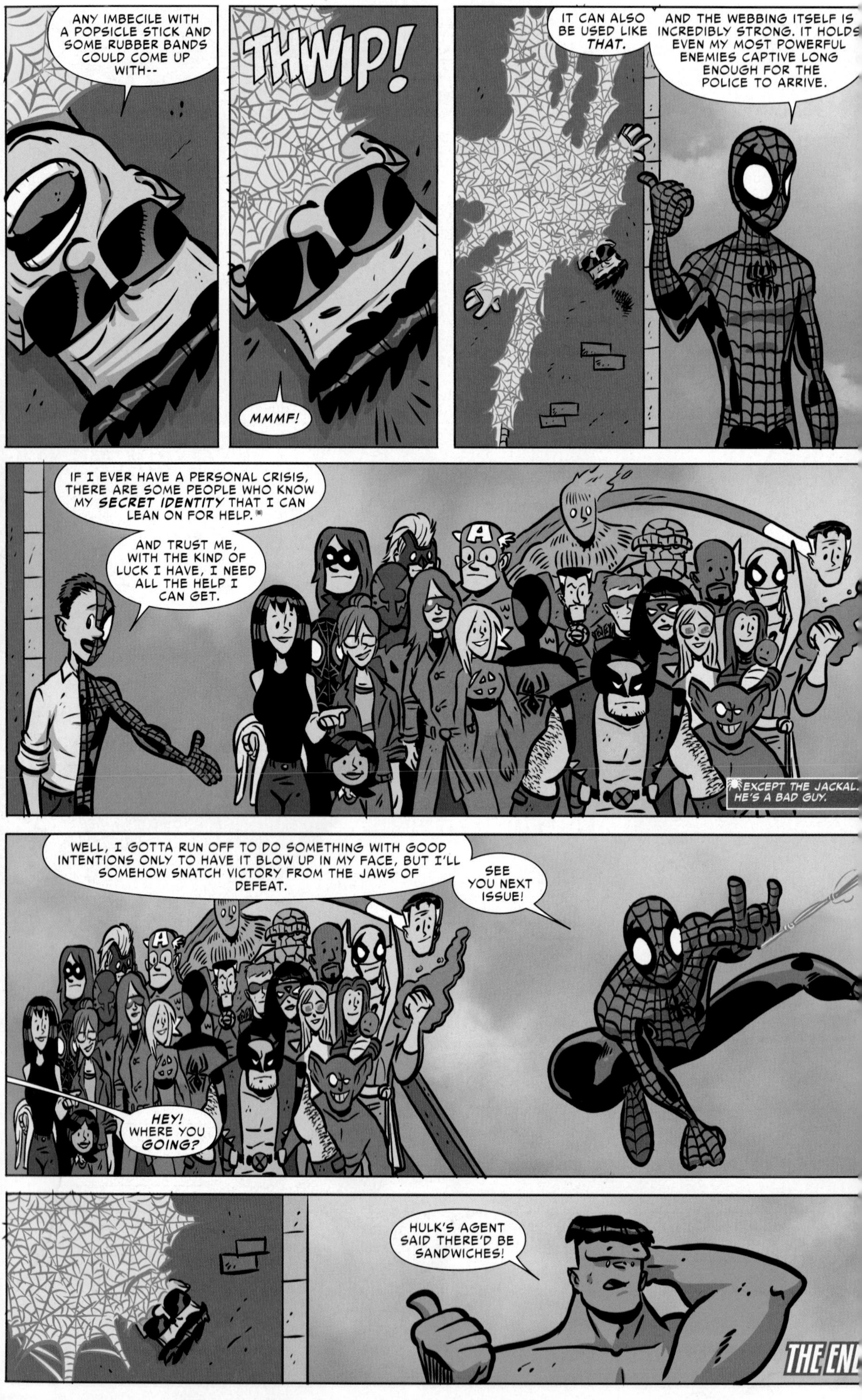
ANY IMBECILE WITH A POPSICLE STICK AND SOME RUBBER BANDS COULD COME UP WITH--
THWIP!
MMMF!
IT CAN ALSO BE USED LIKE *THAT.*
AND THE WEBBING ITSELF IS INCREDIBLY STRONG. IT HOLDS EVEN MY MOST POWERFUL ENEMIES CAPTIVE LONG ENOUGH FOR THE POLICE TO ARRIVE.
IF I EVER HAVE A PERSONAL CRISIS, THERE ARE SOME PEOPLE WHO KNOW MY *SECRET IDENTITY* THAT I CAN LEAN ON FOR HELP.*
AND TRUST ME, WITH THE KIND OF LUCK I HAVE, I NEED ALL THE HELP I CAN GET.
*EXCEPT THE JACKAL. HE'S A BAD GUY.
WELL, I GOTTA RUN OFF TO DO SOMETHING WITH GOOD INTENTIONS ONLY TO HAVE IT BLOW UP IN MY FACE, BUT I'LL SOMEHOW SNATCH VICTORY FROM THE JAWS OF DEFEAT.
SEE YOU NEXT ISSUE!
HEY! WHERE YOU *GOING?*
HULK'S AGENT SAID THERE'D BE SANDWICHES!
THE END

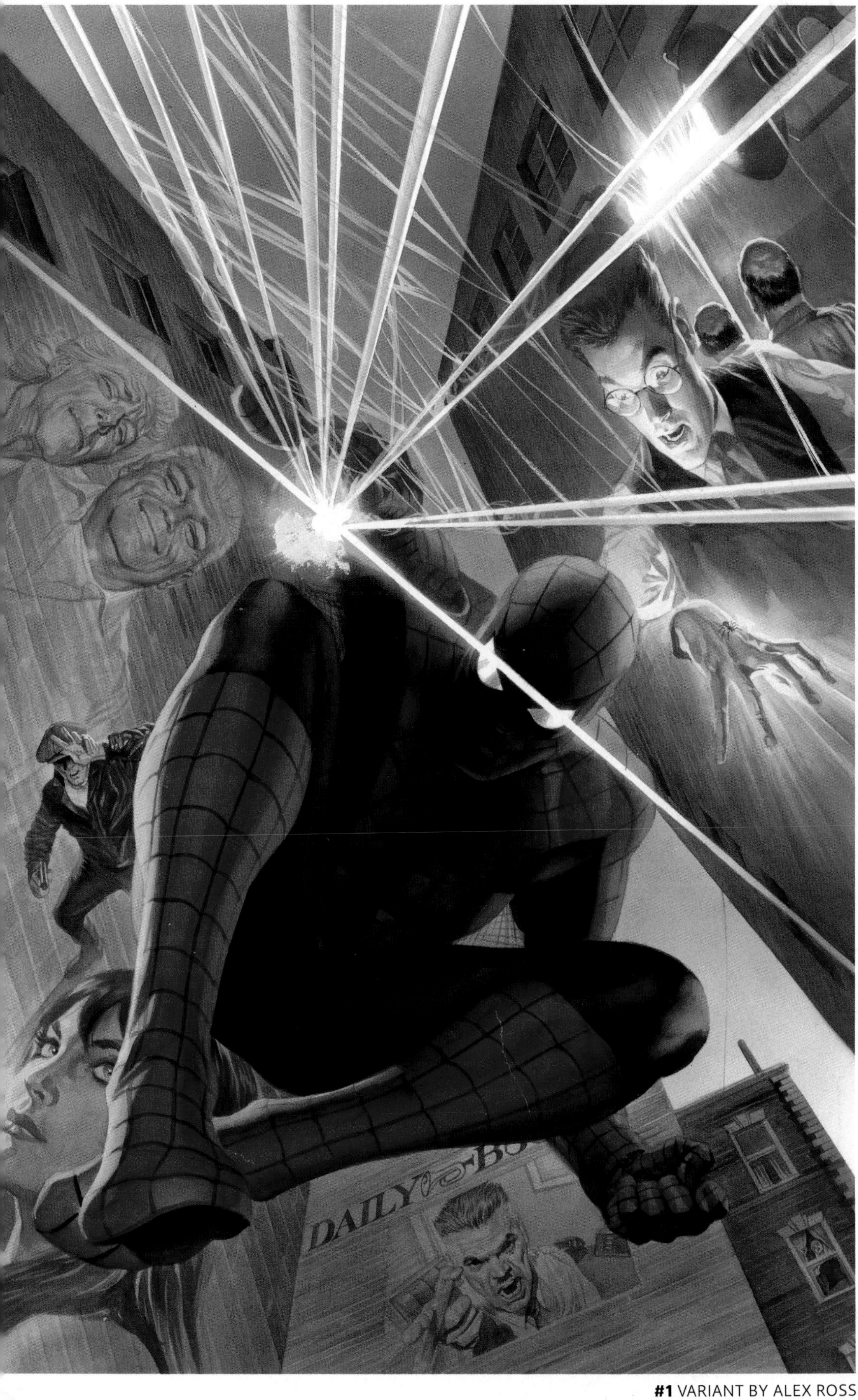
DAILY

#1 VARIANT BY ALEX ROSS

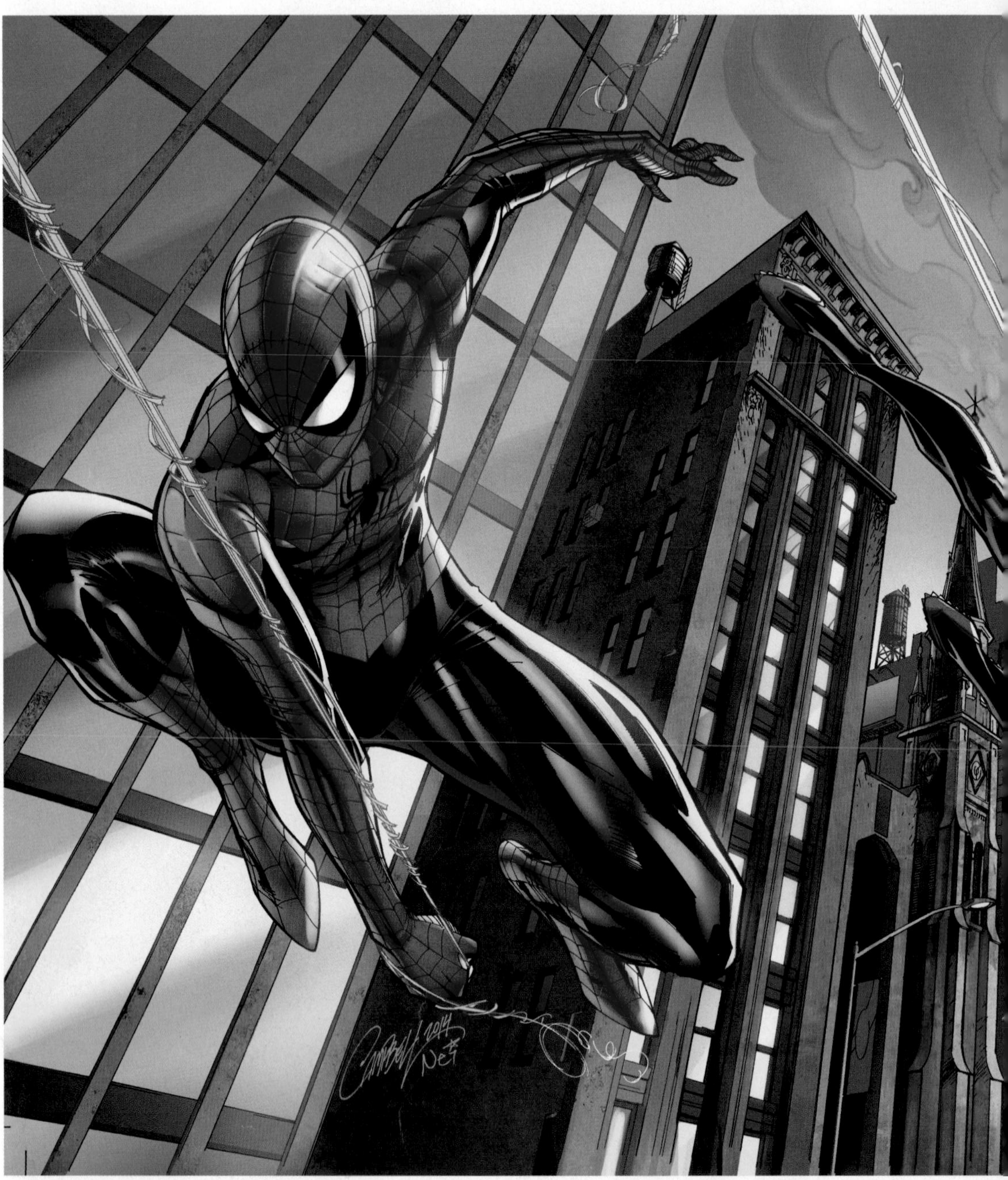

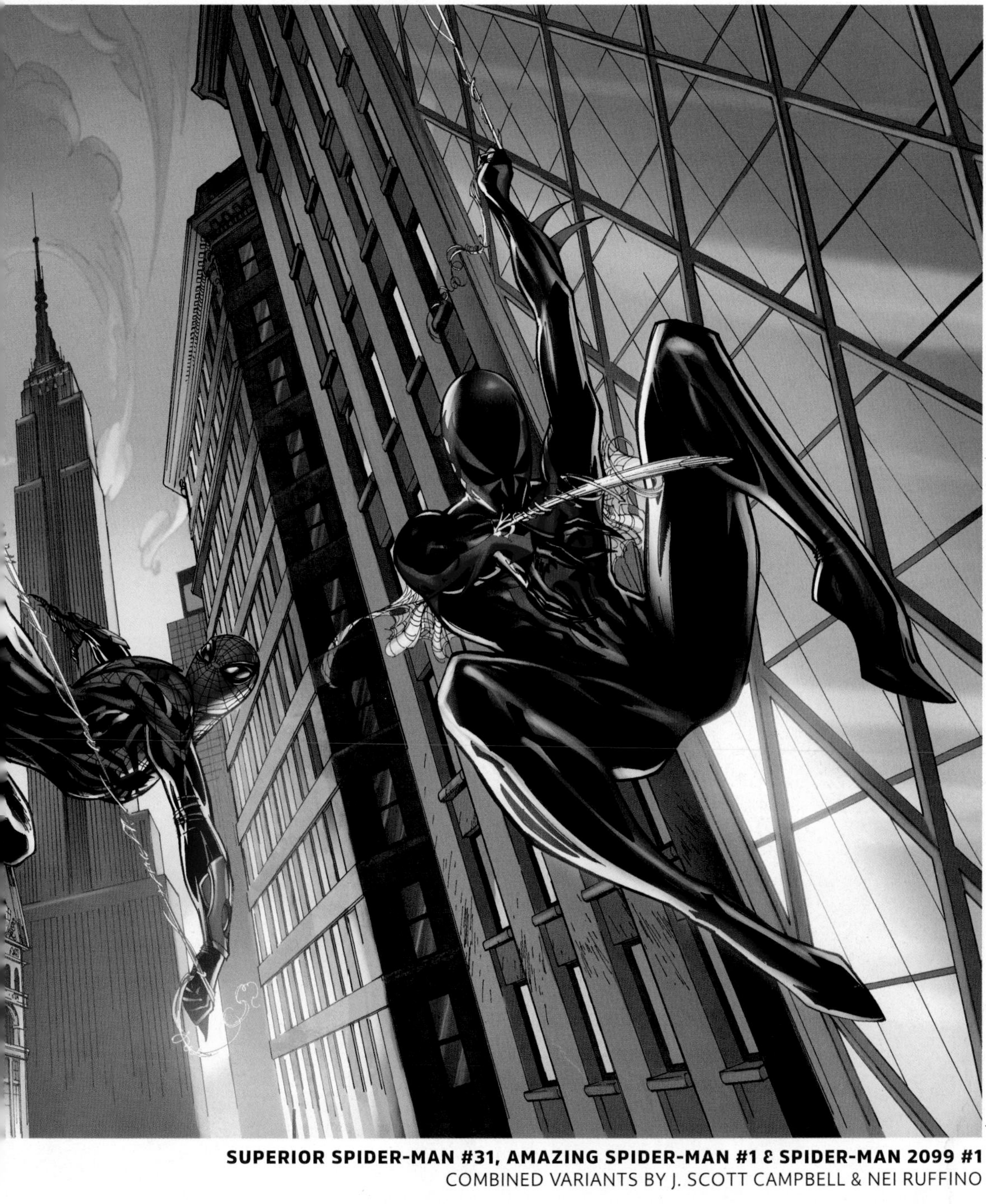

SUPERIOR SPIDER-MAN #31, AMAZING SPIDER-MAN #1 & SPIDER-MAN 2099 #1
COMBINED VARIANTS BY J. SCOTT CAMPBELL & NEI RUFFINO

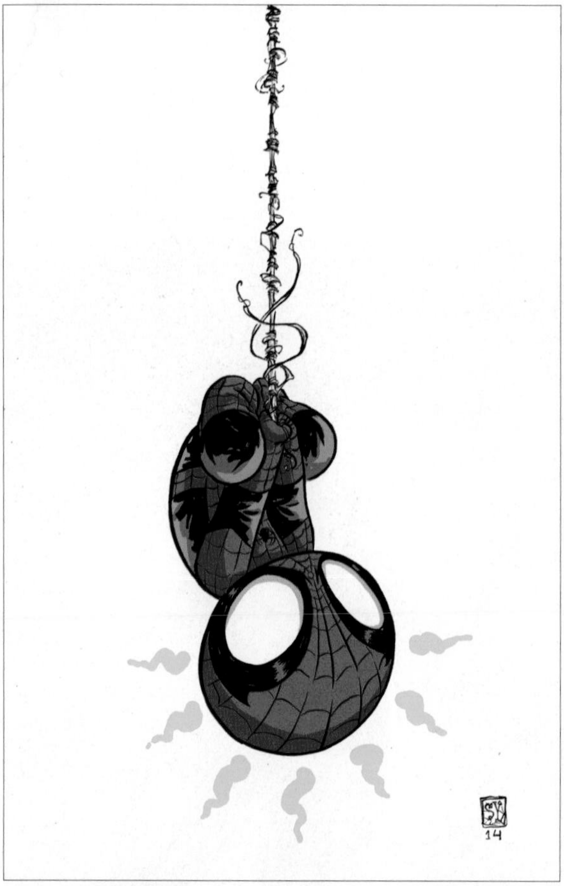

#1 VARIANT BY SKOTTIE YOUNG

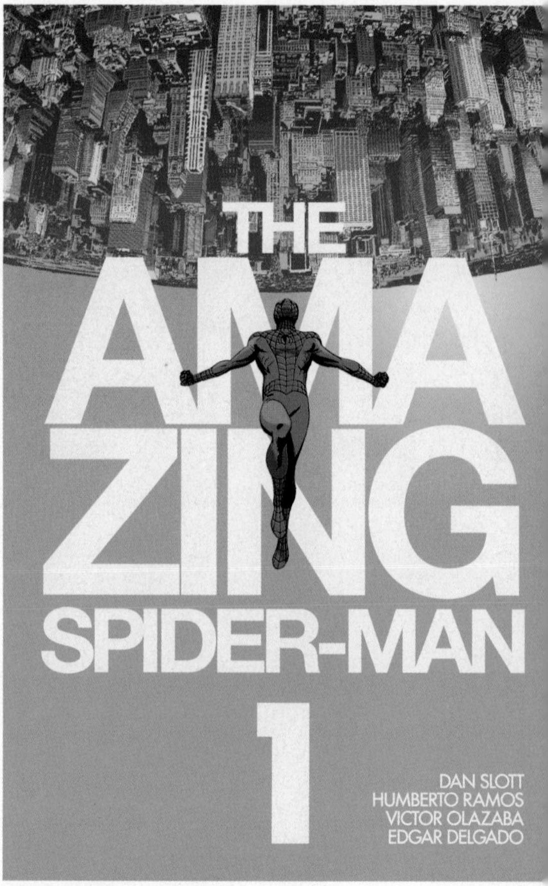
THE
AMAZING
SPIDER-MAN
1
DAN SLOTT
HUMBERTO RAMOS
VICTOR OLAZABA
EDGAR DELGADO

#1 VARIANT BY MARCOS MARTIN

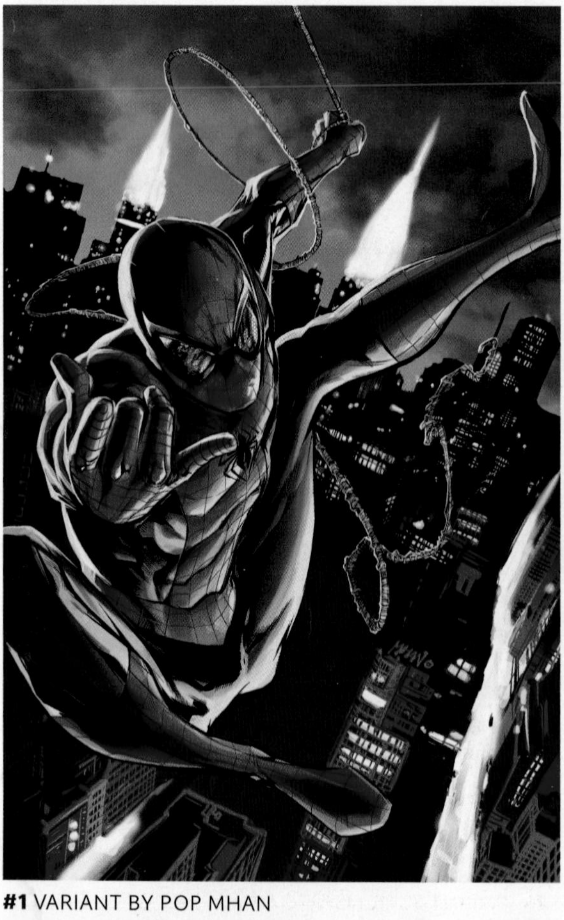

#1 VARIANT BY POP MHAN

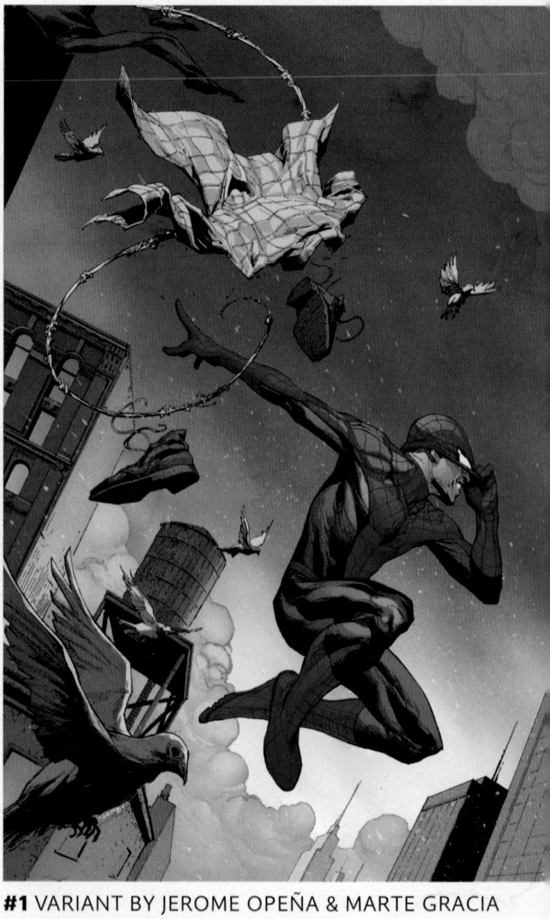

#1 VARIANT BY JEROME OPEÑA & MARTE GRACIA

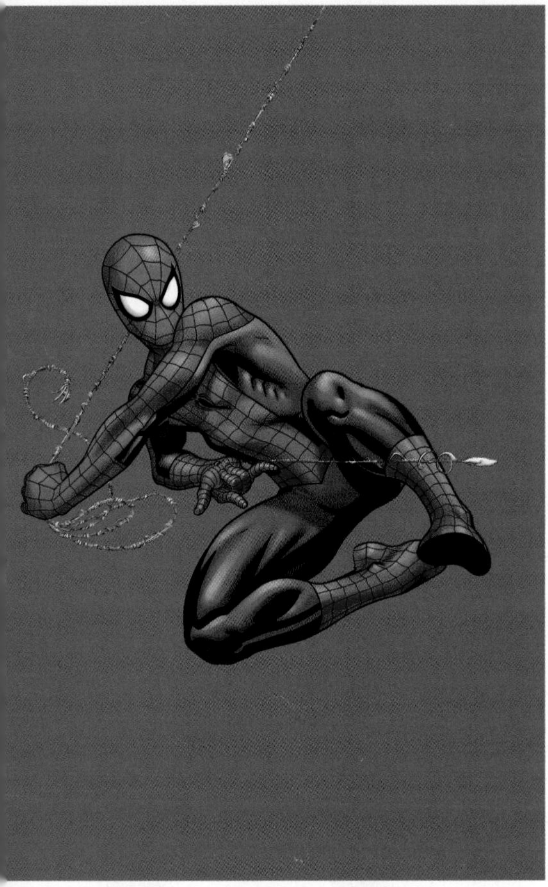

#1 VARIANT BY ED MCGUINNESS

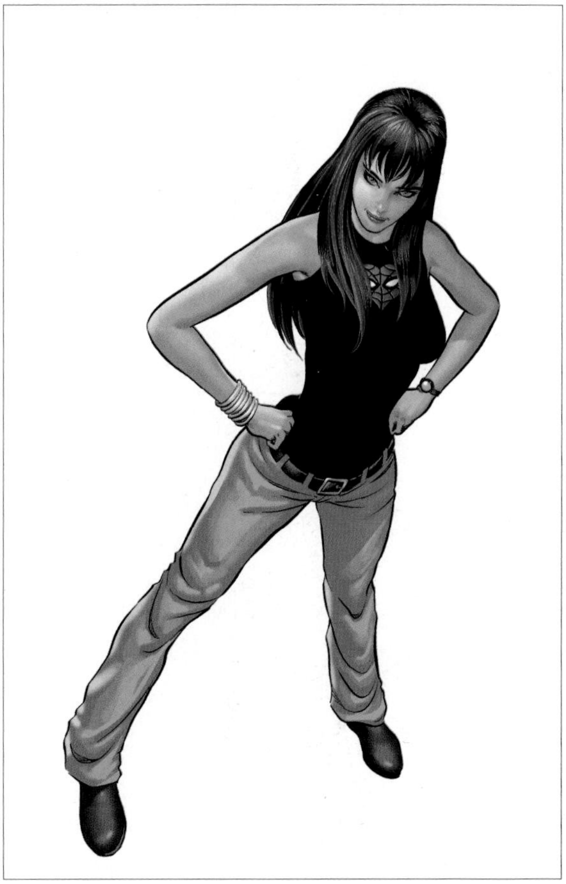

#2 VARIANT BY MIKE DEODATO & RAIN BEREDO

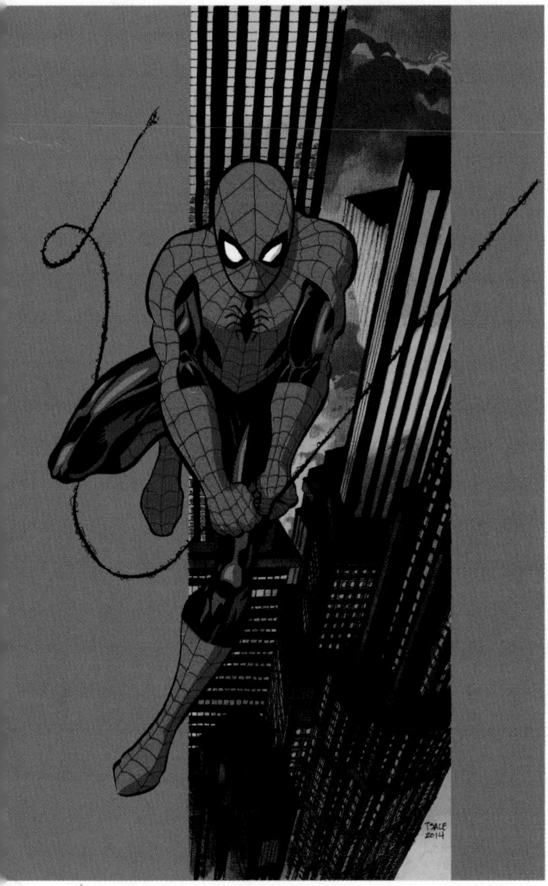

#3 VARIANT BY TIM SALE & DAVE STEWART

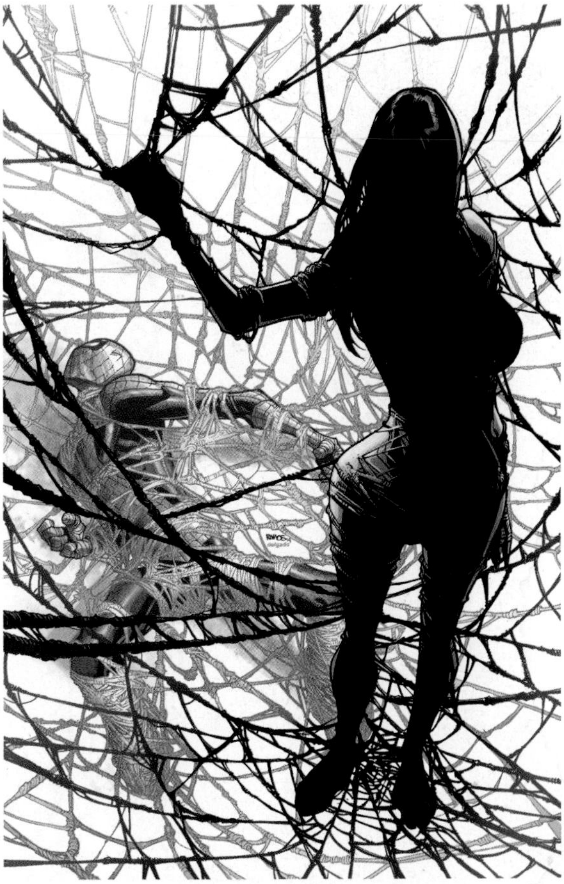

#4 VARIANT BY HUMBERTO RAMOS & EDGAR DELGADO

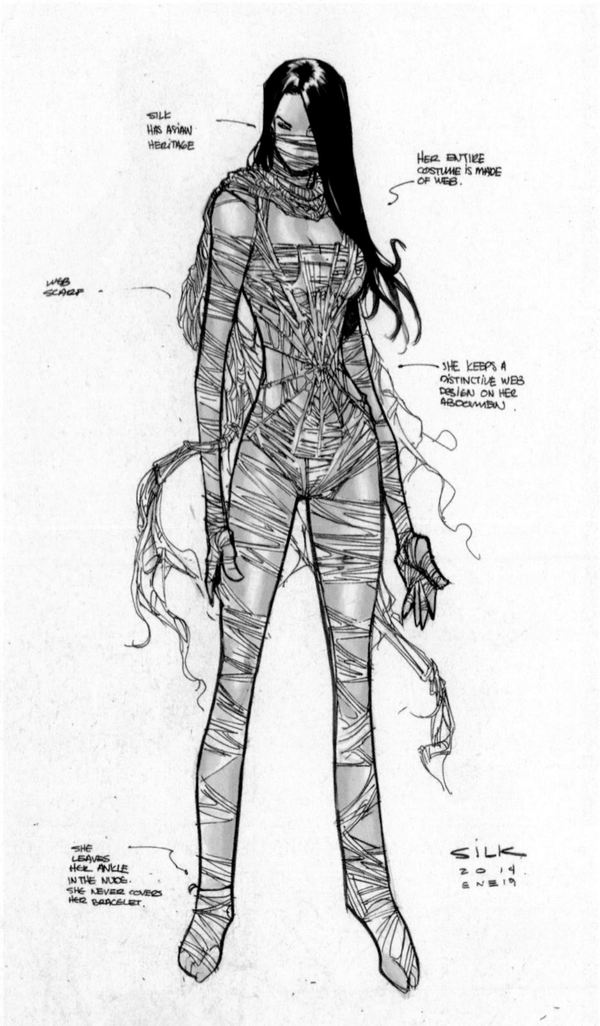
SILK HAS ASIAN HERITAGE
HER ENTIRE COSTUME IS MADE OF WEB.
WEB SCARF
SHE KEEPS A DISTINCTIVE WEB DESIGN ON HER ABDOMEN.
SHE LEAVES HER ANKLE IN THE NUDE. SHE NEVER COVERS HER BRACELET.
SILK
2014
ENE19

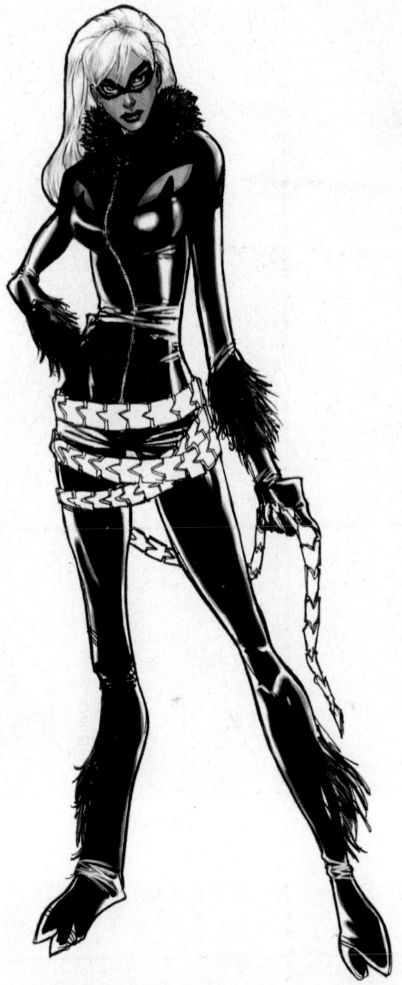

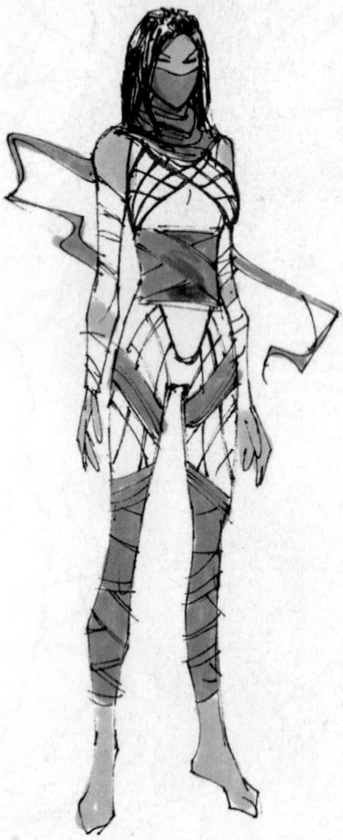

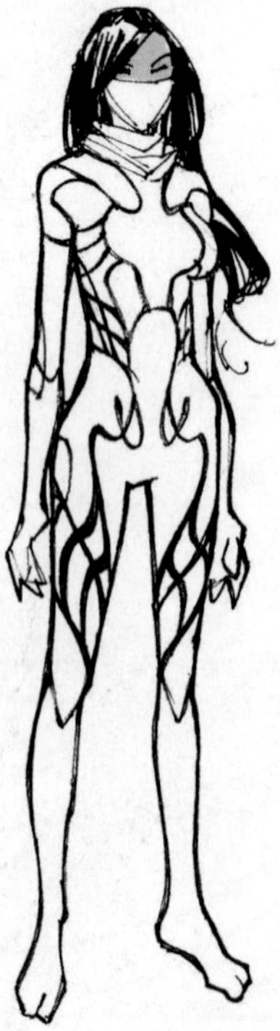

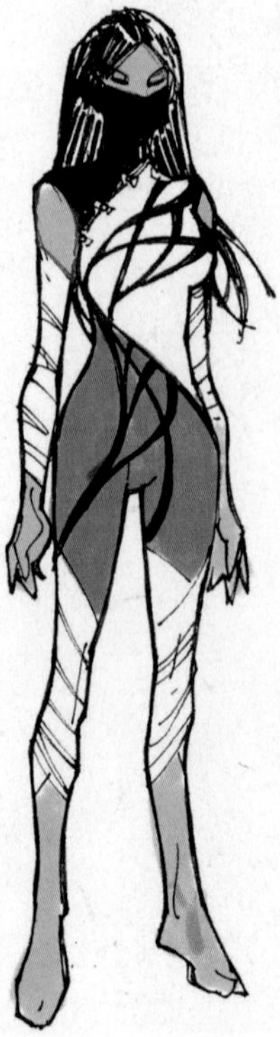

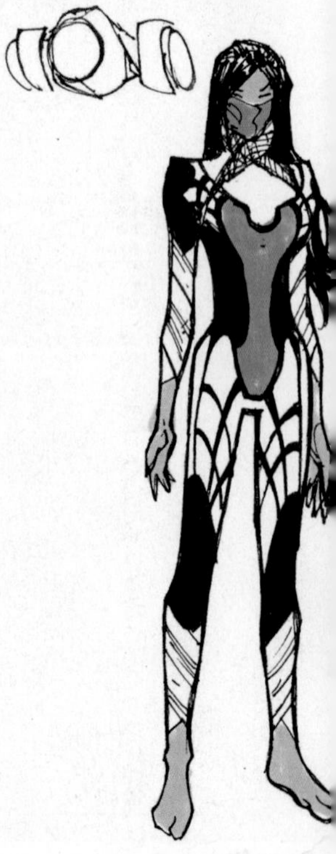

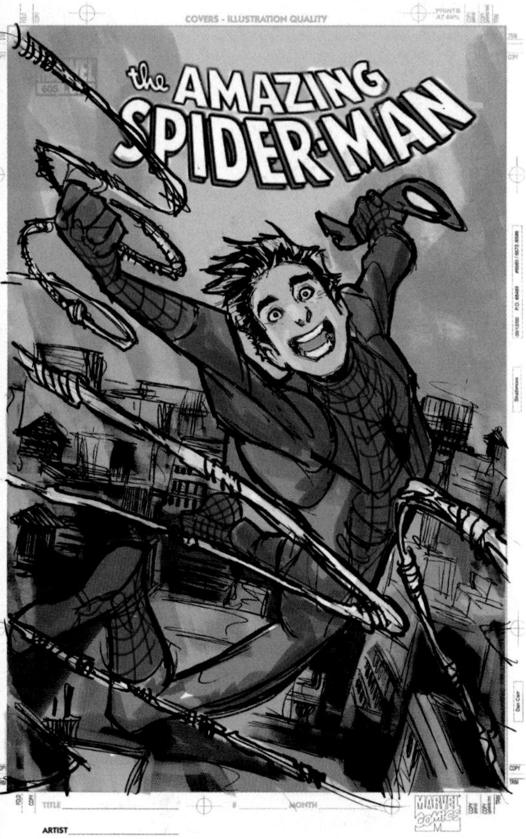
COVERS - ILLUSTRATION QUALITY
the AMAZING SPIDER-MAN
TITLE
MONTH
ARTIST

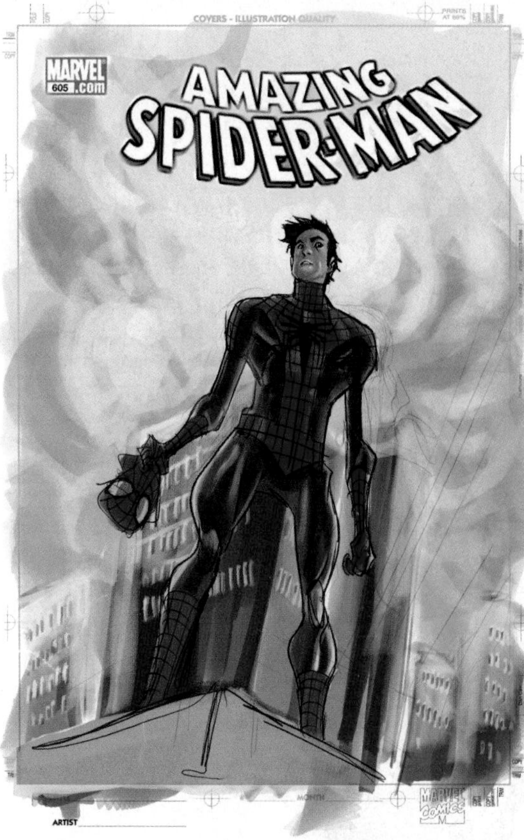
COVERS - ILLUSTRATION QUALITY
MARVEL 605 .com
AMAZING SPIDER-MAN
MONTH
ARTIST

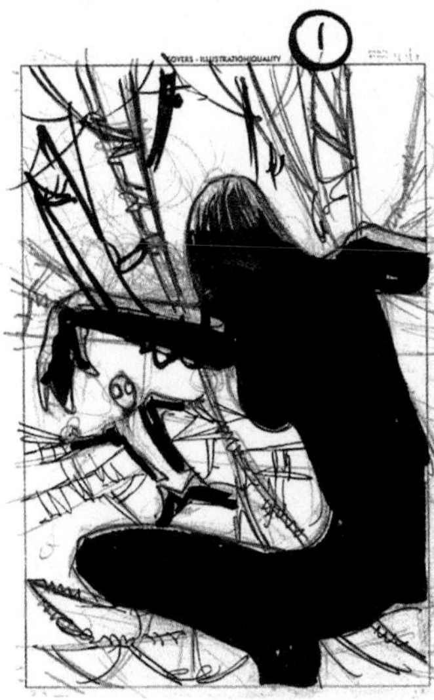
1
COVERS - ILLUSTRATION QUALITY

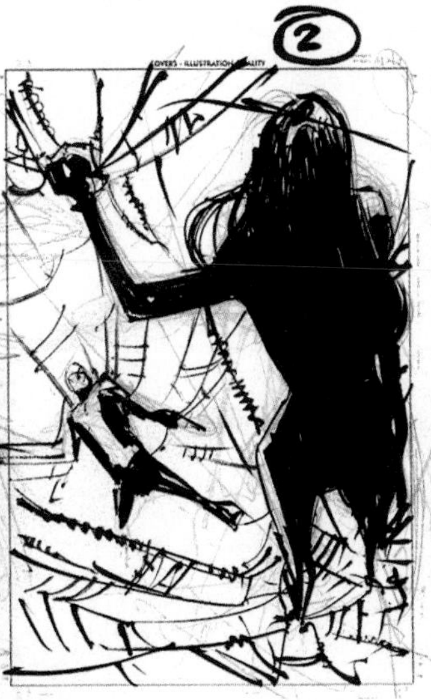
2
COVERS - ILLUSTRATION QUALITY

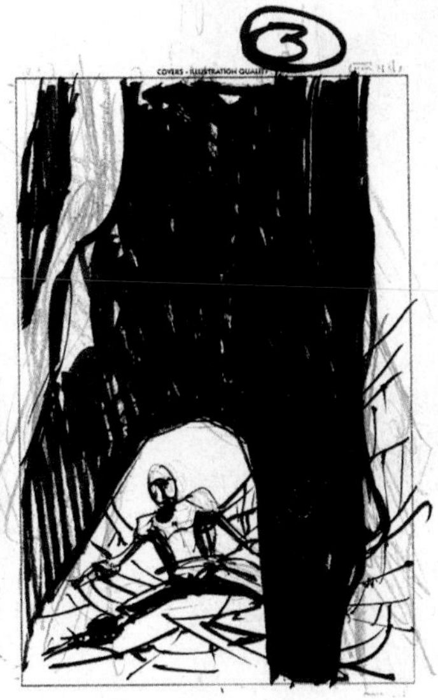
3
COVERS - ILLUSTRATION QUALITY

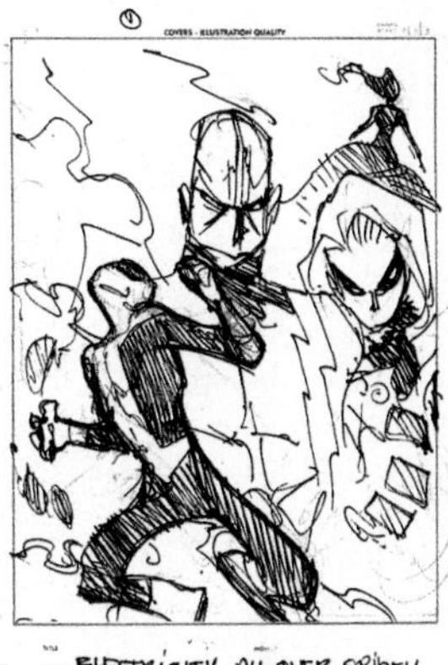
1
COVERS - ILLUSTRATION QUALITY

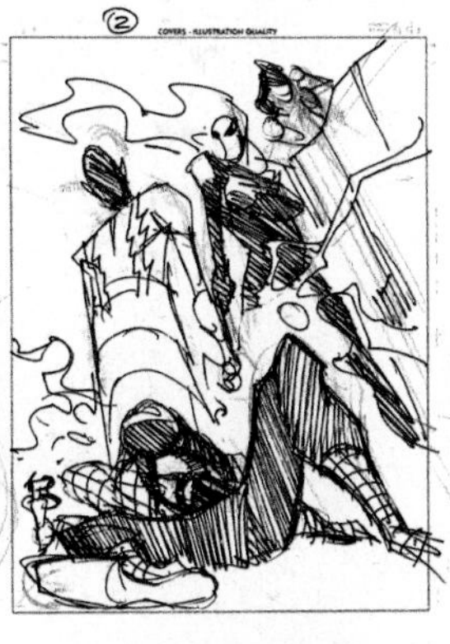
2
COVERS - ILLUSTRATION QUALITY

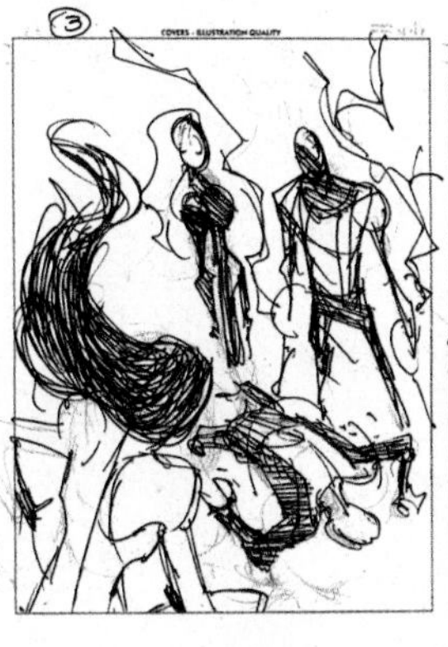
3
COVERS - ILLUSTRATION QUALITY

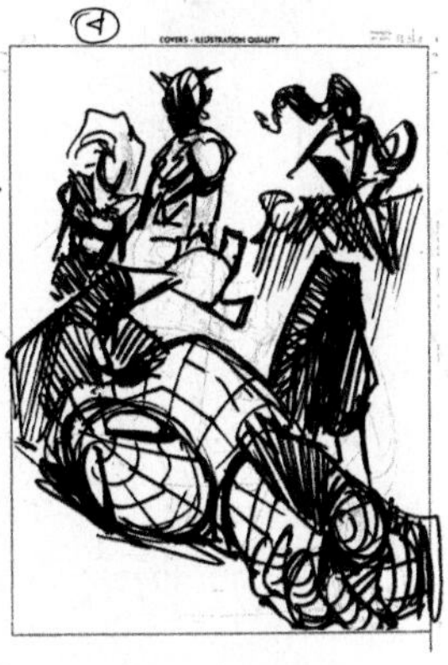
4
COVERS - ILLUSTRATION QUALITY

ELECTRICITY ALL OVER SPIDEY.

MARVEL AR AUGMENTED REALITY

MARVEL AUGMENTED REALITY (AR) ENHANCES AND CHANGES THE WAY YOU EXPERIENCE COMICS!

TO ACCESS THE FREE MARVEL AR CONTENT IN THIS BOOK*:

1. Locate the AR logo within the comic.
2. Go to Marvel.com/AR in your web browser.
3. Search by series title to find the corresponding AR.
4. Enjoy Marvel AR!

*All AR content that appears in this book has been archived and will be available only at Marvel.com/AR – no longer in the Marvel AR App. Content subject to change and availability.

The AMAZING SPIDER-MAN AR INDEX

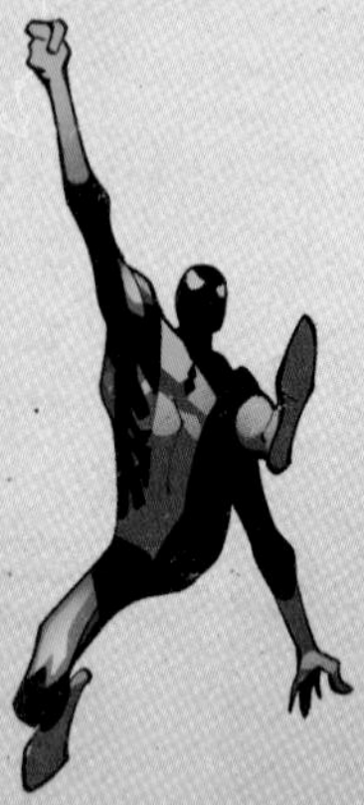

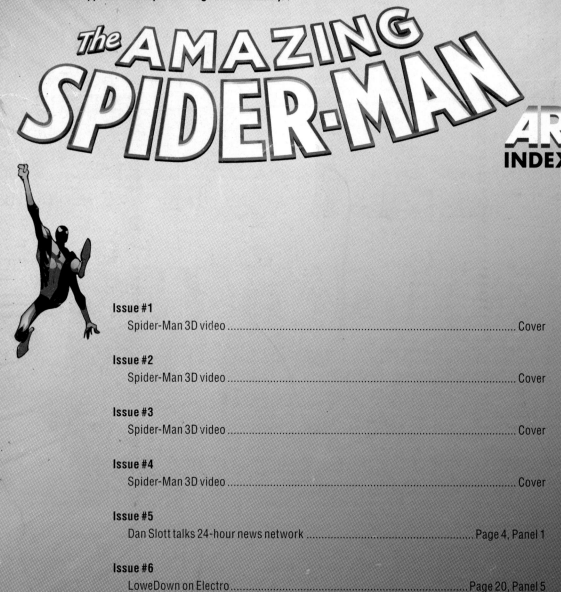